FOOTBALL'S GIANTKILLERS

50 Great Cup Upsets

Derek Watts

Book Guild Publishing

Sussex, England

First published in Great Britain in 2010 by
The Book Guild Ltd
Pavilion View
19 New Road
Brighton, BN1 1UF

Typeset in Garamond by Ellipsis Books Limited, Glasgow

Printed in Great Britain by Athenaeum Press Ltd, Gateshead

A catalogue record for this book is available from The British Library.

ISBN 978 1 84624 281 6

CONTENTS

ACKNOWLEDGEMENTS

I am grateful to the following people who have contributed anecdotes, reminiscences, copies of books, match programmes and match videos to the production of the book. All their help and encouragement is greatly appreciated: Colin Bailey, Martin Ball, David Banks, Eric Berry, Ken Bichard, Dave Boddy, Daniel Brench, Sharon Budworth, Glenn Burvill, Walter Causer, Gary Chalk, Derek Church, Gaynor Collie, Eric Collins, Jean Collyer, Robert Day, Chris Dillon, Brian Flynn, Mark Ford, Nick Fryer, Gillian Green, Ron Greener, Paula Hielscher, Ray Horton, Andy Howland, Matt Hudson, Gareth Hughes, Alan Hutchinson, Barry Jenkinson, Phil Ledger, Peter McKinney, Joseph McNulty, John Moore, A.T. Moran, Paul Nicholson, David Northwood, Ron Parrott, Neil Parsons, Chris Phillips, Richie Pitt, Francis Ponder, Bob Pook, Jill Preston, Barrie Price, D.E. Roberts, Nick Roberts, Trevor Glyn Roberts, Martin Robinson, Colin Rowe, Grahame Rowley, Bill Russell, Andrew Shaw, J.A. Sherratt, Phil Slatter, Alan Sutton, Dave Swallow, David Swindells, Frank Tweddle, Lesley Westmoreland, Lindsey Wainwright, Colin Walters, Kit Walton, Mick Worrall and Clive Youlton.

I am also indebted to the many newspapers whose match reports have been invaluable source material: they are all acknowledged in the text. As far as possible, I have added the team lists for each game: in one or two early games, despite extensive research, I couldn't find them!

Finally I must thank my partner, Gerry – copy-editor and chief critic – for all her support and encouragement. When times were hard she kept me going. When things went well, we shared the joy.

INTRODUCTION

To some, engines, meccano, scientific experiment:
To some, stamps, flowers, the anatomy of insects:
To some, twisting elbows, torturing, sending to un-
deserved Coventry;
To some, soldiers, Waterloo, and miniature Howitzers:
To some, football,
In the sadness of an autumn afternoon
Studs and mud, the memorable dribble,
Rhododendrons at the back of the net
And the steamy dark gathering over bonfires,
The weight of water from the loosened skies.
And fingers too numb to undo laces.[1]

In 1986 Henry Kissinger remarked that English football was in 'nostalgic thrall to a bygone era'[2] – and this book is unashamedly nostalgic. Among my most piquant boyhood memories are Dad taking me to football at the Pilot Field in Hastings on dank, raw November afternoons, the walk home through the freezing fog and the sharp excruciating pain as warmth seeped back into my fingers as I tucked into a crumpet oozing with golden butter and strawberry jam. Then *Sports Report* – da-dum da-dum da-dum da-dum da-diddly dum di-dum – that was football in the early 1950s. I did see the 'Matthews Final' in 1953 on a neighbour's set – and I was irrevocably,

[1] Alan Ross, 'Boyhood', Glanville, p384.
[2] Winner, p. 76.

hopelessly hooked: but apart from the Cup Final, there was no televised football – indeed, for me, till the 1958 World Cup, no television at all. So we kicked about ourselves – there were fields in those days – and there were school games – House matches that seemed life-or-death at the time and then games away at other schools in places as far away as, well, Brighton, Eastbourne and Rye. All this nostalgia is stimulated by the pungent smells of the past. That most evocative of all the senses conjures up the mud, the clinging clods of good Sussex clay, the fresh grass of the early season, my goalie's jersey of wet wool like our shaggy old dog, the faintly medicinal whiff of bay rum, and on your boots the heady tang of polished leather daubed in that most mysterious of substances, dubbin.

We had our heroes, like Stan Matthews, Tom Finney and Billy Wright, but their deeds seemed to take place on some distant Mount Olympus and we learned of them from the radio or grainy photos in the Sunday paper. Or Dad, an accomplished amateur goalkeeper, would tell us of great players he'd admired – Jesse Pye, Alex James, Dixie Dean, Tommy Lawton, and two keepers like him – Frank Swift and Birmingham's Harry Hibbs, the best of them all, he reckoned. He made us feel that football had a sense of history. 'One of the reasons the English love football', according to David Winner, 'is because it is seen as old. The game floats on an ocean of nostalgia, sentimentality, tradition and myth in which its historicity is constantly invoked and celebrated.'[3] Those pillars of the past remain as benchmarks, as icons, so that football fans 'remember players' shirt numbers, their own journeys to stadiums, their team's place in the League on a given day, the texture of the meat pie they ate at half-time, the temperature of the Bovril they spilled. And all of it is important.'[4] To them, football fulfils a role 'not unlike that of the royal family, ruined castles and stately homes: it is a living symbol of stability and heritage.'[5]

Yet since the sixteenth century, football has been seen as 'A devilish pastime. . .and hereof growth envy, rancour, and malice, and sometimes brawling, murder, homicide, and great effusion of blood.'[6] Indeed, until the mid-nineteenth century football matches tended to be played according to an ad hoc set of rules. Captains would agree beforehand on whether to allow 'hacking' (i.e. vicious limb-threatening fouls) and handling of the

[3] Winner, p. 75.
[4] Winner., p. 78.
[5] Ibid.
[6] Philip Stubbes, *Anatomie of Abuses*, 1583.

ball. 'Hacking appeared to cover everything from tackling another player to physical assault, bringing him down violently, whether he had the ball or not. Some preferred this no-holds-barred approach, saying it was a man's game.'[7] There was much debate about the sporting nature of hacking and handling, some feeling, like Mr Campbell of the Blackheath Club, that 'Hacking is the true football game and if you look into the Winchester records you will find that in former years men were so wounded that they were actually carried off the field. I think if you do away with it you will do away with all the courage and pluck of the game.'[8]

In October 1863, football clubs, mostly consisting of ex-public school-boys and Oxbridge graduates and all based in the London area, met at the Freemasons' Tavern in Great Queen Street to form an association 'with the object of establishing a definite set of rules for the regulation of the game'. They called themselves the Football Association and over the next decade the rules were codified until in 1871/72 a tournament for the Football Association Challenge Cup was first staged. The origins of the competition must be seen in context. Conforming to the FA's rules of the game – including the outlawing of hacking and handling the ball – was a pre-requisite for participation in the Cup. The competition was the brainchild of the FA's Secretary, Mr C.W. Alcock, and featured just 15 clubs. It was the first national football tournament anywhere and it remains the bedrock of the modern game. The FA Cup was hugely instrumental in the development of English football. 'It changed some clubs from being places where people could turn up and play football to places where good players could turn up and play football to help the club win matches.'[9]

Although the Cup was won in its first ten years by amateur teams – old boys' sides, Army regiments and on one occasion by Oxford University – the lure of the Cup, the passion generated and the rivalries engendered led subversively but inevitably to the growth of professionalism, whose supporters were largely based in the Midlands and the North and were mainly working class. As more and more spectators turned up to watch, the pressure to win increased: players took time off work to hone their skills and felt entitled to receive compensation for time and wages lost. The game's founder members, mainly upper-class southern amateurs, argued that paying people to play was

[7] Davies, p. 25.
[8] Quoted in Davies, p. 28.
[9] French, p. 16.

against the spirit of the sport and if men's livelihoods depended on the result then cheating would become rife. The argument boiled down to South v North, toffs v workers, old money v new industry.

Cricket, my other sporting mistress, with hazy memories of long summer afternoons redolent of new-mown grass, cloudless skies and sumptuous teas, has always seemed to me a rural pastime, a game rooted in the soil of England's villages and woven into the fabric of their cultural life. When rural workers in their thousands migrated to the growing industrial towns of Lancashire and Yorkshire they took with them the games of their youth. They played the cricket they knew and loved from their rustic past and down the years grafted on to the yeoman stock a harder, grittier, strain. Football, on the other hand, that other temptress, appeared fixed in the warp and weft of the urban life of industrial England. David Goldblatt has pointed out that 'The enduring political, linguistic, economic and cultural differences between the North and the South of England that were played out through the Cup speak to a bigger truth in early industrial football, that at root the phenomenal popularity and success of the game cannot be divorced from the notion of civic pride and civic identity.'[10] Football became an expression of a growing working-class assertiveness and sense of identity. 'The working man, and working families, were finally beginning to lift their eyes up from the most parochial and immediate concerns to assume a wider set of horizons and to claim their rightful place in the national culture. Nothing could do this with more accuracy, simplicity and immediacy than supporting your local football team in the national league and the nation's cup.'[11]

A century on, how times have changed. When Arsenal played Bolton in the Fifth Round replay last season, there were five English players in the starting line-ups. Arsenal are no longer a London team, drawn from boys who sprang from the Hackney Marshes and the Lea Valley, who kicked leather balls about in 30-a-side scratch games in the urban streets of north London, nor even a side wealthy enough to invest in talent from soccer hotbeds such as the North-East or central Scotland. Arsenal are now an international franchise that happens to be based at a swanky new pad in Ashburton Grove.

That is why the Cup exerts such powerful nostalgia for football fans of

[10] Goldblatt, p. 59.
[11] Ibid.

a certain age. Tales of giant-killing deeds force us to confront once again the essential democracy of the game: in a world where moneyed mercenaries ply their trade across continents and oligarchs buy and sell 'franchises' seemingly on a whim, now and again players whose names sound like those we went to school with, players whom we could conceivably rub shoulders with in the pub and whose mums used to make us cups of tea and live down the street, might play out of their skins and put one over the big boys. It's human nature to want to see the mighty humbled, to rub their noses in it. The so-called 'smaller' clubs, essentially non-League, or certainly in the bottom two divisions, existing on annual wage budgets less than a Premiership star earns in a year, have to employ players with names like Green, Smith, or Bunce, Edwards, Heslop or Weaver, though even here, you might be lucky and pick up a loan signing or two from a French Second Division outfit.

Stories of famous Cup upsets remind us of how the game used to be, when we were in short trousers, when we could pronounce all the names, when we listened to Raymond Glendenning's commentaries on the Light Programme and all Cup matches seemed to be played in black and white on *Pathé News*. Historian David Lowenthal has sought to define the links between heritage, nostalgia and history. 'History seeks to convince by truth, and succumbs to falsehood,' he writes. 'Heritage exaggerates and omits, candidly invents and frankly forgets, and thrives on ignorance and error. Heritage is . . . not erudition but catechism – not checkable fact but credulous allegiance. Heritage is not a testable or even plausible version of our past; it is a declaration of faith in that past.'[12]

No doubt the stories of the games become more elaborate in the telling. But it's in the memories of those unforgettable matches that the soul of the game lies. That's why giant-killers are important – they bring the game back to its roots, they restore 'the beautiful game' to the people and they remind us why we fell in love with it in the first place.

Derek Watts
Lewes
October 2007

---

[12] 'Fabricating Heritage', article in *History & Memory*, Vol. 10, No. 1; quoted in Winner, p. 97.

1

NEWCASTLE UNITED 0, CRYSTAL PALACE 1

FA Cup, Round One, January 12, 1907

The Crystal Palace was one of the wonders of the Victorian age. With an interior height of 108 feet and 990,000 square feet of exhibition space, Sir Joseph Paxton's immense glass-and-iron structure symbolised Britain's global pre-eminence in engineering and technological advancement. Originally erected in Hyde Park, the Palace housed part of the Great Exhibition of 1851, designed by Prince Albert to show off Britain as the 'workshop of the world'. Three years later, the Palace was rebuilt in Penge Park at the top of Sydenham Hill and in 1861 workers at Paxton's iconic edifice formed the first Crystal Palace football team. The club was one of the 15 original entrants in the inaugural FA Cup competition of 1871–2 and reached the semi-final only to lose 3–0 to the Royal Engineers in a replay.

The amateur club of the 1860s and 1870s played in a huge grass bowl in the park at Sydenham. By the 1890s, the Cup Final, which had been held at Kennington Oval, Fallowfield in Manchester and Goodison Park in Liverpool, was beginning to attract crowds approaching 50,000. A new venue was needed and though London teams had no Cup pedigree, the FA chose Crystal Palace, with its own natural amphitheatre, for the 1895 Cup Final. In those days the Palace, with its own purpose-built railway station, was a sort of late-nineteenth-century Disneyland attracting two million visitors a year, with the 'Switchback' (a roller-coaster railway), a cinema, dirt-track cycling, a weekly display of fireworks during the summer and the first-ever dinosaur exhibition with life-size models designed and made by the grandly named Benjamin Waterhouse Hawkins. For two decades, between 1895 and the Great War, the finals at the Palace were

1

social occasions. There were small 'flower-pot' stands and in the open grass areas there was 'room to parade and picnic, although some fans only saw the ball when it was kicked 20 feet into the air.'[1] In an atmosphere not far removed from Derby Day at Epsom, spectators took their bikes and had picnics and 'the Cup Final was played after the crowd had eaten their lunch or had a few beers.'[2]

However, the FA was becoming increasingly irked by the idea of the Cup Final hosts running their own club and insisted that a separate company had to be formed. Thus in 1905 the present club came into being and John 'Jack' Robson, a former goalkeeper from Durham, was appointed the first manager of Crystal Palace FC. Robson was an interesting character. With his smart suit, boater and an impressively luxuriant moustache he affected more the air of an Edwardian dandy than a professional football manager. He had begun his managerial career at Middlesbrough where, despite being paid the handsome sum of £3 a week, he declined to travel to away games to save money. Nonetheless, despite this parsimony, he transformed the amateur Northern League side into a professional Second Division club.

Palace, nicknamed 'The Glaziers', entered the Second Division of the Southern League and, after losing their first match against Southampton Reserves when roughly three thousand people paid sixpence to stand or a shilling to sit, they remained undefeated for the rest of the campaign and ended their first season as champions.

In 1907 a new Elementary School was built in Davidson Road in East Croydon, where a year later a newly qualified teacher from Nottingham took up his first post. From the school, across the growing suburban terraces and the tracks into Norwood Junction, D.H. Lawrence could see the 'fairy-like, . . . blue bubble of the Crystal Palace'. The team that played in the shadow of the 'blue bubble' had begun their first season in the Southern League First Division with a 3–0 victory over Northampton but then won only two matches of the next ten.

In January therefore when Palace, having despatched Rotherham County[3] of the Midland League 4–0 before Christmas in the fifth qualifying round, were faced with the daunting prospect of travelling to St James' Park to

---

[1] Butler, *The Official History of the Football Association*, p. 49.
[2] Collett, p. 11.
[3] Now Rotherham United.

face the might of Newcastle United in the First Round proper, the long trip for Glaziers' fans hardly seemed worth the fare. Whether Mr Robson deemed it value for money we are not told.

Palace were languishing second from bottom of the Southern League: Newcastle had won all ten of their home league games and were one of England's most successful clubs before the First World War. They were the Chelsea or Manchester United of their day and had narrowly failed to achieve the League and Cup double in 1905, when Villa beat them in the Final. They hadn't lost at St James' Park for over a year and 'were a side of character and rare ability, strong, well-organised and unpredictable, an attraction wherever they played.'[4]

And yet, on one of those inexplicable afternoons when either lassitude or a collective lack of focus renders even the greatest sides ineffectual, a complacent and out-of-sorts United just never got into their stride. The Geordies did put together one decent moment of football in the first half when Jimmy Howie netted, only for his effort to be disallowed for offside – then Roberts was denied a goal for Palace for the same reason. In the early exchanges, according to the *Daily Mirror*, 'The Palace forwards were always the more nippy and speedily line'[5] [sic], and Scottish keeper Jimmy Lawrence in the Newcastle goal was far busier than Bob Hewitson, the Glaziers' keeper.

Then five minutes before half-time, the Magpies almost fell off their perch when against the run of play, Horace 'Harry' Astley, the former Millwall striker, 'who was an ever opportunist, profited by some indecision on the part of the Newcastle backs' and squeezed his shot past Jimmy Lawrence to give Palace the lead.

In the second half Newcastle established and began to press forward from a beach-head in Palace territory 'and the Palace captain brought a man back into the defence, and decided to play to hold the lead rather than increase it . . . and although Hewitson was frequently hard pressed he kept every shot out.' At the other end only brilliant saves by Lawrence kept George Woodger, Palace's local hero from Croydon, from adding to the visitors' lead. But despite all the pressure from the Geordies, the ball wouldn't go in and, in the florid prose of the *Mirror*, 'the result was the discomfi-

---

[4] Butler *The Official History of the Football Association*, p. 47.
[5] *Daily Mirror*, January 14, 1907.

ture of the Novocastrians'. Palace had given everything and 'It was a glorious victory well played for and thoroughly deserved . . . if the Crystal Palace do nothing more this year in the cup they have made themselves famous.'

The twenty thousand spectators had witnessed the biggest shock in the 35-year history of the FA Cup. As the *Guardian* said at the time, 'the Cup tournament is famed for surprises, but it has certainly never occasioned a more sensational result than this.'[6] It was a match which was responsible for the term 'giant killer' and only Walsall's humbling of the Mighty Arsenal 26 years later or Colchester's demolition of Leeds United in 1971 knocked it off its pedestal as the greatest upset of all time. Their remarkable win on Tyneside launched Palace on a buccaneering Cup run, though they needed replays against fellow Southern League opponents Fulham and Brentford before the quarter-finals saw them drawn at home to First Division Everton. In front of a record Selhurst Park crowd of thirty-five thousand Harry Astley struck once more to give Palace the lead, but Everton, at the time riding high in second place in the First Division, took the tie to a replay where the Glaziers' bandwagon hit the buffers. Everton pulled rank, and their class and professionalism gave them a convincing 4–0 home win.

As for Newcastle, their shattering Cup exit proved to be a temporary blip. The Magpies went on to win the Division One championship for the second time in three years, dropping only one point at home – in their last home match.

Palace's Cup exertions almost certainly took a toll on their League campaign and they finished nineteenth in the Southern League First Division. At the end of the season John Robson left Palace to take over at neighbours Croydon Common and thence, in March 1908, he moved to Brighton and Hove Albion, where six years later, he masterminded yet another giant-killing, this time over Oldham Athletic.

Palace continued to play on the old Cup Final ground till 1915, when they were evicted by army requisitioning, whereupon the club moved to nearby Herne Hill, briefly shared Millwall's Den, before settling at a purpose-built venue, their current home, Selhurst Park, in 1924. They had started life in the League in 1920 with a flourish, winning the Third Division championship, heading a league which included their now-traditional rivals Brighton and Millwall and in the same season they beat Manchester 2–1

---

[6] *Guardian*, January 14, 1907.

in the First Round of the Cup – but it was a deceptively promising start to League life. Four years later, as they moved into their new home, Palace were relegated and spent the next 26 seasons bumping around the bottom division.

In the 1960s and 70s the club became better-known for its off-the-field characters than its results. Palace reached the First Division for the first time in 1969 but within five years, they were back in the Third – years which encompassed the exciting reign of the flamboyant fedora-wearing, cigar-smoking and champagne-drinking Malcolm Allison, featuring a Cup semi-final against Southampton in 1976.

The sharp-suited, fast-talking but shrewd Terry Venables masterminded the team's return to Division One as champions in 1979 but as soon as the press – and the club's own publicity machine – hailed them as the 'Team of the Eighties', Palace were relegated after only just two seasons, which left the field open for the self-confident publicity-seeking 'personality' chairman Ron Noades, who at least had the nous to appoint ex-England and Manchester United star Steve Coppell as manager in 1984 for the first of his three spells at the helm. Coppell, a highly intelligent and effective motivator and a forward-looking coach, created a tough and efficient outfit which won promotion to Division One in 1989. Coppell's men included future England internationals Geoff Thomas, John Salako and Ian Wright and remains the most celebrated in the club's history. The team achieved the club's highest-ever League position, third in 1990–91, a year after losing to Manchester United in an FA Cup final replay. Nevertheless, Palace were relegated again in 1993 and suffered the same fate on two more occasions before the turn of the century.

On November 30, 1936 at six in the evening, the manager of the Crystal Palace, Henry Buckland and his daughter Crystal, named after his love of the historic building, were out walking their dog when Buckland noticed a red glow in a staff lavatory. He called firemen and workmen to extinguish the blaze but, within five minutes, the fire had swept through the whole building. The flames could be seen from Central London, several miles away, and by morning most of the Palace was destroyed. Viewing the ruins, Winston Churchill was said to have remarked, 'It is the end of an era.'

There were doubtless a few times during the mid-1990s, during a period of financial meltdown off the field, when Palace fans must have felt the same. The club had 17 changes of manager since the start of the 1980s and in the boom-and-bust decade of the 1990s Selhurst Park became a rest home for underachieving foreign players in the twilight of their careers.

Unlike Paxton's historic structure however Crystal Palace FC has risen from the ashes. Businessman Simon Jordan restored financial equilibrium and in 2003/04 a sensational late-season dash up the Division One table brought a shock promotion to the Premiership. However, the club seems perennially to be one of those 'yo-yo' teams, like Watford or Sheffield United, destined to shuttle forever between the Championship and the top flight of English football, and the team went straight back down. While the gulf between the second tier and the Premiership seems wider than ever, when the prospect of Palace again playing Newcastle at St James' Park seems a pipe-dream, fans of the Eagles can console themselves with the thought that a century ago their non-League no-hopers dumped the best team in the land out of the Cup on their own patch and their heroes were dubbed the original 'giant-killers'.

2

WEST HAM UNITED 2, MANCHESTER UNITED 1

FA Cup, Round Three, February 25, 1911

'Come on, you Irons!' When the roars of thousands of passionately committed West Ham fans echo round one of the most atmospheric stadiums in the country, I wonder how many realise how closely the nickname expresses the roots of their club's long history, or how intimately the club was bound up with the economic lifeblood of the urban landscape from which it emerged.

In 1880 Frank Hills bought the Thames Ironworks and Shipbuilding Company, taking over a scarcely going concern with a markedly chequered history. The revolutionary impact on transport of advances in the technology of iron and steel building had become increasingly apparent in a century infatuated by scientific progress, and engineers everywhere were exploring new ideas, new materials and new designs. Thames Ironworks was in the forefront, building the *Warrior*, the world's first iron warship, at its Orchard Road works in Blackwall in 1859, but when a grandstand constructed to hold spectators at the launch of another battleship, the *Albion*, collapsed, killing 200 people, the company's reputation was severely tarnished. Furthermore, by the 1890s, the shipbuilding industry along the Thames was under increasing attack from bigger firms on the Clyde, Tyne and Mersey. However, Arnold, Frank's son, was determined to keep his 6,000 men in jobs and maintained the yard at Blackwall when a move downstream to Tilbury would have made more economic sense.

Like many patrician Victorian businessmen, Hills was a devout Christian and in 1895, as part of a campaign to get his workers out of the pubs and on to the playing fields, he founded the Thames Ironworks football team. Two years later Hills invested in a new sports stadium at the Memorial Ground in Plaistow, which boasted a grandstand and hosted athletics and cycling meets as well as soccer. He also arranged the club's early fixtures, including a debut season appearance in the FA Cup and a series of friendlies under innovative artificial lights supplied by the dockyard engineers. The heirs of his legacy, West Ham United, winners of a European trophy less than 70 years later, therefore owe their origins less to an ambition for global sporting dominance than an exercise in Victorian 'muscular Christianity'.

The first players to wear the famous claret and sky blue – the house colours of Thames Ironworks – were shipyard workers and dockers. A generation or so before they might have been farmers, for until the mid-nineteenth century agriculture was the main commercial occupation. Between the Thames to the south, the Lea Valley to the west and the River Roding to the east, this low-lying, marshy area five miles east of the City of London produced market-garden foodstuffs, milk and cheese for the rapidly growing population of the nation's capital.

A major change came in the 1850s with the building of the Royal Docks for the new large steamships. In their time, they were the largest docks in the world and since they were the first directly linked to the railways, London's East End became the most important focus for manufacturing activity in southern England. Thousands of people moved from Britain's countryside, then suffering a severe agricultural depression, into Stepney, Bermondsey, Whitechapel and Poplar, attracted by the multitudes of new jobs that were created. They came from the Empire, too – Indians, Chinese, Africans – and Jews and Italians from Europe, so that today, following the *Windrush* migration of Afro-Caribbean workers in the 1950s and 60s, the London Borough of Newham is the most ethnically diverse in the country. The population of West Ham – 18,817 in 1851 – had grown by 1901 to 267,903 and the borough was heavily industrialised with seemingly endless terraces of jerry-built housing.

By then the Football League had been founded and the game was quickly becoming a huge working-class sport. Meanwhile, the shipyard was in trouble but, paradoxically, as the Ironworks itself began to creak under the weight of competition, its offspring team prospered. They turned professional in 1898 and entered the Southern League Second Division. In June 1900

Thames Ironworks FC was dissolved, but with an issue of 20,000 ten-shilling shares the club was relaunched in July 1900 as West Ham United FC. Four years later the club moved to its current home, the Boleyn Ground, in Upton Park.

Within seven years the great era of the Thames as a shipbuilding river was over, when in 1911 the Ironworks launched the *Thunderer*, the last ship ever built in London. The increasingly rapid mechanisation of ship-building and cargo-handling during the Edwardian decade led to high unem-ployment and more casual daywork in the docks. Ironically though, the year which saw the end of commercial shipbuilding brought the club born of the Ironworks to national attention for the first time. After several years of modest success in the Southern League the Hammers beat three previous FA Cup-winners in reaching the Fourth Round. Their victory in the First Round over Nottingham Forest was played in such a dense pea-souper that newspaper reports described the game as a 'pure farce'. Hammers forward Frank Carruthers later confessed to having 'punched both West Ham goals into the net in full view of several opponents'.[1]

There must have been something subversive in the air that season, when, it seemed, 'The old order changeth, yielding place to the new'.[2] Sunderland and the two Sheffield teams fell against non-League opposition – Norwich, Darlington and Coventry respectively. First Division Bristol City, finalists only two years before, were beaten by a team from the Birmingham and District League – Crewe Alexandra – and in Round Two, 'Proud Preston', whose 'Invincibles' had been one of the pre-eminent teams in the late nine-teenth century, were the visitors to the Boleyn Ground and were soundly despatched 3–0.

In 1911 Manchester United were en route to their second League title in four years. They had made a wonderful start to the season, winning seven out of their first eight matches and, in the words of the *East Ham Mail*, 'The draw was undoubtedly the tit-bit of the third round, for Manchester United are looked upon as the best team in England this season.'[3]

The gate was officially 24,800, but as 'Rambler' reported, 'Every point of vantage was seized upon by the spectators. Some climbed up the tele-graph pole, others sat on top of advertisement hoardings and looked every

---

[1] Lyons and Ronay, p. 431.
[2] Tennyson, 'The Passing of Arthur', I. 407.
[3] *East Ham Mail*, March 3, 1911.

minute as if they would topple over while others seated themselves on top of the covered stands.'[4]

The pitch was heavy and it was felt that the visitors' superior fitness would tell as the Hammers started nervously. Yet, against the run of play, they opened the scoring when Webb 'took the ball well down the field and neatly tricked the opposing backs before passing to Shea, who sent in a screw shot, the ball going into the far corner of the net. It was a lovely goal', writes Rambler. Local euphoria was short-lived, however, for a few minutes later Manchester forced a corner from which Turnbull headed the equaliser. 'Then commenced a ding-dong struggle for the mastery. Webb again broke away, and his shot struck the upright, and for a couple of minutes the ball was hovering round Manchester's goal. Shea struck the crossbar, and then Butcher headed, the ball dropping dead on the goal-line, Edmonds just saving it in time, and then Caldwell sent over.'

In the second half West Ham were the better team and had most of the play. On one occasion Rambler records that 'Webb got through and was pushed in the back by an opponent. There were loud appeals for a penalty, but the referee did not give a foul, much to the crowd's disgust': *plus ça change, plus c'est la même chose.*

With both sides pressing for a winner, the game became 'very scrappy and of the traditional cup tie order. West Ham were triers all the time, and now had the best of things. The crowd yelled their disgust when Ashton was given offside after making a fine run.' Even then Manchester were renowned for a sophisticated attacking game, but Rambler noted that they 'now played a game quite foreign to their recognised style, and kicked out at every chance'. Just as everyone was composing mental sick-notes for a long trip north for the replay, with only three minutes left, 'Ashton sent over to Caldwell, who netted with a first-time shot. The remaining few minutes saw the visitors going for all they were worth', but the Hammers' defence held firm.

It was all over – Southern League West Ham had won. The First Division leaders had been beaten – narrowly, in a close-fought encounter, but they had been beaten by a more determined side on the day. The scenes at the close were 'indescribable. Thousands dashed across the pitch to shake hands with the Hammers, while some were carried shoulder high into the pavilion.'

Sadly, one cannot record that the crowd greeted the momentous triumph

---

[4] Ibid.

with resounding choruses of 'I'm Forever Blowing Bubbles', now one of the most recognisable club anthems in English football – for the song did not see the light of day until the Broadway musical *The Passing Show of 1918*, and while it was certainly played over the newfangled Upton Park tannoy in 1927, nobody knows for sure just how 'Bubbles' fell into the hands of West Ham.

In the 1920s the lilting waltz became a music-hall favourite and was a popular number at the piano singalongs in the pubs of the East End. One can imagine the dockers on a Saturday lunchtime, flushed with a few pints and the song's schmaltzy optimism, carrying the lyrics with them from the taverns to the terraces at Upton Park. It was also known to have been sung about a schoolboy footballer at the local Park School, one Billy J. Murray, so-called because of his singular resemblance to the boy in *Bubbles*, the famous painting by Millais. Corney Beal, Park's headmaster, was a mate of Hammers' coach Charlie Paynter and is widely credited with introducing 'Bubbles' to the Upton Park faithful.

Whatever the origin of the links between 'Bubbles' and the Hammers, they sang it when Bobby Moore led them out in the FA Cup Final at Wembley in 1964 and Ronnie Boyce headed in a stoppage-time winner for a 3–2 victory over Preston. 'It was one of the first times that supporters had burst into spontaneous song at a Cup Final without being hectored by a man in a white coat.'[5] These terrace songs – like 'Keep Right on to the End of the Road' at Birmingham and 'Blaydon Races' at St James' Park – were stylistic forerunners to the chants that have since become a trademark of the game – early expressions of the clannish communality which is part of the folklore of the football supporter.

The tribal character of football, notably in the cities of industrial England and Scotland, gave rise to fierce and implacable rivalries. West Ham's early players included Charlie Satterthwaite, reputed to be one of the fiercest strikers of the ball in the country, who in 1906 took part in the first of many fiery Derby games with Millwall. Separated only by three or four miles and the A13, the two clubs held each other in such antipathy that the *East Ham Echo* report describes a game in which 'all attempts at football were ignored', climaxing in West Ham's Jarvis 'smashing the head of Millwall's Deans against a metal advertising board, seriously injuring his opponent, for which he received only a caution.'[6]

---

[5] Irwin, p. 199.
[6] Lyons and Ronay, p. 431.

11

Life in the East End had always been tough, a battle for survival among rapid changes in industry and the urban landscape. It is hardly surprising that its football reflected that reality. As recently as 2006 a Channel 4 television documentary noted high crime rates, lower-than-average school results, high pollution levels, low economic activity and depressed property prices. A century before, Arnold Hills dreamed of a thriving ironworks and a successful football team, preferably made up of sober vegetarians. In reality, his legacy to the people of Blackwall was certainly very different. When he died in 1927, the jobs in his ironworks had gone but they still had the Hammers to cheer.

The club still pays homage to its engineering roots in the two crossed hammers on its crest. And that is why to this day you will hear the crowds at Upton Park shouting 'Come on, you Irons', a chant and a nickname that dates back to the great shipbuilding days of the Thames.

3

BRIGHTON AND HOVE ALBION 1, OLDHAM ATHLETIC 0

FA Cup, Round One, January 14, 1914

In 1750, when he was practising medicine in Lewes, Dr Richard Russell, an eminent physician, published his treatise *Glandular Diseases, or a Dissertation on the Use of Sea Water in the Affections of the Glands*. He recommended especially that people try the water on the coast, near a small fishing settlement called 'Brighthelmstone',[1] where in 1753 Russell built a house on the site of what is now the Royal Albion Hotel. His advocacy of the benefits of sea-bathing and the chalybeate water led to the town's becoming the fashionable resort for London society, patronised by George III's flamboyant eldest son, the Prince Regent, who first visited the town in 1783, using it as an informal retreat from the stifling atmosphere of the court in London. The contribution of 'Prinny' to the town is summed up in a delightful painting by Rex Whistler in the Royal Pavilion. Called *The Prince Regent Awakening the Spirit of Brighton*, it shows the almost-naked prince lifting the veil from a sleeping girl.

With the coming of the railway from the capital in 1840, Brighton became a Mecca for the day-tripper and the country's most popular resort. Nonetheless, despite almost a century of royal patronage, and having virtually created the seaside holiday, as the nineteenth century drew to a close Brighton was undergoing a depression. Its economic base was largely seasonal, with a sizeable industry centred on the railway workshops. The town, with a population of around 120,000, was as densely populated as any northern city and entertainment was provided largely by the many theatres, music

---

[1] It became 'Brighton' in the early nineteenth century.

halls and taverns – although local 'kinematic' pioneers were giving moving-picture shows at Hove Town Hall and other venues.

Until 1898 the only football of any importance to be seen in Brighton was at Preston Park where amateur teams like Brighton Hornets, Brighton Athletic and North End Rangers played purely for fun. The Sussex County Football Association, founded in 1882, comprised public-school sides and 'professional' men and it was not until the formation of the East and West Sussex Leagues in 1896 that the influence of the upper- and middle-class teams diminished with the emergence of club sides like Southwick, Shoreham, Hastings & St Leonards, Worthing and Hove. But Brighton, by far the largest town in Sussex, had no single side to represent it. Compared with the industrial Midlands and Lancashire, where professionalism flourished, what was happening in Brighton was very small beer indeed.

Against this unpromising background enterprising men like Edgar 'Chippie' Everest, a local tobacconist and SCFA Secretary, saw the value to civic pride of a professional football team, and in 1898 the semi-professional Brighton United was formed – 'a good advertisement for a seaside town in the doldrums'[2] – and was elected to the Southern League. Despite beating Thames Ironworks – the forerunners to West Ham United, 4–1 in the FA Cup, by March 1900 – 'United' was dead. Heavy rain had led to small gates at the unsheltered cricket ground but a team was formed from members of North End Rangers, who in 1901 were invited to join the Second Division of the Southern League.

Rangers were the Brighton and Hove Albion in embryo and looked across the town with envy at Hove FC, a local amateur club, who had secured themselves a private pitch close to the railway station. The Goldstone Ground was by far the best site in the town and Rangers, camping like cuckoos at the County Ground, desperately coveted a home of their own. In 1901 they changed their title to Brighton and Hove amidst objections from the amateur club, fearful lest their supporters might see a sell-out to the professional game. Their fears were somewhat dispelled when the name 'Albion' was adopted in July 1901. The true origins of the name 'Albion' are now shrouded in the mists of time. Right-winger Bert Baker claims he thought of it. The former Brighton United manager and landlord of the Farm Tavern had been associated with West Bromwich. Whatever the truth

---

[2] Vinicombe, p. 5.

was, the colours were changed from green to the blue-and-white stripes worn at the Hawthorns – but not until 1904.

Brighton and Hove Albion FC was formed at the Seven Stars in Ship Street in June 1901, and the Albion marked their debut season in the Southern League by finishing third. This promising start badly affected Hove FC and the Albion approached them with a view to sharing the Goldstone. It was an inevitable move given the growing professionalism within the game and they moved to the Goldstone in 1902 and were promoted to Division One of the Southern League in 1903. Their arrival was greeted by the more established clubs with some disdain. They were regarded as upstarts. The club, much like the town, was acquiring a swagger in its step.

Not only were Albion's prospects brighter, but Brighton as a town had started to pick up. In 1901 Harry Preston, an important figure in the sporting and theatrical world, rebuilt the derelict Royal York Hotel, and the social pulse started to beat with renewed vigour. The world and his wife (or somebody else's) could enjoy themselves in Brighton and a local detective agency regularly took several columns in one of the weekly newspapers extolling the proficiency of their lady cyclist investigators.

As the Edwardian era began, Brighton was a town with a risqué reputation, which produced handsome profits for the booming hotel and catering business. The town strutted with an ineffable brio, and a century later has never quite thrown off the air of raffishness conveyed in Whistler's picture, even if it ever wished to. In the immortal epithet of writer and former resident Keith Waterhouse, Brighton always looks as though it is helping the police with their inquiries. It has the aura of a town of no fixed abode, loitering with intent, the sort you'd think twice about taking home to meet your parents.

In the years before the Great War, crowds flocked to see Fred Karno's troupe at the Hippodrome, and rocked with laughter at a funny little man at the foot of the bill – Charlie Chaplin. The Grand Theatre was the most popular because it was lit by electricity and you could puff on a Woodbine. You could lunch at Sam Isaacs' restaurant in West Street on sausages, mash and onions for fourpence halfpenny and go to Eastbourne and back on the excursion paddle steamer for ninepence. 'With donkey rides for the

---

[3] Vinicombe, p. 13.

15

children and the pub for mum and dad, Brighton was a working-class heaven.'[3] As if that was not enough, Ranjitsinji was thrilling the aficionados at the County Ground with his graceful, wristy stroke play. When King Edward visited three times in 12 months around 1908, it was the final accolade.

The Albion won the Southern League championship in 1909/10, playing regularly against teams like Portsmouth, Southampton, Crystal Palace, Millwall, QPR and West Ham United. In the FA Charity Shield they defeated the Football League Champions Aston Villa 1–0 at Stamford Bridge, one of the club's greatest-ever achievements. Albion opened the 1913/14 season confidently, losing only three of the first sixteen games and were in third place when they drew Oldham Athletic away in the first round of the Cup. Just nine months before, the Athletic had reached the FA Cup semi-final, going down 1–0 to Aston Villa at Ewood Park. This was the golden era in Oldham's history and the team included several internationals, notably Charlie Roberts, their centre-half. In the immediate prewar years, Albion's solid defence made the Goldstone Ground a fortress, although the forward line lacked punch – but would they get the chance to play the Athletic at home?

For the game at Boundary Park, the London and North-Western Railway Company ran 'a splendidly-equipped train', reported the *Evening Argus*, which was 'electrically-lighted, and steam-heated', to take two hundred Albion supporters north. 'Nothing could have looked more cosy in contrast to the murky atmosphere outside than the well-lighted carriages as they drew their sinuous trail out of the station at midnight.' The atmosphere among travelling soccer fans has changed little down the years. 'No-one breathlessly dashed in at the last moment or did anything creating incident except sing songs and raise a cheer as Brighton was left behind.' But a delightful comment shows how the game has moved on: – 'Colours were freely worn and a few ladies in the party showed that even the weaker sex are real enthusiasts.'

The fans' long journey was rewarded when, 12 minutes from time, Bill Miller, Albion's centre-forward, equalised Scottish left-winger Joe Donnachie's first-half goal. The return train left at 6.30 and even at 1.15 in the morning, a sizeable crowd had gathered at the station to greet the team. The replay was scheduled for the following Wednesday, with a 2.15 kick-off, which would, in the *Argus'* elegant prose, 'admit of an extra half-hour being played if there is no deciding score at the expiration of the regulation hour and a half.'

The club's directors decided to increase admission charges to a shilling for the replay, as the Aldershot board did 73 years later. Despite impassioned letters in the local press,[4] there were queues at the Goldstone 'over an hour before the commencement, and the turnstiles continued to click merrily until after the kick-off'[5] and according to the *Brighton Herald,* another thousand fans stood outside, 'content to hear the shouting and get an occasional sight of the ball as it was kicked high'.[6]

About an hour before kick-off, the Oldham fans paraded their mascot, a goat, around the ground. 'The goat was drawing a blue chair gaily decorated with the Club's colours, and also displaying a facsimile of the English Cup filled with blue and white flowers.'[7] In response one of Albion's programme sellers 'decked out the groundsman's bulldog in blue and white and ushered it onto the pitch. On spotting the Oldham mascot the bulldog gave a sudden leap, broke away from its leash and uttering furious and menacing noises chased the goat round the ground.'[8]

It was a bitterly cold afternoon, when a biting north-east wind 'played havoc with the intentions of the players, and reduced the game to a matter of opportunism rather than of science.'[9] It was a dour defensive struggle in which the Albion matched their illustrious opponents in all departments, with their skipper, Joe Leeming, outstanding at left-back. Occasionally, their forwards, led by Billy Miller, put the Athletic on the defensive and 'Jones, Miller, and Longstaff figured in the smartest combined movement of the game so far. They put in a neat passing run half the length of the ground, and Jones, who was given the shot, sent just outside the left post with a capital cross-drive.'[10]

In the second half the wind continued to make 'accurate combination and shooting being well-nigh impossible under the circumstances'[11] and the game went into extra time with neither side looking likely to score.

---

[4] Mr D. Torrance of Hove joined in 'the universal protest at such a charge for a replay, because I can assure you that on all sides is the same remark – "If they charge a shilling I shan't go."'
[5] *Evening Argus,* January 14, 1914.
[6] Ibid.
[7] Ibid.
[8] Vinicombe, p. 25.
[9] *Brighton Herald,* January 17, 1914.
[10] *Evening Argus,* January 14, 1914.
[11] *Brighton Herald,* January 17, 1914.

However, the Albion were pressing: Miller went close with a smart header and, with only eight minutes to go, they forced a corner. In the teeth of a blizzard, Bert Longstaff's corner scraped the crossbar, David Parkes prevented the ball from going out of play, screwing it back across the goal. The Oldham defenders tried frantically to clear, but Billy Booth got in first, 'rushing the ball through from the exciting melee that followed in the goal-mouth'[12] and steered the ball into the net.

At the final whistle the crowd hurled their hats and sticks into the air and the players had to sprint for safety as Albion fans poured over the barriers, seizing upon Joe Leeming and shouldering him off in triumph. With the town in the grip of Cup-fever, the official gate of 10,700 for the Oldham replay was smashed when in the second round at the Goldstone three weeks later, Albion clashed with Second Division Clapton Orient. A goal down at half-time, when a long shot was deflected off Gunner Higham with Whiting stranded, Brighton rampaged back in the second half. Charlie Webb equalised in the 57th minute, gave the Albion the lead six minutes later and 'Bullet' Jones clinched the tie fifteen minutes from time, with a quarter of an hour left on the clock. The club had reached the last 16 for the first time.

In the Third Round, Albion travelled north again, this time to Hillsborough, to meet a Sheffield Wednesday side, who, despite having won the trophy twice before, were struggling in the First Division. The four hundred fans who made the journey to South Yorkshire were quietly confident, an optimism boosted by a first-half performance in which Longstaff and Webb threatened the home defence on several occasions. After half-time, however, the wheels began to fall off and, when Dave McLean gave Wednesday the lead, Albion's dreams of Cup glory began to unravel. Gill and Burkinshaw added further goals and the Albion were left with the significant consolation of £1,700 from the Cup run, a welcome financial boost to a hard-up non-League club.

After the Great War, Brighton remained a solid Third Division club, gaining a reputation between the wars for FA Cup adventures, knocking out seven First Division opponents. Promoted to Division Two in 1958 as Third South champions, on December 27 Albion faced promotion favourites, Fulham, who had an all-star line-up including George Cohen and Johnny

---

[12] Ibid.

Haynes, but the biggest attraction was the first return appearance of Albion's legendary former skipper, Jimmy Langley. The crowd was a staggering 36,747, the ground record at the Goldstone. Albion walloped the Cottagers 3–0, with Tommy Dixon scoring twice and Adrian Thorne slotting home the third ten yards from me as I sat with my dad in the front row of the South Stand.

A quarter of a century later, I stood amazed at Wembley in May 1983 as Scottish midfielder Gordon Smith attained immortality, responsible for the second most famous piece of football commentary in history, after 'They think it's all over!' It had been a pulsating final against Manchester United, with Gary Stevens equalising for the Seagulls four minutes from time. In the last minute of extra time Michael Robinson slipped the ball to Smith, unmarked inside the United penalty area. 'And Smith must score!' shouted BBC Radio's Peter Jones as Smith hesitated fatally, allowing goalkeeper Gary Bailey time to block Smith's low drive.

The Albion succumbed meekly in the replay, going down 4–0. Since then the club has come close to going out of business. The Goldstone Ground, stalked by the ghosts of the club's nine decades of history, was built, like many stadiums, on land which was a prime target for retail development. Property developers Chartwell Land convinced the gullible souls in charge of the club 'to sell up and use the money made from the nice town centre development to wipe out the club's debts and build a shiny new out-of-town ground.'[13] There was just one problem – the hated Chief Executive David Bellotti sold the much-loved old ground before ensuring that the club had a new one. The Albion's decade-long struggle to move to a new ground at Falmer, via a two-year exile at Gillingham and an uneasy lease of a converted municipal athletics stadium, is a microcosm of what has gone wrong with football since the Secod World War, the game and the clubs which form its lifeblood increasingly falling prey to accountants and businessmen with little interest in or commitment to football, more dedicated to the balance sheet than the game.

Now, with the prospect of moving to their new 22,000-seat stadium in 2010, Seagulls fans look forward to a future supporting a club with a deep

---

[13] French, p. 160.

local taproot, and a history in which games like the victory over Oldham stand as landmarks in a respectable and sometimes glorious past.

BRIGHTON: Whiting, Spencer, Leeming, Booth, Parkes, Higham, Longstaff, Jones, Miller, Webb, Tyler
OLDHAM: Taylor, Hodson, Cook, Moffat, Roberts, Wilson, Tummon, Walters, Gee, Woodger, Donnachie

4

SWANSEA TOWN 1,
BLACKBURN ROVERS 0

FA Cup, Round One, January 9, 1915

Swansea means different things to different people. To the Welsh it means 'Abertawe', where the River Tawe flows into the great sweep of Swansea Bay. To devotees of industrial history, it was a tiny harbour and fishing village until the early nineteenth century, when the Morfa Copper Works were built on the river above the town, exploiting the abundance of cheap local coal and deposits of copper ore. The harbour was expanded and by the middle of the nineteenth century more than ten thousand ships used the port each year and Swansea had become the largest exporter of coal in the world. By the 1880s, 60 per cent of the copper ores imported to Britain were smelted in the Lower Swansea valley and arsenic, zinc and tinplate works added to the town's industrial importance.

To aficionados of popular song, it was the home of Pete Ham, the man who wrote 'Without You', Harry Nilsson's biggest hit and the leading light in Badfinger, the first band the Beatles signed to their Apple label. Husky-voiced songstress Bonnie Tyler was born a couple of miles up the Neath road in Skewen, and the suburb of St Thomas, east of the city centre, produced tenor and arch-Goon Sir Harry Secombe. To the holidaymaker it is still something of a seaside resort, where, along with the hotels, pubs, shops and amusement arcades, it is the gateway to the Gower Peninsula, unspoilt haven of small fishing villages and delightful coves. To the railway buff, the Mumbles was the terminus of one of Britain's earliest railways, a hybrid affair – a sort of seaside tramway and a genuine railway, which ran beside the beach eight miles to Swansea from early in the nineteenth century until the mid-1950s. The railway ran into Swansea hard by St Helen's cricket ground, forever immortalised for cricket fans as the place where in 1968 Sir Garry Sobers hit Malcolm Nash for six sixes in one over – the first time this had been done in first-class cricket.

To followers of the national game – almost the national religion – the same St Helen's ground was the home of Swansea Rugby Club, who once played in front of gates of 10,500, many seated in the celebrated east stand, whose cloisters arched over part of the Oystermouth road. It was here that the 'All-Whites' became the first-ever club side to beat the All Blacks in 1935 and world champions Australia were vanquished 21–6 in 1992.

Oh yes – and to the literati, it was the birthplace of Dylan Thomas. He was born in October 1914 in Cwmdonkin Drive, Uplands and there is a memorial to him in the nearby Cwmdonkin Park, where he played as a child. Dannie Abse, the best-known living Welsh poet, once met Thomas when Abse was a medical student in wartime London. Thomas, for once sober on licensed premises, joined him at a table in a Swiss Cottage pub and seemed less than enthralled when Abse introduced himself, mentioning that Thomas knew his cousin, the Swansea painter Leo Solomon. This awkward encounter failed to lessen Abse's admiration for the great man and much of his early work was profoundly pervaded by Thomas's language and cadence. In a 1959 poem, Abse, a lifelong Cardiff City fan, describes Saturday afternoons at Ninian Park, where, 'waiting, we recall records, legendary scores,' and evokes a 'memory of faded games, the discarded years; talk of Aston Villa, Orient and the Swans.'[1]

'The Swans' (the all-white colours and their name led logically to the nickname) were formed in 1912 when Swansea Town Football Club came into being as a professional outfit. But soccer was being played in Swansea many years before and children would kick a ball about on a patch of waste ground covered in vetch.[2] In 1911 a committee of the Swansea League, which had been formed in the same year, rented the field and the club began playing on a clinker surface[3] – the result of the ground being the site of the former coal store for its former owners, the Swansea Gas and Light Company. The ground was hemmed in by terraced housing, with the 'shambolic mix of stands'[4] overlooked by a Territorial Army depot and Swansea Prison. This

---

[1] From 'The Game', published in *Presenting Welsh Poetry* (Faber, 1959).
[2] Any of a group of trailing or climbing plants belonging to the pea family, usually having seed pods and purple, yellow, or white flowers, and including the fodder crop alfalfa (from www.tiscali.co.uk).
[3] With players wearing pads to protect their knees.
[4] *Observer*, p. 22, January 6, 2008.

position, near the seafront and the town centre, made the tight little ground boisterously atmospheric. As many other South Wales towns were already represented, the Swans were invited to join the Second Division of the Southern League and played their first professional match against Cardiff City at the Vetch Field on September 7, 1912; the result was a 1–1 draw.

The club was immediately successful. The Welsh Cup was won in 1913 and two years later, against the backdrop of the carnage of the Western Front, the Swans were drawn to face League champions Blackburn in the First Round of the FA Cup.

Football continued for a time after the outbreak of the First World War: there was no conscription until January 1916. For some among the traditional officer class, football began to be seen as 'a key element of the metaphorical experience of war. Boys at Marlborough College thought the war was like a glorified football match in which, if peace did not come, they might take their places in the England team.'[5] Writing of the experiences in the trenches of the East Surrey Regiment the *Illustrated London News* published this:

> On through the hail of slaughter
> Where gallant comrades fall,
> Where blood is poured like water,
> They drive the trickling ball.
> The fear of death before them
> Is but an empty name;
> True to the land that bore them
> The Surreys play the game.[6]

The continuation of the football programme caused a great deal of controversy. Some felt that it was good for morale, but by January 1915 most believed it to have been a bad idea. Nonetheless, a soldier with the 7th Royal Field Artillery wrote to his local paper in Swansea, on the eve of the Swans' First Round tie, 'I see they are trying to stop football. I think it is a wrong thing to do, as we out here follow the play in the papers. If football was stopped they might as well stop sending papers to the troops, as we eagerly wait for the papers, with accounts of the League matches.'[7]

---

[5] Richard Holt, *Sport and the British: A Modern History*, (Oxford University Press, 1989), p. 256; quoted in Goldblatt, p. 173.
[6] *Illustrated London News*, July 29, 1916; quoted in Goldblatt, p. 173.
[7] *Swansea Football Post*, January 9, 1915.

However, as the reality of war began to hit home and the telegrams started to arrive on doorsteps up and down the country, criticism of football as a worthless distraction intensified. Clubs were accused of helping the enemy, and the Dean of Lincoln wrote to the FA railing against 'onlookers who, while so many of their fellow men are giving themselves in their country's peril, still go gazing at football'.[8] Footballers, fit young men compared to many of their contemporaries, were seen by many virtually as cowards, using their profession to avoid volunteering for King and Country.

Nonetheless, many players did quit their clubs to go to war and the work of the FA almost ground to a halt. Attendances had halved but the League decided to carry on with their programme. However, professional football was in abeyance: 'a hierarchy of priority given concrete form when the War Office commandeered the FA's office space at 42, Russell Square.'[9]

The FA had consulted the War Office before going ahead with the 1914/15 Cup and against this surreal background, with a major war being waged with bloody intensity just two hundred miles away, Swansea prepared to do battle with the League champions. They were lying fourth in the Southern League's Second Division and took the field to enjoy their afternoon against the league champions. Victory was clearly out of the question, as Rovers, albeit with several players on the injured list, were at the time third in Division One, with three successive away League wins. 'Freelance', the *Swansea Football Post's* writer, expressed local concern 'with regard to the reshuffling of the Swan's front rank for the purpose of adding to its effectiveness.' He also noted a fact that now seems astounding but existed until the 60s – that club directors picked the team. 'If the Swans lose today against the Rovers, every one of those critics will observe: "I told you so", but if the Swans win these critics will say the directors were wise in sticking to the same team. This is part of what the directors have to go through.'[10]

A week later, Freelance summed up an astonishing result. 'Had we searched the whole 32 matches on Friday with the admitted object of looking for a staggering miracle we could not have chosen a more amazing event than that which happened at Swansea. It must not be assumed that Rovers underrated their opponents, or were too confident of winning. The result is one of those accidents which occur in any sport. If there were no such

---

[8] *Daily Telegraph Football Chronicle*, p. 32.
[9] Goldblatt, p. 73.
[10] *Swansea Football Post*, January 9, 1915.

uncertainties there would be no charm in this magical Cup.'[11]

Understandably, perhaps, Freelance indulged himself in some journalistic hyperbole. 'Swansea has become famous in many ways. Everything its inhabitants undertake is done well. They seem instinctively to do the right thing at the right moment and this sets people talking all over the country. . . .For its size Swansea has sent as many men to swell Lord Kitchener's army as any other town. We had the first Welsh VC' and for the Swans '. . .in bringing about the downfall of Blackburn Rovers last Saturday they accomplished a performance which has amazed the whole athletic world.' For Freelance, even in the hour of triumph, the war was not far away: '. . .the very idea of the Swans knocking out Blackburn Rovers, the English champions, in the first round of the English Cup, seemed too absurd to be true. It all sounded like a German "official" wireless . . .'

Swansea's game plan was to force the Rovers to 'adopt a style of play which was least likely to bring them success'. They went out to stifle Rovers' expensive forward line, sticking to their men like grim death so that 'even if opponents got away they kept worrying them so much that when chances of shooting came along the players had to take lightning shots without having time to accurately judge length and direction.' The Swans themselves played 'with fine opportunism and skill' and when Benyon gave the Swans the lead, Rovers, despite the best efforts of their star striker, Danny Shea, couldn't respond.

Blackburn Rovers had won the Cup five times in the 1880s and 90s and, in defeating them, Swansea became the first Welsh team to reach the Second Round of the FA Cup. Their shock victory was the last instance of the reigning league champions' elimination by a non-League club.

In the Second Round, the Swans were drawn away after a remarkable and record-breaking run of 11 consecutive home draws, a record unequalled in the Cup since its inception. A fortnight later they went up to Newcastle and drew 1–1 after extra time, Lloyd scoring, then lost the replay a week later at home 2–0.

It was truly a remarkable result for a club only three years old – and the best was yet to come. Five years later, the double-tiered West Stand was built, Swansea Town were elected to the Football League and won promotion to Division Two in 1925. In their first season in the Second Division, they knocked out Arsenal on the way to the semi-finals of the Cup for the

---

[11] *Swansea Football Post*, January 16, 1915.

first time. Ten other top-flight clubs have fallen victim to the Swans in the years since, most notably the 2–1 victory over Liverpool in the quarter-finals in 1964 and West Ham in 1999. In the early 1980s the club soared like a shooting star, reaching sixth place during a two-year stay in Division One, with current Wales manager and ex-Liverpool favourite John Toshack leading the way. The crash was just as spectacular and by 1986, the Swans were back languishing in Division Four, having survived a dice with death when Christmas 1984 saw them staring bankruptcy in the face.

Twenty years later, the record attendance of nearly 33,000 at the Vetch Field had been reduced to an official capacity of nearer 11,000. The condition of the club's old fortress was deteriorating rapidly and the West Stand roof had been removed for safety reasons, with the remaining main terrace acting as a roof for the lower tier.[12] The Vetch Field was no longer an acceptable venue but, in what was to be the final game ever played there, at the end of the 2005 season, the club did manage to collect £100,000 for winning the FAW Premier Cup.

In 2003 the club went into partnership with Swansea City Council to develop a site for a new stadium as part of a retail and leisure complex a couple of miles from the city centre. The Morfa Athletics Stadium and adjacent playing fields had been the site of heavy industrial exploitation since the fourteenth century and the home of the Morfa Copper Works and Landore Silver Works, with production dating back to 1835. Thus on the very site which was the wellspring for Swansea's Victorian prosperity, has arisen a state-of-the-art sports and entertainment arena, a 20,000-seat bowl called the Liberty Stadium. In August 2005 the Swans played their first competitive game at their new HQ, beating Tranmere Rovers 1–0.

The ground-share situation with Neath–Ospreys Rugby Club, along with facilities for conferences, weddings and major rock concerts, is perhaps a direction sign for other similar community-based ventures in the future. And if it can be done with rugby, why not with other football clubs, as happens most prominently in Milan? As David Conn writes so perceptively in *The Beautiful Game*, 'the breaking of that English football taboo might help solve the local problems of clubs which have outgrown their historic but cramped inner-city neighbourhoods'[13] – and there were few grounds as cramped or historic as the Vetch.

---

[12] The stand was finally demolished in 1990.
[13] Conn, p. 75.

5

CARDIFF CITY 2, OLDHAM ATHLETIC 0

FA Cup, Round One, January 10, 1920

Cardiff – the Arms Park and Sospan Fach, Max Boyce and Barry John – throughout the sporting world the city's name is synonymous with the passion and skill, the singing and the humour, the tradition and the *hwyl* of Rugby Union football. Since 1999, however, the magnificent stadium built for the Rugby World Cup has also been home to soccer – Cup finals, internationals and vital play-off matches. Yet the city's professional soccer club 'The Bluebirds', as Cardiff City are known, grew out of cricket, that most English of games. The evocative sound of leather upon willow around the fields of Sophia Gardens in late-Victorian summers seems far away from the hurly-burly of Association football. Nonetheless it was from a desire to give the gentlemen of the Riverside Cricket Club something to keep them active during the winter, to keep them off the gaslit streets of the rapidly growing town, that the idea of starting a local soccer club was born. Bristol-born lithographic artist, Bartley Wilson, was a keen member of the cricket club, and he set up a meeting of all interested parties at his home in the shadow of Cardiff Castle in the autumn of 1899. That meeting resulted in the formation of Riverside FC and Wilson was duly elected secretary of the new club. Friendlies with local teams were arranged during that first season with home games being played at their Sophia Gardens base, until in 1900 they were admitted to the Cardiff and District League for their debut season of competitive football and in 1908 they were at last allowed to change the name to Cardiff City.

City moved to Ninian Park in 1910. The ground itself had been carved out of waste ground and allotments between Sloper Road and the railway

27

sidings and was formally opened with a friendly match against Division One champions, Aston Villa. The 2nd Marquess of Bute, a visionary entrepreneur who initiated the development of Cardiff as a coal-exporting port in the age of mid-Victorian industrial expansion, owned much of the land in the centre of the city. His son, Lord Ninian Crichton-Stuart, agreed to become a guarantor and in recognition of his financial support, the new ground was called Ninian Park. The acquisition of a purpose-built stadium by the club, attracting new spectators expecting to watch a higher class of football, made the change to professionalism inevitable. Coincidental with the opening of Ninian Park, Cardiff City was admitted to the Second Division of the Southern League and finished a respectable fourth in their first season.

The years just before the First World War were a golden age for the game. Aston Villa won the Cup in 1913 before a record crowd of 120,081 and the 1914 Final was the first to be watched by a reigning monarch. Within four months, however, the nation was at war. Inevitably, attendances fell away as men were called to the front and, as the horror of the war unfolded, the 1915 Cup final between Sheffield United and Chelsea at Old Trafford was played on a dark, dank day before a muted crowd. When Lord Derby presented the trophy to Sheffield United, the winners of what has become known as the 'Khaki Cup final',[1] 'his parting words touched the resolute heart of the game and the nation: You have played with one another and against one another for the Cup. It is now the duty of everyone to join with each other and play a sterner game for England[2].'

When competitive football returned in 1919, Cardiff were luckier than many other British clubs as only one player, full-back Tom Watts, perished in the conflict. Manager Fred Stewart re-engaged most of the pre-war team and then began the task of recruiting new players despite money being in short supply. The club's ultimate ambition was to join the Football League and a successful run in the first FA Cup competition after the war would do their cause no harm at all. The nation's footballing drought ended on January 10, 1920, with the First Round of a revived FA Cup competition. The Football League had been expanded, with 22 clubs now in each division, but the Cup had lost none of its allure and the Bluebirds faced formidable

---

[1] So-called because thousands of servicemen in uniform were among the 50,000 crowd, many of them bearing injuries sustained at the front.
[2] Butler, *The Official History of the Football Association* p. 49.

opponents in Oldham Athletic from Division One. In the last full League season before the outbreak of the First World War the 'Latics', as Oldham were popularly known, had been runners-up to Everton.

Sadly for Oldham, by the time League football resumed in 1919, many of the players who had taken the Latics to the threshold of the championship had either retired from football or been killed in the war. Those who remained, however, were an experienced professional outfit. 'Arthurian', of the *South Wales Echo*, recorded that Oldham had arrived in Wales on the Tuesday before the match, noting 'The directorate propose making Penarth their headquarters for the week, and naturally the hope is held by them that the team will be thoroughly acclimatised by Saturday.' They would have done better to stay at home in Lancashire. On a pitch made greasy and unpredictable by a week of heavy rain, a rampaging Cardiff side played out of their skins.

They had an early fright when Smith failed to cut out a cross and Burrows could not convert the opportunity, but the home side dominated the first half. Matthews in the visitors' goal kept his side in the game with great saves from Beare, Cox and Smith and the First Division team held out until a quarter of an hour from the end. Just as Cardiff were envisaging a long train journey and a replay at Boundary Park, West headed home from a corner in goalmouth melee. Seven minutes later, the game was settled. Evans was found by West with a long cross-field pass and his first shot rebounded from a defender. Not to be denied, he latched on to the rebound and hit a powerful drive into the roof of the net via the underside of the bar.

The general opinion in the Principality's capital was that 'there was far better class football seen in the game than is generally produced in Cup-ties[3], according to Arthurian. 'There was an entire absence of that "kick and rush" style that seems to be a feature of Cup games and the City players settled down with a determination to show their cleverness in the finer phases, and they succeeded in reproducing the class of good football that has made them so successful a side in League engagements.' City were practitioners of quick, short-passing game later adopted by Arthur Rowe's successful Spurs side of the early 1950s, a game, as Arthurian pointed out, 'that can, however, only be indulged in successfully when the players work

---

[3] *South Wales Echo*, January 17, 1920.

harmoniously together. It must not be thought that there was such a rigid adherence to the orthodox as to bring their movements into stereotyped order. Such was not the case, and their strategy in varying their methods was one of the reasons why their attacking work could not be coped with by the opposing backs.'

Arthurian goes on to observe in his charmingly dated prose, that for those, like him, who were campaigning to popularise the Association code in South Wales in the face of an overwhelming passion for rugby football, a particularly gratifying aspect of Cardiff's great day 'was the remarkably fine attendance at the match. Everyone, of course, knows how bad were the conditions, and it is a tribute to the loyalty of the club's supporters that, despite the disheartening effect of a continuous down-pour of rain, so many thousands turned out to show their love of the game and their keenness with which they looked forward to their team's success.' The game, being the first Cup encounter since the horrors and deprivation of four years of conflict, was of course unique, but was prof-fered as evidence 'of the contention that Soccer is not only thoroughly established in Wales, but that is rapidly becoming the chief national sport.'

The iniquities of myopic officials have been the main topic of post-match seminars in public bars down the years. On occasion, the referees them-selves have become the story and today, more than ever before, the media are always dissecting their performances, their judgements analysed and scrutinised by endless replays on television. It was no different nearly nine decades ago. In language far more temperate than that offered by the likes of the *Sun* or the *Mirror*, Arthurian describes an incident

> that serves to show how necessary it is for a referee to be well up with the play. Spectators will recall that on one occasion when Cardiff City were filling the role of defenders a long pass was sent out towards Beare. The alert outside-right had seen the ball travelling his way, and very properly set off at full pace so as to take it on the run. He effected his purpose, and after dribbling well ahead was prevented from shooting by being pushed down in the penalty area. With one voice there was an appeal for a penalty, and doubtless the referee would have made the award had he not decided that Beare was offside when he broke away from the halfway line.

In the same paper a week before Arthurian had bemoaned Beare's fate: now, in a vital Cup match, it had happened again 'and all because the referee does not notice his rapid movement off the mark when the ball is in the air'.

The unlucky outside-right must have timed his runs right in the next round, when three weeks later he scored the winning goal against Second Division Wolverhampton Wanderers at Molineux. He also got the Bluebirds' only goal as they exited the Cup in Round Three, beaten 2–1 by Bristol City at Ashton Gate.

In the following season, Cardiff became members of a restructured Second Division, reaching the Cup semi-finals and winning promotion, just 21 years after their formation and only ten years since becoming a professional club. Within six years, the Bluebirds would feature in two Wembley finals, famously beating Arsenal in 1927 – the only time the Cup has left England.

And Oldham? The club never really recovered from the Great War and, after struggling against relegation for several seasons, the inevitable finally arrived in 1923. Ironically enough, the Latics' last Division One game was away at Cardiff City – a game that would prove to be their last in the top flight for 68 years.

CARDIFF CITY: Kneeshaw, Layton, Barnett, Hardy, Smith, Kennor, Beare, Grimshaw, Cox, West, Evans
OLDHAM ATHLETIC: Matthews, Wolstenholme, Stewart, Dougherty, Pilkington, Wilson, Walters, Bradbury, Burrows, Hopper, Wall

6

WALSALL 2, ARSENAL 0

FA Cup, Round Three, January 14, 1933

If Manchester United were the team of the 1990s and Liverpool were the team of the 1970s, then without doubt the 1930s belonged to Arsenal – and their legendary manager, Herbert Chapman. Chapman's grasp of new techniques of tactics and physical training brought the League title to Highbury five times (1931, 1933–5 and 1938). The Gunners were runners-up in 1932 and third in 1937; they won the Cup in 1930 and 1936 and were beaten finalists in 1932. Interestingly, there are resonances of today's barely disguised antipathy towards Chelsea, as Bryon Butler points out: 'They were the sovereign power in English football, their success envied and resented by all but their own. Here was London's riposte to the North and the Midlands.'[1]

In January 1933 Arsenal were the League leaders: Walsall were struggling in Division Three (North). If it had been a boxing match when the Third Round draw brought them face to face at Fellows Park, the bout wouldn't have been allowed. It would have been deemed a mismatch. Arsenal won their last game before the Cup tie 9–2 over Sheffield United. Walsall hadn't won for a month, though they had despatched Mansfield and Hartlepool comfortably enough in the earlier rounds and were unbeaten at home in 21 games since the previous February – though, as Cliff Bastin, Arsenal's classy left-winger, pointed out, 'the opposition against which the record had been achieved was hardly of the highest calibre. Besides, Walsall had not managed to win away from home that season, and a team which could not even bring off a victory on the ground of a Third Division opponent would hardly seem to have much chance

---

[1] Butler, *The Official History of the Football Association*, p. 65

of holding the mighty Arsenal – even if they were playing at home.'[2]

Walsall FC, furthermore, was scarcely 40 years old. The town itself lies in the heart of the Black Country, an area north-west of Birmingham and east of Wolverhampton whose energy and productivity powered the Industrial Revolution of the early nineteenth century. Towards the end of the Victorian age, organised football began to reflect 'a deep-rooted social revolution in industrial society, involving the freeing of the lower strata to enjoy the first meagre benefits of a technically advanced and relatively sophisticated society.'[3]

The village of Walsall had been a Saxon farming settlement, but by the fourteenth century there was a metalworking industry and coal was mined near the town. From the seventeenth century, with raw materials like ironstone locally available, Walsall's iron foundries produced nails, pots and pans, locks, chains and buckles, as well as stirrups, bits and saddles, and by the nineteenth century, as the coal mines became worked out, factory production made Walsall internationally famous for the leather trade and the traditional home of the English saddle manufacture industry. Walsall Town (founded 1877) and Walsall Swifts (1879) had merged as Walsall Town Swifts in the 1887/88 season and, three years after joining Football League Division Two in 1892, changed their name to plain Walsall, with the nickname of 'The Saddlers'.

The FA apparently were unable to decide whether Walsall, quintessentially a Midlands club, should play in Division Three (North), where they spent their early years, or Division Three (South) where they spent four seasons from 1927.[4] It was during this 'southern sojourn', in January 1930, that Walsall travelled seven or eight miles to Villa Park for a Fourth Round Cup tie. Before a crowd of 74,600, the biggest gate Walsall have ever played to, the Saddlers gave a spirited account of themselves before going down 3–1 to First Division Aston Villa.

The year 1931 saw Walsall back in Division Three (North): the Saddlers had spent their entire League history as the poor relations of more fashionable clubs – Aston Villa and Birmingham City to the south and West Bromwich Albion and Wolverhampton Wanderers to the west. Indeed, it was claimed that Arsenal, the southern aristocrats, had spent more on their

---

[2] Glanville, *The Footballers' Companion*, p. 137.
[3] Walvin, p. 69.
[4] They ended up between 1936 and 1958 back in the Southern section.

bootlaces than Walsall had on their entire team. Yet the Gunners had misgivings about the draw. 'We never liked to play against Third Division teams,' said Bastin. 'Such teams ... would fling themselves into the game with reckless abandon, and, win, lose, or draw, the gashed, bruised legs of the Arsenal players, after the game was over, would bear grim testimony to their misguided enthusiasm. The Third Division footballer may not be a Soccer artist, but when it comes to a heavy tackle, he ranks with the best.'[5]

So Herbert Chapman brought his galaxy of stars up the A6 with his side in an uncharacteristic slough, having not won for three games on the road. They had gone down to Brighton as usual to tune up for the Cup tie. Perhaps the sea air didn't agree with them in that grey winter during the Depression: certainly an influenza epidemic was sweeping the country. *Time* magazine for January 20 reported that London had 1,100 postal workers sick; Leeds curtailed its tram service and could not get its gas meters read; in Oxford a coroner's jury could not determine the cause of a violent death because all the jurymen and most of the witnesses had influenza; and a London bride with a 30-foot train to her gown lost a bridesmaid at the eleventh hour. The virus that did for the postmen, the bridesmaid and the jurymen had also struck down Arsenal first-team regulars Eddie Hapgood, Jack Lambert and Bob John. With England winger Joe Hulme out of form as well, Chapman called on four reserves who had only one first-team appearance between them: half-back Norman Sidey had made his League debut against Leeds United barely a fortnight before.

The 11,500 fans in foggy Fellows Park that January afternoon saw one of the most memorable encounters in Cup history, yet in truth it was far from being a classic. On a narrow, muddy pitch Walsall's roughhouse approach forced the skilful, swift-passing Londoners out of their stride and, according to *The Times*, as a result of the home side's 'hard tackling, great speed and boundless energy', the illustrious visitors 'were quite unlike themselves'. To add to Arsenal's woes, the inexperienced players Chapman had drafted in all had nightmares.

Outside-right Billy Warnes, an amateur international from Isthmian League club Woking, the stand-in for the speedy Hulme, was quite unable to cope with the rugged defending. He was, said Bastin, 'an artistic footballer ... and he was very chary of involving himself in a full-blooded tackle.'[6] Charlie

[5] Glanville, *The Footballers' Companion*, p. 138.
[6] Ibid.

Walsh had long been trying to convince Chapman that he was the best centre-forward on Arsenal's books – but he was so nervous he nearly took the field without any socks and spurned two golden chances. In the first half, Bastin put a centre right on his head – but 'His nervousness was pitiable to behold.'[7] With a defender nowhere near him, he missed the ball completely and it bounced harmlessly off his shoulder. In the second, David Jack was about to pick his spot and plant a perfect cross from Bastin into the Walsall net when 'who should come thundering up from behind like a runaway tank but . . . Charlie Walsh! The astonishing leap through the air with which he ended his run deserved a better fate than it actually received. Alas, all Charlie did was to divert the ball away from David Jack, far, far from the Walsall goal.'[8]

And it was the fate of Scottish full-back Tommy Black, who replaced England captain Eddie Hapgood, to feature in the decisive moment of the game, deep into the second half. By that time, however, the writing was on the wall.

Walsall took off from the whistle at full throttle. On the right flank, Ball and Coward ran rings round Sidey and Black, and 'only the untiring efforts of Roberts and the reliability of Male kept Walsall from setting up a winning lead before half-time'.[9] In defence, the uncompromising Leslie, the Saddlers' centre-half, kept Alex James and David Jack in control and Salt completely mastered Warnes. Only once did the visitors threaten when Bastin who, 'alone of the Arsenal forwards, played up to his usual standard', tested Cunningham in the home goal 'with perhaps the best shot of the match'.

Half-time came without any score, though boxing judges would have had the underdogs ahead on points. After the interval, however, Arsenal had their best spell. Warnes was free in front of goal but hesitated fatally, 'and before he could shoot Salt bowled him over' and Charlie Walsh bungled several chances before, on the hour, Walsall took the lead.

Ex-Coventry[10] centre-forward, 25-year-old Gilbert Allsop, headed in a corner taken by the outside-left, Lee. 'Their full-back, Black, was marking me,' said Alsop. 'He didn't get up. The ball was just a big plum-pudding that day and I headed it straight into the corner of the net.' The resultant

---

[7] Glanville, *The Footballer's Companion*, p. 139.

[8] Glanville, *The Footballer's Companion*, p. 141.

[9] *The Times*, January 16, 1933.

[10] In fact, the whole Walsall forward-line against the Gunners that day were all ex-Coventry players: manager Bill Slade had been at Coventry as director and acting manager till 1931.

roar was heard two miles away. Unsurprisingly, Alsop became an instant legend at Fellows Park. He scored Walsall's record 40 goals in the following season and had spells with West Bromwich Albion and Ipswich, before rejoining Walsall in November 1938, netting 151 goals in 195 League games. Later, Alsop became groundsman and lived just long enough to see a stand named after him at the Saddlers' new Bescot Stadium, where Walsall moved in 1991 from the dilapidated Fellows Park. He died the following year.

Arsenal were now stung into action though they foundered on the pillars of Leslie and Salt at the heart of the Saddlers' rearguard. Then Walsh pinched Jack's gilt-edged chance to equalise literally from under his nose. Nonetheless, with half an hour left it seemed inevitable that Arsenal would at least force a draw. Then, 25 minutes from time, Tommy Black, who had been floundering for most of the game, having 'neither the speed nor the resource to hold in check the fast wing opposed to him'[11] hacked at Alsop, his cynical challenge on the Walsall centre-forward leaving a scar that Alsop still proudly displayed 50 years later. Bastin felt the penalty award 'thoroughly deserved' and Walsall inside-right Bill Sheppard's hard, low shot gave the Gunners' goalkeeper, Frank Moss, no chance. The Saddlers' improbable victory was sealed.

'The Swift' of the *South Staffordshire Advertiser* could not believe what he had seen:

Is it true? Is it not a dream that I shall awake and smile at? No! Even now I cannot quite grasp that my little Walsall – the team I gaze upon so anxiously every week – has had the cheek, the impudence, to wipe the great and mighty Arsenal out of the English Cup and send them back to the Metropolis bewailing a whipping at the hands of a insignificant club in the Northern Section of the Third Division.

Under the banner headlines 'SENSATIONAL GAME' and 'COMPLETE FAILURE OF MIGHTY ARSENAL', *The Times* wrote of the Walsall players being 'mobbed and carried shoulder high to the cheers of some twelve thousand excited spectators, who, with the final whistle, rushed on the pitch.' The *Daily Mirror* described how 'a struggling Third Division team created a sensation of the century' and declared that 'Saturday

---

[11] *The Times*, January 16, 1933.

may have been a dream to the small teams in the Cup-ties, but it was something of a nightmare for the "big noises". It was rumoured that voices of the BBC's newsreaders shivered with surprise when they announced the score that evening; at Highbury, where Arsenal's reserves were playing, 'the result was greeted with roars of laughter. They thought it was a leg-pull.'[12]

Yet it was true. Walsall 2, Arsenal 0. Nothing could change those figures. Arsenal had played with a woeful lack of spirit and cohesion. In spite of that, Bastin knew 'we had still been presented with enough chances to have won'.[13] He felt they had been beaten 'by a fifth-rate side. Napoleon must have felt like that in Russia, a hundred and twenty-one years before.' As the baby of the side at 20, he felt the loss most keenly.

> On my way home to my lodgings that night, in the Underground Railway, I felt positively suicidal. Visions of the Arsenal goals that might have been rose up before my eyes; hopes that the events of the afternoon had been nothing but an evil nightmare would delude me for a brief moment, only to be banished away by the cold, grim reality.

He had never seen his boss so dreadfully unhappy. 'He made a brave, desperate, but unavailing effort to cheer us all up. "Never mind, boys," he said, "these things do happen."' His team knew before kick-off that Walsall would make up for their lack of skill by rugged tackling but a forward line containing David Jack, Alex James and Cliff Bastin should have had sufficient ammunition to break down a Third Division defence, some of whose challenges were rash even by the more robust standards of the 1930s.

Few of the Arsenal side left Fellows Park without some scars of battle and Tommy Black, along with most of his teammates, reported to the treatment room on Monday morning. At once he was sent to the manager's office. A furious Chapman turned on the hapless Scot. 'Tommy,' he said, 'you will never put an Arsenal shirt on ever again, for what you did was disgraceful.' Within the week he was transferred to Plymouth: Charlie Walsh was packed off to Brentford within a fortnight.

The calamity at Fellows Park signalled the nadir of Chapman's distinguished career. Arsenal, dubbed by the press the '£30,000 aristocrats', had been humbled by a Third Division Midlands team that cost £69 in all. It

[12] Butler, *The Official History of the Football Association*, p. 65.
[13] Glanville, *The Footballer's Companion*, p. 142.

was his last FA Cup game as Arsenal manager: within a year the man whose charisma shaped the club of the decade, whose strength of personality persuaded the London Electric Railway to change the name of Gillespie Road Tube station to Arsenal, had died of pneumonia.

That season, Arsenal recovered to win the first of three consecutive League titles. There have been many glorious days since. Yet in the club shop at the Bescot Stadium, replica match programmes are still on sale, for the tale of the day when 'Herbert Chapman's omnipotent Gunners . . . were bullied to defeat by a little Black Country club from the shadowy mid-region of the Third Division (North) . . . is a story which gets better with every telling'[14] – but for Arsenal fans down the years the saga of the debacle that raw January afternoon is one they prefer to forget.

WALSALL: Cunningham, Bird, Bennett, Reed, Leslie, Salt, Coward, Ball, Alsop, Sheppard, Lee
ARSENAL: Moss, Black, Male, Hill, Roberts, Sidey, Warnes, Jack, Walsh, James, Bastin

---

[14] Butler, *History of the FA Cup*, p. 140.

7

MILLWALL 2, MANCHESTER CITY 0

FA Cup, Quarter-Final, March 6th, 1937

'We're building up for Millwall and it's going to be nasty, yet we respect Millwall somehow, deep down, though we'd never say as much, knowing New Cross and Peckham are the arseholes of London. . . As far back as our memories go Millwall have always been mad. Something special, mental, off their heads. They've got their reputation and they deserve it, raised on docker history spanning the century.'[1] Thus wrote a Chelsea fan from his west London perspective in 1996. He could have been living in a different city.

There are very few clubs in British football that enjoy as close a symbiosis with the area and the community which spawned them as Millwall, where history, myth and reality go hand in hand:

> South-east London therefore enjoys a specific position in those folk-taxonomic schema which so characterize life in the city. And its close association with crime and plebeian entrepreneurialism, in themselves central themes in historical relations between the metropolitan classes, marks it out as an especially significant site in the ongoing dialectics of class and culture of social identities embodied and ascribed.[2]

Any club which can inspire such intense sociological jargon is to be taken seriously, and as Robson goes on to point out, the historical environment from which the club sprang has always exerted a profound influence:

---

[1] King, p. 225.
[2] Garry Robson in an essay in Armstrong and Giulianotti, p. 68.

This particular tradition and iconography, from medieval criminal quarter and pleasure ground to pick-pocket Fagin and the definitive Dickensian criminal warren at Jacob's Island in Bermondsey, from the original nineteenth century 'Hooligan' to the first 'Teddy Boys', from classical gangland enclave to home of the archetypal football thug at Millwall, marks south-east London out as a very particular and historically significant place.[3]

The West India, opened in 1802, was London's first trading dock and soon expanded into the West India Import and Export Docks and, on the western side of the Isle of Dogs, the Millwall Docks (so-called from the presence of a large number of windmills on the river wall). In the 1850s, in his *London Labour and the London Poor*, Henry Mayhew described the docks

> as being the 'real hell', where men with 'sweaty faces dyed blue from the cargoes of indigo' and others 'coughing and spluttering as they stacked the yellow bins of sulphur and lead-coloured copper-ore' all battled to earn a living. He writes of the dark vaults that were the warehouses, where men inhaled 'fumes of wine, the fungus smell of dry rot, and the stench of hides.'[4]

Life may have been harsh in late Victorian London, but the river and its commerce were 'the very lifeblood of the East End, and the labour and services needed to keep trade going – from stevedore to carpenter, from rat-catcher to brothel-keeper, from pawnbroker to rope-maker – were provided by the cockneys in their riverside parishes.'[5] Those parishes soon acquired the reputation of being the most decadent and dangerous of all the neighbourhoods east of the City. It was hardly surprising that the 'labouring poor, with their daily grind of getting by in the best way they could in the overcrowded, vermin-ridden slums, packed into narrow, dung-slicked streets and foggy alleyways, all reeking of Dickensian deprivation'[6], would become stereotyped as the essential images of London's East End.

---

[3] Ibid.
[4] Quoted in O'Neill, pp. 22–23.
[5] O'Neill, p. 24.
[6] O'Neill, p. 25.

For the working classes of the East End, spectator sports – bear-baiting, bare-knuckle fighting – had always offered an ephemeral escape from the rigours of everyday existence. However, from the 1870s a more cohesive industrial labour force emerged with the time, money and penchant for organised leisure and the recently codified and organised game of Association Football offered a dramatic new attraction. Hence, many London clubs had their origins in the last two decades of the century as teams developed from traditional institutions or new commercial enterprises.

Millwall Football Club was no exception. It started life in 1885 as 'Millwall Rovers' at the Islanders pub in Tooke Street. It was a working man's team, founded by young Eastenders who worked at Morton's jam and marmalade factory in West Ferry Road – a place where seasonally unemployed match-girls could find summer jobs. It is a myth, however, that Millwall FC came into being as a product of missionary work by émigré Scottish football fans in England's capital. True, J.T. Morton *was* a Scottish firm, founded in Aberdeen in 1849. Morton's supplied food to sailing ships and with the growth of the canning process the company expanded into the world's premier mercantile port in 1870, opening a new plant on the Isle of Dogs.

A second deep-rooted myth can also be scotched (if that is the right word) – the one that Millwall's club badge is derived from the Scottish Rampant Lion emblem. In fact, Millwall were known as 'The Dockers' until about 1900, when the club's triumphant run to the semi-finals led to their being dubbed 'The Lions' for their giant-killing. The name stuck and was adopted as the club's nickname and emblem, though it did not appear on club shirts until the 1930s.

The club had four grounds in its first quarter-century, at one time playing at the back of the Lord Nelson pub. In 1910 the Lions relocated to The Den in Cold Blow Lane, a bleak and unforgiving ground in a bleak and unforgiving neighbourhood, 'a wicked place full of nutters. . .'[7] Eighty years later, when the club had relocated to the New Den on the Isle of Dogs, time had stood still: 'There's no colour in the buildings, bricks identical and wasteland overgrown, rows of broken walls and broken wire, smashed glass and rusted metal, dull new houses. . . Full of decaying dockers in flat caps bombed and left to rot under a collapsed London.'[8]

Millwall is still the most urban of London's football clubs: indeed, until

---

[7] King, pp. 225–7; quoted in Armstrong and Giulianotti, p. 61.
[8] Ibid.

the early 1960s, Millwall was the only club permitted to kick off home games at 3.15 instead of three o'clock, to allow the dockers to arrive on time after work. Originally, the bulk of its support derived from its traditional catchment area between New Cross and Bermondsey, including Rotherhithe, Deptford – and Peckham:

> My father's side [of the family] all lived in Peckham. They were Millwall supporters and . . . would mostly meet on a Friday night to talk about the match, and then they would all meet up at the same spot at the ground every week. After the match, they had a sequence, one uncle one week, another uncle another week. We would go back and have tea, which invariably was winkles and shrimps and some watercress sandwiches, and they would curse the team and swear and say they'd never go and see them again they were so bad, but the following Saturday they were there. They never missed.[9]

Millwall's fans began to acquire an extreme and raucously voluble abrasiveness, and from the 1920s on their reputation for unbridled passion and intimidation were expressed in outbursts of occasional violence.[10] By the late 1940s, in the post-war football boom, 'the "Lions' Den" was, in fact, already well-established as a site of proto-hooligan activity, and had been so since the early decades of the century'.[11] So much so that the very word 'Millwall' has become a metaphor for mob violence, overt masculinity, unabashed racism and working-class 'fascism', which in the football subculture excites an uncomfortable mix of fascination, fear and loathing.

It has always been so. Southwark-born writer Michael Collins believes that, as Millwall's fan base has always been the white working class, it has been easy and at times fashionable for the press and media to demonise that culture of support. He writes: 'At the end of the 19th century around the time Millwall FC was formed, middle class journalists used to descend on the area like Baudelaireian flaneurs,[12] to report on the urban working

---

[9] Taylor and Ward pp. 11–12.
[10] In 1920, following a fractious encounter, the visiting Newport County goalkeeper was pelted with missiles before being 'flattened' by a 'useful right hook' (Murray, p. 83).
[11] Quoted in Armstrong and Giulianotti, p. 63.
[12] The nineteenth-century French poet and aesthete Charles Baudelaire saw the *flâneur* – 'a gentleman stroller of city streets' – as having a key role in understanding, participating in and portraying the city, whilst remaining a detached observer.

class as though they were discovering natives from the remote islands of the Empire.'[13]

The club from the marmalade factory, originally known as Millwall Rovers and then Millwall Athletic, won its first trophy, the East End Cup, in 1887 and reached the semi-finals of the FA Cup in 1903 while still a Southern League side, losing 3–0 to Derby County. Following its move to New Cross in 1910, the Lions became founder members of Football League Division Three in 1920 and eight years later won promotion to the Second Division as champions of Division Three (South), having beaten Middlesbrough 3–2 in a fifth round FA Cup tie the previous season in front of a crowd of 42,250 at The Den.

A decade later, the 1936/37 Cup campaign began modestly enough, with a 6–1 victory at Aldershot, then, on a groundswell of expectancy, the Lions played every tie at Cold Blow Lane. Gateshead were thrashed 7–0, Second Division Fulham 2–0, First Division Chelsea 3–0 and Derby County 2–1 in front of a 48,672 crowd – a ground record. It was Ken Sheehan's very first game as a boy – 'but I never saw the match. We got as far as the gates and there was such a crowd milling around that my father said, "There's no way I'm taking you in there," and we had to go home again.'[14] Thousands were locked out and concern was expressed in the local press ahead of the Sixth Round clash with First Division Manchester City. 'I hope the management at The Den will close the gates in time to prevent a recurrence of the crowd problems which manifested itself at the Derby game.'[15]

At the time, City were on course for their first League championship and, after their convincing dismissal of Bolton in the previous round, were, like Arsenal, in a position to make twentieth-century history and win the Cup and League double. However, 'AJJ' pointed out that, 'Millwall will be full of fight and confidence and will take some beating, so that there is every prospect of a stirring struggle' and his colleague 'Olympian' echoed his sentiments: 'most of all in favour of the South Londoners is their terrific spirit. Having tasted blood whilst slaughtering the Pensioners and Rams, Lions are not going to be thwarted of another appetising meal without putting up a great struggle.'

---

[13] Collins, *The Likes of Us: A Biography of the White Working-Class*, (Granta, 2004).
[14] Taylor and Ward, p. 9
[15] AJJ in *South London Press*, March 5, 1937.

Certainly, for many clubs of whatever standing, Cold Blow Lane was never the away ground of choice and already Chelsea and Derby had already shown little stomach for the fight. Manchester City, with Frank Swift in goal, one of the best pairs of full-backs in the First Division and the finest attack in the country, should have been well capable of coping with the Third Division side, but veteran striker Dave Mangnall, with seven goals already in the campaign, scored twice as before a crowd of 42,474 the Division Three side dumped City – Swift, Peter Doherty, Alex Herd, Eric Brook and all – out of the Cup.

Millwall's run of success was widely expected to come to an end but, on a slippery surface, the result was 'in little doubt after the first quarter of an hour', according to *The Times*. 'Millwall set the pace and their distinguished opponents were soon in difficulties. Playing good football, Millwall swung the ball about and in spite of the experience of Barkas, at left back, and the energy of Marshall, the centre-half, the Manchester defence was at times almost overrun.'[16]

The pace of Millwall's early attacks had the Lancashire defence chasing shadows and after ten minutes the entire Manchester rearguard bought a dummy from Dave Mangnall, whose fierce drive struck a post from an acute angle. Two minutes later, the City walls were breached when, after three successive comers, the inevitable Mangnall headed Ken Burditt's corner-kick well out of Swift's reach. For most of the first period, Millwall's half-backs dominated City's forwards and AJJ, from the *South London Press*, indulged himself in some purple passages: 'Tackling with immense speed and force, and snapping up infinitesimal inaccuracies by the northerners, Millwall knocked proud Manchester City sprawling off their balance . . . Talk about Nero fiddling whilst Rome burned. That was nothing compared with the way the City fiddled whilst the Lions tackled.'[17]

Indeed, Millwall's defence was in little difficulty. Wallbanks snuffed out the threat from City's prolific scorer, Fred Tilson, and Ernie Toseland and Alex Herd, Manchester's renowned right flank, looked utterly ineffective against Inns and Forsyth. On the other hand, the Lions' inside-left, McCartney, and the 'small, sallow'[18] Reg Smith, who came into the side at the last minute because Thorogood was injured, led Dale a merry dance.

[16] *The Times*, March 8, 1937.
[17] *South London Press*, March 9, 1937.
[18] Ibid.

Smith was an interesting character. The son of a Springbok Rugby international, he had joined Millwall from amateur side Hitchin Town only 18 months before, and according to AJJ, 'calmly outmanoeuvred Rogers and Dale time and again'.[19] Eighteen months on, he played twice for England, scoring two on his debut against Norway in a 4–0 win.

The Third Division side kept up the pace and 12 minutes after half-time Frank Swift, City's goalkeeper, flapped at a centre from McCartney and Mangnall's head was there to put Millwall two up. Manchester then rallied and AJJ takes up the story:

> Herd, for once escaping Inns, hit the ball at Burke, head-high. The goalkeeper knocked the ball up against the underside of the bar and fell on his face. Meanwhile the ball bounced down behind him on the goal-line and Burke, turning round scooped it up as it jigged up and down. With a few minutes to go. Brook, appearing from nowhere, fired in a great, rasping drive which Burke, flinging himself full-length, punched wide of the post.

When it was all over swarms of Millwall fans seethed on to the ground, sweeping aside the police. 'McCartney headed a rush for safety, but Mangnall and Wallbanks were caught in the tide and, amid ringing cheers, were carried off the ground shoulder high.' For the second time since 1900, Millwall had muscled their way into the semi-finals of the FA Cup, and 'none can say that they have not deserved their place in the last four. In the last three rounds they have beaten First Division sides – Chelsea, Derby County, and now Manchester City – and they have beaten them convincingly by good football by a total of seven goals to one.'[20]

Thus Millwall became the first Third Division team to reach the FA Cup semi-finals and on April 10, they faced defending League champions Sunderland at Huddersfield in front of a crowd of 62,813. Mangnall gave the Lions the lead after ten minutes but it was a step too far and they went down 2–1, while Sunderland went on to win the cup. The dream over, Millwall finished the season eighth in the Third Division (South). A year later Millwall won the Third Division (South) championship again but the Second World War intervened just as the Lions were developing a very strong side.

---

[19] Ibid.
[20] *The Times*, March 8, 1937.

Many clubs suffered a grievous loss of personnel during the global conflict and Millwall did not escape – but the club's Dockland location meant it was virtually on the front line. The Den sustained severe bomb damage during the Blitz and in the immediate post-war decades the club's form was poor and the Lions endured three relegations. But between 1964 and 1967 the club enjoyed a remarkable run of 59 successive home games without defeat and The Den became a fortress in more ways than one. In the 1970s 'a violent element, apparently attracted less by the club than by the chance to cause trouble, became associated with Millwall's core support.'[21] The truth was that it had always been there and the chant of 'No One Likes Us – We Don't Care', which emanated from Millwall supporters in the early 1980s as a reaction to what the Millwall fans saw as exaggerated and unjust criticism of their behaviour and the stereotypical image of all Millwall fans as hooligans, was a verbal two-fingered salute to the press and the media.

Mind you, the papers and TV had a case. In March 1985 Thatcherism was at its zenith:

> In the garden of middle England, now blooming on easy credit and rising house prices, the only demon that remained was football, one of the few cultural zones in which the people and the disorder of rust-belt Britain clung on. In the spring of 1985 these beliefs were confirmed by a series of violent and catastrophic incidents. In March the nation had a ringside seat for the televised battle at Luton Town, between the massed ranks of police and visiting Millwall fans.[22]

During the late 1980s, with The Den at its most formidable, and with the club's fans at the peak of their notoriety, the Lions under George Graham and John Docherty finally reached Division One in 1988, and in 1989 even topped the League briefly. After a couple of seasons the club were relegated, but had a recent flowering in 2004 when under the feisty leadership of Dennis Wise, the Lions reached the Cup Final for the first time.

Ironically, Millwall's first final was not in London, but 'abroad', in Cardiff – ironic, for Millwall remains essentially an inner-city club, based in that part of London that has undergone dereliction and regeneration, its workforce and population reinforced and enriched with successive waves of

---

[21] Lyons and Ronay, p. 260.
[22] Goldblatt, pp. 567–8.

immigration. The move to the New Den at Senegal Fields in 1993 represented a symbolic attempt by the club to soften the atmosphere in and around the ground and to encourage harmonious support from all parts of the local community while remaining true to its heritage by introducing 'Docker Days', and archiving the club's dock roots in the club museum.

Mark Ford, Professor of English at University College London, is a former Millwall fan. He now follows Arsenal. 'The switch followed my moving from just near the old Den to just near the old Highbury. The Emirates is something else, more like going to the ballet than a football match.' While Ford's move epitomises the gentrification of football in the last ten years, his poem, Passion Play, evokes the roots of Millwall's stark, uncompromising, often violent past and reminds us that football 'remains what it has always been – the people's game. Those who forget the strength of its roots who seek to remove it from the social warp and weft which have fashioned football for more than a century – may find that it is a game which has a life of its own.'[23]

> Can we hear you Bury? Noooeoooe!
> Your tide is out
> And drift-wood fires our cause.
> We chip the keeper, and ram the ball home.
>
> Our bicycle has been stolen. Thieves
> Came in the night and took it;
> Now I'm tanked up, and celebrating.
> We chip the keeper, and ram the ball home.
>
> To be sleepless on a starless night
> In Croydon, begets a sound defence,
> And vicious attack. Why lie? you wearily inquire.
> We chip the keeper, and ram the ball home.[24]

---

[23] Walvin, p. 210.
[24] From *Landlocked* (Chatto and Windus, 1992).

MILLWALL: Burke, C.E. Smith, Inns, Brolly, Wallbanks, Forsyth, Burditt, Barker, Mangnall, McCartney and J.R. Smith

MANCHESTER CITY: Swift, Dale, Barkas, Rogers, Marshall, Bray, Toseland, Herd, Tilson, Doherty and Brook

8

BURNLEY 0, SWINDON TOWN, 2

FA Cup, Round Three, January 10, 1948

I had, in racing parlance, 'spread a plate'. Pretty apt, four miles from the thoroughbred gallops above Lambourn, as I sprawled, minus a sandal, on the right foreleg of a 3,500-year-old equine epic. Four years old, on a family day out from our holiday at the Matthews' dairy farm, I cared more about the loss of my sandal, my mother's wrath and the pain of my grazed shin than the splendour of the White Horse of Uffington. On the northern slopes of the Berkshire Downs, the elegant creature, outlined by ramming chalk into trenches cut into the turf, is but one of many reminders of ancient people on the Marlborough Downs of Wiltshire and the downs of Berkshire and Hampshire. The ridges of these ancient hills are linked by the Ridgeway, a prehistoric track skirting the bustling commercial town of Swindon, which began as a Saxon village in a defensible position on the crest of a limestone hill. During the Middle Ages Swindon became a small market town but, by 1697, Swindon's population was still only 791, tiny even for Britain at the end of the seventeenth century. Until the early Victorian era, Swindon remained a provincial centre for barter trade, exchanging the wool and sheep of the Cotswolds with the wheat and dairy produce of the vales to the east.

Britain's Industrial Revolution at the end of the nineteenth century was built on the harnessing of new sources of power to the technology of mass production, together with a massive expansion in the canal network, enabling raw materials such as coal, cement and timber, as well as manufactured goods, to be moved efficiently across the country. As the towns and cities at the heart of the coalfields grew rapidly, in the rural areas those towns which lay at the junctions of the canal system profited from this rapid commercial growth. Swindon was no exception, although in 1830 it was still a quiet market town, 'pleasantly seated on the banks of the Wilts and Berks Canal, by which navigation the trade of this place is much facilitated . . . The population of the entire parish, according to the census of 1821, consisted of 1,580 inhabitants.'[1]

This was to change markedly with the coming of the Great Western Railway. In 1835 Parliament approved the construction of a railway between London and Bristol, with Isambard Kingdom Brunel as chief engineer. After running through the Goring Gap, where the Thames cuts between the Chilterns and the Berkshire Downs, the line was originally routed through Savernake Forest to Marlborough, but the Marquess of Ailesbury, who owned the land, objected. The Marquess, a kind of Victorian nimby, had previously also objected to part of the Kennet and Avon Canal running through his estate and, as it was cheaper to transport coal for trains along canals at this time, the railway needed to run near to the Kennet and Avon. As a result, Swindon was the next logical choice for the works, 20 miles north of the original route.

To the east, towards London, the line was gently graded along the Thames valley, while westwards there was a steep descent from the edge of the Cotswolds towards Bath. Swindon, therefore, was situated at a point where engines would need to be changed and in 1840 the town became the site of the vast engine workshops for the Great Western Railway, which transformed the town into a true railway junction: indeed, until 1895, every train had to stop at Swindon for at least ten minutes to change locomotives. As a result, the station boasted the first recorded railway refreshment rooms with the upper floors housing the station hotel and lounge: the building survived until 1972.

Along with the workshops and the railway station, and because the town of Swindon at that time was over a mile away on top of the hill, the Great Western built a small railway 'village' to house some of its workers. It became the focal point for 'New Swindon' and over the next 50 years the town continued to grow rapidly, dominated by the railway works. By 1881 the population of Swindon exceeded 15,000 but 'New Swindon' would remain both physically and administratively separate from 'Old Swindon'

---

[1] Pigot & Co, *National Commercial Directory for Cornwall, Dorsetshire, Devonshire, Somersetshire and Wiltshire*, (1830).

until 1900. The town continued to grow, reaching 54,000 by 1921 – while 'Old Swindon' still retained – and does to this day – the atmosphere of a provincial market town, with Georgian inns and townhouses.

A 'Swindon Association Football Club' was in existence in 1879: a match report from the *Swindon Advertiser*, dated December 13, showed a Revd William Pitt of Liddington playing for the club in a 4–0 defeat against Rover FC. Thereafter it appears there were two changes of name – Swindon AFC changed their name to Spartans between 1879 and 1881, whereupon after a match between Spartans and St Mark's Young Mens' Friendly Society the good Reverend, now widely credited with founding the modern club, convinced the two clubs, from the fractious farming and railway communities of Old and New Swindon, to resolve their differences and merge. This they did, renaming themselves 'Swindon Town' in 1883, settling on red shirts after giving up on finding a suitable green dye for their old white kit, and were accordingly nicknamed 'The Robins'.

The club's first home was a field next to a quarry in Old Town but the ball would regularly vanish and in 1884 the club was forced to move to The Croft when a young spectator fell to his death down the quarry. Although the club was now professional, having joined the Southern League, there were no facilities near the pitch. The teams changed in the Fountain Inn on Devizes Road, tickets were purchased from a pigeon-hole in the Royal Oak Inn, and the supporters were forced to stand on wooden footboards. Eventually, in 1896 Town moved to the County Ground when local brewer Thomas Arkell lent the club £300 to build a stand, which stood until the 1970s.

Before the Great War Harold Fleming, a skilful winger who is said to have walked 30 miles from his home in Andover to join Swindon in 1907, inspired the club to two FA Cup semi-finals and in 1910 scored both goals in Swindon's 2–1 win in the Dubonnet Cup (an FA Cup third-place play-off) at the Parc des Princes in Paris. The Town also won two Southern League championships. In 1911 their Charity Shield match with Manchester United proved to be the highest-scoring Charity Shield game to date, United winning 8–4. Fleming scored four times in Swindon's first game in the Football League as a founding member of Division Three (South), when the Robins beat Luton Town 9–1 at the County Ground. He is commemorated in the naming of a road that radiates from the confusing and aptly named Magic Roundabout outside the County Ground.

In the Second World War the club shut up shop and the County Ground was used as a POW camp. As a result, when soccer resumed in the autumn of 1945, the Town were at a disadvantage to other clubs and manager Louis Page had a job building a cohesive team as many players still needed permission to play as they had not yet been demobbed. In the circumstances, the Robins' fourth-place finish in 1946/47 was a real achievement. However, Swindon made an unexceptional re-entry to the Cup in the first two seasons, but 1947/48 saw a 4–2 win over Ipswich in Round One and a 2–0 win in a replay over Aldershot. Hopes of a money-spinning run seemed to have foundered when they were drawn against First Division Burnley in the Third Round. What was more, as the *Swindon Advertiser* pointed out, 'Eight of the players who took part in last season's Wembley Cup Final are included in Burnley's team to oppose Swindon Town in the third round of this season's competition at Turf Moor on Saturday.'[2] Burnley were going strong in the League (they would ultimately finish third) and were confidently expected to dispatch a mediocre Swindon side from Division Three South.

Robins manager Louis Page, however, had done his homework, having seen the Clarets at Bolton the week before. He was an interesting man. A former Burnley player, he had won seven England caps in 1927/28 and had once scored six in a 7–1 win at Birmingham. He was one of four brothers from Liverpool, all of whom represented their country at baseball, a popular sport in England in the 1920s and 30s. When league football resumed after the Second World War, he was appointed manager of Swindon, having previously managed Yeovil, Glentoran and Newport County. His plan was to 'Play football and beat Burnley to the punch'. He noted among other things the 'vulnerability of Burnley right-back Woodruff to a winger cutting on his inside and the danger of the scheming inside forward Knight'.[3]

His best-laid plans were followed to the letter, as the *Advertiser* reported. 'Swindon beat Burnley to the ball and never gave them a chance to settle down and manoeuvre for long enough to develop their own plans. Apart from odd spells, they made the Northerners look quite an ordinary side, and the hard first-time tackling and kicking of the defence upset the home attack. . .'[4] In a delightfully punning headline,

---

[2] *Swindon Advertiser*, January 8, 1948.
[3] *Swindon Advertiser*, January 12, 1948.
[4] *Ibid.*

given Burnley's long history as a cotton town, the *Advertiser* told its readers: 'SWINDON GOT WEAVING, PUT BURNLEY THROUGH THE MILL.'

The Robins were ahead inside two minutes, when Jones put centre-forward Maurice Owen through Burnley's defence with a perfect pass. Owen slipped the ball to Jackie Dryden, who had sneaked closer in. The winger went straight for goal and Strong did not get anywhere near his flashing, low cross-shot. Owen himself scored the second five minutes from the interval, as Burnley keeper Strong 'dashed out to intercept a loose ball with Owen in hot pursuit. . .' In a fierce tussle, 'Owen forced the ball out of his possession and while still partly on the ground, performed a contortion which enabled him to hook the ball into the empty net.'

Burnley came hard at the Third Division side in the second half but found Robins goalkeeper Boulton 'cool and completely safe'. He even saved a penalty from future Burnley manager Harry Potts, his third miss in successive matches. Swindon's defence stood firm and, in the final analysis, Burnley had been beaten by a side 'with more craftsmanship, with more enterprise, and with unquenchable enthusiasm and team spirit'. Louis Page said it had been 'a wonderful experience to take the team back to my old club and give them such a tanning. The Burnley chairman told me that Swindon were the best side that has played at Turf Moor this season.' About three thousand jubilant supporters joined the Deputy Mayor at Swindon Junction Station on the Sunday night to welcome the team as they returned home.

It had been an amazing day for Cup shocks as Colchester beat Huddersfield and Arsenal went out to Bradford Park Avenue. *The Times* assessed Swindon's win as an 'even greater' surprise, a victory all the more remarkable in view of Burnley's home league record that season. They conceded only 12 goals at home and only three teams managed to net twice.

More was yet to come, however. The Swindon faithful were rewarded with a home tie in the Fourth Round against Notts County, 'a popular draw as it gives Town supporters a glimpse of famous international centre-forward Tommy Lawton. It will give Swindon a chance of revenge for it was the County who knocked them out during the second round last season at Meadow Lane after the Town had given a fine performance.'[6]

---

[5] *The Times*, January 12, 1948.
[6] *Swindon Advertiser*, January 12, 1948.

Swindon were in the middle of an unbeaten run of 11 games, and two weeks later swept aside the game's oldest League club when 'an astute flick by Owen gave Lucas a chance to score the winner'.[7] Three games from Wembley, on February 2 the Town lined up at The Dell against Second Division Southampton. They suffered a grievous blow, losing right-half Kaye after only eight minutes with a broken ankle and goals by Wayman, Curtis and an own goal put them out for another year.

The Robins' greatest-ever day came two decades later, when the Arsenal team which won the European Fairs Cup in 1970 and the 'Double' in 1971 were humbled on a Wembley pitch resembling a rice paddy after a week of heavy rain and the Horse of the Year show. Four minutes from time Bobby Gould's header equalised Smart's first-half strike, but in extra time Don Rogers scored two breathtaking solo goals and the image of Rogers scoring his second in a spotless white shirt remains an iconic image in Swindon: 'A proud ocean liner sailing on a sea of mud', according to a poem in the *Advertiser*. The Robins even won in Europe that year, as they lifted the Anglo-Italian League Cup Winners' Cup.

The late 1980s saw a resurgence and under the little Argentine Ossie Ardiles the Town won promotion to the old Division One via the play-offs in 1990, only to have its achievement rubbed out ten days later when the club was demoted because of financial irregularities. Nothing daunted, three years later a memorable 4–3 play-off win against Leicester saw Swindon promoted to the Premiership. In 1994 Gerry Boon, an accountant at Deloitte and Touche, produced a report noting that 'the English professional game was making massive money compared to pre-Sky days', but that this huge influx of cash 'determined playing success, because the better players were only attracted with more money. United, which made the most money, won the Championship again. The three clubs with the lowest wage bills, Sheffield United, Oldham and Swindon Town, were all relegated.'[8]

Thereafter the club has survived two spells in administration but 'remain the epitome of an unfashionable provincial club, short on cash and high on hopes'[9] – and there, as Hamlet so wisely mused, lies the rub. The real

---

[7] *Swindon Advertiser*, January 26, 1948.
[8] Conn, p. 107.
[9] Lyons and Ronay, p. 400.

agony lying at the heart of OSS, or 'Obsessive Supporter Syndrome', is not the unremitting poor form, the despair or the disillusion. It's the hope, 'that deep-rooted nagging shred of optimism that this will be the day when your boys will turn into world-beaters'.[10]

Colin Irwin, in his admirable book *Sing When You're Winning*, describes meeting Derek, an amiable middle-aged bloke from Northampton who hasn't missed a single Swindon Town match in almost 25 years:

> He's gratifyingly vague about how someone from Northants became a Swindon obsessive. Something about a friend of the family taking him to the County Ground when he was a kid and that was it – Swindon till he dies. Poor bloke had no say in it. It's the old cliché: you can change your wife or husband, but you can't change your football team . . . Like all proper football fans, he's at a loss to explain why he careers all over the country supporting a moderate League One side who've broken his heart more times than they've made his day. 'They're just my team, that's all,' he says limply, fully aware of how naff it sounds. 'You often go thinking, well, it can't possibly be as bad as that again.'[11]

Ah, that's the trouble – it often is. . .

BURNLEY: Strong, Woodruff, Mather, Attwell, Brown, Bray, Billingham, Potts, Harrison, Knight, Hays
SWINDON TOWN: Boulton, Young, Emery, Kay, Ithell, Painter, Dryden, Lucas, Owen, Jones, Maguire

---

[10] Irwin, p. 46.
[11] Irwin, p. 45.

9

YEOVIL TOWN 2, SUNDERLAND 1

FA Cup Round Four, January 29, 1949

It's a daft name really. Only a marketing genius whose lift didn't reach the top floor could have reckoned that Subbuteo would be a catchy sort of name for his new football game.[1] Yet a few years after it was first announced in the August 1946 edition of *The Boy's Own Paper* the game had captured the imagination of schoolboys searching for fun in post-war Britain. Its unique genius was that, while most games feature only two teams, Subbuteo created hundreds of team kits. My brother and I had a couple – he was Wolves and I was Arsenal – and there was even one of a Southern League team we used to watch playing Hastings United. In honour of their Cup exploits,[2] Yeovil Town became the first non-League club to have a Subbuteo set made in their colours. There weren't just teams, either. Later you could buy accessories, such as new balls and goals, referees and linesmen, physios, stands and crowd, policemen, floodlights, TV cameras – and even streakers.

Any self-respecting streaker – a contradiction in terms, surely? – would have kept themselves to themselves on a clear but bitterly cold afternoon in January 1949, when First Division Sunderland, the moneybags of English football at the time, came calling at tiny Huish Park in Yeovil. Whatever other garments they had discarded, they would have needed a pair of the sheepskin gloves for which the market town in south Somerset was widely renowned.

Glove makers had first been mentioned in the town in the early fourteenth century, and in the Middle Ages Yeovil had two annual fairs, attracting

---

[1] The game's creator, Peter Adolph, chose the name Subbuteo, it being derived from the neo-Latin scientific name *Falco subbuteo*, a bird of prey known as the Eurasian hobby, after he was refused as trademark to call the game 'Hobby'.
[2] Beginning with a match against Plymouth in 1928/29, they reached the first round of the Cup on over 40 occasions and knocked out League teams a record 20 times.

customers from all over the West Country. Its prosperity was based on the flourishing woollen and linen industry and it became a centre of glove making. In the seventeenth century, however, the town suffered during the Civil War and its wool and linen both faltered through competition from Europe. The town's fortunes revived during the eighteenth century and by the 1830s it was said that three million pairs of gloves were made in Yeovil each year. Communications improved dramatically, with three railways serving the town by the 1860s; light engineering had developed by 1900; and, today. Yeovil is the only industrial centre of any size in a region of secluded villages and small country towns. Even the huge Westland Aircraft complex does not have an undue impact upon the surrounding hills.

The Westland Aircraft Works was founded in 1915 as a division of Petters Limited to build Short seaplanes and in the same year Petters United, the works team, merged with Yeovil Town to form Yeovil and Petters United. Yeovil Town, formed in 1907, had had two incarnations, first in 1890 as Yeovil Football Club, then as Yeovil Casuals, playing their home games at the Pen Mill Athletic Ground. In 1922 the new club progressed from the Western League to the Southern League, reverting to the name Yeovil Town in 1946.

The 1948/49 season rolled on like any other. By the end of January, Yeovil were sixth from bottom in the Southern League. They had beaten Romford and Weymouth, both 4–0, in the first two rounds of the Cup and then out of the blue, they walloped Second Division Bury 3–1 at Huish Park. A one-off, said the pundits. Lightning couldn't strike twice – not when you're quoted at 5,000–1 to win the Cup and your next game is against Sunderland. Lying eighth in Division One, Sunderland were dubbed the 'Bank of England club'. They had spent £20,000 on Len Shackleton, 'celebrity, showman, rebel, eccentric and brilliant inside-forward'.[3] What is more, they had had the cheek to pinch the most talented player of his generation from Newcastle, their arch-rivals. Great players and illustrious achievements graced Sunderland's history and, in an age of austerity, their spending on players beggared belief, whereas Yeovil's wage bill for their part-timers was £100 a week.

On the last Saturday in January, 17,000 spectators – a remarkable turnout for a town of only 23,000 – packed into the ground. By the time the gates

[3] Butler, *The Official Illustrated History of the F.A. Cup*, p. 168.

60

opened at noon, the queues were six deep and half a mile long. Near the front stood 13-year-old Ray Horton, who had left home for Huish Park about nine o'clock, wearing three small green-and-white rosettes which his father had made and carrying a large wooden wartime gas rattle. He recalls rushing in 'to get a good position. Along the top touchline, opposite the grandstand, wooden beer crates with planks between them had been placed inside the boundary wire. Us lads made a beeline for a seat on these. I was near the halfway line with an unobstructed view of the pitch.' Eleven-year-old Jill Preston had a rattle too, 'one of those lovely old-fashioned wooden rattles that make such a satisfying racket, as well as a green-and-white scarf especially knitted by mum.'[4] Jill was desperate to go to the match and, though her mum 'never went to football matches, she decided on this occasion to come with me so that I could go. She even queued for the tickets! As the crowd built up the young, smaller children were summoned to sit on benches right near the touchline in front of the stand.' Along the touchline, too, scores of newspaper reporters were squashed into little desks borrowed from a local school.

As kick-off drew near, cinema newsreels filmed cheering supporters and Ray Horton remembers being filmed 'twirling my large rattle but don't remember seeing myself on the big screen.' He also recalls a character dressed in green and white placing two green-and-white balloons on the centre spot. 'He then pointed his arms towards each goal and tried to kick the balloons but seemed to be a little unsteady on his feet – perhaps too much local scrumpy.' Perchance he was just overexcited: for weeks all over town people had talked of little but the big match. Fans had begun queuing from 9 in the morning for a 2.00 kick-off. There were no floodlights then and allowance had to be made for extra time: under the government's post-war austerity measures, to save energy and lost working days, there was to be no replay. Not that the home fans ever dreamed of holding the star-studded visitors to a draw.

After all, the only Yeovil player with League experience was their captain and player–manager, the intelligent and articulate Alec Stock. A Somerset lad from the mining village of Peasedown St John, Stock had been a creative inside-forward with Charlton and QPR before the war, which ended his professional career when he was injured in Normandy. He had been a major

---

[4] She wasn't alone – I still have the rattle which my dad painted in the Hastings colours of claret and blue.

in the Royal Armoured Corps and brought to the role of player–manager a flair for military-style organisation and an off-beat approach to nutritional techniques, insisting on a diet of glucose, sherry and eggs for his team. Ralph Davis, who played left-back against Sunderland, described him later as 'a great manager, a father of eleven boys if you like'. As for Stock himself, he viewed player-managership as 'violent exercise on top of a pile of worries'. In later years, he would manage Leyton Orient, Arsenal, AS Roma, Queens Park Rangers, Luton, Fulham (whom he managed to the Cup Final in 1975) and Bournemouth.

Stock was also not above the judicious use of psychology. The Huish pitch had a famous eight-foot slope, which ran from the side of the pitch under the main stand over to the far touchline, and Stock refused Sunderland permission to train on it. Speaking to the press before the game Stock exaggerated the slope so much that when the Wearsiders arrived they 'must have had the idea that we played on the North Face of the Eiger'.

As the game began, hundreds more fans outside the ground listened on police car radios and a few spectators climbed trees at the back of Huish Park. Several people without tickets were invited into houses in Queen Street which backed on to the ground and watched the game from bedroom and attic windows behind one of the goals. On a crisp winter afternoon they would have seen the ground bathed in bright sunlight but they might also have heard with dismay that the Glovers' keeper, Stan Hall, had been hurt in training and would be replaced by 23-year-old solicitor's clerk, Dickie Dyke, with only one senior game to his name. Many locals had never heard of him and Yeovil's hopes were further lessened when winger Jack Hargreaves pulled a muscle after ten minutes and became a passenger.

Yet in the 28th minute, centre-half Les Blizzard pushed a free kick to inside-left Ray Wright, who drilled a waist-high ball towards Stock on the edge of the penalty area. The player–manager swivelled on his right leg before striking a left-foot shot past the diving goalkeeper, Johnny Mapson. Gaynor Collie's mother-in-law rarely missed a match but she was at a local pantomime that afternoon and, though she missed Stock's goal, she knew the score – when Yeovil went 1–0 up, a character in the panto managed to work the score into his lines.

Sunderland were worried and, in the face of some tough tackling by the Yeovil defence, they just could not settle to their fluid passing game: 'Individually, they looked like a Test cricketer playing on a bumpy country pitch.'[5] Thus it was hardly a surprise that Yeovil continued to hold their ascendancy till half-time.

Then, just after the hour, the Wearside aristocrats hit back. Dickie Dyke, who had played superbly throughout the first period, showed his nerves for the first time when he failed to cut out Barney Ramsden's long ball and dropped it at the feet of centre-forward Jackie Robinson. A pre-war England international at the age of 19, Robinson gratefully tapped the ball into an open goal. Sunderland were on level terms.

Then just before the final whistle, the first tendrils of a menacing mist eddied around Huish Park and, with the part-timers tiring, in 'a riotous whirlwind of Cup-tie soccer . . . it looked as if the sands of ambition were running out.'[6] However, as the murk deepened, Alec Stock's experience and his side's tight marking and fierce tackling took the game into extra time, with the Glovers still in the fight.

Len Shackleton, the Paul Gascoigne of his generation, was the most gifted but the most mercurial forward of the post-war years, his skill and individualism brightening many a dour Saturday afternoon in the age of austerity. He had had a quiet game, well shackled by an unyielding Yeovil rearguard. After 104 minutes, he had a chance to control the ball and set his strikers on their way. On the halfway line, in acres of space, he chose to juggle the ball and tried an overhead kick in the general direction of Jackie Robinson. Unfortunately for the Wearsiders, his aimless and ambitious pass into the fog was seized upon by Yeovil's Ray Wright. His through ball put Eric Bryant in the clear and from 15 yards the centre-forward thumped the ball home as Mapson rushed out. Ron Hunt, standing near the corner flag on a wooden box at the Queen Street end, never saw the winning goal. 'I'd bought the box for 6d from one of the boys in the backyards of the Queen Street houses backing on to the ground. In the thickening fog I couldn't see the goal at the Brewery end, but the roar that went up from that end was enough.' Jill Preston saw it and 'when the ball went into the net I leapt to my feet waving my wooden rattle around and dancing about like crazy. Grinning from ear to ear I turned round to mum to find she was clutching her nose which was pouring blood. As Bryant had scored I had caught her smack on the bridge of her nose!! Needless to say that was her first and last match and I don't know from that day to this what happened to that rattle.'

---

[5] *Sunday People*, January 30, 1949.
[6] Ibid.

How many of the seventeen thousand fans actually saw Eric Bryant score Yeovil's winner is not known. Many feared that the thick fog which now enveloped the ground might cause the tie to be abandoned. Left-back Ralph Davis couldn't see a thing. 'I felt sure the referee would call it off.' But mindful of the situation regarding replays, the significance of the occasion and the record attendance, he allowed the game to go on. The fog disappeared as quickly as it had come, with Sunderland laying siege to the Yeovil goal.

Time slowly ticked away and, during the second period, Yeovil's rearguard seemed to care little for the beautiful game, hacking away anything played into their penalty area. In a frantic last few minutes Sunderland threw everything at the home defence, prompted by Len Shackleton, perhaps trying to atone for his costly error. Then, with two minutes left, the referee blew his whistle for a free kick to Sunderland; the crowd rushed on to the pitch, thinking it was the final whistle. Ralph Davis feared the match would be abandoned and 'the greatest day of my life would all count for nothing'. So he and the other Yeovil players helped the officials shepherd the excited fans back behind the touchlines. At last Sunderland could take the free kick. It summed up their afternoon, ending not with a bang but a whimper. The last seconds were played in a frenetic atmosphere but Alec Stock's ragbag assemblage of publicans, glove-cutters, clerks and warehousemen held on till the final whistle, when hundreds of people, including 13-year-old Ray Horton, ran on to the pitch to congratulate the players. 'It seemed to take ages for the ground to empty and when it did I made my way home, still twirling my rattle and shouting the score to everyone that I met.'

Another Yeovil fan, Ken Rogers, recalls that 'Sunderland took defeat very sportingly; that evening, Yeovil people and Sunderland supporters enjoyed each other's company in the pubs and clubs, playing skittles, darts etc. There was no sign of any bad feelings.' To give Sunderland credit, their long-serving manager Bill Murray sought no excuses: 'We were beaten by a better side on the day.' His team had had no answer to Yeovil's strength of resolve and 'in every department were outmanoeuvred, outpaced and outclassed.'[7] 'Argus' of the *Sunderland Echo*, one of the press corps squeezed into a school desk on the touchline, wrote: 'Occasionally a bugle sounded. Whether Sunderland thought it sounded the retreat I don't know.'

A fortnight later, after the Wearsiders had retreated back up the A1 to

---

[7] Ibid.

lick their wounds, 81,565 people – the largest FA Cup crowd outside of a final – saw the Glovers come down to earth with a bump in Round Five. At Maine Road – Old Trafford was still not ready after the war – Cup-holders Manchester United hammered Alec Stock's men 8–0, Jack Rowley scoring five of them. However, 'the score was not important. That huge crowd . . . gathered to pay tribute to a team of part-timers from the green and pleasant acres of Somerset that had captured the respect of the nation. . .'[8]

It would take another half-century or more however for Yeovil Town to be granted the respect of League status. They had been founder members of the inaugural Alliance Premier League in 1979, the top tier of non-League football, but despite being the best-supported club, they were relegated for the first time in their history six years later. In their relegation season, Somerset cricket hero Ian Botham, who had been to school in the town, turned out occasionally for the Glovers and boosted the crowds, but Alec Stock, now at the Huish as a spectator, was less than impressed: 'As a footballer, he's an exceptional cricketer.'

Eventually, in 2003, Yeovil won promotion to the Football League as Conference champions and were promoted to League One two years later. It was no surprise that, when the side who as a non-League club had beaten 20 League sides in the Cup were drawn against non-League opposition for the first time, one newspaper ran the headline 'poacher turned game-keepers'.

The 'poachers' of 1949, says Ray Horton, 'are still household names with some of the oldies of the town'. As football fans we need heroes who embody our hopes and fears, champions whose feats of skill and daring transcend our everyday existence and, while we imbue them with almost godlike qualities, it is somehow extra special if they walk the same streets we walk and breathe the same air. As Chris Oakley writes, 'we are drawn to individuals whom we like to see something of ourselves in, or something that we aspire to.'[9] Fifty years ago, you could probably bump into Eric Bryant or Ralph Davis in the pub or on the bus – and when 'we gaze so intently at our heroes or demonise our villains'[10] it is ultimately reassuring to see they are rather like us.

---

[8] Butler, *The Official History of the Football Association*, p. 98.
[9] Oakley, p. 40.
[10] Ibid., p. 41.

YEOVIL TOWN: Dyke, Hickman, Davis, Keeton, Blizard, Collins, Hamilton, Stock, Bryant, Wright, Hargreaves
SUNDERLAND: Mapson, Stelling, Ramsden, Watson, Hall, Wright, Duns, Robinson, Turnbull, Shackleton, Reynolds

10

PORT VALE 2, BLACKPOOL 0

FA Cup, Round Five, February 20, 1954

The novelist and critic Arnold Bennett wrote in his *Journal* for 1897 of 'the grim and original beauty of certain aspects of the Potteries. . .' He had been born thirty years earlier in the heart of the North Midlands, in Hanley, 'one of the Potteries towns that fashioned and fired the Empire's table-ware'.[1] His *Journal* goes on: 'Down below is Burslem, nestled in the hollow between several hills, and showing a vague picturesque mass of bricks through its heavy pall of smoke. . . It is not beautiful in detail, but the smoke transforms its ugliness into a beauty transcending the work of architects and of time.'

This vivid evocation of the landscape of his childhood forms the backdrop to his first major achievement, *Anna of the Five Towns*, in which the fictional Hanbridge and Bursley are each only a single syllable away from the real Hanley and Burslem. To Bennett, 'Nothing could be more prosaic than the "Huddled, red-brown streets"; nothing more seemingly remote from romance. Yet be it said that romance is even here – . . . The grass grows; though it is not green, it grows.' And, in 1897, where there were mills, factories and kilns – hard, smoky and unforgiving – 'huddled, red-brown streets' and a patch of grass, men played football:

Moor Road, which climbs over the ridge to the mining village of Moorthorne and passes the new Park on its way, was crowded with people going up to criticize and enjoy this latest outcome of municipal enterprise in Bursley:

---

[1] Elmes, p. 110.

. . .' What stacks of folks!' Agnes exclaimed. 'It's like going to a football match.'

'Do you go to football matches, Agnes?' Mynors asked. The child gave a giggle.

Agnes might have been a regular supporter of Port Vale, the local professional club. Formed in 1876, Port Vale became the 'Kings of geographical minimalism',[2] as the club took its name from Port Vale House, the single dwelling in Longport which hosted the inaugural meeting. Together with Arsenal, Port Vale is one of only two professional clubs in England not to be named after a place, though when the club moved to Burslem in 1884 it changed its name to 'Burslem Port Vale', just as Arsenal were originally 'Woolwich Arsenal'.

A flourishing pottery industry existed in the late twelfth century, based on the high-quality local clays. Six hundred years later, in the Industrial Revolution and at the height of the 'Age of Canals', Josiah Wedgwood, who was born in Burslem, set up his own business in 1759 and built the world-famous Etruria factory in 1766, which produced three iconic ceramic designs – Queen's Ware, Black Basalt and Jasper. Burslem – Bennett's 'Bursley' – became known as 'The Mother Town' of the six towns that make up the city of Stoke-on-Trent. The others are Hanley, Longton, Stoke itself, Tunstall and Fenton, 'the forgotten town'.[3] Today, the industrial area of Burslem remains a district where people still live within walking distance of a single heavy industry. As a result, a good deal of the town's industrial heritage and its Georgian and Victorian architecture has survived intact.

So has Port Vale FC – more or less, for the football club, in common with countless others, has continually been beset by financial difficulties. Vale began life in the Midland League, but, after becoming a founder member of the Football League Division Two in 1892, had to resign from the League in 1907 and almost went into oblivion. The prefix 'Burslem' was dropped from the name as a new ground several miles away was acquired and the new club, Port Vale, returned to the Football League in 1919, when Leeds City were thrown out of Division Two because of illegal payments.

It was still an unrelenting struggle, however. Stoke City, only five miles

---

[2] Seddon, p. 170.
[3] To Bennett, 'Five Towns' had a more mellifluous ring. Thus Burslem was 'Bursley', Hanley 'Hanbridge', 'Longton' Longshaw, Stoke 'Knype', Tunstall 'Turnhill', plus Fenton, 'the forgotten one'.

away, had moved within six short seasons from Division Three (North) to Division One and had Stanley Matthews, the George Best of his generation, dazzling on the wing as a major attraction. In 1928/29, the club experienced relegation for the first time – but only two seasons later Vale finished fifth in Division Two, which still remains the club's highest-ever League position. They were again relegated in 1936, but in 1950 the club moved to their present home at Vale Park. The ground, planned before the Second World War to hold 70,000, was to become the 'Wembley of the North'. However, construction had been slow owing to post-war demand for materials and the perennial lack of funds, and it was considerably smaller on its completion.

In 1951 Vale appointed Freddie Steele, once a teammate of Matthews at Stoke before the war, and fortunes began to look up. The team acquired a solid and dependable spine. Geordie Ray King arrived from Ashington and became an England 'B' goalkeeper. Roy Sproson, a huge centre-half seemingly hewn out of the Millstone Grit quarried near Biddulph a few miles north of Stoke, became Vale's most loyal servant, making 761 appearances in a 22-year career. Upfront, Albert Leake, a local lad, joined Vale from Stoke City in February 1950 and began banging in the goals. The side was skippered by Tommy Cheadle, who gave his name to a celebrated watering-hole, situated right outside Vale Park, next to the away end.

By the turn of the year in 1953, Vale were runaway leaders of Division Three (North). In the Cup, after routine victories over Darlington, Southport and QPR, they saw off First Division Cardiff 2–0 at a snowbound Ninian Park. By the time Blackpool arrived at Vale Park for the Fifth Round clash on February 20, Vale hadn't conceded a home goal for nearly six months. The Seasiders had won the Cup the previous May in what came to be dubbed the 'Matthews Final' and the eponymous hero of that victory over Bolton was returning to his home town. On a winter's day when 'even the harsh, scarred countryside of the Potteries, where vast kilns and chimneys point upwards like chubby fingers, took on a kindly, gentle look',[4] the Cup-holders, Matthews and all, walked into a frenzied atmosphere full of heightened expectation. Though there was never any love lost between Stoke and Port Vale, for the locals, wrote *The Times*, 'Here was a pretty problem': much as 'they wanted their idol to remain on his pinnacle', they longed for a Port Vale victory.

---

[4] *The Times*, February 22, 1954.

Freddie Steele knew his man. He devised a cunning plan to nullify Matthews' ability to dribble at speed and reach the byline. The core of Steele's strategy was to force him away from the drier areas on the wing where left-back Reg Potts was to hug the touchline and make Matthews and the inside-forwards play through the midfield mud, where Sproson and Dickie Cunliffe formed a human roadblock.

The tactic worked so well that Matthews seemed a prophet without honour in his own country, or, in the words of *The Times*, 'a stranger in a friendly land'. None of the Blackpool forwards could get to grips with the tough Vale half-backs. By contrast, Vale forced three corners in the first quarter of an hour, and from the third, local lad Albert Leake, making the most of his height advantage over left-half Hugh Kelly, headed Cunliffe's looping cross to the far post wide of keeper George Farm. Ten minutes later Ken Griffiths and Cunliffe combined to send centre-forward Basil Hayward down the left and, as the Blackpool defence hesitated, hoping for an offside decision, Leake dashed in to side-foot his diagonal low centre pass past George Farm in the visitors' goal.

To all intents and purposes the game was over, though the Seasiders' pride was hurt and they had several chances to come back into the game. They gave the home defence a moment of alarm on the half-hour when Cheadle slipped and left centre-forward Stephenson with ball in front of goal. His sharp drive was tipped one-handed over the bar by King. Five minutes later, Matthews almost scored from Blackpool's third corner, but was blocked his shot on the goal-line by right-back Stan Turner. For an hour Turner kept Blackpool winger, Bill Perry, the match-winning hero at Wembley a year before, well under lock and key but in the 66th minute Perry slipped his marker and shot narrowly wide.

Usually, in Cup ties like this one, the home side will come out of the blocks at a hundred miles an hour, throwing everything at the much-vaunted visitors. Away from home on a small pitch and faced with a fiercely partisan crowd, the 'class' side's game plan is to hold on till half-time and then crank up the pressure in the second half as the home side tire. If that was Blackpool's strategy, it misfired. Indeed, it was a measure of how rattled they were that after 70 minutes, the normally controlled and fair-minded Matthews gave away a free kick for holding back Cunliffe. However, his customary equanimity was restored on the final whistle: he was the first to shake hands with Tom Cheadle as policemen faced the fruitless task of keeping the ecstatic crowd off the pitch.

Blackpool captain Harry Johnston was equally magnanimous in defeat, telling the *Daily Express* he 'envied his *[Cheadle's]* coolness and the way he steadied a team undergoing a tremendous ordeal'. There was no doubt among the national press that on the day, the Cup-holders had been beaten 'by better football, by a team superior in all the arts and crafts – ball control, teamwork, passing accuracy – the lot,' said Henry Rose of the *Express* and its sister Sunday paper admired Vale's 'clean efficiency and beauty which was staggering. They were faster on the ball. Their covering and tackling were superb while the home defence was as treble-padlocked as a bank vault.'

Three weeks later the Vale were in the capital, in a quarter-final against a fellow Third Division side, Leyton Orient, at Brisbane Road. The Os had had their own triumphs en route to the Sixth Round, beating Fulham and Doncaster Rovers of the Second Division. But in a dour struggle characteristic of many a close Cup tie, Sproson and Cheadle marshalled what was now nationally dubbed the 'Iron Curtain' defence and Port Vale won by the only goal of the match, joining Millwall in the distinction of being the only Third Division clubs to have reached the semi-final of the FA Cup.

They were helped because the home forwards, who were unable to pass their way through the Vale's solid barricade on the ground, persisted in the long high ball, where 'the unusually tall Port Vale defenders were always supreme. Thus Leyton Orient enjoyed three-quarters of the game territorially, a pattern that was relieved from time to time by sporadic raids on the part of the Port Vale attack'[5] – and, in their first serious onslaught on the home goal, Port Vale forced a corner. Left-winger Colin Askey floated over a cross, Basil Hayward nodded it on and Leake – yes, him again – half-volleyed the ball past Groombridge. In the second half, Orient piled on enormous pressure, but Vale's defence never seemed likely to crumble and a few minutes from time, 'a glorious shot by Poulton was somehow turned aside by King at full stretch': the match had been won.

Vale were a step nearer Wembley but in the semi-final they came up against a West Bromwich Albion side containing former Vale hero Ronnie Allen, who had played 123 games for the club between 1946 and 1950. For three seasons in the early 50s Allen's intelligence, vision and ball-control made him the outstanding centre-forward in the country, though

---

[5] *The Times*, March 15, 1954.

he was capped only five times for England. This Midlands derby took place at the end of March, in front of a 68,000 crowd at Villa Park, and, with the twin towers in sight, Albert Leake, who had scored in every round since the third, gave the Vale the lead. They were still very much in the game, even when Jimmy Dudley equalised, and it was only a debatable late penalty, converted ironically enough by Allen, that ended the Valiants' dream.

Half a century on, Port Vale play their football in the League's bargain basement. They remain, however, one of football's 'Don Quixote' clubs, redolent with nostalgic black-and-white Pathé News memories of the glory days, the 'Iron Curtain' side, and the season when they tilted at giants.

PORT VALE: King, Turner, Potts, Mullard, Cheadle, Sproson, Askey, Leake, Hayward, Griffiths, Cunliffe
BLACKPOOL: Farm, Shimwell, Frith, Fenton, Johnson, Kelly, Matthews, Taylor, Stephenson, Brown, Perry

11

YORK CITY 3, TOTTENHAM HOTSPUR 1

FA Cup, Round Five, February 19, 1955

The Roxy at Silverhill is long gone. Some sort of carpet warehouse now, I think. But in Hastings in the 1950s it was one of those small picture houses which showed the big films weeks after the main cinemas. It made its money from a rapid turnover of programmes and a nice line in those black-and-white B-movies which featured Wolseley 6/80 police cars with chrome bumpers, silver bells, running boards, doors which opened the wrong way and policemen in trilbies and long raincoats. The villains sported pencil-thin moustaches, used rather too much Brylcreem, wore ties which were just too narrow and just too loud, always spoke out of the corner of their mouths and smoked Woodbines cupped in their hands. The heroes, in impeccable Savile Row suits, called each other 'old boy' and usually smoked Balkan Sobranies held between their fingers whilst pouring a generous Scotch. The ladies in the films were always impossibly glamorous, wore 'hets', looked as if they'd stepped out of a late-1940s fashion magazine, smoked monogrammed cigarettes elegantly in long tortoiseshell holders, wired their girlfriends to meet them for luncheon and always seemed to live in flats in Mayfair or possibly Maida Vale.

I remember being riveted at the Roxy by the swaggering Robert Newton and unnerved by the deranged Ben Gunn in *Treasure Island* and thrilled by Richard Todd in *The Story of Robin Hood*. On another planet – almost literally – I was knocked out by the submarine, the monsters and James Mason as the sinister Captain Nemo in *20,000 Leagues under the sea*. Late February 1955 it was. It must have been, for in the snow, in monochrome, York City were shocking the football world on Pathé News. There on the silver screen, with the triumphantly crowing rooster and Bob Danvers-Walker's insistent cut-glass delivery, was the only national football I ever saw. These were still the radio days, as Peter Hennessy recalls with nostalgia:

For a radio generation boy like myself, the sound of Big Ben striking . . . remains evocative of that pre-television era, as do snatches of long-gone signature tunes. Fifties Saturday afternoon . . . are inseparable in my memory from the Central Band of the Royal Air Force playing in Eamonn Andrews and 'Sports Report' on the Light Programme to the sound of 'Out of the Blue'. Andrews' pleasing Dublin voice, too, is indistinguishable from such gems as 'Accrington Stanley 3, Port Vale 2.[1]

Or incredibly, in that last week of February: York City 3, Tottenham Hotspur 1'. Apparently City were no strangers to Cup glory. I didn't know it at the time – I gleaned what I knew about football from the radio or my dad's *Daily Mirror* – but in 1937/38 they had beaten Halifax Town and Clapton Orient in the first two rounds after replays. They then put out Second Division Coventry City 3–2 at Bootham Crescent in Round Three, and First Division West Bromwich Albion were knocked out by the same score, local lad Reg Baines hitting a hat trick. Middlesbrough were beaten 1–0 at Bootham Crescent in Round Five and in the quarter-finals a record crowd of 28,123 saw City hold Huddersfield Town to a goalless draw before a valiant 2–1 defeat in the replay brought the Cup run to an end.

In that last pre-war season, the club had been in existence only three decades – a mere babe-in-arms in a city nearly two thousand years old. Founded as Eboracum in AD 71 by the Romans, the city became Jorvik after the Vikings captured it in 866 and it wasn't until about AD 1000 that the city became known as York. Since the city was dominated by the Gothic splendour of York Minster, England's largest medieval cathedral, the football club perhaps inevitably acquired the nickname of 'The Minstermen'. Some sources assert that the club's origins can be traced back to 1897, but certainly in 1908 York City FC were founded as an amateur side, joining the Northern League. When they entered the Midland League in 1912 the club turned professional, but on the outbreak of the Great War in 1914 it

---

[1] Hennessey, p. 108.

folded, to be reformed in 1922. Seven years later, when Ashington failed to gain re-election to the Football League, City took their place in Division Three (North).

In those days, York City played at Fulfordgate on the outskirts of the city but towards the end of the club's third season in the Football League, it was anxious about the mediocre gates and, interestingly, when nowadays clubs are increasingly aiming to relocate from their cramped, Victorian, inner-city stadiums, the club decided to move to a ground nearer the city centre. For several seasons York Cricket Club had played at Bootham Crescent but in 1932 they moved to new headquarters at Wigginton Road. Thus Bootham Crescent became vacant and, at the start of the 1932/33 season, York City moved to its present home.[2]

In the club's debut season in the League, in 1929/30, they finished a creditable sixth but they had only moderate success just before and after the war. Indeed, in 1949/50 they had to apply for re-election. By the early 1950s, however, things were looking up: in 1952/53 they finished fourth, their highest placing in the old regional Division. Furthermore, the team were in a rich vein of form, having suffered just two defeats in their previous 23 games. But nothing could have prepared the Minstermen's supporters for what happened a couple of seasons later.

By the time City faced the Spurs at Bootham Crescent on February 19, 1955, Arthur Bottom, a 25-year-old centre-forward from Sheffield, had already scored six goals in the Cup run. Routine victories over non-League Scarborough and Dorchester Town had taken City to Bloomfield Road to face Blackpool, winners of the Cup just 18 months previously and with England stars Stanley Matthews and Stanley Mortensen in their line-up. Blackpool had found themselves Goliaths to Port Vale's David just a year before and were cast in the same role in January when York triumphed 2–0 with goals from Storey and Fenton. In Round Four two goals from Arthur Bottom and another by Storey gave City a 3–1 win over leading amateur side Bishop Auckland, Cup giant-killers themselves, having beaten Crystal Palace and then Ipswich 3–0 in a replay played in a blizzard.

The winter of 1955 was the coldest and snowiest between the two Big Freezes of 1947 and 1963. In the second half of February, snow lay 60 cm deep in northern Scotland and the wintry weather extended to England

---

[2] In 2005 Bootham Crescent was renamed KitKat Crescent, after the club signed a sponsorship deal with Nestlé.

and Wales too. In Yorkshire, after eight days of snow and frost, the game was in doubt but a local building firm levelled out the frozen ridges and rolled tons of sand into the surface. On the morning of the game, the York ground staff shovelled away more snow and, though the surface was a mixture of ice, snow and slush, the referee had no hesitation in declaring the pitch fit. Even so, a heavy snowstorm started about an hour before the kick-off and it seemed even then that the match might be called off, but the line had been meticulously marked in blue paint, and, although it was still snowing when the match started, the sun soon broke through and, it seemed, the natural order of things was re-established as Spurs took an early lead.

The capacity crowd of 21,000 had no early inkling of the sensations to come when, in the 11th minute, Alf Ramsey set up a smooth attack down the right. The move was carried on by Sonny Walters and George Robb, storming in from the left wing, netted Len Duquemin's centre from five yards. 'There', wrote *The Times* in momentous prose, 'seemed the beginning of the end. But the afternoon held its own secret and that in point was the end of Tottenham's beginning.'[3]

The contest was won and lost in 60 pulsating seconds right on the half-hour as York, following on a flurry of corners, struck back. After 29 minutes, Fenton set off, with Ramsey in pursuit, on a clever diagonal 30-yards run before back-heeling to Hughes wide out on the right. Norman Wilkinson, City's all-time leading record goal scorer, met Hughes's swift centre and headed it firmly past Ron Reynolds into the top corner of the net. The Minstermen were level.

A minute later, Bottom seized the ball in midfield and set up a chance for Wilkinson. His fierce cross-shot was parried by Reynolds and, while the Spurs keeper lay prone in the snow, Billy Fenton nipped in to score an opportunist goal and give the home side the lead.

City continued to dominate the play in the second half. They launched wave after wave of attacks and Reynolds kept the Londoners in the game with a string of brave saves. Duquemin went close with a great header but that was all. Though half the Spurs team were internationals, they had been drifting dangerously close to the First Division relegation zone, prompting the purchase just before Christmas of the Irish international Danny Blanchflower from Aston Villa for £30,000. Blanchflower worked hard,

---

[3] *The Times*, February 21, 1955.

probing for weaknesses in the home defence, but the visitors' forwards could make no headway against the likes of Gordon Brown and George Howe. 'Long before the finish', wrote *The Times*, 'all that we saw were the cherry-red shirts of York. Tottenham, in white, had disappeared, merged in the wintry scene, and melted away like the early flurry of snowflakes that fled as the sun came out to smile on a great and unquestioned triumph.'

Nine minutes from the end York applied the coup de grace. Once more Ramsey was left for dead by Fenton, 'who, with Hughes on the opposite flank, was a constant threat to a nervous Spurs defence'. Not for the first time that afternoon, 'Ramsey, indeed, was ... not in the same county as Fenton showed him his heels' and his centre found Wilkinson, who slid the ball home past Reynolds with ease. A deafening roar rent the darkening afternoon sky and 'If the bells of the minster did not actually peal ... there was an indefinable ring in the crisp evening air of York as the city, half disbelieving, hugged its famous victory to itself.'[4] What made the moment even sweeter was that the victory was no fluke. While the visitors had begun by trying to play their unruffled and precise passing game, they were forced out of it by York's pace and strength in the tackle. It was the Third Division side who played the more constructive football and that, along with their more flexible movement and greater team spirit, was the foundation of their win.

The Minstermen's reward was a visit to Meadow Lane to meet Notts County in the Sixth Round on March 12. For the princely sum of 12 shillings[5] City fans could take advantage of the British Railways special excursions from York to see their heroes tackle a challenging assignment, for County had beaten Middlesbrough at Ayresome Park, and then put out two First Division clubs in Sheffield Wednesday and Chelsea.

The match was the expected grim battle but 'Spartan', the correspondent for the *Yorkshire Gazette and Herald*, could declare in the paper's next edition 'YORK CITY have done it! A hard-earned 1–0 victory over Notts County, at Nottingham, on Saturday carried them into the semi-final of the FA Challenge Cup for the first time in their history.'[6]

It was not pretty, City's football never reaching the heights of the previous rounds against Blackpool, Bishop Auckland and Tottenham Hotspur. The

---

[4] Ibid.
[5] When an industrial worker earned around £8 a week.
[6] *Yorkshire Gazette and Herald*, March 18, 1955.

Minstermen won with a disputed goal from Arthur Bottom 12 minutes from time. In a typical Cup-tie encounter, man-to-man marking and rugged tackling ensured that the defences were always on top, but York showed they were as equal to this kind of craggy Cup football as they had been to the more artistic, measured game of the Spurs.

Both left-wingers, Fenton for York, and Broadbent for the County, had gone close before Bottom secured the vital breakthrough. Out on the right, Scottish winger Billy Hughes floated a free kick which was nodded down to Sid Storey. 'The inside left side-stepped two players,' wrote Spartan, 'pushed the ball through the crowd and saw it bounce off centre-half Leuty's leg to Bottom as he emerged from the group of players to shoot past Bradley.' Once again, City's eleven thousand travelling supporters 'cheered themselves almost hoarse' and, as they poured into York station, they were joined by more crowds waiting to greet the conquering heroes on their return by coach.

They now joined Millwall and Port Vale as the only Third Division clubs to reach the Cup semi-finals, where they would meet First Division Newcastle United at Hillsborough a fortnight later. An all-ticket crowd of 65,000, including 21,000 City fans, saw a classic encounter. By now, City were everyone's favourites and they were unfortunate to go behind after 13 minutes to a goal by Vic Keeble. However, their grit and endeavour brought them a deserved equaliser 20 minutes later when the inevitable Bottom chalked up his thirty-third goal of the season, his eighth of the incredible Cup campaign.

City had earned a replay, the first Third Division club to do so – a feat later emulated by Norwich City and Chesterfield. They ran out of steam four days later at Roker Park when goals from Keeble and White sent United on to beat Manchester City at Wembley.

In later decades, other York City teams have occasionally tapped into their club's proud tradition of giant-killing. In January 1985 the Minstermen beat Arsenal in the Fourth Round at Bootham Crescent, courtesy of a late penalty by Keith Houchen, whose diving header two years later helped Coventry City claim the Cup in an epic battle with Spurs. More recently – and perhaps even more extraordinarily – City beat Manchester United 3–0 in a League Cup clash at Old Trafford in September 1995.

Later in 1955, at the Roxy, I was gripped by Olivier's grotesquely seductive Richard III, the son of the 3rd Duke of York. A century before he bawled vainly for a horse and expired on Bosworth Field, his predecessor, Richard II, wanted to make York the capital of England. In the world of football, for a month or two in the almost Arctic winter of 1955, it very nearly was – and, though Pathé News has gone the way of the Roxy, for fans of the Minstermen nothing can erase the memory of the day they knocked the Spurs out of the Cup.

YORK CITY: Forgan, Phillips, Howe, Brown, Stewart, Spence, Hughes, Bottom, Wilkinson, Storey, Fenton
TOTTENHAM HOTSPUR: Reynolds, Ramsey, Hopkins, Blanchflower, Clarke, Marchi, Walters, Baily, Duquemin, Brooks, Robb

12

NOTTS COUNTY 1, RHYL ATHLETIC 3

FA Cup, Round Three, January 5, 1957

British seaside resorts are all about nostalgia – something to do with youth, escape and freedom. They're about the sea, of course, and its smells – the seaweed, the salt and the sand. They're also about sun and fun – swimming, rock pools, candyfloss, ice cream, shrimps, fish and chips, sticks of rock, kiss-me-quick hats and donkey rides. Before political correctness emasculated the Punch and Judy shows, the pierrots, the black-and-white minstrels and the naughty postcards, summers in seaside resorts a generation or more ago were joyously and unashamedly vulgar. The postcards still exist and, here and there, the raucously energetic clamour of the fairground organ, seagulls, drunken day trippers, ice-cream sellers and the screams of pretty girls pretending to be frightened by the waves while being chased by young blades down the beach to the sea.

Between the wars – and after – posters advertising seaside resorts, depicting a sunlit landscape of golden beaches, harmonious families and bonny children were produced for regional railway companies (and later for British Railways) and are now hugely collectable. A 1955 poster for London Midland Region promoted the North Wales resort of 'Sunny Rhyl' as an ideal holiday destination for families. Beneath a montage of postcard-like images a family are paddling in the sea – Dad is in his shirt sleeves with his trousers rolled up, Mum is wearing a floral frock and the three kids are happily splashing in the foam.

Rhyl reached the height of its prosperity as a resort a decade later, though the town had been welcoming visitors for 150 years. In 1800 the small village of Rhyl at the mouth of the Clwyd had only 300 inhabitants but

40 years later it had become an elegant Victorian resort and its population had grown twentyfold, to about six thousand. Many titled people took rooms for months at a time at this fashionable watering place and, even today, a walk along the promenade can evoke images of Victorian tourists in their top hats or crinolines enjoying the same bracing sea air.

By the end of the 1960s, however, once the British had learned to over-come their suspicion of all things foreign, the package holiday – and the charter airlines – took off for Spain, Greece and Portugal. Rhyl, in common with many other traditional British resorts, fell into decline, though it still had its passionate devotees. Marilyn from Cheshire recalls that her Sunday-school trips were always to Rhyl: 'My dad always booked a week's holiday there for us all too in the 1950s. We went to shows at the Pavilion and saw many famous people there, including Tommy Trinder, the singer Eve Boswell and Danny La Rue . . . Endless things to do. Loved it. Happy memories.' John Turner of Formby has vivid memories too: 'from owning caravans in the marine caravan park to holidays with my parents at Sunny Vale holiday camp'. Twenty years later, Bill Bryson couldn't agree with these rose-tinted reminiscences: 'From the train, north Wales looked like holiday hell – endless ranks of prison-camp caravan parks standing in fields in the middle of a lonely, windbeaten nowhere. It seemed an odd type of holiday option to me, the idea of sleeping in a tin box in a lonesome field miles from anywhere in a climate like Britain's. . .'[1]

Nonetheless, Rhyl has an eminent past as a small but perfectly formed resort, and its sporting antecedents are equally distinguished. The football club now known as Rhyl FC plays in the Welsh Premier League and has at various times been known as Rhyl Athletic, Rhyl Town and Rhyl United. Its origins lie in a group of lads who, in 1876, when the town had been a fashionable watering hole for half a century, formed a club called Rhyl Skull and Crossbones: the team wore black jerseys bearing the traditional pirate logo, intended to strike fear into their opponents. In 1879 they moved to the Green Field in the heart of the town, where the very first floodlit football match in Wales was staged in December of that year by Thomas Edison.

The club moved to its present home, Belle Vue, in 1900 and its first few decades were characterised by changes of name and colours (white shirts,

---

[1] Bryson, p. 248.

black shorts),[2] amalgamations and bewildering switches between the Welsh League, the North Wales Coast League, the Anglo-Welsh Combination and, after the Great War, the North Wales Alliance, before Rhyl became founder members of the Welsh National League (North) in 1921. They did have a modicum of Cup success. In 1927 (incidentally, when another Welsh side won the trophy), following wins over Stoke and Wrexham (what a local derby that must have been), they reached Round Three, going out by the odd goal in three at Darlington.

In the early 1930s the holiday towns and the Flintshire coalfield in North Wales did not escape the impact of the Great Depression, which had devastated the mining communities in the South Wales valleys. The Welsh League was in turmoil and Rhyl joined the Cheshire County League in 1936. After the war the club won two league titles and the Welsh Cup twice. In 1952 they beat Merthyr Tydfil 4–3 and in Coronation year they became the first non-League side to retain the trophy since Wrexham before the First World War when they defeated Chester 2–1.

Attendances were never high even for a successful amateur side in a strong league and being adjacent to the major conurbations of Liverpool and Manchester was a double-edged sword. While many would-be fans were lured away to Anfield, Goodison Park or Old Trafford, in the 1950s Rhyl's proximity to Merseyside and Lancashire meant that many former pros signed for clubs along the North Wales coast. Whereas few if any of today's Premiership stars will ever be forced to end their careers in the semi-professional game, it wasn't always so. As Rhyl fan Gareth Hughes points out, 'When the term "Player Power" was little more than a distant dream and the pay differential between top-and lower-level players was not so great, players found themselves having to play in their twilight years to earn their bread and butter.' The 1956/57 season was a good example. Rhyl attracted a number of former stars: the first was Stan Hanson. He joined the club at the age of 40 in October 1956 having made 384 Football League appearances for his only ever club – Bolton Wanderers. He was the goalkeeper on the losing side in the famous 'Matthews Cup Final' of 1953 when Blackpool came back to win 4–3 at Wembley. He may not have been as agile playing for Rhyl as in his Bolton days, but his mere presence was enough to inspire those around him. Another former Wanderer

[2] The colours gave rise to the club's nickname, 'The Lilywhites'.

to find his way west along the A55 was Ulsterman Billy Hughes who had made his one appearance for Northern Ireland in 1951 against Wales in Belfast.

That season the Lilywhites had other players with League experience – Harry Williams had arrived from Swindon after spells at West Ham and Bury, left-half Les Donaldson had come from Hearts, Clyde and Wrexham. Other émigrés from the Racecourse Ground were right-back Phil Spruce and Brian Roberts at right-half.

An interesting character was inside-right Billy Russell, then a 21-year-old student at Aberystwyth, who was on Manchester City's books and had turned out for the Welsh Universities. His father had been player–manager of Rhyl before the war and had taken the team to its post-war Cheshire League successes, but had moved on to Flint Town United in the 1950s, winning the Welsh Cup in 1954. Russell junior, back home for a funeral in November, was pressed into service by manager Freddie Roberts against Midland Counties League side Frickley Colliery in the Fourth Qualifying Round of the Cup. He scored one of the goals in a 2–0 win and kept his place a fortnight later against Scarborough in the First Round (Proper). The young German-language student bagged a brace in the 3–2 win at Belle Vue but he was still away at university and could play only the Cup games. Thus his next appearance was in the Second Round tie against Bishop Auckland, the leading amateur side in the country. Goals from Harry Williams, Donaldson and Billy Hughes saw the Lilywhites home and in the hat for the Third Round draw on the Monday. Russell hadn't scored but 'I must have made a good impression because later that season the Bishops asked me to play for them in their Amateur Cup Final at Wembley. I scored the first goal – we beat Wycombe Wanderers 3–1 – and I still have my winner's medal.'

So, on the Monday, December 10, the Rhyl players and their fans gathered round the wireless to hear the traditional lunchtime draw, which sounded like one more mundane item on the Agenda of the Challenge Cup Committee: 'We come to item six, the draw for the third round of the Football Association Challenge Cup. . .' Once the balls had been plucked from the bag at Lancaster Gate, Rhyl were faced with a visit to the East Midlands, and a game at Meadow Lane, home of the world's oldest League club, Notts County, then a Second Division side. Manager George Poyser had taken County to the Cup Quarter-Finals in 1955, where they were beaten by York[3] but they were having a dreadful season. They propped up the table with only ten points from a possible fifty and by the time Rhyl arrived at Meadow Lane on the first Saturday in January they had lost their last six games: indeed, they had won only three games all season.

So the 1,500 Rhyl supporters who set off for Nottingham in two specially decorated trains were full of optimism. As a 12-year-old boy, Barry Jenkinson travelled with Billy Russell's mother. He was lodging with his father at the Russells' guest house in Rhyl. 'Stan Hanson and Billy Hughes would some-times stay over at our house after midweek matches and my boyhood claim to fame is that I have played snooker with an FA Cup Final goalkeeper!' Derek Church, Rhyl-born but newly married and living in Derby, got the local train to Nottingham. 'As we waited the Rhyl football special pulled in and for some reason it stopped for a short time. As the heads popped out I seemed to know practically everyone including my own father. The front of the engine was decorated with "Rhyl FC Football Special". We followed on the next train, and I joined my father at the match. My wife went shopping!'

Also on board the football special were the Rhyl Silver Prize Band, who played the Welsh National Anthem as the Rhyl players ran out at Meadow Lane. 'To add to the festivities, visiting fans planted a succession of leeks in the centre circle before kick-off. They really knew how to enjoy them-selves in those days.'[4]

The match programme (black-and-white on buff paper, price 3d) appealed to County supporters in quaint terms: 'Your encouragement can help to extricate us from this crisis and we only hope that your efforts to help us will be rewarded by something better on the field of play.' And, 'today we hope that as supporters of the oldest League club in the country you will extend ... a very great welcome to our visitors Rhyl. Let them go back to North Wales full of praise for the sportsmanship of the Notts County fans and let us hope that we have made new friends in that part of the country.' The programme also announced that County would play in 'black and white striped shirts' and, as was standard in 1950s programmes, 'black knickers'[5]

---

[3] See York City v Tottenham Hotspur, pp. 73–79.

[4] Tibballs, p. 80.

[5] Victorian players had worn 'knickerbockers', knee-length trousers fastened at the bottom, and though 'foot-ballers quickly dispensed with the fastenings so that knickerbockers effectively became shorts, the abbreviation "knickers" lived on in football regulations for decades – much to the amusement of schoolboys, aware from the 1880s that it also meant "women's underpants".' (Seddon, p. 67.) Yet the term was still used until the early 1960s.

and Rhyl would turn out in 'blue shirts, white knickers'. It also showed that County gave a debut to 18-year-old left-winger Peter Bircumshaw, who had scored 11 goals in 20 reserve games, while the visitors had a couple of team changes – Ken Reynolds in at left-back and Graham Meakin, a Welsh schoolboy cap and friend of Billy Russell, in on the left wing.

From the first whistle, Rhyl undaunted by the occasion, went on the attack and as early as the fifth minute, Harry Williams headed against the underside of the bar while County's relatively inexperienced team seemed beset by 'Cup nerves'. Rhyl continued to press and their fast, aggressive football had its reward when, in the 20th minute, Les Donaldson's long pass found Harry Williams. The creative inside-left teed up a shot but, before he could pull the trigger, he was bundled off the ball by County's right-half, John McGrath. County lined up a wall on the edge of the penalty box to defend the free kick and County's keeper Jimmy Linton chose to stand behind it. Williams simply lobbed the ball past the unsighted Linton into the unguarded corner of the net.

For most of the first half the Rhyl defence was untroubled and keeper Hanson had little to concern him until, in the 37th minute, County's centre-forward, Gordon Wills, crossed for Ron Wylie to head goal-wards. Hanson fumbled Wylie's header and Peter Bircumshaw scrambled the rebound into the net. For a while, Notts held the upper hand but, after half-time, under the floodlights and in driving rain, Rhyl dispelled any hopes among the home supporters that the Cheshire League side would run out of steam. The Williams brothers both shot narrowly wide, while, at the Rhyl end, County's ham-fisted forwards bungled several easy chances.

It was no surprise therefore that, on the hour, Rhyl regained the lead, albeit through a disputed penalty. As Harry Williams ran on to Brian Roberts's through ball, the County centre-half Peter Russell was deemed to have pushed him. Outside-right Billy Hughes calmly stroked the ball inside Linton's left-hand post but had to retake it because Russell was encroaching inside the penalty box. Hughes easily beat Linton at the second attempt and from then on County looked all over a beaten team. They had a golden opportunity to level the scores when Reynolds cleared off the line from Wills but the final crushing blow fell six minutes from time, when County's left-back Frank Cruickshank tried to play the ball out of defence, only to lose it to Harry Williams. His delightfully floated cross to the far post was met by the young outside-left Graham Meakin, who totally unmarked, sealed the home side's fate with a neat header inside the far post. The die was cast and the final whistle signalled the inevitable pitch invasion as hundreds of excited Rhyl supporters poured on to a rain-soaked Meadow Lane.

Seventy-nine-year old James Sherratt, a Rhyl supporter from the age of five, who still does the odd job as a joiner at Belle Vue, was not among them: 'I forgot to book the day off from work at the Courtaulds factory and a few of my mates beat me to it. They arrived back between 11 p.m. and midnight, singing and a bit worse for wear.' Among the tales they told James was that the game at the City Ground, where Nottingham Forest were thrashing Goole 6–0, had started half an hour before Rhyl's match and Forest fans, hearing that Rhyl were winning 2–1, decided to call into Meadow Lane where they were overjoyed to see Rhyl score again. At the end of the game, James heard, Notts County supporters were so unhappy they broke the windows in the back of the stand. Two days later George Poyser was sacked as County manager.

The wheels came off Rhyl's bandwagon three weeks later at Ashton Gate, where two goals from John Atyeo and a third from Bobby Etheridge sent another Second Division side, Bristol City, through to a money-spinning glamour tie away at Villa Park.

Half a century later, in April 2008, the then Minister for the Cabinet, Ed Miliband, visited Rhyl on a fact-finding mission. 'As the man responsible for the government's policy on social exclusion,' wrote local journalist David Rutland, 'he was keen to see some of the worst areas in the UK. Naturally,' he adds unkindly, 'Rhyl was at the top of his list.' Apparently, he spent the whole of his tour wearing a Rhyl FC scarf. Did he fall in love with the team while on a seaside trip as a child? Or had he, as Rutland muses, 'caught the team's performance against Llanelli AFC on TV and was so impressed, he immediately bought a scarf from E-Bay?'

He may have been aware that down the years the club has produced players of the highest calibre – players like Graham Williams (West Bromwich Albion), Barry Home (Everton), Andy Jones (Charlton Athletic), Andy Holden (Oldham Athletic) and recently Craig Bellamy and Lee Trundle, of Newcastle United and Bristol City respectively. Or did he know that once, 50 years ago, Rhyl had humbled and beaten Second Division Notts County in the Third Round of the Cup?

Perhaps he was just cold.

NOTTS COUNTY: Linton, Southwell, Cruickshank, McGrath, Russell, Loxley, Lane, Wylie, Wills, Carver, Bircumshaw
RHYL: Hanson, Spruce, Reynolds, Roberts, Rogers, Donaldson, Hughes, Russell, J. Williams, H. Williams, Meakin

13

DARLINGTON 4, CHELSEA 1

FA Cup, Round Three replay, January 29, 1958

It is January 25, 2008. Fifty years ago to the day Ron Greener was at Stamford Bridge playing centre-half for Darlington in the fourth round of the FA Cup. On that weekend half a century ago Elvis Presley's 'Jailhouse Rock' became the first single to enter the British music charts at No. 1 and 'Oh Boy!' became Buddy Holly's third Top Ten hit. Today, Holly's sheer class and Presley's magnetic sexuality have assured them iconic status in twentieth-century popular music. Rock 'n' roll, like Ron Greener, is here to stay. Today, the former club captain has a suite named after him at Darlington's new stadium. Like old rockers, old footballers too never die – as the wags on the terraces have it – they just lose their balls. . ..

Darlington's adventure that season in the Cup, in the days of black-and-white telly, Pathé News, Housewives' Choice and 78s, remains the high point in the history of a football club whose origins go back to July 1883, when representatives from the amateur and part-time teams met at Darlington Grammar School and decided to form one club to represent the town.

Darlington itself has a far longer history. Originally the Saxon village of 'Deornoth ing tun', it later fell victim to waves of Viking pillaging – indeed, there are still many place names of Viking origin in Northumberland and Durham. Medieval Darlington was a small market town where wool was woven and dyed, part of the estate of the Bishopric of Durham. However, in the middle of the 1600s – the 'Century of Dissent' – when people began to claim the right to think for themselves, Darlington became a popular retreat for members of the Religious Society of Friends, or the 'Quakers'. In a society riven by political and religious ferment, the movement faced opposition and persecution. By the time of the Industrial Revolution, the

Quakers in Darlington were an influential and wealthy community, prominent in banking, iron-ore mining and the linen and woollen industries.

The best-known member of this Quaker fraternity was wool merchant Edward Pease, who in 1821 formed the Stockton & Darlington Railway Company with the aim of carrying coal from the collieries of West Durham through Darlington to the River Tees at Stockton. Pease had been an early convert to steam power and offered George Stephenson the post of chief engineer on the new line, providing the capital for Stephenson and his son Robert to build steam locomotives. Hence, on September 27, 1825, the Stockton and Darlington railway, the world's first passenger line, opened: as well as carrying coal, the train included 600 passengers, most travelling in coal wagons. Some commuters might claim they still do.

At the beginning of the nineteenth century Darlington was still only a small market town but it grew rapidly and had reached a population of fifty thousand by 1900. The linen industry had died, but there were many iron foundries and Darlington became an important centre for railway manufacturing, with three significant works, the largest of which, the main-line locomotive workshops, opened in 1863, closing a century later.

Coincidentally, it was in 1863 that workmen on the North Staffordshire Railway formed a team which later became Stoke City. We have seen elsewhere in this volume how many of today's professional teams owe their origins to local industries and that early professional footballers were generally part-timers who worked in them. Other railway workers founded Crewe Alexandra and in a northern suburb of Manchester, workmen of the Lancashire and Yorkshire Railway Company formed the Newton Heath team in 1880; in 1902 they became Manchester United.

Churches, factories and schools gave rise to sports teams of all kinds. 'It was natural enough,' as James Walvin observes,

> that new forms of social activities in working-class communities should emerge, where possible, from existing institutions and traditions. By the late nineteenth century a number of inter-related institutions dominated and formed the geographical and social limits of working-class life; the home and immediate neighbourhood, the work-place, the church, the union and, later, the local school.[1]

---

[1] Walvin, p. 64.

This was the case in Darlington, where, in 1883, Darlington Football Club was founded at the local grammar school.

Having won the Northern League twice in the 1890s, the club turned professional in 1908, joining the North-Eastern League. Three years later Darlington reached the last 16 of the FA Cup. When football resumed after the Great War, within two seasons the side had won the North-Eastern League and were elected to Division Three (North) for the 1921/22 season. In 1925 they were promoted to Division Two as champions only to be relegated two seasons later.

In 1885/86 the club's goalkeeper was Arthur Wharton, a fascinating character and the first black footballer to play professionally in England. Wharton was born in Jamestown in 1865 in the Gold Coast, now Accra, the capital of Ghana. His father was half-Grenadian and half-Scottish and his mother was a half-Scottish member of the Ghanaian royalty. He moved to England in 1882 to train as a Methodist missionary, an ambition soon discarded in favour of becoming a full-time athlete, fast enough to set a new world record of ten seconds for the 100 yards at Stamford Bridge in July 1886. He then joined Preston North End as a semi-professional, playing in the FA Cup semi-final in 1887. Throughout the 1890s he drifted from club to club to try to make a living, eventually retiring in 1902. His is a sad story, for he died in 1930, a penniless alcoholic who had spent the last 15 years of his life as a colliery haulage hand.

His first English club, inevitably nicknamed 'The Quakers', lived out a similarly humdrum if somewhat less lurid existence for the next 30 years, once having to reapply for re-election to the League. They did achieve a footnote in FA Cup history when on November 28, 1955, Darlington played Carlisle United at St James' Park, Newcastle in a First Round, second replay: it was the first FA Cup match to be played under floodlights.

By the 1958/59 season, however, the club was at a low ebb – 'frankly, rubbish',[2] according to some Cup historians – ambling along in the lower reaches of the Third Division (North). They had only ever twice been beyond the Third Round, and that was two decades before, while Chelsea, admittedly with no great Cup pedigree themselves, had won the League in 1955,

---

[2] Lloyd and Holt, p. 197.

so a home draw in the Third Round against Darlington looked a formality.

Nonetheless, on a waterlogged pitch, 'Chelsea paid the penalty for defensive errors but Darlington took their openings in fine style. Harbertson, their centre-forward, shot the first goal with a powerful drive after four minutes.'[3] Ronnie Harbertson had already notched up five goals in that campaign, scoring in every round. Ron Greener remembers him as 'quick, with a good shot' and, like Alan Shearer, he 'used to play off the shoulder of the last defender'. After 29 minutes Dave Carr, Darlington's left-winger, scored another. Two–nil up at half-time, the Quakers were on course for one of the biggest shocks of the post-war FA Cup. The massed ranks of the Chelsea faithful stood in stunned silence and when Morton, the outside right, flicked the ball past an uncertain Reg Matthews in the Chelsea goal in the 51st minute, the impossible threatened to become a reality. 'Then Chelsea retaliated and goals came from the outside-left Lewis, the centre-forward, Tindall, and the inside right, McNichol.'[4]

The second half was a siege and Jimmy Greaves could have settled the tie with a powerful shot which struck a post. In fact, as Ron Greener recalls, 'he hit the bar three times in the last ten minutes.' He has vivid memories of the game against Chelsea: 'Our legs were heavy and at the final whistle, we were down-hearted, thinking we had thrown a chance away and that we wouldn't get Chelsea on a bad day again.' Darlington manager Dickie Duckworth told his lads not to worry. 'It was the best result we could have had. Your supporters will see you beat them.' Duckworth had skippered York City in their run to the FA Cup quarter-final in 1938, when they lost to eventual finalists Huddersfield Town. 'He was strict,' says Ron Greener, 'but he was the only one who ever gave us a Christmas present – a tie – and he gave the wives a box of chocolates.'

Chelsea had had a narrow escape. 'We really should have beaten them,' says Ron Greener, and Jimmy Greaves remembers a difficult afternoon: 'What everyone saw as a straightforward tie for Chelsea proved anything but. I didn't score and Ted Drake obviously thought I hadn't had the best of games because he dropped me for the replay at Feethams.'[5]

From the 1860s amateur soccer had been played at Feethams, but it was only in 1883 that Darlington FC made it their home. From 1827 it had

[3] *Manchester Guardian*, January 27, 1958.
[4] Ibid.
[5] Greaves, p. 77.

been – and still is – the home of Darlington Cricket Club, the venue for Durham's first-ever home victory in the County Championship, against Somerset in June 1992. At Feethams the football ground backs on to the cricket ground, in much the same way as the Leeds Rhinos' Rugby League ground backs on to Headingley, the spiritual home of Yorkshire.

Feethams was a peculiar ground altogether. After entering the turnstiles, through the famous Twin Towers (built in 1913, they were unrelated to those at Wembley and were still there when the club moved in 2003), spectators had to walk round the cricket pitch until they reached another set of ornamental gates, beyond which lay Feethams. On the east side the River Skerne flowed past a row of fine Victorian villas, while to the west of the ground 'the cobbled Polar Lane runs to an ornate footbridge that leads over the river to a Victorian lodge and a leafy park.'[6] The ground exuded 'an aura of prim conservatism'.[7] This cannot be said of most League grounds, which in the lower leagues at least are functional remnants of the urban industrial landscape of late Victorian England. There are exceptions. One corner of Everton's Goodison Park, the first purpose-built football stadium in England, is actually formed by a church, St Luke the Evangelist's. At Goodison, the Bullens Road Stand and the original Main Stand were designed by the celebrated football ground architect Archibald Leitch, who also designed what is now the Johnny Haynes Stand and a new pavilion, named the 'Craven Cottage', at Fulham, both now designated as Grade II. listed buildings.

It is a unique setting for a football ground – and uniquely for Jimmy Greaves – Chelsea's teenage talisman was named only as the travelling reserve: 'It was the first ever time I had been dropped from a team.'[8] Perhaps manager Ted Drake felt that the slightly-built 17-year-old would struggle on a pitch that was a quagmire in places.

As the Quakers had no floodlights, the match had to be played at 2.15 on a weekday afternoon and over fifteen thousand spectators turned out to see Darlington open positively with long passes out to the wings, where Tommy Moran and the bricklayer from Wheatley Hill pit, Dave Carr, forced several corners early on. This early pressure brought its reward when, after 35 minutes, Moran drove past Sillett on the left and fired an angled drive

---

[6] Greaves, p. 78.
[7] Ibid.
[8] Ibid.

just inside the far post. Darlington's faithful went mad but their joy was short-lived. Three minutes later Ron Tindall headed goalwards from a corner and Johnny McNichol equalised. With honours even at half-time Chelsea were confident of finishing the job in the second half.

It didn't happen. As so often in any giant-killing act, the underdog's goalkeeper is a hero and Joe Turner stepped into the role when he managed to touch Peter Brabrook's drive on to the bar. Throughout the second half, skipper Ron Greener and Brian Henderson proved to be the rocks on which the waves of attacks from the more talented Chelsea forwards foundered time and again. Right-half Ken Furphy, who later went on to manage Blackburn Rovers, Sheffield United and New York Cosmos, describes Greener and Henderson as the best players he ever played with. 'I can't separate them. Ron was great in the air and as for service to the club – well, he played a record 442 League games.'

Darlington had their chances, too, but, with the extra half-hour looming, their six part-timers would now surely crumble. As the man on the Light Programme said, 'The first division side's superior skill, stamina and fitness will be crucial in extra-time.' It proved a crucial misjudgement. Darlington dug deep. 'We were quicker into the tackle, every ball,' recalls Ron Greener. 'I just think we wanted it more than they did.' The longer extra-time went on, the more Chelsea struggled and, in an incredible six-minute spell, the Quakers scored three times.

After only five minutes Darlington's final push began. Harbertson worked his way past two defenders on the right, his powerful shot was blocked, and Tommy Moran again put the Quakers ahead when Pensioners keeper Matthews dropped the ball at his feet. Three minutes later from a corner on the right Tommy Moran's shot was pushed high into the air where Dave Carr's looping header, blessed with that touch of luck which every Cup side needs, soared gracefully beyond Matthews into the Chelsea net.

With Chelsea's coffin already seriously damaged, Darlington hammered in the final nail two minutes later when Ken Furphy put Moran through on the left wing. The little Scot beat Sillett and his cross was met six yards out by Ron Harbertson and Darlington's ace goal scorer made no mistake. It was all over.

The Londoners' goal ace had sat huddled in his worsted overcoat in Darlington's East Stand, yearning to be part of the action – yet, at the final whistle, Jimmy Greaves thought this might not have been a bad one to miss. 'That's the way it is with players. When they have been dropped, deep down they're torn between wanting the team to do well and not so well in order that they might regain their place in the side.'[9] Ted Drake, needless to say, was not a happy man. He tore into Greaves' teammates. 'Normally, following a mid-week match in the North country, we didn't hang about. The players would wolf down some sandwiches and grab a cup of tea while trainer Albert Tennant gathered up the muddy kit and threw it into the wicker skip in double-quick time as there was always a train to catch. Not on this night. . . Ted was blazing mad.'[10] When a Chelsea official put his head around the door to remind Drake it was time to leave, the manager bellowed, 'I don't care if they [the players] spend the night on Darlington station or have to walk back to London. They ain't leaving till I've told them some home truths!'

In hindsight his selection may have contributed to the debacle. Without a constructive inside-forward – a play-maker, in modern parlance – the exclusion from the Chelsea attack of perhaps the most naturally gifted goalscorer in the history of the English game seems a serious blunder. But it was more than that. According to *The Times*, Darlington's shock victory was 'earned by combination of sound tactics and an enthusiasm that Chelsea never equalled'.[11] Ron Greener sums it up succinctly: 'On the day they just didn't fancy the contest.'

He still has a photograph of the team in the communal bath. Some are drinking what may or not have been mineral water; several have cigarettes in their hands. It was hardly the champagne lifestyle of today. You had to get rid of the rats first. 'They were terrible, you could tell when they'd been in because the soap was all nibbled away. If we'd been out training, we had to kick the door first to chase them. Dickie Deacon, the trainer, was also the rat catcher and the only man who could light the boiler.' Greener and the late Brian Henderson were the heaviest smokers. 'We'd light up from the moment we got on the bus to the moment we got off. When you think I was down the pit as well and played more than 500 matches, I must have been doing something right.'

Unfortunately, that was as good as it got in 1958, as on February 15, as the world of football mourned the loss of eight 'Busby Babes' in the Munich

---

[9] Ibid/ p.79.
[10] Ibid.
[11] *The Times*, January 30, 1958.

tragedy, the Quakers were put in their place by Wolverhampton Wanderers at Molyneux, where Jimmy Murray scored a hat-trick. He was Wolves' leading goalscorer that year as the club won the League title, which they retained the following season. Darlington, routed 6–1, finished in the lower half of Division Three and ended up in the newly formed Fourth Division the following year.

Since then the Quakers have wandered about the lower tiers of the League, spending an ignominious year in the GM Vauxhall Conference in 1989/90. In May 1999 George Reynolds, a former bank robber turned multimillionaire fitted-kitchen tycoon, promised to change all that. A talented self-publicist, with a mouth as big as his wallet, Reynolds moved the club from Feethams to a new purpose-built stadium on the outskirts of town. The George Reynolds Arena – what else? – cost £20 million to build, boasted marble sinks, state-of-the-art lifts and 27,000 seats – reminiscent of the vainglorious flights of fancy of Ken Bates at Oldham in the late 1960s. For a club with average attendances of around five or six thousand the new ground was such a severe drain on resources that shortly after Christmas 2003 the club went into administration.

Once again, however, the fortunes of this historic club are on the rise. At the time of writing, the Quakers lie third in Division Two of the Football League, with another promotion in prospect and visits from the likes of Sheffield Wednesday, Millwall and Leeds United – all former First Division clubs.

Fifty years ago they laughed at Stamford Bridge when, before the first game, Darlington's officials brought down tickets for the replay. Instead, the laugh was on them. In the words of the *Daily Mail*, 'Chelsea wear the cap and bells – the Cup clowns of 1958.'

DARLINGTON: Turner, Green, Henderson, Furphy, Greener, Rutherford, Moran, Milner, Harbertson, Bell, Carr
CHELSEA: Matthews, Sillett, MacFarlane, Casey, Mortimore, Saunders, Brabrook, McNicol, Tindall, Stubbs, Lewis

14

NORWICH CITY 3, MANCHESTER UNITED 0

FA Cup Round Three, January 10, 1959

Helping Mum make the mustard for Sunday lunch was a special treat. It felt great to be entrusted with an important job, mixing the fiery golden powder with just the right amount of water into a smooth paste – 'Don't make it too runny, mind' – and I came to love the red-and-gold tin with the bull's head on the side. We had it so often that it seemed to me Mr Colman must have been a rich man if everybody ate as much as our family did. Dad put me right on that one: 'Oh no,' he told me. 'He made his fortune from the bit that you left on the side of your plate.'

Whatever, as they say: it's now a British institution. It was in 1814 that Jeremiah Colman, a flour miller, who made his mustard at a watermill on the River Tas, four miles south of Norwich, first advertised his product in the *Norwich Chronicle*. Fifty years later the firm received the ultimate accolade when Queen Victoria granted a Royal Warrant as Manufacturers to Her Majesty and in July 1902 the company produced a special commemorative tin to mark the Coronation of King Edward VII and Queen Alexandra.

Just a month before, at the Criterion Café in White Lion Street, Norwich, two Victorian schoolteachers, Robert Webster and Joseph Cowper Nutchey, founded Norwich City Football Club. Wearing blue-and-white-halved shirts and calling themselves 'The Citizens', Norwich played their first fixture competitive game in an FA Cup preliminary round, away at Lowestoft Town on Saturday, September 20, 1902, losing 5–0. At a public meeting at the Agricultural Hall in Norwich in March 1905 a motion was passed to accept professional status and the Citizens were admitted to the Southern League.

Although East Anglia lacks the dense urban population of the game's established heartlands, Norwich City has survived as a professional football club for a hundred years, a proud outpost in a largely agricultural hinterland, with 'a history enlivened by occasional cup-chasing feats, periodic financial meltdowns and a tradition of stylish attacking football.'[1] In the Middle Ages the city was one of the largest in England, its prosperity based on the wool trade and its proximity to the great trading cities – Antwerp, Ghent and Amsterdam – in the Low Countries. When a great wave of Flemish refugees arrived in Norwich in the mid-1500s, fleeing from Spanish persecution, they brought with them sophisticated technical skill in weaving, engineering and gardening. They also brought with them their pet canaries, and by early Edwardian times the breeding of canaries had become a popular local pastime – so much so that by 1907, with Norwich City becoming known more and more commonly as the 'Canaries', the club adopted their distinctive yellow shirts with green collar and cuffs – the nickname has stuck.

On January 11, 1908, a record crowd of 10,366 filled the club's Newmarket Road ground, a venue still used by local schools for hockey and rugby matches, to see City defeat FA Cup holders Sheffield Wednesday 2–0 in a First Round tie. Three years later they beat Sunderland 3–1: the Canaries were establishing a distinguished Cup-fighting pedigree. After the First World War, the club secured promotion to the Football League in 1920, playing at The Nest, a ground bordered by a chalk cliff that rose sheer a yard from the touchline. They won the Division Three (South) title in 1934 and moved to City's present ground at Carrow Road, then home of the Boulton and Paul Sports Club, the following year, when players at The Nest were warned to beware of falling rubble from the crumbling chalk cliff when taking corners. After three ordinary Second Division seasons, City began the 1938/39 campaign in woeful form and, by the time war clouds loomed, they were relegated on goal average. Having begun post-war football in Division Three (South) largely under Duggie Lochhead, the first half of the 1950s saw the Canaries, now managed by Norman Low, again challenging for promotion, scoring a club record 99 League goals in 1952/53.

Most notably, however, in the early 1950s Norwich City emulated the giant-killing feats of their Edwardian forebears. In January 1951 they beat

---

[1] Lyons and Ronay, p. 277.

Liverpool 3–1 at Carrow Road and more famously, knocked out Arsenal at Highbury in the Fourth Round in January 1954, by two goals to one.[2] However, in 1957 City almost went bankrupt after installing inordinately expensive floodlights: a public appeal fund quickly raised the £25,000 but the gloomy season ended with the Canaries having to apply for re-election to the League after finishing bottom of Third Division (South). Change was needed and the former Scottish international Archie Macaulay took over as manager from ex-Arsenal skipper Tom Parker. Macaulay had had a distinguished playing career with Brentford, Arsenal and Fulham and joined the Canaries from Guildford City in the Southern League. Taciturn and impassive, Macaulay installed a steely self-belief in his players and his shrewd grasp of his opponents' strengths and weaknesses gave him strategic judgement – but with sufficient flexibility to change tactics, even in mid-match.

In spite of this, the 1958/59 campaign opened like any other and gave few signs that it was to be one of the truly sensational great seasons in the club's history. The Canaries lost six of their first ten League matches and bumbled along in mid-table through the autumn.

In the First Round of the FA CUP at Carrow Road, City trailed 1–0 at half-time home to Isthmian League Ilford, but two goals from Bobby Brennan and one from Jimmy Hill (not the one with the beard) saw the Canaries home. Macaulay's master plan was taking shape. He had moved Hill to inside-left from the right wing and told Terry Allcock to lead the forward line from the front, and not from a deep-lying position. Two weeks later Macaulay's astuteness paired the steady Bryan Thurlow and Canaries legend Ron Ashman at full-back and moved Roy McCrohan from full-back to wing-half.

A week later, in the Second Round of the Cup at Swindon, the Canaries held the Robins to a 1–1 draw and five days later the Canaries were on song, a goal from Errol 'Cowboy' Crossan giving them a plum Third Round tie at home to Manchester United. While their results in the League on either side of Christmas continued to be patchy, the Cup run was the catalyst for an astounding change of form and as 1959 dawned Macaulay's side were playing with increasing confidence, skill and power.

Thus, by the time Manchester United trotted out at a snowbound Carrow

---

[2] See Hastings United v Swindon Town, pp. 361–365.

Road on January 10, Macaulay's Canaries were ready for them. They had won their last three home games and, while it was less than a year since the Munich tragedy, which had deprived United of eight of the immensely talented 'Busby Babes', the Old Trafford stars had won eight games on the run in the First Division. Going head-to-head in the dugouts were a pair of canny Scots – Matt Busby, the legendary genius who achieved near-immortality at Old Trafford, and Macaulay, the man who sought to outwit him. Busby had watched City beat Swindon but any plans he may have formulated before his squad arrived in East Anglia did not take into account the ice rink that was the Carrow Road pitch and the yellow-and-green tsunami which swept the Reds out of the Cup.

The all-ticket gate of 38,000 cheered as one when Ron Ashman, who was equalling Joe Hannah's club record of 431 appearances, led the Canaries out and an even bigger one when Ashman, who would eventually set the amazing record of 662 games for Norwich, his only club, won the toss and forced United to play into the low, glaring winter sun. On an afternoon when 35 spectators were treated for the effects of the bitter cold it soon became clear that the players were going to have difficulty keeping their feet. 'Suiting themselves much the better to the snowbound conditions, City harried United unmercifully.'[3] Even so, United were the better side for the first 20 minutes but could not capitalise on their superiority: Bobby Charlton slipped when in a good position and Bryan Thurlow cleared a shot off the line.

Archie Macaulay's strategy was to stifle the threat from United's talented forwards Charlton, Viollet and Quixall and the Canaries' tight marking meant that they never had the space to create any danger. As a result, United looked a very ordinary team. They seemed to have little answer to the rock-hard surface and even less stomach for the fight and their wing-halves, Goodwin and McGuiness, never came to terms with the dazzling work of 'Tiger' Hill and Terry Allcock in the midfield. Neither Foulkes nor Carolan at full-back could cope with 'Cowboy' Crossan's speed down the right flank and Bobby Brennan's clever creativity on the left.

City's hero was centre-forward Terry Bly, a local lad from Fincham, a tiny hamlet in west Norfolk between Swaffham and Downham Market. Never was a defender more inaptly named, for United's Ronnie Cope just

---

[3] *Eastern Daily Press*, January 10, 1959.

couldn't as Bly gave him an unnerving afternoon. Like most footballers, Bly was deeply superstitious. 'He always kissed his daughter Karen exactly three times before leaving for a game and told his wife to stay away from Carrow Road because her presence invariably seemed to bring him bad luck.'[4] Using his speed and balance, he had 'all the room he needed in the middle', said Macaulay afterwards, 'and could have had half a dozen goals.' In the event he had to settle for two, the first coming after 31 minutes. Terry Allcock made progress down the left and sent Bobby Brennan scurrying to the byline. His pull-back was perfectly placed for Bly to run in and hammer the ball past Harry Gregg.

As for United, they had only one more chance to equalise before the interval, Dennis Viollet heading wide after Quixall had managed to outwit Ashman. For the rest, Matt Crowe controlled the midfield and skipper Ron Ashman was a tower of strength at the back, leading a defence so effective 'that Nethercott was seriously extended only once when he dealt in grand style with a curling shot from Scanlon'.[5]

At the start of the second half, City bombarded United's goal. Terry Bly's header rattled the crossbar, dislodging a layer of snow; Bobby Brennan's shot hit the foot of a post and, from the rebound, Allcock's attempt was scrambled off the line.

The Canaries' constant pressure made a second goal almost inevitable and just on the hour Bly beat Carolan on the halfway line and set off down the left touchline. When his cross came in, Gregg could only parry it to Errol Crossan, who, loitering with intent, nodded home despite the Irishman's brave effort to atone for his error.

But a 2–0 lead was not enough for Macaulay's men, who continued to surge forward. A diving save from Gregg denied Bly; Terry Allcock shot narrowly wide and Crossan had a 'goal' disallowed. Eventually, two minutes from time, their positive football had its just reward when Bly shook off Cope's challenge down the left and cut in to beat Gregg with a searing right-footed drive from a narrow angle.

A few minutes later, 'IT WAS GLORY, GLORY ALL THE WAY', as the *Eastern Daily Press* declared in its late 'pink un' that afternoon: 'Charlton was but the palest of shadows of his great self of the Under-23 International,

---

[4] Tibballs, p. 91.
[5] *Eastern Daily Press*, January 10, 1959.

and only once did City have to indulge in the rankly unceremonious to stop him. If City had had the luck they deserved, or Gregg had not been in his best form, the rout must have been the most staggering of all the feats of giant-killing in Cup history.' Macaulay summed up the win:

> They all laughed when I said we could beat Manchester United but I knew our men to be capable of winning. I planned two lines of defence. Right-half Roy McCrohan stayed back with the centre-half and full-back while Matt Crowe operated in front. As soon as a Norwich move broke down, inside-right Terry Allcock doubled back with Crowe. That way we were able to break up most of their moves before they started. I reckoned Billy Foulkes could be beaten so I told inside-left Jimmy Hill to stay on the wing with Bobby Brennan and that was where our goals came from. It worked to perfection.

Overnight, Bly, once an amateur with City who had started the season in such poor form that he had played one game as full-back in the reserves, had become a 'danger man', feared by defences throughout the land. Bly cemented his growing reputation by scoring 29 goals in the next 30 games, of which the Canaries lost just three, becoming only the third-ever Third Division team to reach an FA Cup semi-final. Following the victory over Manchester United, the whole of East Anglia was in the grip of soccer fever and City's Secretary, Peter Dash, and his office assistants faced a continuing barrage of requests from a growing army of fans – and the national media – for tickets, interviews and personal appearances.

A fortnight later it was a case of the Bluebirds against the Canaries as Second Division Cardiff City travelled east to Carrow Road in Round Four. The visitors from the Principality had the temerity to lead the nation's favourite giant-killers at the interval, whereupon Crossan and Bly then put City ahead, only for Joe Bonson, later to find Cup fame with Newport County,[6] to equalize for the Bluebirds. Hanging on desperately for a replay at Ninian Park, Cardiff fatally lost concentration three minutes from the end and let in Bly to hit the winner with a screamer that Ron Nicholls in the Cardiff goal could scarcely have seen.

City were now being feted as local, even national, heroes, but neither

---

[6] Newport County v Sheffield Wednesday, pp. 131–137.

Macaulay nor skipper Ron Ashman would allow their men to be distracted from the task in hand. Three weeks later at White Hart Lane, an estimated twenty thousand City fans saw Cliff Jones force home a last-gasp equaliser – and four days later a crammed Carrow Road roared to the rafters when Terry Bly (who else?) scored the only goal to send City into the quarter-final away to Sheffield United.

At Bramall Lane, the Blades took an early lead before Canaries keeper Ken Nethercott dislocated his right shoulder early in the second half. He courageously continued and kept United out, by using his body and good arm and amazingly, the Canadian winger, 'Cowboy' Crossan, netted a well-deserved equaliser. The replay was just as close and hard-fought, but, back at Carrow Road, Bly scored two more to take City through by three goals to two.

In the middle of March, only Luton Town stood between City and a day of glory at Wembley. Once again that season the Canaries found them-selves in a Cup battle at White Hart Lane and dominated the semi-final, Bobby Brennan getting City's goal in a 1–1 draw. They also had the upper hand in the replay at St Andrew's where they just could not score and, in the 56th minute, a goal from Luton's Northern Irish international winger Billy Bingham shattered the Canaries' dream. It was the team's first defeat in a run of 19 games since Christmas. Though Macaulay's men bounced back with tremendous character and were undefeated in their next nine games, the backlog of games eventually sapped the team's mental and phys-ical resources and City missed out by four points and two places on promo-tion to Division Two.

The Canaries' incredible Cup run had captured the nation's imagination. Every sports fan loves an underdog and the unfashionable team from one of League football's outposts had won new fans and attracted nationwide media coverage. The nation loved their boldness in taking on the 'big boys' and their anthem, 'On the Ball, City', was one of the sounds of the season.[7] Years later the Canaries' campaign inspired the 'Ballad of Crossan & Bly' by Paul Wyatt, a heartfelt paean to the team of 59:

---

[7] It is believed to be the oldest football song anywhere in the world still in use today; the song is in fact older than the club itself having probably been penned for Norwich Teachers or Caley's FC in the 1890s and adopted for City by 1902.

You can keep your 4-2-4, your lying deep, your sponsored gear
Your million-pound prima donnas in fancy shorts and puffed up
    hair
They get £1,000 a week, no wonder the game's gone wrong
Who'll take their kid to stand in a cage where a load of thugs
    belong?
You can keep your coloured playbacks, your electric scores in
    digital time
I'll just have my memories of 1959
And the yellow and green army reaching for the sky
Which'll always be the year of Crossan and Bly.[8]

Wyatt expresses every schoolboy's anguish at the death of a dream and every football fan's indefinable commitment to the cause, his almost elemental sense of history and his innate nostalgia. Like the smell of Sunday roast as I mixed the Colman's mustard for Mum.

NORWICH CITY: Nethercott, Thurlow, Ashman, McCrohan, Butler, Crowe, Crossan, Allcock, Bly, Hill, Brennaniy
MANCHESTER UNITED: Gregg, Foulkes, Carolan, Goodwin, Cope, McGuinness, Bradley, Quixall, Viollet, Charlton, Scanlon

---

[8] Quoted in Irwin, p. 203.

15

WORCESTER CITY 2, LIVERPOOL 1

FA Cup, Round Three, January 15, 1959

Forget the pies and the burgers – for me, football goes hand in hand with apples. When my Dad took me to watch Hastings in the early 1950s, we always had an apple in our pocket to crunch on at half-time. The small, sharp russets, the juicy Coxs – they were great but Dad's favourite was the Worcester Pearmain. They were coarse and crisp, smelt gorgeous and tasted vaguely of strawberries.

The city of Worcester stands in the centre of a huge fruit-growing area, a fertile plain whose soil is tinged with the red of the sandstones which underlie the region between the Vale of Gloucester and the Midland Plain. The Pershore plum comes from the town of that name just south of Worcester and the city's coat of arms features three black pears, representing a rare local variety, the Worcester Black.

Down the centuries Worcester, one of the great cathedral cities, has touched English history at significant points. Worcester was important for the Romans as a fording point on the Severn, providing access to the Malvern hill forts and by the late Middle Ages it had a population of around ten thousand, many working in the cloth-making trades. The final, decisive battle of the English Civil War was fought in and around the city in 1651 and put paid to Charles II's hopes of regaining the Crown. Exactly a century later, the Royal Worcester Porcelain Company was founded by Dr John Wall at Warmstry House on the banks of the Severn. While the Industrial Revolution which so transformed towns in the nearby West Midlands largely bypassed Worcester, by 1755 the company was making the finest blue-and-white tea ware money could buy.

Mention 'Worcester' today, however, to the man in the street and the chances are he'll call to mind the city's most famous product, Lea & Perrins Worcestershire Sauce. The label is so iconic, like the HP bottle, the Marmite jar and the Tate & Lyle tin and, though the sauce is one of the many legacies of the British Raj, the product is so quintessential English. First sold in 1838 by John Wheeley Lea and William Henry Perrins, who were dispensing chemists in Broad Street, it is still made at the factory built some 60 years later, out along the Midland Road.

Worcester, however, has not only contributed products like fruit, pottery and sauces but also people to the nation's cultural life. Revd Geoffrey Kennedy, famously known as 'Woodbine Willy', who acquired his nickname from his habit of handing out Woodbine cigarettes to the soldiers in the trenches of Flanders, was for some time the vicar of St Paul's in the city – but Worcester's most celebrated citizen was arguably that most English of composers, Sir Edward Elgar, born in Broadheath, a few miles west across the Severn and whose father ran a music shop at the end of the High Street. And in January 1959 city's football team wrote a page in the history of English football 'which captures the essence of the FA Cup and the vagaries of the English weather'[1] – two national obsessions for the price of one.

Over half a century before, Worcester City Football club had been formed in September 1902 playing at a compact ground north of the racecourse and east of the Avon in St George's Lane, Barbourne. City began life as a member of the Birmingham League but at the start of the 1938 season city joined the Southern League.

While the club had no great Cup pedigree, having reached the First Round only a couple of times previously, in the 1920s and again in 1950/51, manager Bill Thompson's side had taken Third Division Aldershot to a second replay in November 1957. Three shrewd signings in the following summer, Les Melville, a centre-half from Oldham, Bernard Gosling, a young inside forward from Portsmouth, and Tommy Brown, a forward from Walsall, made instant impacts and by Christmas 1958 the side had lost only three out of eighteen games in League and Cup.

The Cup campaign opened with a routine 3–0 win over Brierley Hill, followed by victory over Chelmsford City after a replay. The fans' optimism began to turn into genuine hope when Fourth Division Millwall were walloped 5–2 at St George's Lane in Round Two, centre-forward Harry

---

[1] Ward, p. 110.

Knowles scoring twice. Twenty-six-year-old Knowles, who had scored 18 goals in as many games, was being watched by a posse of Football League scouts and the locals were desperately hoping to hold on to him at least till the summer.

The Third Round draw on the Monday lunchtime gave City 'a plum as juicy as those from the Vale of Evesham just down the road – a home draw against Liverpool'.[2] Strange as it may now seem, between 1954 and 1962 Liverpool were a Second Division club, albeit with some outstanding players – Alan A'Court, capped five times for England in 1958, Scottish international goalkeeper Tommy Younger and a true Anfield legend, Billy Liddell, the colourful and free-scoring winger. Liddell played 24 times for Scotland and, with the possible exception of another Scot, Kenny Dalglish, is thought by many on Merseyside to have been the greatest player ever to play for the club.

January 1959 experienced one of those typically icy spells which seemed to afflict football in the black-and-white era and many of the 32 Third Round ties, including City's, were postponed because of frozen pitches. The fixture was rearranged for the following Thursday afternoon and as a result of the extensive media interest a temporary press box had to be erected on girders above the old main stand. Liverpool had to return tickets they couldn't sell, Worcester sold them and a club record home gate of over fifteen thousand crammed into St George's Lane that Thursday, the city's early closing day. The weather was still bitterly cold: the pitch had been covered with sand and salt and the fog swirling around the trim little ground intensified the already-electric atmosphere.

Liverpool were Second Division promotion favourites and had lost only two of their last sixteen games but, in a decision which smacked of complacency, their manager Phil Taylor inexplicably rested Liddell for the trip to St George's Lane. On the other hand, his counterpart, City manager Bill Thompson, a wing-half with Portsmouth in the Championship-winning side of 1948/49, had devised a cunning plan: his side would concentrate on keeping the ball on the ground, making Liverpool's defenders twist and turn on the half-frozen pitch. It was a master stroke. Both Worcester goals came from what Alan Hansen, later a distinguished Liverpool defender himself, would call 'schoolboy errors'. As the Worcester *Evening Times* put

---

[2] From the Worcester City FC website.

it: 'The Liverpool rearguard were as nervous as old ladies on icy pavements.'

By contrast, City's 39-year-old captain Roy Paul commanded his defence with an air of unruffled confidence. He had led Manchester City to a Cup Final victory at Wembley three years before and several of his colleagues had also had Football League experience – but it was the baby of the side, 18-year-old Tommy Skuse, who stepped into the foggy limelight after only ten minutes.

City full-back Eddie Wilcox hit a low centre into the visitors' penalty area from the right and Liverpool full-back John Molyneux tried to divert the ball back to his keeper. In scrambling to reach it, Younger panicked, turned suddenly on the treacherous surface and lost his footing. Liverpool's centre-half Dick White and Skuse tussled for the ball but White could only nudge it on to the City forward, who stabbed the ball in the net and promptly fell over. It was a great moment for the young Skuse who was so nervous that he was physically sick at half-time. 'It was the biggest thrill I've ever had,' he said. 'White and I ran for the ball together; he jabbed at it with his foot and simply teed it up for me. If he hadn't touched it, I'd never have reached it!'

Liverpool rallied over the next 20 minutes and the gulf in class began to show. City's keeper John Kirkwood made a couple of fine saves and Melville had his hands full containing Liverpool centre-forward Louis Bimpson. Little by little, however, City gained more possession of the ball and urged on by Roy Paul, together with his fellow wing-half, Sammy Bryceland, Worcester managed to reach the interval still a goal to the good.

Liverpool came out for the second half with a more focused intent and for about ten minutes pummelled the home goal. Geoff Twentyman hit a post and Johnny Kirkwood pulled off three crucial saves. Then manager Thompson made a decisive tactical switch, capitalising on Knowles' pace down the wing and using outside-right Brown's extra control in the middle to unnerve the defence.

As the freezing fog gripped St George's Lane ever more firmly, Wheeler and Twentyman beavered away to regain the initiative. Worcester's defence, however, marshalled by Paul, weathered the storm until, eight minutes from time, came the game's turning point.

Harry Knowles took a pass from Bernard Gosling out on the right, cut inside and clipped the ball into the goal area. The hapless Liverpool centre-half Dick White tried to cut out the danger but only succeeded in slicing it high over Younger. The keeper's gymnastics in attempting to reach the deflected cross were to no avail and he collapsed in a heap in the back of the net a split second after the ball.

City were amazingly on the brink of a major victory – but all was not quite done. A minute later Melville bundled untidily into Liverpool's Freddie Morris in the penalty area and Twentyman scored from the penalty spot. The locals naturally felt it was a harsh decision and the last six minutes must have seemed like six hours to City supporters. When the referee blew his whistle for a free kick, City fans began to storm the fence on to the field only to be shepherded back by police and officials.

Worcester held out comfortably and, at the end, jubilant spectators hurled their hats in the air, swallowed up their heroes and bore goalkeeper Johnny Kirkwood and captain Roy Paul in triumph from the field.

To give Liverpool manager Phil Taylor credit, he declined to use the pitch as an excuse for the fiasco in the frost: 'Worcester deserved to win. They outfought us on a pitch that may have reduced the odds against them, but was still as good a playing surface as you can get in England right now. We lost because our forwards refused to fight.' City manager Bill Thompson could not have asked more from his men, eight of whom had been working on the morning of the game. His tactics paid off in spades. As The 'Times' put it:

> They played the right football on the frozen turf, tackling strongly and moving the ball about quickly. Their defence were magnificent. Always cool under pressure, Worcester covered slickly to such effect that Liverpool could rarely get in a direct shot at goal. In contrast, the Liverpool defence were often uncertain when Worcester forwards were on the move and defensive errors led to both the non-League team's goals.[3]

City's win was a headline writers' dream. While The Times restricted itself to 'Worcester Dismiss Liverpool From FA Cup', others in Fleet Street hailed the upset with 'What Sauce', 'Saucy Worcester' and 'Worcester Too Hot for Liverpool'.

Years later Harry Knowles told BBC Hereford and Worcester of the

---

[3] The Times, January 11, 1959.

players' reward for the biggest win in the club's history: 'I was getting £7 a week and we had a £5 bonus for beating Liverpool – mind you, we'd have played for nothing in those days.' Furthermore, Harry had his own particular arrangement with a local fish and chip shop: 'every goal I scored, I had free fish and chips.'

Nine days later another Division Two side, Sheffield United, were due at the Lane for the Fourth Round tie, and Harry Knowles recalls that during the build-up to the match 'we had two or three farmers come in on training nights and they brought us chickens and bags of potatoes and swedes and cabbages.' Though City's players doubtless relished this locally sourced traditional fare, it availed them little in their clash with the men from South Yorkshire. As 17,042 City fans feared, lightning was unlikely to strike twice in the same place and, in an efficient professional performance, United won 2–0. City did win the Worcestershire Senior Cup later that season, beating Southern League champions Hereford 2–1 on aggregate in the final, but it was something of an anti-climax.

Later that year, just before Christmas, Phil Taylor left Liverpool for health reasons, to be replaced by Bill Shankly, whom many regard as the greatest manager of all time. So, perhaps the debacle in the West Country on a freezing January afternoon was the true origin of the Merseyside club's golden years under its most charismatic leader. Every cloud, they say, has a silver lining.

WORCESTER CITY: Kirkwood, Wilcox, Potts, Bryceland, Melville, Paul, Brown, Follan, Knowles, Gosling, Skuse.
LIVERPOOL: Younger, Molyneux, Moran, Wheeler, White, Twentyman, Morris, Melia, Bimpson, Harrower, A'Court.

16

IPSWICH TOWN 2, PETERBOROUGH UNITED 3

FA Cup, Round Three, January 9, 1960

There must be something in the waters of the River Nene. Hereward the Wake, whose uncle was alleged to be the Abbot of Peterborough, has gone down in British history as an outlaw, a resistance hero who, from his base in the Fens east of Peterborough, led revolts against William the Conqueror. A thousand years later, the local football team, too, has repelled invaders and made a name for themselves as feisty Cup fighters, having sent a wave of giants back home with their reputation in tatters.

Peterborough, through which the Nene flows east to the Wash, had been a fortress in Roman times, when the garrison town of Durobrivae was founded on Ermine Street in the first century AD. In the 1850s the Great Northern Railway's main line from London to York and Edinburgh was routed through Fletton, just over the river from Peterborough. Over the next few decades the provincial market town became an important railway hub and the exploitation of Oxford clay led to the growth of the brick-making industry. By the early 1900s there were as many as 19 brick works operating around Fletton and the area became the UK's leading producer of bricks.

By the 1860s long campaigns in a wide variety of industries had resulted in the granting of the free Saturday afternoon, seen as the sine qua non for a better personal and social life. Until then, 60-hour weeks were commonplace and working men and women faced a short, brutish life of drudgery and toil in the factory, down the mine, at the mill or on the farm, with Sunday, their only day off, dominated by church or chapel. The working classes began to have time for organised recreation: 'thus those sports, notably football, which came to dominate the Saturday afternoons of working men, tended to be watched and played by workers in the heavier industries – textiles, metals, engineering, mining, shipping and port industries.'[1] Workers in expanding industries like the Fletton brickworks had money to spend and on their free Saturday afternoons 'Football emerged as an industrial game, not as a palliative to the grimness of industrial life, but largely because industrial workers, unlike others, had free time.'[2]

That Saturday half-day resulted in employees at the brickworks forming a football team, Fletton United, inevitably known as 'The Brickies', who played at the present club's London Road ground. In 1921 Pat Tirrel, the player–manager, announced that he was looking for 'Posh players for a Posh team' to compete in the Northamptonshire League (later the United Counties League) – and the epithet has stuck. When in 1923 Peterborough United and Fletton United amalgamated the new team were dubbed 'The Posh', despite the fact that because of the cramped changing accommodation at London Road, they changed at The Peacock and walked across the road to the Glebe Road corner of the ground.

The merged club's most notable achievement was in 1928 when, after winning an away Cup tie at Botwell Mission (now Hayes FC), the club beat Aldershot at London Road and were drawn against First Division Birmingham in the Third Round. In a seven-goal thriller, the Posh lost 4–3 at St Andrew's after leading 3–1, Joe Bradford scoring a hat-trick for Birmingham. Players in the late 1920s included Harry Salt, who moved to Walsall in 1932 and played left-half for the Saddlers when they knocked Arsenal out of the FA Cup.[3]

Following suspension by the FA for financial irregularities, the club was disbanded in August 1932, leaving behind debts of £248 1s 11d, by no means a trivial sum in those days. Two years later, a crowded meeting in the Angel Hotel decided to form Peterborough United Football Club to fill the void. They were still called 'The Posh', as one old supporter recalls: 'A popular song of the period was "Yes! We have no bananas" and I recall the adapted version going something like this:

[1] Walvin, p. 56.
[2] Ibid.
[3] See Walsall v Arsenal, pp. 33–39.

> Yes!, we have some Posh players,
> We have some Posh players today
> When you're reading the 'Pink-un'
> Of old Andy Lincoln
> who scored the only goal today.

Thus, when Peterborough United made their Midland League debut against Gainsborough Trinity they were greeted with cries of 'Up the Posh' from the crowd.

There followed 26 years in the semi-professional Midland League. There were hard times, as in the early 1940s when the club came uncomfortably close to losing its London Road home. The 1950s however were immensely more successful: in the second half of the decade the Posh won five successive League titles and went undefeated throughout the 1958/59 League season. Frustratingly though for the loyal fans, Peterborough were repeatedly refused League membership in the annual re-election vote.

This annual rejection was especially unjust considering that Peterborough United achieved national fame through their regular exploits in the Cup, in which as a non-League club they almost invariably reached at least the Second or Third Rounds. In 1953/54, with the former Newcastle goalkeeper Jack Fairbrother as player–manager, the Posh were drawn away to Cardiff City, then going well in the First Division. A Ninian Park crowd of more than thirty-eight thousand were stunned to see Freddie Martin give the Posh an early lead. Welsh international centre-forward Trevor Ford equalised but only in the dying minutes did another goal from Ford and one more by Andy Northcott finally clinch the tie for the Welshmen.

Three years later another goalkeeping star, Arsenal's George Swindin, led the Posh to a Third Round meeting at London Road, when Denis Emery's two goals were cancelled out and the Second Division outfit secured a replay with a fiercely disputed late penalty. History repeated itself in the replay, necessitating extra time in which Andy Donaldson completed his hat-trick and Emery and Ray Smith also struck for the Posh. Suddenly the underdogs led 5–2. Lincoln then responded with a couple of their own to make it 5–4 but in a cliffhanger of a finish Peterborough clung on, their reward a Fourth Round visit to Huddersfield Town. The Second Division side proved too strong but the ten thousand travelling fans of the Posh could console themselves that, unknowingly, they had seen the birth of a legend, 16-year-old Denis Law, who that day scored his first ever FA Cup goal.

If Law became a Scottish legend, Johnny Haynes is up there in England's pantheon. This creative and elegant inside-forward, described by Pele as 'the best passer of a ball I've ever seen', captained England 22 times and, with World Cup winner George Cohen and TV pundit Jimmy Hill, was in the Fulham side in January 1959, when the Posh travelled to London for a Third Round tie. The Midland Leaguers held Haynes's men to a goal-less draw at Craven Cottage but a fortnight later a London Road crowd of 21,600 saw the Posh's solitary defeat in an otherwise invincible season when Mick Johnson put Fulham through with the only goal of the afternoon.

The Posh, managed by former Sheffield United stalwart Jimmy Hagan, a Geordie who went on to take Benfica to three Portuguese League titles in the early 1970s, were becoming the best-known and most feared Cup fighters outside the Football League. In 1959/60, what were by now almost routine victories over Shrewsbury Town and Walsall brought the Posh face to face with East Anglian rivals, Second Division Ipswich Town away at Portman Road.

The 'Tractor Boys' from Suffolk were in rampant form, having just crushed Leyton Orient 6–0. Nonetheless, in 1955 when Ipswich were a Third Division club Peterborough had put them out in the First Round and their shrewd manager, Alf Ramsey, never one to underestimate his opponents, prepared his side for the fixture with his customary thoroughness.

However, from the first whistle, a heavy blizzard sweeping in from the steppes seemed to freeze his team's resolve. Though they had the wind and snow at their backs, Ipswich plodded through the opening exchanges, failing to attack the nervous Peterborough defence, who seemed strangers to one another. Their best chance in the opening spell fell to Ray Crawford,[4] whose sharp drive was plucked out of the air by Posh keeper Tom Daley.

Gradually they warmed to the task and in the 20th minute, Ted Phillips' shot from a corner was cleared off the line by left-back Jim Walker only as far as Doug Millward, who netted from close range. Ipswich were still taking time to come to terms with the challenging conditions and the tackling of the Peterborough defence, who were like a pack of Jack Russells snapping at their heels. On the half-hour, Crawford spurned a chance of a

---

[4] See Colchester United v Leeds United, pp. 163–168.

second, when he screwed a shot wide of the open goal after dribbling around Daley.

Soon Peterborough were pressing in the opposing half and three minutes before half-time, they were level, centre-forward Jim Rayner finishing off some smooth inter-passing involving Billy Hails, Peter McNamee and Ray Smith. They could have gone ahead just before the whistle when Hails' shot was headed clear by Reg Pickett.

As the blizzard continued to rage through the break, Posh fans could warm themselves not only with their half-time Bovril, but with the thought that their side had been equal to the task. However, Jim Walker had been off the field before the interval with a twisted right knee and, if he was a passenger in the second half, could the ten men hold out for a replay? Their fears were deepened when within two minutes of the restart – the home side were ahead again. Winger Jimmy Leadbetter slipped a smart through-ball to Ted Phillips, who struck a left-foot shot against the post and slotted home the rebound.

Walker's injury had reduced the Posh to virtually ten men and a side with less backbone would have crumbled: however, Hagan's men never threw in the towel. They continued to pressure the Ipswich goal and after 55 minutes Denis Emery scored a second equaliser, rounding off a fine run by McNamee.

The last ten minutes were epic. In the driving snow Peterborough, driven on by the indefatigable Ray Smith, harried the home defence, which began to sag in the face of the relentless onslaught. Three minutes from the end, McNamee crossed a hopeful ball into the Ipswich penalty area, Andy Nelson mis-kicked and Denis Emery pivoted and cracked the ball in past Roy Bailey.

Ipswich's hopes were buried in the blizzard and suddenly 'The little ground was suddenly full of bobbing Peterborough heads, a youth with a ginger crew cut became hysterical, and three schoolboys rushed on to the pitch before the game was allowed to wind out to the finish.'[5]

In the crowded Posh dressing room, the press besieged the heroes from the Fens. Skipper Norman Rigby, the captain, puffed on a cigarette as he mused about future Fourth Division battles. A reporter put it to Ray Smith, towelling down after his bath, that Peterborough's second goal had been beautiful. The Yorkshireman gave a weary grin: 'They're all beautiful when

---

[5] *The Times*, January 11, 1960.

115

they're in the back of that net.' As the man from *The 'Times'* walked back to the station, 'shivering in the snow and darkness, a tall, tired man with an accordion was playing a sad little French tune. Jinking their way round him, clusters of wildly excited Peterborough supporters moved towards their special trains and left behind a stricken East Anglian town.'

Peterborough's win had been no fluke. In the proud tradition of their forebears, they had cocked a snook in the snow. This Midland League club, not for the first time since the war had had the cheek to challenge a successful Second Division club. They had played better football and had tussled like terriers to come twice from behind to win.

The Posh faithful faced a long trip to South Yorkshire three weeks later for a clash with First Division Sheffield Wednesday. Nonetheless, more than 20 special trains and dozens of coaches took roughly twenty thousand to Hillsborough where a crowd of 51,144 saw Posh hold their own till 15 minutes from time, when Wednesday's Bobby Craig netted twice without reply. The dream was over for another year but the Posh's shock victory assumed even greater significance when Ipswich won the Second Division title the following season and the League Championship the year after that.

The Posh's Cup run had its reward when the door on which they had been knocking for years finally opened in 1960, when, at the expense of Gateshead, United strode into the Football League. However, their accession to the Fourth Division failed to dim their passion for Cup glory. Routine wins away against Dover, Torquay and Portsmouth gained them an attractive Fourth Round home draw against Aston Villa and only a disputed late penalty gave the Villa a replay, after Billy Hails had put the Posh ahead. Four days later several thousand fans, among them hundreds of Posh supporters, were locked out but the 64,531 crowd inside saw Hagan's side battle hard before going down to a 2–1 defeat.

During the club's first season as a League side they marched to the Division Four championship with Terry Bly,[6] acquired from Norwich City, scoring an unbelievable 52 League goals, which still stands as a record for any division below the top flight. In 1965 they reached the Cup quarter-finals, beating Arsenal in the Fourth Round before being steamrollered 5–1 by Chelsea.

---

[6] See Norwich City v Manchester United, pp. 97–104.

Three years after that quarter-final, Peterborough was designated a 'New Town' to absorb London's overspill population and in the 1970s the town's population almost doubled. The large influx of newcomers might have been persuaded by a TV campaign featuring Roy Kinnear as a Roman legionnaire – a reminder of Peterborough's long military history as a town on the frontier of the Fens which confronted the invader, 'And sent him homeward', as the Scots sing, 'tae think again.'

IPSWICH TOWN: Bailey, Carberry, Malcolm, Pickett, Nelson, Elsworthy, Owen, Millward, Crawford, Phillips, Leadbetter
PETERBOROUGH UNITED: Daley, Stafford, Walker. Banham, Rigby, Chadwick, Hails, Emery, Rayner, Smith, McNamee

17

CHELSEA 1,
CREWE ALEXANDRA 2

FA Cup, Round 3, January 7, 1961

Most towns which are now part of the tapestry of England's urban landscape – port towns, fort towns, religious towns, market towns, seaside towns, industrial towns – evolved organically from an earlier site, an ancient settlement, a religious foundation. Towns like Liverpool, Colchester, Canterbury, Dorchester, Brighton and Manchester all had identifiable *raisons d'être*. In the Victorian age, towns came into being where no settlement had existed before as a result of the entrepreneurial drive for the expansion of railways as a commercial imperative. Haywards Heath in Sussex is one example and another, much better known, is Crewe.

Knutsford, a few miles north of Crewe, is Elizabeth Gaskell's 'Cranford', and she describes in her vividly engaging novel the impact of the railway as its pushes relentlessly towards the town from Manchester, arousing fears among the provincial ladies of marauding bands of itinerant navvies, the collapse of law and order, and the imminent end of civilisation as they knew it. Susie Conklin, co-creator of the BBC series in 2007, says: 'The railway for the people of the mid-nineteenth century was like the silicon chip for us. We are terrified of change, of social structures breaking down, and yet we are rather thrilled by it as well.' Something of the atmosphere of the fictitious Cranford must have been felt in Crewe in the 1840s.

In 1837 the Grand Junction Railway was opened to link the four largest cities of England by joining the existing Liverpool and Manchester Railway with the proposed London and Birmingham Railway. The line was not intended to serve towns en route but a station was built in fields near Crewe Hall in the parish of Monks Coppenhall in Cheshire, where the line crossed the turnpike road linking the Trent and Mersey and the Shropshire Union canals. Since the land was bought from the Earl of Crewe, whose mansion stood nearby, the station was called Crewe, which was the first to be built independently of the need to serve a town and the first to form a junction between more than two companies. More than that: to the poet WH Auden, it was the junction between two worlds. In a magazine article published in 1947 he wrote: 'Crewe Junction marks the wildly exciting frontier where the alien South ends and the North, my world, begins.' It was also the first station in the world to have its own railway hotel, The Crewe Arms, built in 1838 and still in use. At this time the population was about 70, scattered among a few dairy farms but by 1871, the town, laid out by GJR's chief engineer, Joseph Locke, had grown to forty thousand and was a major junction with a bustling railway works.

By the 1870s, then, Crewe was a railway town with a high proportion of migrant male workers, and in 1877 an amateur football club was formed. It took the name 'Alexandra', either from Princess Alexandra, wife of the future king Edward VII, or (rather more likely) from a pub of that name where early members – mostly rail workers – met. They were inevitably nicknamed 'The Railwaymen' and in 1884 lost their first-ever match in the FA Cup, 10–0 against Queens Park of Glasgow. Four years later, however, they reached the semi-final, beaten at Liverpool by Preston North End: a fine achievement for what was still an amateur club.

In the 1890s, for England's growing urban working class, football was an 'escape, of course, from drudgery, misery and uncertainty'.[1] The industrialisation and politicisation of Britain's working class in the last quarter of the nineteenth century underpinned the emergence of football as a professional occupation in important ways. When a combination of parliamentary legislation and local industrial action achieved the Saturday half-day holiday, working men had the time to watch games. While lifestyles were hardly profligate, real incomes rose about 30 per cent in the last quarter of the century and working men could afford to pay to watch football. Moreover, Goldblatt noted, 'within cities, the spread of the bicycle down the social scale and the development at the turn of the century of horse-drawn trams and then electric trams massively increased the radius from which football crowds could be gathered together.'[2]

---

[1] Goldblatt, p. 52.
[2] Goldblatt, p. 53.

Goldblatt also observed that 'the presence of railway stations was a factor in determining where new grounds and clubs were based.' This was, of course, fundamentally true for Crewe, which had by the 1880s achieved national importance as a railway junction. In 1893 George LeBrunn wrote Marie Lloyd's music-hall classic 'Oh! Mr Porter', whose lyrics include this chorus:

> Oh! Mr. Porter, what shall I do?
> I want to go to Birmingham
> And they're taking me on to Crewe.

In the same year, against the backdrop of miners' strikes in Yorkshire, as clubs encompassed the growing wave of professionalism, Crewe's players became aware that they, too, were worthy of their hire and, after a threat to strike, forced the club's directors to offer them professional terms.

Not that their new professional status improved their results. The Railwaymen dropped out of the League in 1896 and it was not until a quarter of a century later that the club rejoined, taking its place in the nascent Division Three (North) in 1921. During the first half of the last century games were often played against a background of steam from trains on the tracks behind the ground in Gresty Road and Alexandra were once reported to have scored 'against a bemused Hull City under cover of almost total invisibility, after clouds of steam from a shunting locomotive had engulfed the pitch'.[4]

Crewe's greatest achievement over 70 years of almost exclusive occupation of the lowest division was successfully avoiding tumbling out of the League altogether. From 1946 the town was the home of Rolls-Royce motor car production. The team, however, were hardly a high-class luxury machine, purring with well-oiled efficiency. They had won the Welsh Cup in 1936 and 1937 and in 1947/48 defeated Sheffield United in the Third Round of the Cup, but in 1955 Crewe embarked on a sequence where they did not win away for 56 matches and for three years in succession they had to apply for re-election.

The onset of the new decade saw one of the club's most famous matches, when a new record attendance of twenty thousand at Gresty Road saw the

---

[3] Ibid.
[4] Lyons and Ronay, p. 100.

121

Railwaymen hold Spurs to a 2–2 draw. In the replay, Tottenham steam-rollered the Fourth Division side, storming to a crushing 13–2 win – still a record defeat for the club. Three players scored hat-tricks – Les Allen (5), Bobby Smith (4) and Cliff Jones, and it made entertaining viewing on Pathé News, sandwiched between the B-feature and the spectacle and passion of *Ben-Hur*.

In the following season they were drawn against another London club, Chelsea, who two years earlier had fallen foul of a banana skin, going down 4–1 at Darlington. In their last two League games they had been thrashed 6–0 at Old Trafford by Manchester United and 6–1 at Wolves. Nevertheless, they fielded star forwards in Peter Brabrook, Jimmy Greaves and Bobby Tambling, with Terry Venables at right-half, 'Chopper' Harris at left-back and Peter Bonetti in goal. Far from overawed, however, six thousand supporters of the Railwaymen climbed aboard their football specials entrained at the famous old junction for the Bridge and a reunion with their former hero, son of a railway ticket inspector, the blond winger Frank Blunstone. In the match programme, Chelsea manager Ted Drake wrote:

'However, we have personal ties going back for nearly eight years, when in February, 1953, Frank Blunstone moved from Crewe to Stamford Bridge. He played his first League match for Crewe when only sixteen and was one of the first players that I signed after my appointment as Manager here. Frank, I know, will be eager to do well against his old team, though it will be with a mixture of feelings that he will view the outcome of the match, whoever is the winner.'

For so long the Aunt Sallies of the lower divisions, Crewe were a more formidable proposition in 1961 and as they travelled south to London, the team stood sixth in the Fourth Division. The side had a judicious blend of youth and experience and several of Crewe's regular first-team players had played at a higher level than the Fourth Division. Their new manager, Jimmy McGuigan, felt the secret to success lay in snuffing out one of the game's greatest instinctive goal scorers, Jimmy Greaves, and in ex-Gateshead goalkeeper Brian Williamson and centre-half Eric Barnes he had the right men to do the job.

The Railwaymen took the lead after only five minutes when Terry Tighe sent a superb pass out to Shepherd, who put Foster clear. His cross eluded

Peter Bonetti in the Pensioners' goal and Billy Stark, a summer signing from Glasgow Rangers, netted with ease. Twenty minutes later, the lead was doubled when Tighe fed Stark down the right wing. His cross was met with crisp precision by leading scorer Barry Wheatley, who headed past a despairing Bonetti. With a nice line in irony, Blunstone, Chelsea skipper for the day, gave the First Division side a glimpse of daylight four minutes later when he outpaced the defence and hammered home a screamer.

Chelsea camped in Crewe's half for most of the second period, Greaves seeing a shot hit a post and roll agonisingly along the goal-line. Alexandra's defenders hacked two other efforts off the line and their only threat was when Stark clipped a post with Bonetti well-beaten. But, the Railwaymen, as the *Crewe Guardian* reported, 'down to nine men in the dying minutes when both wingers Stark and Jones were off for treatment, held out in worthy fashion'.

At the final whistle Jimmy Greaves trudged dejectedly from the field he had graced for the past three seasons. Mike Langley, football writer for the *Daily Express*, who had begun life with the *Crewe Guardian*, described the side that day as 'the best Crewe I ever saw' and the *Crewe Chronicle*'s headline proclaimed 'EVERY MAN IN A RED SHIRT WAS A HERO'. The *Crewe Guardian* praised 'a defence which covered superbly and rarely lost its composure, asserting that it was 'Crewe's half-back line which laid the foundation for victory'. Next to its match report, the local paper carried the traditional picture of the team, in sharp haircuts, slim ties and raincoats, a couple of bottles of bubbly to hand, huddling round a transistor radio, waiting hopefully for the chance of revenge over Tottenham Hotspur in Round Four. In one of those exquisite Cup coincidences, the Railwaymen were granted their desire – but proved the truth of the old adage, 'Be careful what you wish for. . .' For all manager Jimmy McGuigan's brave talk in the local paper of fearing nobody and 'having nothing to lose', at White Hart Lane three weeks later five different Spurs players netted as the eventual Double-winners cruised to a 5–1 win. At least, however, the grisly spectre of 13–2 had been banished – well, sort of.

In the later years of the twentieth century, the club enjoyed something of a renaissance. Promoted from Division Four in 1992, Crewe rose steadily, reaching the First Division and Championship, before slipping into League One in 2005/56. Dario Gradi, who has spent nearly a quarter of a century as manager at Gresty Road, has developed an almost unparalleled reputation for finding and developing local talent. The conveyor belt of players whom Gradi nurtured into League football includes Bruce Grobbelaar, Rob Jones, Seth Johnson, Neil Lennon, Danny Murphy, David Platt, Robbie Savage, Geoff Thomas, Ashley Ward, Dele Adebola and Dean Ashton – a roll-call of footballers impressive enough to put paid to the argument that English clubs cannot produce players of the highest quality – given, of course, the inspiration and patience of a gifted and experienced coach. And how many of those are there around?

CHELSEA: Bonetti, Sillett, Harris, Venables, Evans, Anderton, Brabrook, Greaves, Tindall, Tambling, Blunstone
CREWE ALEXANDRA: Williamson, McGill, Campbell, Keery, Barnes, Shepherd, Stark, Tighe, Foster, Wheatley, Jones

18

NEWCASTLE UNITED 1, BEDFORD TOWN 2

FA Cup, Round Three, January 4, 1964

For most people, Bedford is not so much a destination as a motorway junction. Two of the main arteries of modern British commerce, the A1 and the M1 motorway, pass a few miles to the east and west of the town, as if each had forgotten that Bedford exists. Indeed, 'this peaceful region appears to have absorbed history rather than reacted to it.'[1] The county town of Bedfordshire, lying on the A6 and the Great Ouse, received its borough charter in 1166 from Henry II and from the early Middle Ages Bedford was the market town for its rich agricultural hinterland. We are in cattle country here. The vast belt of Tertiary clays, formed over 150 million years ago when the area was under the sea, stretches from the Cotswolds through Trowbridge to Oxford and Bedford, producing a landscape dominated by glimpses of water, oak stands and meadowland.

With a population of about eighty-five thousand for its size Bedford is one of the most ethnically and linguistically diverse towns in the world. Every thousand residents, give or take, speak a different language, including Punjabi, Turkish, Polish, Portuguese and both Cantonese and Mandarin Chinese – and Italian. Nearly 30 per cent of Bedford's population can boast some Italian descent, the largest concentration of Italian immigrants in the UK. In the early 1950s, after the Second World War, the rebuilding and reconstruction of the country's towns and cities created a huge demand for bricks. Labour was short and the London Brick Company recruited from the southern Italian regions of Puglia, Campania, Calabria, Molise, Abruzzo

---

[1] *AA Illustrated Guide to Britain*, p. 216.

and Sicily. The brick industry has long been associated with Bedfordshire, thanks to the extensive clay deposits. By the 1930s there were 135 chimneys in the Marston Vale and the London Brick Company employed over two thousand people and produced over 500 million bricks per year.

Although by the end of the century, the industry's fortunes were declining, threatened by new technologies and products, bricks remained among Bedford's most famous products, along with Olympic athletes Harold Abrahams, 100 metres champion in 1924, Tim Foster, coxless fours gold medallist, Paula Radcliffe, the current world record holder for the women's marathon – and one of Britain's literary and religious heroes, John Bunyan. For 12 years, from 1661 to 1672, Bedford's prison housed John Bunyan for refusing to give an assurance not to preach. In his most celebrated work, *The Pilgrim's Progress*, Bunyan wrote:

> No lion can him fright,
> He'll with a giant fight,
> But he will have a right
> To be a pilgrim.

Three centuries later, the town's football club was about to fight its own giant.

Bedford Town Football Club, nicknamed 'The Eagles' after the bird of prey on the ancient town crest, was founded in 1908 and in the early years played in the United Counties League and its predecessors, the Northampton League and Northampton Alliance. In 1945 the Eagles moved to the Southern League but, having achieved little during the immediate post-war years, the club received a welcome lift when in February 1951 Ronnie Rooke was signed as player–manager. This signing fired the enthusiasm of the locals: 'Rookie' was a national name, having played for Arsenal, Fulham, Crystal Palace and England. There was a crowd of 4,790 for his first game in charge and when he made his debut for the reserves, when he scored a hat-trick, three thousand turned up.

However, in 1954 Rooke departed for Haywards Heath FC, where he teamed up with Sussex and England cricket legend Jim Parks and it was not until 1955/56 that the Eagles began the first of three or four thrilling adventures in the FA Cup which brought them national fame as 'giant-killers'. Having beaten Watford in Round Two at home 3–2, they then faced

Arsenal at Highbury. True successors to Bunyan's hero, Christian, the Eagles achieved what some supporters would deem their greatest-ever result. In front of a crowd of over fifty-five thousand, Bedford held the Gunners to a 2–2 draw, with goals from Steel and Moore. The Eagles nearly caused a major shock in the replay leading 1–0 until four minutes from time before going down 1–2 after extra time, having had two goals disallowed for offside. The following season Norwich were despatched 4–2 in the First Round.

By 1963 Rooke, who had returned as manager in the late 50s, had finally gone and Basil Hayward was now in charge. Town's Cup run that season began routinely enough, with 1–0 wins over fellow Southern League sides Weymouth and Chelmsford City. The Third Round draw pitted the Southern Leaguers against a true Cup giant. Winners of the trophy three times in the 1950s, they were managed by Joe Harvey, the Magpies' skipper, in two of those Wembley triumphs.

It was the sort of day out which fans of the likes of Bedford never forget. 'For me,' recalls Trevor Lloyd, 'the Newcastle affair was the greatest trip of them all. The supporters hired two trains, each holding 800 people and overall there were 40 coaches. The first train left Midland Road at six o'clock in the morning, the second one at about eight.' Tony Moran remembers 'there was snow on the ground and my carriage wasn't particularly warm.' He was lucky to be going at all. When he got to the Eagles' shop in Queen's Park on the Friday evening before the match it was closed. 'I was on my bike in those days, and looking for a ticket. An American fellow drove up in his limousine and we compared notes: I needed a ticket and he had one to spare, which he sold me at less than face value. The ticket was valid for the return rail fare and admission to the ground at Newcastle.'

The Eagles fans were far from optimistic and consoled themselves with liberal supplies of Charles Wells ale. So much so, says Trevor Lloyd, 'We'd run out of beer by York and they had to phone ahead to Newcastle to restock for the return journey.' The 'football special' was policed by the supporters' club and despite the consistently determined drinking, there was no trouble. The Eagles' fans arrived in Newcastle well before kick-off and Tony Moran headed for a pub on the way to St James' Park. 'The Geordies I met couldn't have been kinder,' he recalls. They may have been patronising their southern guests from the sticks. As Sue Pass says, 'Their fans were saying: "It's a long way for you to come to see your team lose" and comments like that, taking pity on us.' Nonetheless, they walked up to

127

the stadium with Tony Moran 'and I stood on the terraces with them. There was no crowd segregation in those days.'

'Leazesmag', writing on the Newcastle United message board in 2006, sums up the eternally naive optimism of a Toon fan. 'It was FA Cup time, 1963, New Year's Eve probably and my dad, uncles and grand-dad were discussing the Toon's prospects of winning a 3rd round FA Cup tie against non-League opposition. Remember, those sitting round the fire/table that evening still had FA Cup wins fresh in the mind, only eight short years previously.' Sitting in his short trousers, only nine years old, he heard the grown-ups. Although Newcastle at the time were struggling unsuccessfully to escape from Division Two, 'they should beat them all right'. Those words struck a chord. 'I was totally oblivious to the fragility of the Toon in this situation (or the curse that was about to engulf us for decades to come during my life span) I thought to myself "well, we must be going to win then", as all the grown ups knew what they were talking about.'

Our Toon fan reckoned without the fickle fates of the FA Cup. Eagles fan Mick Spavins didn't think the game would be on. It was sunny but bitterly cold and 'there was a layer of frost on the pitch. They covered it with straw and I remember there being a smoky atmosphere because someone had set fire to the straw.' Not for the first time in the Cup, the pitch was the true democrat, wiping away the difference in class and literally ensuring a level playing field. Tony Moran remembers clearly John Fahy, the Bedford centre-forward, scoring the first goal. 'He challenged the Newcastle goalkeeper who fumbled the ball and Fahy, goal-hanging, scored! Was he offside? No, the goal was given. The Newcastle fans congratulated me. There I was alone with my blue-and-white scarf surrounded by black-and-white ones.' Fahy, soon to be transferred to Oxford United, impressed throughout with his direct running. His goal prompted some of the Magpies' fans, Mick Spavins recalls, to throw apples at the away supporters, trying to hit a cut-out cardboard eagle being waved about. 'Someone next to me threw an apple back at them and luckily it hit their ringleader! After the match, their fans were friendly, but they did try to take the cut-out eagle as a souvenir.'

Bedford added a second, a messy deflection off Bill McKinney, and the second half was all Newcastle. Tony Moran remembers Newcastle playing 'some brilliant attacking football under the lights. They deserved to win but Bedford defended really well and if all else failed Wallace, their goalkeeper saved them.' Twenty-five minutes from time, he flung himself to tip a waist-high shot by Stan Anderson round the post but in the 89th minute was unable to prevent the same player from scoring a consolation for the Geordies. The goal, however, came too late and flattered their display. Despite a few late alarums the Eagles held out. The Second Division side had been outclassed and outmanoeuvred. 'Newcastle's worst Cup moment was still to come, but this was a shocking performance'.[2]

For Jack Eagles (his name was a coincidence, though he had played a couple of times for Bedford in 'midweek, end-of-season games when some of the regular players couldn't leave work early enough to play away'), his 'most vivid memory was the friendliness of the Newcastle supporters after the match. No cross words, no punch-ups, just a "well done!" and "the best team won"'. Tony Moran had an even more close-up and personal experience: 'The Geordies took me back to the pub and bought me a couple of pints. They were magnificent! Generous in defeat, they wouldn't let me pay for anything, congratulated me and my team, but had hard words for their team and their manager.'

Tony remembers the train was cold on the journey home and the Eagles' fans huddled together in the buffet car for warmth. When it left Tyneside, the train had plenty of Newcastle Brown Ale aboard but as Trevor Lloyd recalls, 'we got as far as Leicester when the buffet ran out again!' The Supporters' Club train beat the team home by half an hour. Delayed by a derailment near Peterborough, the conquering heroes eventually arrived at St John's station by a special train from Cambridge. Mick Hull remembers – just – welcoming them home and the huge celebration in George Senior's café in London Road well into Sunday morning.

On the Monday, Lloyd, who had ordered the special trains, took a phone call at work from the manager of British Rail. 'First of all', he said, 'I'd like to congratulate you on your win on Saturday... The other thing is that you now hold the record for the most drink drunk on British Rail.' He went on to praise the football club for the behaviour of the fans; there had been no trouble at all. The *Bedford Record* printed its own accolade: 'In these times when one hears so much of vandalism and hooliganism on football trains, it was pleasant to hear the buffet car attendant pay a tribute to Bedford supporters for their good behaviour and control, without losing any of their conviviality.'

The Eagles' fans had witnessed a small piece of history that January day

---

[2] Lloyd and Holt, p. 220.

in the North-East and as Sue Pass says, 'We had the last laugh!' Leazemag was dumbfounded. Sitting watching the teleprinter on *Grandstand*, he saw the cursor dance its way across the screen like the finger of doom. He remembers 'a sense of puzzlement. How did we lose and how come they were all wrong? I think from that point my curiosity had been woken and I was interested in Newcastle United.' A lifelong obsession had been born and shortly after he attended his first game – 'April 8, 1964, at home to Rotherham and we won 5–2.'

Bedford's hopes of a glorious Cup run soared when the Fourth Round draw gave them a home tie with Fourth Division Carlisle, 'but the lure of the last sixteen proved too great a distraction.'[3] The Cumbrians, at the time the highest goal-scoring side in the Football League, cruised to a comfortable 3–0 win.

After the euphoria of the win at St James' Park, there was more Cup success in the following couple of seasons with wins over Exeter, Brighton and Oxford. But a series of managers came and went, including Barry Fry in 1977 and the Eagles went the way of Accrington, Maidstone and Aldershot. When the owners of the football ground terminated the lease, plans to move to a new ground in the Bedford area failed and Bedford Town folded after 74 years.

Eagles' fans were determined not to turn their backs on three-quarters of a century of history. The supporters, like those of Wimbledon and Aldershot, resolved to take back their club and on May 5, 1989 a campaign was launched to re-form Bedford Town FC, which was so successful that they obtained Council permission to play their home games on a public pitch in Queen's Park not a stone's throw from the old ground in Ford End Road. 'With all the money washing through football,' writes David Conn about Bury, though he could easily have been referring to Bedford, 'there is no reason why clubs like Bury, still serving their towns, should be so starved of money, have to work so nerve-shreddingly just to stay alive. . . It's no way to run a sport, in a boom.'[4]

NEWCASTLE UNITED: Marshall, McKinney, Dalton, Anderson, McGrath, Iley, Hockey, Hilley, Thomas, Renman, Suddick
BEDFORD TOWN: Wallace, Coney, Avis, Goundry, Collins, Anderson, Lovell, Sturrock, Fahy, Heckman, Miles

---

[3] Ibid.
[4] Conn, p. 209.

19

NEWPORT COUNTY 3, SHEFFIELD WEDNESDAY 2

FA Cup, Round Three, January 4, 1964

The Workmen's Institute in Tonyrefail, a former coal-mining village in the Rhondda Valley, once spent £45 on a copy of the *Oxford English Dictionary*. By the late 1930s the Tredegar Workmen's Institute circulated 100,000 books a year, housed an 800-seat cinema, ran a film society and put on a popular series of celebrity concerts. As Jonathan Rose points out, 'The miners' institutes of South Wales were one of the greatest cultural institutions created by working-people anywhere in the world.'[1] Many had begun in the mid-nineteenth century as mechanics' institutes, temperance halls, or literary societies under the patronage of the Victorian middle class. It might seem surprising that such a richly varied and vibrant cultural life could flourish in an environment permeated by such hard, unyielding, dangerous, grubby toil. In 1932, however, a miner offered H.V. Morton, England's early twentieth-century William Cobbett,[2] a pretty basic explanation. The British working man, he claimed, was an obsessive hobbyist. While some gardened, played football, or bred dogs, others pursued literature, philosophy, or classical music. 'The miner', he said, 'works in a dark, strange world. He comes up into the light. . . He wants to do something. It may be . . . pigeon racing, fretwork, whippet racing, carpentry, music, choral singing, or reading.'[3]

Or rugby. A man from Llwynypia, four miles up the valley from Ton-yr-efail, claims that it was the very nature of the miners' work which made

---

[1] Rose, p. 237.
[2] Journalist, farmer and MP (1763–1835), author of *Rural Rides* (1830).
[3] H.V. Morton, *In Search of Wales* (Methuen, 1932); quoted in Rose, p. 240.

rugby particularly attractive. 'Mining was tough, rough and hard. . . These qualities were to develop a sense of camaraderie. . . among workers, who tended to take their sport far more seriously than others. . .' Indeed, in the late nineteenth century, the South Wales valleys, in common with other industrial areas of Britain, were obsessed with organised sport. Games such as handball and quoits were very popular, and gamblers were drawn to pursuits like boxing and foot-racing.

The most popular sports, however, were association and rugby football and by the early 1880s rugby had become a vital part of working-class culture in the mining villages and valleys in South Wales. The game was first introduced by boys returning from public schools in England and the few public schools which existed in Wales itself. Despite this upper-class background it soon took hold in the South Wales valleys. The new industrial middle class began to devote their entrepreneurial vigour to developing a classless and semi-professional Rugby Union culture. As the man from Llwynypia asserted, 'taking part in the game gave the miner an opportunity of gaining more social prominence as a player for was he not rubbing shoulders with the elite and surpassing or overcoming them at their own game?' Rugby began to lay claim to being the national game of Wales even in the mining districts that were the natural breeding grounds of soccer talents elsewhere, such as the Black Country, Lancashire, Yorkshire and the North-East.

However, historian Dr Martin Johnes in his *Soccer and Society: South Wales, 1900–39*,[4] argues that despite South Wales's reputation as a rugby hotbed, football was an equally important and popular part of the region's culture. Historically, however, soccer was more popular in North Wales, having arrived from across the border with Cheshire and it was probably the migration of so many North Walians into the South Wales coalfield, along with Englishmen, which made soccer so popular in the valleys. Nonethless it was not until the early 1900s that organised, professional football developed in South Wales. Cardiff City FC was founded in 1910 and within ten years had been admitted into the Second Division of the Football League. Thousands travelled by train from the valleys to see Cardiff City, Newport County and Swansea Town play and by the 1920s in many valley communities soccer had outstripped rugby in support.

---

[4] Published by University of Wales Press, 2002.

'To begin', as Dylan Thomas wrote, 'at the beginning.' In the late nineteenth century coal from the eastern valleys of South Wales and iron and steel from foundries in towns like Merthyr and Ebbw Vale were transported by rail down the valleys to Barry, Cardiff and Newport. The Romans had built a port at Caerleon to defend the crossing of the Usk: a millennium later, the Normans built a castle and the town was a significant medieval port. The Industrial Revolution of the late eighteenth century necessitated larger ships: the Usk became no longer navigable and in 1796 the Monmouthshire Canal was opened and in the 1840s new docks were built.

In the late nineteenth century, ironworkers in Newport undertook missionary work to establish football in a rugby stronghold and in 1912 the first Newport County was formed, originally taking the title 'Newport & Monmouth County FC', joining the Southern League's Second Division. When football resumed after the First World War in 1919/20, County were elected to Division One, which became Football League Division Three a year later.

The economic depression in the early 1930s hit South Wales harder than anywhere and in 1931 County became the third club from the area to lose its League membership,[5] though they returned to the fold a year later, playing their home games at the new Somerton Park. In 1938/39, after almost 20 years in Division Three (South), the club won promotion to Division Two as champions. However, after only three games, with County just above halfway in the embryonic table, world war put paid to league football for the second time in a generation.

Saturday, August 31, 1946 saw League football underway again and County soon found themselves out of their depth, incurring their record defeat – by 13–0 at Newcastle following a 7–2 thrashing at home to West Bromwich – and were relegated to Division Three (South). One highlight for the Welsh fans in a dismal decade – apart from the greyhound racing and speedway which were regular features at Somerton Park – was the Cup run in 1948/49 when their side reached the Fifth Round, featuring in a glamour tie at Fratton Park against a Portsmouth side on their way to the League Championship. County led 2–1 and would have earned a home replay had it not been for the rule allowing for extra time in the first game and Pompey squeezed through 3–2.

---

[5] In 1927 Aberdare Town had been voted out, and the former Merthyr Town failed to be re-elected in 1931.

County spent the 1950s in Division Three (South) until, in 1962, with only seven wins all season, the club fell into Division Four, which is where they found themselves when First Division Sheffield Wednesday came visiting in the Third Round of the Cup in January, 1964.

Although Wednesday were missing their England goalkeeper Ron Springett and gifted inside-forward John Fantham, the Hillsborough side were in form[6] and still had England internationals Peter Swan and Ted Holliday, England B international Alan Finney, as well as England Under-23 cap Colin Dobson. County fans feared the worst and, while the players were more optimistic, having despatched Hereford United, after a replay, and Watford in previous rounds, they knew they would have trouble thwarting Finney and Holliday.

Nonetheless, despite their fears, a crowd of twelve thousand turned up to see only the fourth First Division side to play at Somerton Park since the war. Before kick-off, they were entertained by Ricky Ford and the Crossfires, described in the quaint idiom of the mid-1960s, as 'a rhythm group', and when the home crowd gave voice to the inevitable Welsh hymn-singing the thousand blue-and-white-scarved Wednesday supporters who packed the area behind the goal at the railway end must have imagined they had wandered into Cardiff Arms Park by mistake.

From the whistle, County set off like greyhounds from the traps, forcing a couple of corners and Wednesday were clearly hassled by County's fear-less panache. In the opening exchanges, honours were just about even: 'the quality of the County's play was remarkably good, and they interpassed with speed and precision',[7] Swan, Megson and Hill having to keep a watchful eye on Hunt, Sheffield and centre-forward Joe Bonson. Wednesday were always dangerous on the break and one raid by 'Bronco' Layne and Dobson County's centre-half Graham Rathbone was forced to head behind for a corner, from which left-back Walters cleared a shot from the former Manchester United inside-forward Mark Pearson, off the line. At the other end Ralph Hunt saw his first-time shot clutched gratefully by MacLaren as it was heading for the top left-hand corner of the net.

Then, after 20 minutes, Ted Holliday gave the visitors the lead. Dobson broke clear and his cross-shot seemed to be going wide when Newport keeper Len Weare, playing his 355th game for the club, dived to save but

<hr>

[6] They eventually finished sixth.
[7] *Football Argus*, January 4, 1964.

succeeded only in palming the ball into the path of Holliday, who tapped it in.

Though Wednesday were on top, their fast and penetrative forwards inter-passing skilfully, County pressed strongly for an equaliser before half-time. Once there was a reminder of how football used to be when Wednesday keeper, Roy MacLaren, having gathered a corner, successfully resisted the former Wolves and Cardiff player Bonson's attempt to shoulder him and the ball over the goal-line. The tall and powerful Peter Swan was also a rock in Wednesday defence, 'though occasionally he was inclined to play the man before the ball'.[8] A free kick given for one of his robust challenges ended in Walters forcing a corner, which Rathbone headed against the Wednesday crossbar. Just before half-time, Sheffield's fierce drive from 25 yards clipped the bar, 'with MacLaren looking a very surprised man'.

As the whistle blew for the interval, County left the field to more hymns and a deafening ovation from the crowd. They had given the First Division side plenty to think about and on the balance of play deserved to be on level terms.

Three minutes after the break, they were. Colin Webster took a corner from the right and County skipper Joe Bonson, lurking at the far post, beat Wednesday's right-back Hill to head the ball beyond MacLaren's reach. Bonson, a Newport legend, played only two seasons for County after his move from Doncaster Rovers but scored 47 goals in 83 games before moving to Brentford at the end of the season. He was overwhelmed by his team-mates and 'scores of excited County supporters swarmed on to the pitch to congratulate him'. Nowadays, such a mass pitch invasion would result in arrests, fines, disciplinary enquiries by the FA, columns in the broadsheets bemoaning the end of civilisation and rent-a-quote politicians demanding that 'something must be done about soccer hooligans'. In the 1960s, when fans ran on the pitch, they were shepherded off and their ecstatic celebrations accepted as part and parcel of high-spirited crowd behaviour.

And in any case, such euphoria seldom lasted long. County's fans were quickly silenced as, in the 56th minute, Alan Finney sped through the home defence, weaved his way past two defenders and beat Weare with a brilliant shot from the angle of the box to restore Wednesday's lead.

[8] Ibid.

County fought back from this reverse with the fiery spirit of the Welsh dragon and, within a quarter of an hour, they had clinched the tie. In the 69th minute Joe Bonson scored his second, pouncing on a feeble clearance from MacLaren to drive home from 12 yards: two minutes later the crowd swarmed over the walls once more. Left-winger Smith cut in, Maclaren could only parry his shot and Ralph Hunt, who sadly died in a car crash ten months later, raced in to prod the ball over the line.

Cue more choruses of 'Cwm Rhondda' and 'Sospan Fach'. Against the background of thunderous hymn-singing, Wednesday strove hard to get back into the game and gave County's defence several nervous moments, none more so than in the 80th minute, when Len Weare leapt like a salmon in the River Usk to turn a shot from Holliday behind for a corner.

Then suddenly, amazingly, County had done it. 'What a game! And what a County triumph!' wrote Willis Huntley in the *Football Argus*, who can be forgiven his hyperbole: 'There was no doubt another County's right to victory today. From the start they stood no nonsense from the First Division club and although there were times when the Wednesday looked the more polished side, they could never match Newport in dash, determination and fighting spirit.'

Summing up the game, the Mayor of Newport chose not to analyse the tactical reasons for County's famous victory, concentrating instead on leading the crowd in a full-throated rendering of 'Cwm Rhondda'. Well, he was Welsh – and it's a belter of a hymn that can't be sung quietly. The unofficial Welsh national anthem, it embodies the essence of the virtually untranslatable *hwyl*, the Welsh love of homeland and of culture. There must have been something in the air that day, for 300 miles away on Tyneside, Bedford Town were creating their own piece of Cup history.[9] But County's delirious fans were not to know that, as they walked home through the darkening streets of their ancient port town.

What they also could not know was that, two decades later, County had a breathtaking squad who won a promotion and Welsh Cup double. John Aldridge and Tommy Tynan became local legends as the club flourished in Division Three and reached the quarter-final of the European Cup Winners' Cup. On Easter Monday, 1983, County beat Cardiff City at Somerton Park to go top of the Third Division in front of 16,052 fans.

---

[9] See pp. 125–130.

Within four years however, Newport became the second team to suffer automatic relegation from Division Four and the bailiffs moved into Somerton Park after the club was expelled from the Football Conference for failure to fulfil fixtures.

Throughout the football world, whether in Aldershot or Wimbledon, supporters of small non-League clubs invest in their teams a huge degree of emotional energy, and as a result of the passionate desire of County fans not to see their club vanish from the football scene, a replacement club, Newport AFC, was formed in June 1989. The new club began the 1989/90 season in the Hellenic League, playing at Moreton-in-Marsh and over the next six years endured a peripatetic existence. The bizarre move to the Cotswolds was followed by two years back at Somerton Park, until the historic old ground was sold for redevelopment. The next two seasons were played in Gloucester, as the FAW refused to countenance Newport's participation in the English football pyramid. Finally, in 1994/95, the club settled at Newport Stadium in the council-owned sports complex at Spytty Park.

Before that proud day four decades ago Wednesday manager Vic Buckingham previewed the game: 'We are doing reasonably well in the First Division, so I do not think we shall worry unduly about meeting Newport. I know it never does to underestimate opponents but surely we cannot be anything other than confident of winning.' Today Newport County now play in the second tier of non-League football, in the Blue Square Conference (South), a far cry from the afternoon when the club's legendary predecessor took on one of the best teams in the land – and with characteristic Celtic cussedness stuffed their manager's arrogant words back down his throat.

NEWPORT: Wearer, Bird, Walters, Rowland, Rathbone, Hill, Webster, Sheffield, Bonson, Hunt, Smith
WEDNESDAY: MacLaren, Hill, Megson, McAnearney, Swan, Young, Finney, Dobson, Layne, Pearson, Holiday

20

OXFORD UNITED 3, BLACKBURN ROVERS 1

FA Cup, Fifth Round, February 15, 1964

A Clerk ther was of Oxenford also,
That unto logyk hadde longe ygo.[1]

This couplet from Chaucer's humorous, rumbustious, humane and philo-sophical Prologue to the *Canterbury Tales* gives us a clue to the origins of the ancient town of Oxford. Sited where the Cherwell flows into the Thames, it was a place where a ford allowed oxen to cross the river. A Roman and then a Saxon settlement, pillaged by the Danes in the eleventh century, by the time of the Norman Conquest and the Domesday Book 20 years later, it was a trading centre and by 1200 had an abbey, a castle and a growing community of scholars.

The Domesday Book of 1086 also records 'Rex tenet Hedintone' (The King holds Headington). A small village on the London road two or three miles east of Oxford, through the Middle Ages Headington became a service centre furnishing the increasingly important urban centre of learning and political power to the west. In Victorian times, the men of Headington still provided Oxford with its market-garden produce, its bricks and its stone. The women (who were noted for the 'Headington hump', acquired by years of bending over the washtub) did Oxford's washing, despite the fact that there was no piped water until 1902.

The working village of Headington, now rather a backward rural area

---

[1] A university student from Oxford there was, too, who had studied logic long ago.

compared to the international centre of academia down the hill and across the Cherwell, nonetheless contained its middle-class professionals and in 1893 two Headington worthies, the local physician, Dr Robert Hitchings, and the vicar, the Revd John Holford-Scott, met in the Britannia Inn. Among many of the clergy, 'belief in athleticism was almost as striking as their belief in God. . . Few doubted the needs for large-scale recreation as part of the Churches' solution to the nation's ills. Clergymen seized on football as an ideal way of combating urban degeneracy.'[2] The two men were doubtless devotees of the Victorian ethic of 'muscular Christianity', which held that vigorous games could 'bring strength, health and a host of qualities badly needed by deprived working people – especially the young'. As a result many of today's leading clubs had their beginnings as church teams. Aston Villa originated in 1874 from members of the Villa Cross Wesleyan Chapel who already played cricket but wanted a winter sport. Thus it was that, in the village pub, the doctor and the vicar launched Headington United, a village team known locally as 'the boys from up the hill'.

For the next half-century United were happy to compete in the local county leagues. The club moved to the Manor Ground on the London Road in 1925 but while Headington's population grew 79 per cent in the 1920s as the Cowley car works expanded, it had to wait until 1926 for gas and 1929 for electricity. After the Second World War the club were still a small amateur outfit playing in the Spartan League until its ambitious president, Vic Couling, took the premeditated gamble of turning Headington professional and in 1949 the club was elected to the Southern League. Ex-Wolves and Sunderland player Harry Thompson was appointed manager and given the job of transforming Headington United into one of non-League football's leading forces. His start in August 1949 was far from auspicious. Playing away at Hastings United, Headington were trounced 5–2. It was indicative of the club's ambition that in December 1950, when the village had had electricity for only 20 years, Headington United became the first non-League club in the country to install floodlights when only a handful of Football League clubs had done so.

By 1953 the side had won its first Southern League Championship and in the following season they reached the Fourth Round of the FA Cup

---

[2] Walvin, p. 59.

with victories over League clubs Millwall and Stockport County, before going out 4–2 to Bolton Wanderers. In 1957 the Beech Road Stand – one of the most modern stands in the country at that time – was erected at the Manor Ground ready for the much-hoped for arrival of League football. The appointment of the former Birmingham City manager Arthur Turner as manager in 1959 was another watershed in the club's history. A year later, to broaden the appeal to the whole of the city and to raise its national profile, the club's name was changed to Oxford United.

In the early 1960s Turner's men secured two successive Southern League championships and, when Accrington Stanley folded in 1962, Oxford United was the natural choice to replace them. This, however, was only the beginning. Oxford were an ambitious club and in 1964 Turner – and club skipper Ron Atkinson – led the side into the Sixth Round of the FA Cup – the first of only four Fourth Division sides to ever get that far. Folkestone, Kettering, Chesterfield, Brentford – all these had been seen off either side of Christmas, Billy Calder getting both goals in a replay at Griffin Park in Round Four, before the Manor Ground welcomed Blackburn Rovers for the most exciting fixture since Oxford's admission to the League. Among the visitors were the skilful Bryan Douglas, former England captain Ronnie Clayton and international players like Fred Pickering (England), Mike England (later of Spurs and Wales), Mick McGrath (Eire) and the prolific scorer Andy McEvoy (Eire).

The home side were toiling in the depths of Division Four: by contrast, Rovers, second in the First Division, hadn't conceded a goal in their two cup ties against Grimsby and Fulham and had won 8–2 at West Ham (Bobby Moore and all) on Boxing Day – but they had lost their last two League games away from Ewood Park.

Come Saturday, February 15 and the record crowd of 21,000 was crammed on the terraces and heaving noisily along the touchlines. Rovers were unable to include their classy full-back Keith Newton, injured in an England training session, but United's first-choice side included ex-Villa wing-half and chief enforcer Ron Atkinson, deputed to mark Bryan Douglas, the fulcrum of all Blackburn's creative menace. Arthur Turner, however, had a cunning plan. Whenever Douglas received the ball, Atkinson was all over him like a rash. The England man had a frustrating afternoon and in the florid prose of *The Times*, 'he scurried back and forth *[and]* took a buffeting which would have broken the heart of many twice his size. Now all his superb control and delicate, fluted artistry were crushed before they had time to blossom.' The visitors started confidently, stroking the ball around with ease, without seriously troubling United's keeper Harry Fearnley. United, knowing the first 20 minutes were vital, snuffed out this early threat and actually produced the game's first shot after four minutes when right-back Cyril Beavon forced Fred Else to tip his drive over the bar. When the Rovers 'tried to step up the pace and power they found the United a stride ahead of them and there were long periods when the visitors, including their hitherto all-conquering inside forwards, seemed completely bewildered by what was going on.'[3]

Their bewilderment deepened in the 13th minute when John Shuker's throw found winger Peter Knight and his superb pass sent Longbottom away up the right. As Blackburn's defence retreated, Longbottom's centre was mis-controlled by Calder, but it ran on to ex-Birmingham City amateur Tony Jones and he gratefully slotted the ball home.

United were now on top and almost at once Longbottom's 30-yard drive was confidently dealt with by Else. Rovers continued to play composed football in the belief that their superior class would bring them goals but United centre-half Maurice Kyle restricted England prospect Fred Pickering to only two chances in the whole game. Five minutes before the interval, Knight's low cross only narrowly evaded Calder's lunge, then the same man fired wide of the far post seconds before United left the field at half-time to a standing ovation.

The pressure continued on the Blackburn goal early in the second half, though McEvoy should have equalised soon after the restart but sliced his shot wide. It was a costly miss, for two minutes later Calder nodded a long free kick from Atkinson on to Jones, who drifted in to wallop a second past Else from eight yards.

With United now 2–0 up, Blackburn rallied briefly. Pickering's powerful header flew only inches over the bar and Atkinson then hacked the ball off the Oxford line. Rovers were now playing with purpose and the Oxford defence came under increasing pressure. The dam was breached in the 68th minute when Harry Fearnley punched a right-wing corner only as far as the edge of the United penalty area, where Mike Ferguson volleyed into the net through a gaggle of players.

For the next ten minutes, Rovers strove frantically for the equaliser, but,

---

[3] *Oxford Mail*, February 17th, 1964.

shortly after Bryan Douglas had headed into Fearnley's hands, Pat Quartermain led a swift counter-attack, charging determinedly down the left wing. With a minute left and the Rovers' defence absent without leave, Billy Calder tapped in his low centre with a fine flourish to clinch the tie for the Fourth Division outsiders, prompting a pitch invasion. The remaining minute was played out amid chaotic scenes but, in the words of *The Times*, 'there were too many people on the pitch for anything to matter much'.

At the final whistle hundreds of Oxford fans swarmed on to the pitch and chaired Ron Atkinson off. His men had become the first side from the basement to reach a Cup quarter-final. He had been United's inspiration. Affectionately known as 'The Tank', on account of his girth, Atkinson's iron will was the team's driving force and 'his tackling was swift and strong, his distribution and control sure, not least when he swung the ball across for Calder to lay on Jones's second goal'.[4]

John Parsons, writing in the *Oxford Mail*, was understandably euphoric: 'This was no ordinary Cup shock with the underlings sneaking success from the masters but an impressive, clear-cut and exhilarating triumph by a superior side. . . United's unheralded men from the Fourth Division not merely overcame but out-smarted and for lengthy periods outclassed and out-played Blackburn.' The staff man from *The Times* expressed it rather more lyrically. 'A team immeasurably richer in skill and imbued with the traditions of greatness had been swept aside by courage and selfless determination, a driving, unquenchable spirit.'

Hero of the hour, two-goal Tony Jones, said afterwards, 'Kettering was much harder than today', and skipper Ron Atkinson commented that, 'Workington in the League gave us a harder game than Blackburn.' Left-back Pat Quartermain added, 'I still can't believe how easy it was. It's the greatest thing that has ever happened to me in football.'

Blackburn Rovers manager Jack Marshall and skipper Ronnie Clayton agreed that United were the better side on the day. Marshall said, 'We have no excuses. Oxford deserved their win and we wish them well.' Ron Clayton conceded: 'Oxford played it hard and played it well and we wish them the very best of success in the next round. From our point of view it was just one of those days which come to every club in turn. Oxford fully deserved their win.'

---

[4] Ibid.

On Leap Year Day, an all-time record Manor Ground crowd of 22,750 saw United go down 2–1 in the quarter-final to the eventual finalists Preston North End. The club from Lancashire, the League and Cup giants of the late Victorian era, played classy attacking football and from the kick-off troubled the home defence, so redoubtable against Blackburn. A breakthrough was inevitable and when United keeper Harry Fearnley hesitated in collecting a through ball, centre-forward Alec Dawson nipped in to put the visitors ahead. He could have made it two a few minutes later, heading wide when unmarked in the goal area. A second was not long delayed, however, as Godfrey finished off a smooth passing move to fire home from 12 yards. Oxford's spirit urged them on to besiege the visitors' goal throughout the second half and they gained their just reward when Tony Jones scored from eight yards following a melee in the Preston area. However, it was not enough and the men from Deepdale cruised confidently into the semi-final.

Atkinson and Turner led the side to Division Three in the following year and to the championship in 1968. They clung on in Division Two for eight years but in 1972 Atkinson left for the player-managership at Kettering and eventually to Old Trafford, and gradually the modest crowds at the Manor Ground, their home since 1925, blunted the club's ambitions. In 1982 newspaper magnate and MP Robert Maxwell took over as chairman with his crackpot scheme to merge United with Reading as the 'Thames Valley Royals'. Nonetheless, during his reign as chairman, with Jim Smith as manager, Oxford won the Division Three and Division Two championships in successive seasons – an unprecedented feat and the club survived for three years in the top flight under new manager Maurice Evans. A leaky defence was bailed out on numerous occasions by the prolific goalscorers John Aldridge and Dean Saunders and in 1986 the Manor Ground faithful had a marvellous day out at Wembley as United crushed QPR 3–0 to win the League Cup. However, eventually Maxwell took his ball home and debt-ridden Oxford slithered down the divisions.

The history of the club is almost unique in English football. Only the story of Wimbledon, who rose from non-League football to Division One and a Cup win at Wembley, thence to oblivion, all in 25 years, can compare with that of Oxford. In less than half a century United have joined the League, risen from the Fourth Division to the First in 20 years, won the League Cup and then suffered a slow but steady decline. There was a brief renaissance at the end of the 1990s when the club moved to the smart new Kassam Stadium on the southern ring road, named after the former chairman Firoz Kassam. Fortunes on the field, however, continued to deteriorate and in 2006 the club was relegated to the Conference.

An American scholar from Maryland once wrote of the city of Oxford: 'It's not just that the school buildings themselves are beautiful; the architecture of the entire town is breathtaking. On every street the buildings are ornately decorated with carvings, ornaments and gargoyles. Cathedrals, domed roofs and spires sweep up to the sky and deep green gardens dot the campuses.' This is Matthew Arnold's 'city of dreaming spires'. For one afternoon in 1964, for the faithful fans of Oxford United, the cramped and humble terraces of the Manor Ground in the once rustic backwater of Headington were just as beautiful and just as inspiring.

And for them at least, unlike the loyal fans of Wimbledon FC, their club still exists.

OXFORD UNITED: Fearnley, Beavon, Quartermain, Atkinson, Kyle, Shuker, Knight, Longbottom, Calder, Jones, Harrington
BLACKBURN ROVERS: Else, Bray, Joyce, Clayton, England, McGrath, Ferguson, McEvoy, Pickering, Douglas and Harrison

21

NORTH KOREA 1, ITALY 0

World Cup, Group Four, Ayresome Park, July 19, 1966

Middlesbrough Ironopolis to Kim Il Sung – something of a leap of the imagination, you might think, but in the link between the two lies one of the biggest upsets in football ever seen in Britain. The match took place at Ayresome Park in Paradise Field, opened in 1903 next to the old stadium of the former Northern League side 'Middlesbrough Ironopolis', who had spent one season in Division Two a decade earlier and whose glorious appellation derived from Teesside's major industry.

Football came home in 1966 when the nation that gave birth to the world's favourite game played host to the 'World Championship, the Jules Rimet Cup', as my dog-eared ticket for the semi-final calls it. 'The World Cup' (as most fans knew it) welcomed 16 teams from around the globe and, in the days when foreign teams and international stars were scarcely seen live on our TV screens, it promised a festival of fabulous football. Group Four, which comprised the USSR, Chile, Italy and North Korea, was played in the North-East, and the six games were shared between Ayresome Park and Roker Park in Sunderland. Middlesbrough's home, then over 60 years old, was beginning to look its age but the club, cashing in on its status as a World Cup venue, upgraded the old ground in Paradise Field, which became one of the best-appointed stadiums in the country.

At Ayresome Park, the opening game of the group – a kind of Marxist–Leninist local derby – saw the USSR comfortably beat North Korea when, on the half-hour, two goals in a minute settled the match. The Soviets added a third in the dying minutes and the gutsy Koreans, 1,000–1 outsiders to win the tournament, were dead and buried. Their 1966 World Cup anthem, proclaiming 'We can beat everyone, even the strongest team', indicated the pride and the spirit of these unknown players from an impenetrable, totalitarian society. For the average British football fan, the Democratic People's Republic of Korea might as well have been on another planet. Few could have found it on a map and even fewer were aware that they played football. The Korean War had ended just over a decade before and, as Britain had no formal diplomatic relations with North Korea, the Foreign Office regarded the team with deep suspicion. On the football front, 'Some people thought it ridiculous that a team of no-hopers like North Korea could be allowed to qualify for the 1966 World Cup Finals, whereas other, more proven nations, like Czechoslovakia, Yugoslavia and Scotland, would not be there.'[1]

Russia's easy victory seemed to vindicate that opinion but for the North Koreans, who had been preparing for the tournament for three years, the opportunity to play in the World Cup tournament was not only a chance to prove themselves as footballers. They were also standard-bearers for North Korea's communist system and its 'Dear Leader', Kim Il Sung. Defender Ring Jung Sun recalled Mr Kim's words of support. 'Before we left our homeland, the Great Leader invited us to see him. He embraced us lovingly and said: "Europeans and South American nations dominate international football. As the representatives of the Africa and Asian region, as coloured people, I urge you to win one or two matches."'

The Koreans' next game was also at Ayresome Park, where a crowd of only 15,877 saw Chile take a first-half lead, then struggle to apply the coup de grâce. With the clock ticking away, North Korea's inside-right Pak Seung Zin, to the delight of the friendly Middlesbrough crowd, scored a tremendous equaliser with a couple of minutes left. The Asians, showing tenacity in defence and pace in attack, had come out of their shells and the draw, as well as boosting the Koreans' confidence for the final Group game against Italy, gave them a chance of at least qualifying for the quarter-finals.

As for the Italians, they were in poor form, and even their team manager, Edmondo Fabbri, felt the side, with the vultures of the Italian press circling overhead, had 'lost faith in their own ability and were frightened of failure.'[2] He urged them to rediscover the kind of performance which had made them one of the favourites to lift the World Cup at Wembley at the end of the month. In Fabbri's view, all the North Koreans had to offer was speed

---

[1] Ward, p. 133.
[2] *The Times*, July 19, 1966.

and the received wisdom was that swift, flexible defenders were needed to deal with it. Astonishingly, therefore, Fabbri stuck two ponderous players, Janich and Guarneri, at the heart of his defence and compounded the error by calling on his manifestly unfit captain and play-maker, Giacomo Bulgarelli.

The Italians seemed to have taken Fabbri's strictures to heart as in the first half-hour they could have put the game beyond the Koreans' reach. Barison, Mazzola and Bulgarelli combined in a smooth-flowing move leaving Marino Perani clear with only the keeper Li Chan Myung to beat but he froze, scuffing his shot from only ten yards and it was scrambled away.

Then came the incident which in the view of many Italians cost them the match. In the 35th minute, Bulgarelli, already carrying an injury, collided with Pak Seung Zin in midfield and had to be carried off on a stretcher with torn knee ligaments. To give the Italians credit, they responded well to this reverse, their star striker, Sandro Mazzola, urging his teammates to redouble their efforts. However, in the days before substitutes the loss of their leader and most influential player was a grievous blow and it was the North Koreans who drew first blood. Three minutes before half-time, a Korean attack was only half-cleared and Pak Doo Ik, latching on to Pak Seung Zin's fierce header back into the box, beat Rivera and slammed the ball well out of the reach of Enrico Albertosi just inside his far post. The goal was greeted with a noise like thunder as the Middlesbrough crowd roared on their new favourites.

In the second half the Italians were forced to take the game to the Asians and they threw in all they had. For all their possession, however, they could make no impression on a resolute Korean defence, who appeared to grow in stature. Mazzola, Perani and Barison were being hustled and harried, and when they did manage a shot at goal, Li Chan Myung was equal to the challenge. Once, early in the second half, Rivera, 'with a splendid burst of individualism, flicked the ball over his head to beat one man, accelerated past two more, and sent in a superb shot which the little goalkeeper almost nonchalantly fisted over the top.'[3]

The Koreans were matching the stars of Serie A blow for blow and were still hungry for goals. Once, the great full-back Giacinto Fachetti, the pride of Inter-Milan, had his pocket picked in his own penalty area by Han Bong Zin, who barely reached his shoulder. Zin put Kim Bong Hwan through

---

[3] *Guardian* July 20, 1966.

on goal but he was off balance and the chance was missed.

With time running out for the Italians to save the game, their tournament and their reputations, Mazzola, who had never stopped working like a Trojan, Facchetti and Landini – and at the end, even Janich – poured forward in search of the equaliser. 'But ability was tinged with desperation and the ability was not of such quality as to be able to control the desperation.'[4] As the minutes ticked away, the Boro crowd, who had taken the 'little men from the land of the morning calm'[5] to their hearts, chanted '"KO-REA", "KO-REA", drowning the forlorn cries of "ITALIA", "ITALIA" and, from the roars which greeted the final whistle, you would have thought that Middlesbrough had won the FA Cup.

This remarkable victory, the culmination of three years of intensive preparation, reduced a North Korean commentator to floods of tears as he flashed the incredible news back home. The Asians had already impressed the British fans with their pace and fitness and, on a night of raw emotion, against the supreme professionals of Serie A, 'they played with splendid spirit and refreshing sportsmanship; the kind of "professional" foul to which the World Cup exposed them clearly filled these straightforward little men with pained surprise.'[6] In one week they had learnt a lot about the world game. Their midfield pair of Pak Seung Zin and Im Seung Hwi had been tireless and the defence, with Ha Jung Won bringing much-needed height, made few mistakes. Now, if Russia could avoid defeat against Chile, the Koreans would face the talented Portuguese – Eusebio et al. – at Goodison Park on Saturday for a place in the World Cup semi-final.

The Koreans were both thrilled and perplexed by the support they received. 'It still remains a riddle to me,' said Ring Jung Sun. Dennis Barry, a Middlesbrough fan, explained. 'They played good football – you know they were all small and that was a novelty in itself. It was like watching a team of jockeys playing,' he said. 'But they moved the ball around really well. I think they took people by surprise, and they were very positive in their approach – they played attacking football, there was nothing defensive about their game, and the crowd got behind them from the way that they saw them play.'

---

[4] *The Times*, July 20, 1966.
[5] 'The Land of the Morning Calm' is an English-language nickname roughly derived from the 'hanja' characters for Joseon, the name of the Joseon Dynasty and the earlier Gojoseon. 'Hanja' is the Korean name for Chinese characters.
[6] Glanville, p. 147.

As for the much-vaunted Italian stars, the departure of Bulgarelli was a devastating loss, for he was the centre-pin of their tactical game and the mainspring of most of their attacks. Yet why did a side with such a wealth of talent fail so badly? *The Times* had a theory: 'Fear of defeat has turned giants into pygmies. Concentration on defence has stifled the flair of their game.'[7] Whatever the explanation, knowing the kind of reception they would receive from their rabid press, the Italian camp planned to sneak back home at one o'clock in the morning at an unscheduled airfield. However, the Italian media were a step ahead: smelling blood, they were already camped at Genoa airport to greet the squad with a torrent of rotting tomatoes and for many months afterwards, the mocking cry of 'Ko-re-a!' would echo over Italian stadiums when Fabbri or any of his World Cup men appeared.

For half an hour, on Saturday, July 23, 1966, the Koreans stood on the brink of a World Cup semi-final against the hosts at Wembley. By 3.30 the world of football seemed to have been turned on its head. This wasn't meant to happen. North Korea, 'clever, methodical and disrespectful,'[8] were three goals up against Portugal. Were their opponents too complacent or supremely self-confident? After all they were 'only playing North Korea'. It was impossible to say, yet the truth was undeniable.

Archive commentary confirmed that: 'There's no question about it . . . these boys are turning form upside down. They look more the favourites now than Portugal do . . . the crowd are calling for more . . . and we believe that's possible.' Three thousand Middlesbrough fans at Goodison Park saw the Koreans go a goal ahead in the first minute. Im Seung Uwi slipped the ball to Pak Seung Zin who slammed the ball past Pereira. The scorer glanced quickly at the referee, the linesmen and their opponents, afraid it had been some kind of mistake. They need not have worried – the crowd saluted the goal with a roar normally reserved for a winning goal against Liverpool. The Goodison Park faithful, accustomed to cultured, intelligent football with a touch of steel, saluted the Koreans' neat, constructive play as twice more the Portuguese defence was pierced before the half-hour.

In the 20th minute Yana Sung Kook's centre evaded both Pereira and Morais, and Li Dung Woon made it 2–0. 'We want three,' chanted the

---

[7] *The Times*, July 20, 1966.
[8] Eric Todd, *Guardian*, July 25, 1966.

Merseysiders: they had no need to worry. Three minutes later Yang Sung Kook scored a beautiful individual goal, highlighting the flimsiness of the Portuguese defence.

Portugal's pride was hurt – and the Koreans had reckoned without Eusebio. Too concerned with scoring goals, they paid little heed to the greatest player to emerge from Africa. Born in Mozambique, a Portuguese colony till 1975, Eusebio had everything. Intelligent, elusive, fast and strong, with a skilful dribbling touch, he decided that enough was enough. With half an hour gone, Augusto created an opening for Eusebio who gave an opponent several yards' start and still managed to zip past him to stab home Portugal's opener.

Two minutes before half-time, Torres, five yards from goal, was tripped from behind by Oh Yoon Kyung as he prepared to shoot and Eusebio scored with the penalty kick. When he swept in Simoes' pass on the run in the 57th minute to bring the scores level 'Eusebio's elusive brilliance was hoisting Portugal's challenge and at the same time pressing the Koreans into hurried clearances.'[9] The final outcome was no longer in doubt.

The 'Black Panther', as he was dubbed by the British press, scored his fourth goal of the match two minutes later, converting his second penalty when he himself was brought down. Ten minutes from time Eusebio's precise corner was nodded down by Torres and Augusta's crisp finish completed North Korea's misery.

In defeat, North Korea had won many new admirers. The Portuguese applauded the skill of Li Dong Woon and Yang Sung Kook and the bravery of goalkeeper Li Chan Myung: in the second half, when Portugal lay siege to the Koreans' goal, the defensive heroics of Lim Zoong Sun and Oh Yoon Kyung saved the day time and again.

It would have been easy for English football fans to sound patronising as they spoke of the little men from the Far East, the underdogs with the funny-sounding names. The Koreans, however, earned respect through their football and deserved on merit to beat Italy and rock Portugal, and the North-East fans in particular had taken them to their hearts. Following England's Wembley mauling by Hungary in 1953, and the European Cup Final of 1960 in Glasgow between Real Madrid and Eintracht Frankfurt, the giant-killing feat of the men from North Korea was one more reminder

---

[9] The Times, July 25, 1966.

that there was vibrant, skilful, tough and exciting football beyond the often parochial horizons of the English football fan.

NORTH KOREA: Li Chan Myung, Lim Zoong Sun, Shin Yung Kyoo, Ha Jung Won, O Yoon Kyung, Im Seung Hwi, Pak Seung Zin, Han Bong Zin, Pak Doo Ik, Kim Bong Hwan, Yang Sung Kook
ITALY: Albertosi, Landini, Janich, Guarneri, Fachetti, Bulgarelli, Fogli, Perani, Mazzola, Rivera, Barison

22

OLDHAM ATHLETIC 1, SOUTH SHIELDS 2

FA Cup, Round One replay, December 9, 1969

Are you sitting comfortably? Then I'll begin. For a long time, I couldn't get algebra. To me, maths was numbers, and I was good at mental arithmetic. I just couldn't see how you could add up letters and multiply 6a by 2b – and what were those brackets for? I mean, come on. . .

Until, that is, Tommy Cookson took me for maths. Once he'd explained that the letters could stand for anything you like – apples, bananas, doughnuts or koala bears – I'd cracked it. Maths had become a language and I was happy with that.

Fascinating, I hear you cry. What's it got to do with football? Well, it was like this. Tommy Cookson's wife was Catherine and she wrote books – gritty tales about fisher folk and cobbled streets, boats coming in, betrayal, death, misery and warm, salt-of-the-earth humour among the down-trodden poor of the North-East. And she came from South Shields, born at 5 Leam Lane in 1906.

Mind you, the area had a history long before Catherine's tales tugged at the heart-strings. Nearly two millennia before, the Romans built their fort of Arbeia on a hill on the southern bank of the Tyne as a granary for the Roman garrison defending Hadrian's Wall. However, the earliest reference to *scheles*[1] (fishermen's huts) occurs in 1235, and the actual town was founded by the Prior and Convent of Durham in 1245. For centuries, because the burgesses of Newcastle stipulated that no ships should be laden or unladen

---

[1] A.D. Mills, *The Oxford Popular Dictionary of English Place-names* (Parragon, 1991): 'from Middle English, *schele*, temporary sheds or huts (used by fishermen).'

at Shields, and that no wharves or quays should be built there, South Shields slumbered, then developed, as a fishing port.

Towards the end of the eighteenth century the Industrial Revolution transformed the face of Britain, and South Shields was in the vanguard of this sea-change in British commercial and industrial life. Salt panning along the Tyne had begun in 1499, and by 1767 the town had 200 salt pans where sea water was boiled away to leave the salt. These pans consumed 1,000 tons of coal from the Northumberland field every year and produced hydrochloric acid that caused terrible pollution as well as smoke that could be seen for many miles. At one time, too, an alkali works, opened in 1822, was the largest in the world, meeting the growing demand for chemical products such as soap, bleach and dyes for the cloth market. Furthermore, alkali could be mixed with other substances to produce glass. Glass manufacturing was begun ironically enough by Isaac Cookson in 1650 and by 1845 South Shields was producing more plate glass than anywhere else in England.

In the mid-Victorian era the growing population was putting pressure on land in the lower Tyne valley, and in 1859 Tyne Dock was opened with the capacity to hold 500 vessels. South Shields became famous for its shipyards and its coal mines and in common with other ironworking and shipbuilding towns in the coalfields of North-East England did not escape the spread of the people's game. For although, as David Goldblatt writes, 'In the early 1870s . . . football remained a minor recreational pastime for a very narrow stratum of Victorian society,'[2] within little more than a decade, 'football had become the sport of the industrial working-class; a social change of major proportions,'[3] the socio-economic roots of which have been explored elsewhere in this volume.[4]

The history of South Shields FC is lengthy and complex but reports in the local *Gazette*[5] suggest that the South Shields football team's first recorded result was a 2–1 win in September 1889 against Gateshead Albion, though the paper had reported three games the previous season. South Shields Athletic formed in 1897 to play in the Northern Alliance, but folded in 1902. In 1899 South Shields Adelaide, nicknamed 'The Laddies', were

---

[2] Goldblatt, p. 32
[3] Walvin, p. 53.
[4] See 'Introduction' and Stoke v Blyth, pp. 223–228.
[5] The *Shields Gazette*, established in 1849, is the oldest provincial evening newspaper in the United Kingdom.

formed by Jack Inskip, and joined the Northern Alliance in 1907/08. Though the club's origins are blurred by time, it is certain that its three distinct incarnations have played in more leagues than Nicholas Anelka has had clubs and after one season they transferred to the North-Eastern League, dropped the 'Adelaide' in 1910, became South Shields FC and a limited company, applying unsuccessfully in 1913 to join the Football League.

After the Great War, the club joined Football League (Division Two) and contested the post-war Victory Shield alongside Newcastle, Sunderland and others. The first game was a 1–0 defeat at Fulham watched by twenty thousand. Big crowds were common but success proved elusive – though the club did hold the world record for a transfer when, in 1922, Warney Cresswell moved to Sunderland for a then world record fee of £5,500: the record was not broken again for three years. In 1929 the club was relegated to the newly formed Third Division (North), where they played for two seasons before moving nine miles west to Gateshead to become Gateshead FC.

A new club was soon re-formed, and this joined the North-Eastern League in 1936, which the club won twice before the league was disbanded in 1958. Two seasons in the Midland League followed but crippling transport costs forced the club to move to the Northern Counties League in 1961/62, the re-formed North-Eastern League in 1963/64 and the North Regional League in 1967/68, when they became founder members of the Northern Premier League. This ushered in the club's most successful period, and they reached the FA Trophy semi-finals in 1973/74. However, the club's imminent demise was widely expected before the match: only, 1,117 bothered to watch the home leg and Shields lost 3–0 on aggregate to a Morecambe side they had beaten 6–0 and 7–1 in the League. Simonside Hall, the club's home since 1951, was sold and the side moved to Gateshead, becoming Gateshead United, a short-lived incarnation which died three years later. A new club, South Shields FC, arose from the ashes and competed in the Northern Alliance and the Wearside League before being promoted to the Northern League.

Shields had seen many great FA Cup days since the war – a 5–0 trouncing of Crewe in 1958, a 2–1 defeat of Chesterfield in 1959, a victory over York City by 3–1 six years later, not to mention the legendary ten-goal feat by Chris Marron – reckoned to be an FA Cup record – in the 13–0 win over Radcliffe Welfare in 1947. But when the club was drawn against Fourth

Division Oldham Athletic in the second round in 1969, it was against 'a team', as the *Gazette* put it, 'that faces the threat of extinction'.[6] Oldham, a club with a proud Cup history, had achieved promotion to the Third Division in 1963 under Jack Rowley and two years later, a millionaire businessman, Mr Ken Bates,[7] drove up to the club in his Silver Cloud Rolls-Royce and spent £50,000 on new players in two weeks. There was much brave talk of European soccer in at Boundary Park in the 70s and a stadium to compete with anything in the country. The chairman splashed out on new dressing rooms and a fully equipped medical room but the team was just not good enough and narrow escapes from relegation occurred in 1965 and 1966, and in 1968 Jack Rowley, who had been sacked, was brought back as manager.

However, the inevitable relegation back to the basement division finally occurred in 1969 and, as the *Shields Gazette* wrote, 'the scene was set for a bitter fight against financial hardship and mounting disillusion in the town.'[8] Bates had asked for the return of the £87,000 which he invested in the club but 'Oldham do not have that kind of money and unless they can come to some agreement over its repayment extinction is the only possibility. Which means defeat against South Shields in the FA Cup next week could be another nail in their coffin.'

Shields had disposed of Bishop Auckland – not an Antipodean prelate but the most successful amateur Cup team of the century – and Bradford PA, another Fourth Division side, in previous rounds, and at Simonside, on the first Saturday in December, they held Athletic to a dour, hard-fought goal-less draw. The stage was set for a replay three days later, at Boundary Park, reputedly the coldest League ground in the country.

It was a step through the looking-glass, as reporter John Donoghue wrote, into the 'Alice in Wonderland world of a little club daring to venture into the great unknown of the FA Cup' and, on the night, it became 'honest-to-goodness reality for South Shields. Driven on by an indefinable quality some teams can produce from nowhere for the big occasion, the County Durham part-timers contemptuously brushed aside the claim of Oldham for a place in the third round.'

Dick Kirkup, the *Gazette*'s correspondent, described a night when 'Shields would not surrender'.[9] Oldham's captain, Ray Wilson, drawing on his ex-

---

[6] *Shields Gazette*, November 29, 1969.
[7] Yes, the same one who became Chairman of Chelsea and Leeds United.
[8] *Shields Gazette*, November 29, 1969.

perience of winning the World Cup with England in 1966, drove on his team, 'throwing everything but the floodlight pylons at a Shields defence that just flatly refused to go down.' But, as Dylan Thomas once said, 'To begin at the beginning'. . .

After only five minutes Oldham winger Keith Bebbington stunned Shields, hitting the side netting, but a minute or two later the Mariners snatched a sensational lead through former Sunderland midfielder Jimmy Potter. Gerry Donoghue collected a defensive clearance on the left touchline and swung a high cross into the penalty area where Len Smith, his back to the goal, rose to nod the ball down to Potter, who, from 12 yards, stabbed it into the net.

It was the start the non-League side wanted but Bebbington, a constant thorn in Shields' defence, equalised in the 26th minute. Athletic's centre-forward, Jim Beardall, pounced on a ricochet off Bobby Elwell's legs, hitting a speculative ball which eluded two attempted clearances. It ran out to Bebbington, who, from a narrow angle, beat Garrow with a drive into the far corner.

Shields pressed even more strongly and as Donoghue observed, 'The safety-first theme that stuck out a mile in the first confrontation on Saturday was lost in a wave of all-out attacking football.' Eric Johnstone, an outside-right with aims of being a professional sprinter, forced Gordine into a great save in the 33rd minute, a minute later Len Smith struck a free kick into Oldham's defensive wall – then, three minutes before the interval, Johnstone left Wilson for dead, took the ball to the touchline and crossed a perfect centre. Smith was there to bury a fierce header in the roof of the net. 'I've scored 310 goals for the club,' said Smith, 'but this was the greatest of them all.'

In the second half it was literally all uphill for Shields on the sloping Boundary Park pitch but they never weakened, continuing to play with more assurance and calm than their hosts. Athletic 'pounded away vigorously in the second half and after a scrambled save on the goal-line by player–manager Bobby Elwell, goalkeeper Bert Garrow made spectacular life-preserving saves from Ian Wood and Shaw. 'Their last real chance came two minutes from the end when Bebbington's shot soared high over the bar. The Mariners had clinched a famous victory. Afterwards player–manager

---

[9] *Shields Gazette*, December 12, 1969.

Bobby Elwell said, 'We were never in any doubt we would do it. We had a few hectic moments in the second half, but we were always there with a chance of making it three.'

The Monday lunchtime draw, with the team gathered round the traditional transistor, saw the Mariners pitted against Second Division promotion candidates Queens Park Rangers. It was a potentially lucrative tie and, as Elwell quipped, 'We always play better away from home. Don't forget, Queen's Park Rangers haven't a clue who we are or probably where South Shields is. But we know about them. We'll go up to London with our heads high, prepared for everything they have to offer. They'll have to be ruddy good to beat us. Our knee won't bend easily.'

As Dick Kirkup recorded, however, Shields' left-winger Nicky McCallum was doubtful for the tie – and not because of injury. Saturday, January 3 was his wedding day! 'We've already changed the wedding date once,' he said. 'It was fixed for November 29th, but as my sister was expecting a baby we decided to postpone the wedding. As it was, the baby came early. You know all the plans and arrangements that have to be made for a wedding. No, I think I'll miss the game in London.'

Such are the dilemmas of a part-time footballer. As it was, he didn't miss much. Shields supporter Colin Rowe recalls: 'We got beat 4–1 at Loftus Road: Len Smith scored for Shields.' QPR, then a vibrant attacking side with all-round strength, had Rodney Marsh, who scored twice, Terry Venables, Tony Hazell, Ian Gillard, Dave Clement, along with Frank Clarke and Mike Ferguson, who got a goal each. Colin Rowe still has the programmes from these matches. 'I was at all these games with my dad as we were both strong Shields supporters.' Despite the eventual disappointment of defeat, he remembers 'the games were great to watch'.

Colin Rowe stands in the proud tradition of those for whom supporting a football club is not based on salary, citizenship or old school ties. Richard Butler describes artist Peter Howson's similar love affair with Ayr United. 'He said, "My happiest memories are standing on the terrace with my father, drinking weak Bovril, eating mutton pie, watching Danny McLean running rings round the opposition. It made a perfect Saturday."'[10]

Bill Shankly's famous quote – 'Some people think football is a matter of life and death . . . I can assure them it is much more serious than that'

---

[10] Richard Butler, p. 8.

– articulates a fundamental truth for all soccer supporters, as Butler observes: 'Football traverses time. Supporters pass the culture of the club through the generations. . . Supporting a club says something about our self.'[11] In that sense, supporting a soccer club is about folk memory, not only of the club, but of your own life, in all its varied experiences. It is also about memories shared with others. The replica kit, the scarves and other regalia are statements of allegiance and group identity.

> Oh, what happened to you?
> Whatever happened to me?
> What became of the people we used to be?
> Tomorrow's almost over,
> Today went by so fast.
> The only thing to look forward to is the past.

The theme song to *Whatever Happened to the Likely Lads?*, the sitcom set on Tyneside, expresses in utter clarity the nostalgia most people feel for their roots. For many in the industrial towns and ports of the North-East, like South Shields, the days when Da' toiled down the pit, tended his whippets, raced his pigeons and watched the football on Saturday are gone. In South Shields, Readheads, the last shipbuilder, closed in 1984 and the last pit, Westoe Colliery, in 1991. Today the town remains a port of extraordinary contrasts. On one side are the quays, warehouses and factories of its industrial life; on the other six miles of coastline with sandy beaches, promenades and gardens, as well as three miles of river frontage, dominated by the massive but unlovely piers at the mouth of the Tyne.

The Mariners play on in the Second Division of the Northern League, but like thousands of Geordies, they have their memories of days – and games – like the one at Boundary Park.

OLDHAM ATHLETIC: Gordine, Wood, Wilson, McNeill, Lawson, Bowie, Bebbington, Shaw, Beardall, Whittle, Colquhoun
SOUTH SHIELDS: Garrow, Thompson, McLeod, Potter, Ewell, Adams, Johnstone, Ellis, Smith, Donogue, McCallum

---

[11] Ibid.

23

COLCHESTER UNITED 3, LEEDS UNITED 2

FA Cup, Round Five, February 13, 1971

Ask anybody what got them hooked on football and they'll probably tell you 'It was the atmosphere', by which they mean the noise, the fans – or more precisely, as Colin Irwin points out, the singing. 'There is an extra-ordinary tribal spirit that binds fans together as one solid, fiercely united representation of a community'[1] – and in part, that community expresses its collective consciousness, stemming from a centuries-old folk tradition, either by adapting snatches of childhood rhymes or chants or by reworking popular songs of the day. These recycled folk anthems become rapidly assimilated, almost it seems by spontaneous combustion, on the terraces of grounds all over the country: grounds like Layer Road, Colchester, where, in February 1971, they might have sung:

> Leeds United sat on the wall,
> Leeds United had a great fall,
> Poor Don Revie and all of his men
> Couldn't put United together again.

They didn't, but they might have done – and it would have been so appropriate, for Colchester is the most widely credited source of the nursery rhyme, 'Humpty Dumpty'.

In the summer of 1648, during the Second English Civil War, the Royalist stronghold of Colchester was besieged by a Parliamentary army for nearly

---

[1] Irwin, p. 13.

four months, during which a large cannon named 'Humpty Dumpty' was mounted on the tower of St Mary's-at-the-Wall Church. When the church tower was hit by enemy cannon fire the top was blown off, sending 'Humpty' crashing down – 'Humpty Dumpty had a great fall'. Shortly after, the town was lost to the Parliamentarians and 'All the king's horses and all the king's men couldn't put Humpty together again.'

Colchester had been a military stronghold since AD 49–50 when Claudius built the Roman fortress-city of Camulodunum, described two decades later by Pliny the Elder as being 'about 200 miles from the Isle of Anglesey'. This was the earliest known reference to a permanent settlement in Britain: thus Colchester can claim to be Britain's oldest recorded town. And even today, the Colchester Garrison is home to 16 Air Assault Brigade.

Whether the amateur Colchester Town FC was formed in 1867 or 1873 – there is some dispute – it was inevitable the club would be dubbed 'The Oystermen'. The town had been associated with oysters since the twelfth century when Richard I, keen to raise money for a crusade, sold Colchester a charter which confirmed its control over the fisheries on the River Colne. In the seventeenth century Samuel Pepys would order oysters by the barrel and by the 1790s Colchester oysters were on sale all over the country.

In 1909/10 the club played its first match – a friendly against Arsenal – at Layer Road where a new stadium had been built on land rented from the Army, and joined the South Essex League, and later the Middlesex League, which they won at the first attempt. From 1925, 11 seasons in the Spartan League's Division One brought no honours and when the Eastern Counties League was formed in 1935/36, Colchester Town were founder members along with local rivals, Ipswich Town. Over the next two seasons, however, the club finished eleventh out of 12 teams and in 1937, the Oystermen moved to the newly formed Essex County League. However, after six games of the 1937/38 season the club folded and Colchester United was formed as a professional club and elected to the Southern League. Within 18 months they were champions.

Post-war, the Oystermen still played at Layer Road, which saw the club's record attendance of 19,072 in November 1948 for a First Round FA Cup match against Reading, a match that was actually abandoned. Cup fever ran high, for in the previous season the Southern League side had reached the last 16. Unable to escape its military past, the side from the old garrison town was led by Bob Curry, who had been wounded at Dunkirk. With Ted Fenton as coach, Curry scored the goals which beat Wrexham and First Division Huddersfield Town, and, when Bradford Park Avenue turned up at Layer Road in the Fourth Round, Curry scored twice in a 3–2 win.

This barnstorming Cup run had brought United to national attention and, when the League expanded from 88 to 92 clubs in 1950, they were elected to the Southern section of the Third Division. Over the next 20 years Colchester bounced between the League's lower two divisions no less than seven times.

The season 1970/71 began like any other – yet soon after Christmas United, ambling along in the obscurity of Division Four and 75th in the Football League, had charged their way into the Fifth Round of the Cup, disposing of Sussex County League side Ringmer, then Barnet and Cambridge United, and chalking up an impressive Fourth Round triumph over Third Division Rochdale, scoring 15 goals in the process. Drawn at home in the last 16 against Don Revie's Leeds United, all the Oystermen could realistically hope for was an all-ticket sell-out at Layer Road and, given a fair wind, a money-spinning replay in Yorkshire. Three points clear at the top of Division One, Leeds were seemingly on the verge of great-ness with a team, in which, in Colin Irwin's colourful description, 'uncom-promising players like Billy Bremner, Jack Charlton, Johnny Giles, Paul Reaney and Norman Hunter were fashioned with such ugly, ruthless effi-ciency by the shifty-looking manager Don Revie (an *EastEnders* extra before his time) that they were widely reviled outside Leeds.'[2] A battle-hardened brigade of internationals, they had lost to Chelsea in the final the previous year and had missed out on a domestic and European treble. Indeed, Revie's side blew more trophies than they won, though they generally fell only at the final fence, beaten by their peers – Liverpool, Arsenal and Celtic. The Wembley disaster against Sunderland was still two years away.

Consequently, Colchester manager Dick Graham's 'mixture of rejects, hand-me-downs and OAPs (known, affectionately, as Grand-dad's Army)',[3] weren't given a chance against Leeds. Six of Graham's team were over 30 and centre-forward Ray Crawford, whom Graham had rescued from Southern League football and whose goals a decade earlier had led Ipswich to their only League title, was 34. Graham, formerly in charge at Leyton

---

[2] Irwin, p. 237.
[3] Butler, *The Illustrated History of the F.A. Cup*, p. 236.

Orient and Walsall, certainly didn't lack confidence. After all, Colchester had never lost to a First Division team at Layer Road and, though his side would face probably the best team in Europe at the time, his team talks exuded common sense – 'we mustn't be frightened. We must take it in our stride. No nerves, no tension. Just relax. And you know what. I think we can win' – and were leavened with an endearing bravado, when he swore that if his side won, he would climb the walls of Colchester Castle.

'Emerging from the industrial grime into a tiny Colchester stadium lit by sunshine, surrounded by gently swaying trees, its field a luxuriant green,'[4] most of the 16,000 fans who crammed into Layer Road that Saturday had, if truth were told, come out of a sense of grudging admiration, to see a potentially great team cruise to their inevitable victory. They hardly expected a real contest. But they got one. Led by Ray Crawford, Colchester gambled on all-out attack, with Colchester's two Johns, Kurila and Gilchrist, detailed to shadow Allan Clarke and Johnny Giles wherever they went – 'if they went to the toilet I wanted my two men there as well,'[5] said Graham. 'He was really clever,' said Crawford later. 'He knew Leeds liked to play the ball around on wide open spaces and he made our tight pitch feel even smaller by placing chairs and benches around the edges.'

The Oystermen tore into Leeds and for the first hour the spectators were joined by the Leeds defence. Don Revie's side, famous for their ability to 'win ugly', came up against a spirit and experience which on the day would not be denied. There was another factor, too. 'We knew', said Crawford, 'that their goalkeeper, Gary Sprake, was going through a bad time. So we decided to bombard him with crosses' – and after 18 minutes Sprake flapped at a free kick floated in from the left by winger Brian Lewis. Crawford, 'still blessed with the physical presence to match anything Norman Hunter and Jack Charlton could throw at him (and sideburns to die for),'[6] put the home side ahead, leaping unchallenged at the far post to nod in.

Ten minutes later the crowd's euphoria became incredulity. There seemed little danger as Leeds full-back Paul Reaney and Crawford stumbled together on a loose ball, which rebounded off Reaney's back. Lying flat, and swinging a trailing left leg, the striker hooked the ball home via a post. 'The funny

---

[4] Brian Glanville, *Sunday Times*, February 14, 1971.
[5] Lloyd and Holt, p. 255.
[6] Steve Morgan, *FourFourTwo*, January 2007.

thing was that I had always scored goals against Jack Charlton. I really fancied myself to score here – and I'd managed a couple.'

Revie's half-time pearls of wisdom must have fallen on ears deafened by the Layer Road roars. Colchester emerged after the break playing inspired football and within ten minutes an exploratory high lob by Lewis downfield saw the ball bounce comfortably between Sprake and Reaney. It was case of 'After you, Claude', a courtesy not generally associated with Leeds's defence, and, as they debated whose ball it was, Dave Simmons swept through to head past Sprake. Brian Glanville painted a vivid picture: 'Charlton stood, hands dejectedly on hips, like a man contemplating the abyss.'[7] The Division Four no-hopers stood on the threshold of history.

In a last desperate throw of the dice, Revie dropped Clarke deep and pushed Irish midfield general Johnny Giles into attack. At last the visitors began to play the cultured football they were famous for. Colchester's veterans, after an hour of non-stop harrying and chasing, naturally enough began to tire and within five minutes a preoccupied Colchester defence allowed Hunter to head home Lorimer's corner. Then, with 12 minutes to go, Giles nabbed a second. A gambling man would have put good money on a draw but, in an anxious finish, 'Grand-dad's Army' found another hero in goalkeeper Graham Smith. Mick Jones's powerful header from a Lorimer cross seemed like the equaliser but Smith pulled off a stunning reflex save from close range.

Colchester had deserved their victory in one of the FA Cup's most prodigious acts of giant-slaying. On the small playing area at Layer Road, Leeds 'never got their passing game going', said Crawford, 'until about the last 20 minutes when we couldn't get the ball off them'. Geoffrey Green, the distinguished football correspondent of *The Times*, described how the inspirational Brian Lewis switched wings to confuse Reaney and Cooper, how Gilchrist 'reduced Giles to a mere name in the programme' and how Crawford and Simmons rendered Jack Charlton 'a dithering novice'. On the other hand, England's World Cup-winning centre-half remembers there being 'virtually no grass on the ground and the pitch was very bumpy: what we call a great leveller'. Nonsense, retorts Crawford. 'They just never got used to the pitch – it was a fantastic playing surface.'

Colchester's Cup bandwagon rolled on into Round Six with a trip to Goodison Park, where the wheels well and truly came off. Howard Kendall

---

[7] Glanville, *Sunday Times*, February 14, 1971.

scored a couple, and Alan Ball, Jimmy Husband and Joe Royle also made the score sheet in a comprehensive 5–0 home win. However, the 53,028 crowd generated £26,000 and, for a Fourth Division side, their one-third share was something of a bounty.

Layer Road is one of football's oldest grounds and the locals know their history. 'There are still photographs of the game up in the bars and lounges at the club,' Karl Duguid, the present-day captain and longest-serving player, said. 'It is good for the history books but it is not something that affects the lads. It is left to the historians and the people who have been around the club for a long time. It was a great achievement, but it's in the past.' Now, the Oystermen are looking to the future. In 2000 Colchester United announced plans to move to a new 10,000-capacity all-seater community stadium at Cuckoo Farm. It was given the go-ahead by Colchester Borough Council on November 13, 2006, and on April 26, 2008, the last League game at the old ground saw the Oystermen go down 1–0 to a Stoke City side on the verge of the Premiership.

However, the daily reminders around the club mean that February 13, 1971 will never be forgotten nor, in parts of Yorkshire, forgiven. On that famous day, Dick Graham's 'Grand-dad's Army' fixed their bayonets and Ray Crawford, who had been a National Serviceman in Malaya and had twice been capped by England, led the charge. Yet Colchester's success belonged, most of all, to their manager Dick Graham, who knew how to assemble a team which proved to be greater than the sum of its parts.

An idiosyncratic man of football, Graham could also keep a promise. A few days later, he scaled the walls of Colchester Castle.

COLCHESTER UNITED: Smith, Hall, Cram, Gilchrist, Garvey, Kurila, Lewis, Simmons, Mahon, Crawford, Gibbs
LEEDS UNITED: Sprake, Cooper, Reaney, Charlton, Hunter, Lorimer, Clark. Jones, Giles, Madeley

24

HEREFORD UNITED 2, NEWCASTLE UNITED 1

FA Cup, Round Three, February 5, 1972

'The goals made such a difference to the way this game went.' This and countless other 'Mottyisms', as well as his obsessive penchant for statistics and a nice line in sheepskin coats, have endeared the BBC's long-serving commentator to his listeners for over three decades. John Motson is no more of course (at least, not on a regular basis) and he will be sorely missed: for everyone who watches football can 'do' Motson saying 'Extraordinary!' in an incredulous voice, though none can do him so well as Alistair McGowan.

The son of a Methodist minister, 'Motty' first joined the BBC in 1968, following stints as a reporter on the *Barnet Press* and *Sheffield Morning Telegraph*, before joining Radio 2. When he went to cover a much-postponed FA Cup replay between non-League Hereford United and First Division Newcastle in February 1972, his best hope was a five-minute segment at the bottom of the show following the two main games. But the startling events at Edgar Street that afternoon ensured that it was 'the breakthrough game for me', as he once told BBC Sport. 'Sam Leitch must have thought I did all right because I got a contract soon after that. It showed people I could cope with the big game.'

And it *was* a big game. For huge numbers of football fans, the Third Round of the FA Cup is the most eagerly awaited day in the football calendar, especially, according to Colin Irwin, 'if you are a part-time team of bakers and candlestick makers who've clawed your way through 28 qualifying

[1] Irwin, p. 96.

rounds, waded through pitched battles on glorified public parks, had punch-ups with burly blacksmiths and won penalty shoot-outs 15–14 in fading light because you didn't have a florin to feed the meter to turn the flood-lights on.'

Hereford United weren't quite as downmarket as that, but in 1972 they were still a Southern League club less than half a century old, having been formed in June 1924 by the amalgamation of two local sides, St Martin's and RAOC, playing originally in the Birmingham Combination League, joining the Southern League in 1939.

The club's ground at Edgar Street, on the A49 close to the city centre, had been used as a sports field, for athletics and amateur football, since the late nineteenth century. Until the late 1960s, the standing areas on either side of the Merton Stand were known as the 'Cowsheds' and, traditionally, the club's most vocal supporters populated a terrace called the 'Meadow End'. Both of these names allude to an industry for which the city is known throughout the world, for it is surrounded by rich pastures grazed by Hereford cattle, now the cornerstone of the beef economy in every cattle-raising country. The Hereford is founded on the draught ox descended from the small red cattle of Roman Britain and from a large Welsh breed once widespread along the border of England and Wales. The characteristics of the modern Hereford were developed by a group of breeders more than two hundred years ago and today the breed produces some of the finest beef in the world. Almost inevitably, 'The Bulls' became the nick-name of the football club and one of the club's endearing – and enduring – traditions is that a bull is led around the ground before important matches. Another equally rustic tradition before kick-off in Cup games was for some fans to dribble a swede to the Meadow End and score a goal for good luck.

These charmingly bucolic customs worked a couple of times in the 1950s. In November 1953 the Bulls beat Third Division Exeter City 2–0 in a First Round replay before going out at Wigan, and four years later victories over in Heanor Town and Newport (Isle of Wight) set up a Second Round tie with Third Division (South) side Queen's Park Rangers. An Edgar Street crowd of 10,131 saw United storm to an incredible 6–1 win, which still stands as the winning margin for a non-League club against a League club in the FA Cup.

The ceremony of the swede worked its magic again in the 1965/66 season, with victory over Third Division leaders Millwall, when the Bulls did for the Lions through a goal from centre-forward Ron Fogg. The following year the club shook the football world by signing one of the greatest players in the history of the game – the 'Gentle Giant', John Charles, who became manager in 1967. He stayed four years before the former Arsenal and Nottingham Forest midfielder Colin Addison was appointed player–manager in October 1971. One of Addison's first duties was to prepare the side for the FA Cup Fourth Qualifying Round tie against Cheltenham Town and a 2–1 win at Edgar Street secured a place in the First Round proper for the twenty-first successive season. Five games over the next month saw the Bulls make heavy weather of their Cup campaign. Firstly, a hard-fought draw at Kings Lynn was followed by a 1–0 win in the replay and a Second Round tie against Fourth Division Northampton at Edgar Street. Nearly ten thousand fans saw a goal-less draw and three days later goals from Tyler and Owen clinched a 2–2 draw in the replay. Five days before Christmas, United, a goal down with seconds to go in the second replay at the Hawthorns, seemed to be heading for the Cup exit door. But Ken Mallender's strike from 20 yards threw the Bulls a lifeline, then Dudley Tyler scored an extra-time winner and for the first time in six years, and for only the third time in their history, Hereford had won a place in the Third Round, where they were handed a glamour tie against Newcastle United – First Division giants and Cup legends of the 50s – at St James's Park.

January 1972 was in the depths of a bleak winter. The miners were on strike and severe weather over the traditional weekend of Third Round matches meant most of the games were postponed till the following week. However, such was the big freeze in the North-East that Hereford could not take the field at St James' Park till the evening of Monday 24. The Bulls made up for lost time: they were awarded a free kick straight from the kick-off and Brian Owen stole into the box past the end of the Newcastle defence to put the ball past Ian McFaul. For the five thousand Hereford supporters in the crowd, it was a dream start, for, though their team were going well in the Southern League, there were 83 League places between the two and Newcastle manager Joe Harvey had put together their best side for years, led by the bandy-legged but powerful striker, Malcolm Macdonald.

The home side, clear favourites with six internationals in their line-up, quickly overcame the early shock and within 13 minutes, had brought sighs of relief to the Toon Army. Macdonald equalised from the penalty spot and John Tudor made it 2–1. He blotted his copybook later when he managed to scoop the ball over the bar from two yards. The Bulls came more and more into the game and, as Ronnie Radford, who was to have his own moment of glory 12 days later said, 'We came close to winning up there.' With a few minutes to go, Hereford player–manager Colin Addison latched on to the ball 25 yards out and spanked it into the top corner to earn his side a remarkable draw. It was no more than the non-Leaguers deserved. Radford recalls, 'Newcastle boss Joe Harvey admitted we'd been the better side. The Newcastle crowd were fabulous. They applauded our approach work and cheered us off at the end.'

The continuing dreadful weather – and three postponed dates – meant the replay took place on February 5th, the day of the Fourth Round. Newcastle had travelled down to Herefordshire on three separate occasions, in the end staying for 10 days in a hotel in Worcester, training on the concrete at a nearby RAF station and even on the scarcely less wet Worcester racecourse. Now, 'the thaw had reduced the pitch to the consistency of chocolate blancmange.'[2]

By early February the miners' strike was beginning to bite, factories were laying off workers because of power shortages and the mood of the nation was gloomy, but in spite of – or perhaps because of – the general air of despondency and the state of the pitch, the pre-match atmosphere was unprecedented. It was as if the local fans and the football world at large were desperate for something – anything – to cheer themselves up. 'Press attention was huge, as was the demand for tickets,' Radford remembers. 'We wanted to do something for the town as the club's main ambition was to gain League status and the Newcastle match was our chance to show we were a decent side.' Ricky George, another United player destined to become a hero before the day was out, claims that 'it would have been ridiculous to say that we were confident but we were definitely feeling in better shape than we were before the original fixture.'

Once the Saxon capital of West Mercia, Hereford derives its name from the Anglo-Saxon 'here', referring to army or formation of soldiers, and the 'ford' coming from an earlier Roman term for an area of river that soldiers could cross in close formation. In essence, Hereford was a place where a body of armed men could cross the Wye – and early that bleak February,

---

[2] Lloyd and Holt, p. 260.

Joe Harvey's men marched down from the Tyne to do battle, to put the non-League upstarts in their place.

So confident were they of victory that Malcolm Macdonald was said[3] to have bragged that he would beat Ted MacDougall's record[4] and score ten goals against Hereford in the replay. Ronnie Radford recalls that Colin Addison 'stuck Macdonald's comments on the dressing room wall to gee us up but all the Newcastle players were sportsmen. Malcolm never forgot his roots: only four years before, he and our centre-forward Billy Meadows had played together at Tonbridge.'

On the Saturday afternoon Edgar Street was packed to its 14,313 capacity and outside the ground spectators perched in trees and clung on to floodlight pylons. On a very muddy surface which quickly deteriorated into a quagmire, they saw an awful game in dire conditions. Newcastle made the better start, forcing six corners and twice striking the bar. Macdonald should have scored on two occasions but Fred Potter in the Hereford goal made some astounding saves. Newcastle had done everything but score and it was not, as Motty once remarked, 'the first half you might have expected, even though the score might suggest that it was'. But after the interval, the ex-Gunner Addison was controlling midfield while McLaughlin kept Macdonald under control and as the second half wore on without a goal, 'Newcastle's confidence began to wane . . . Hereford took charge and it was against the run of play that Macdonald put the Magpies ahead. . .'[5] In the 82nd minute, Viv Busby crossed from the right and Macdonald rose to head home at the far post. The goal seemed to have asserted the natural order and Motson's positive commentary assumed a more solemn air, as he adopted his 'the minnows' brave effort but. . .' approach.

So, on a pitch like a rice paddy, United's part-timers were trailing, dropping like flies with cramp, though *The Times* correspondent noted one Hereford player shaking his fists and clapping his hands to gee up his teammates as they trooped back to the centre circle.'[6] That man was Ronnie Radford and four minutes from time came an FA Cup moment that is still shown all over the world.

When Colin Addison brought the ball out of defence, it ran loose to

---

[3] He subsequently denied having said it.
[4] See Bournemouth v Manchester United, pp. 245–251.
[5] *Daily Telegraph Chronicle*, p. 136.
[6] Tibballs, p. 139.

Radford, who played a one-two with Owen and, breaking a tackle, he strode on through the mud and let fly from 35 yards. His unstoppable drive flashed into the top corner of the net past the Magpies' Northern Irish international keeper, Ian McFaul.

Radford's arms were aloft before it hit the net. It was only his third goal for the club. A journeyman footballer in his first season with Hereford following an unremarkable spell with Newport County, he told the press later, 'I liked to have a go from a long way out. I never got too many because I played fairly deep. Time was moving on when the ball sat up just right for me. In most cases, shots like that ended up in the car park, but I caught it just right.' Spectators in the trees overlooking the ground risked death as they saluted Radford's screamer. 'A pre-pubescent tide of parkas and flares swarmed over the pitch doubtless ensuring a maternal ticking off for getting their shoes muddy.'[7] For the scorer himself, 'to see the joy on the faces of all the kids streaming onto the pitch meant most of all to me.' It took several minutes to herd the youngsters back to the terraces behind the goal so that the game could be played out with a delirious Meadow End singing 'You'll never walk alone'.

At the final whistle the Newcastle stars, who had been comfortable throughout the game and were playing by numbers, waiting for the final whistle, looked at each other in disbelief. This was not in the script and in atrocious conditions they had to bestir themselves for extra time.

After 12 uneventful minutes in the extra period, the Bulls felt the benefit of a fresh – or even a complete – pair of legs. Full-back Roger Griffiths, the only Hereford-born player in the home side, had been replaced at full-time by Ricky George. It later transpired that he had played nearly 80 minutes with a fracture of the left fibula. On 102 minutes, says George, 'Dudley Tyler knocked the ball in and I got it on the edge of the penalty area. I knew Newcastle defender Bobby Moncur was behind me so I turned to my left into the box. I got the ball under control, expecting a challenge.' But none came and ghosting round a statuesque Newcastle defence, George slid a shot across goal. 'Moncur tried to block the shot but it went under his foot inside the far post. I think it may have unsighted goalkeeper McFaul.'

Once more the parka-clad kids from the Meadow End swarmed on to the pitch and, when they were cleared, for the first time in the match

---

[7] Lloyd and Holt, p. 261.

Newcastle showed some urgency. But 18 minutes later the Magpies, proud invaders from the North-East, were out.

The Bulls' celebrations had only just begun to wind down when, four days later, with the Government declaring a state of emergency and BBC local radio stations warning of domestic power cuts, Colin Addison's men faced another First Division side, West Ham United, at Edgar Street in Round Four.

To the delight of the players, their former manager, the legendary John Charles, had appeared in the dressing room after their historic win and, as Ronnie Radford and Billy Meadows arrived at Edgar Street for the West Ham game, 'there was Charlo, camelhair coat, steely grey hair, permanent suntan and wearing that broad grin. He was resting against the bonnet of his car and showed us an envelope. It read: "Mr John Charles, two tickets, £2 to pay."' Both Radford and Meadows stared at him in disbelief as, in a demonstration of the humility of the truly great, Charles said, 'I wouldn't mind, but I've only got 30 bob on me.'

The Hammers' side that afternoon included winger Harry Redknapp, now the manager of Tottenham. He especially remembers the Bulls' centre-forward Billy Meadows. 'He liked to get stuck in. Right from the start Meadows tried to wind Mooro[8] up, giving him the verbals about every-thing under the sun. Absolutely diabolical remarks. To be honest he drove Mooro mad but Bobby didn't bite.' Nor did his teammates that day, for Hereford secured a creditable goal-less draw.

Such was the interest in the replay at Upton Park that Hereford faced the unusual problem for a non-League club of forged tickets. In any event, the crowd of 42,211 was only 111 short of West Ham's ground record. As for the match, Meadows got his own back on the England skipper, scoring a consolation goal for Hereford, but the Hammers won the tie at a canter, with World Cup hero Geoff Hurst scoring a hat-trick.

The Cup run arguably cost Hereford the Southern League title that season but in the days of election and re-election, says Ricky George, 'a club didn't necessarily have to win the league they were playing in to gain promotion to the Football League, even though it was a rare occurrence for anyone to go up.' Though United finished runners-up, 'our FA Cup run was tremendously significant in the votes we received from Football League

---

[8] Bobby Moore, West Ham and England captain.

clubs'. They won the vote in extra-time as well, for after they and Barrow had tied in the first ballot Hereford won the second and took Barrow's place in Division Four.

They have been up and down and, for nine years, out of the lower divisions ever since, but their win that February afternoon encapsulated everything that the Cup has come to mean for the English football fan. The awful pitch, the tiny, ramshackle ground and the delirious home supporters exemplified the romantic image of a giant-killing – and what a giant! It was the first time a non-League side had beaten a First Division club since 1949.[9]

Finally, it was about a goal – and even if the nation saw it only from the comfort of their armchairs on *Match of the Day* that evening, it went on to win the programme's 'Goal of the Season' competition. Each January, when the Third Round comes round again, grainy images of Ronnie Radford's staggering strike still light up the TV and, for the scorer, the memory never palls. 'This was the most wonderful day,' he says. 'And when I see the videos, with the expressions of delight on those kids' faces as they run on the pitch on the final whistle, it still makes me feel emotional.'

His wonderful goal and the joyous pitch invasion that followed have almost come to define the FA Cup. As Motty said at the time, 'Tudor's gone down for Newcastle. Radford again. What a goal! What a goal! Radford the scorer, Ronnie Radford!' Or, as he said years later, 'That shot might not have been as good as it might have been'.

HEREFORD UNITED: Potter, Griffiths (George), Mallender, Jones, McLaughlin, Addison, Gough, Tyler, Meadows, Owen, Radford
NEWCASTLE UNITED: McFaul, Craig, Clark, Nattrass, Howard, Moncur, Busby, Green, Macdonald, Tudor, Hibbitt

---

[9] See Yeovil Town v Sunderland, pp. 59–66.

25

SUNDERLAND 1, LEEDS UNITED 0

FA Cup Final, May 5, 1973

What's in a name? That which we call a rose
By any other name would smell as sweet.[1]

Or a nickname, for that matter. And it doesn't mean the name's been nicked. Originally it was an *eke-name*, an 'extra' name from the Old English *eac*. It became 'nickname' in the 1400s through mishearing and mis-writing.[2] Almost every football club has a nickname, chosen, according to Peter Seddon, to 'convey a sense of identity, individuality and intimacy.'[3] These names celebrate local crafts and occupations and aim to imbue their teams with unique qualities. Shipbuilding vanished from Wearside 20 years ago yet Sunderland FC has as one of its nicknames 'The Mackems', a term which refers to the accent, dialect and people of Wearside, or more specifically Sunderland. In the North-East, a centuries-old gulf in wealth and social status between Wearside and Tyneside gave rise to the 'Mackems' because the Sunderland shipyards 'make 'em' (ships) whereas Newcastle are 'The Tackems', where they 'take 'em' to be fitted out.

Sunderland, not content with having one of football's most distinctive nicknames, have another, also unique. Since the 1960s the Sunderland Supporters' Association have had the black cat as their emblem and today club mascots Samson and Delilah entertain the home supporters every match day as Roy Keane's 'Black Cats' take on their Premiership rivals. In

---

[1] *Romeo and Juliet*, Act 2, Scene 2.
[2] The process called 'metanalysis', which also gave us "newt"' from "an ewt" and in reverse "a napron" and "a nadder".' (Seddon, p. 203).
[3] Seddon, p. 204.

1805 a gun battery on the River Wear was renamed the 'Black Cat' after men manning it heard a mysterious 'miaow' from a yowling black cat: a century later a black cat was pictured sitting on a football next to Chairman F.W. Taylor and, when Sunderland came from behind to beat Preston in the 1937 Cup Final, a black kitten owned by 12-year old Billy Morris was believed to bring Sunderland luck as it sat in his pocket at Wembley. The place of the black cat as a club legend was assured.

Whether James Allan, an Ayrshire graduate of Glasgow University and a Sunderland-based schoolteacher had a black cat we shall never know but it is to him that the football club owes its origin. In October 1879 Allan called a meeting of schoolteachers from Hendon Board School and formed the Sunderland & District Teachers' Association Football Club. In the following year non-teachers were allowed to join and the name was changed to Sunderland AFC.

A decade later Sunderland were elected to the Football League, kept afloat by money from shipbuilding and coal, but once elected to the League the club needed a bigger ground. The architect was Scottish engineer Archibald Leitch, whose work defined the nature of the early industrial football stadium and on September 10, 1898 Roker Park was officially opened by the Marquess of Londonderry, accompanied by marching pipe bands and a flotilla of steamboats on the Wear.

From that day Sunderland became one of the giants of the early years in the Football League, where they remained for 68 years. The Mackems were the first club to win three championships and made it five on the eve of the Great War. Following the Second World War, the club played to massive crowds at Roker Park until, after a second[4] illegal payments scandal in 1957, they slid down the League and a year later were relegated to the Second Division for the first time. They clawed their way back up in 1964 but in January, 1973, when Sunderland set off on the FA Cup trail yet again, they lay third from bottom in the Second Division, having plunged down again in 1970 under Alan Brown. He was sacked in November 1972 and the former Newcastle half-back Bob Stokoe was lured back to his native North-East from a reasonably promising season at Blackpool. At once, Stokoe's passion, hard work and infectious enthusiasm began lifting the pall of mediocrity from the once-great Wearside club. Renowned throughout the game

---

[4] In 1903/04, six directors were suspended after an investigation into bribery.

for his integrity and competitive endeavour rather than innate grace and skill, he began to get the best out of players like centre-half Dave Watson and forwards Dennis Tueart and Billy Hughes.

Sunderland's long and winding road to Wembley began with a routine 2–0 defeat of Notts County in a replay at Roker Park and another replay at Elm Park saw them cruise past Reading in Round Four. The journey became no easier in the Fifth Round as they pondered a clash with Cup favourites Manchester City at Maine Road. Goals from Micky Horswill and Billy Hughes earned yet another replay where, in a highly charged night at Roker Park, they overcame City 3–1 with two more from Hughes. In the quarter-final, Luton Town travelled to Wearside on St Patrick's Day having beaten Sunderland at Kenilworth Road in the League the week before and the Roker Park crowd of over fifty-three thousand witnessed the nostalgic sight of young children being passed down over the heads of those in front to take their positions at the front of the Roker End.

In the first half the Mackems pounded a resolute Luton defence but ten minutes after half-time Dave Watson powered home a fierce header from Bobby Kerr's in-swinging corner. Eight minutes from the end Billy Hughes's corner from the left was headed on by Richie Pitt and Newcastle-born Ron Guthrie swept the ball wide of the keeper to score his first goal for Sunderland and put them into the semi-final against Arsenal.

Sunderland's odds on lifting the famous old trophy tumbled to just 12 to 1 and, in a welter of excitement, the Black Cats' bandwagon trundled on to Hillsborough, where its momentum proved unstoppable. Roared on by a Kop heaving with Rokerites, Sunderland stormed into a 2–0 lead just past the hour. Vic Halom in the first half and, with his fourth goal of the campaign, Billy Hughes, heading past Bob Wilson in the 64th minute, shocked the Gunners, who gained a consolation six minutes from time when Jim Montgomery could not get his fingertips to Charlie George's low drive. At the final whistle, the Roker faithful refused to move until Bob Stokoe took their salute, and his unashamed tears as he returned to the dressing room captured the imagination of the nation. In the town itself, with the Wembley final a month away, he became the Messiah, on the verge of leading his disciples to the Promised Land, unvisited since 1937, and the team's success energised local industry, with ships being painted in the team colours and productivity booming in the factories.

The 1973 FA Cup Final, in Wembley's 50th anniversary year would be fought out between Leeds United, the Cup holders, and the totally unfancied Black Cats. Leeds, hardened and honed in the crucible of the First Division and in the final of the European Cup-Winners' Cup, were a supremely efficient unit, containing ten international players, and were playing in their third final in four years. No Second Division side had won the Cup since West Bromwich Albion in 1931 and, while few football pundits gave Sunderland anything but the remotest chance of winning, the Wearside fans rode to Wembley on a wave of euphoria. Manager Bob Stokoe, extrovert and lively, waged a brilliant psychological war on Leeds boss Don Revie, who managed to look overwrought and beleaguered even on a good day. By the day of the final, Stokoe's men were relaxed but ready to scrap for their lives whereas Leeds were the side with everything to lose.

The turf was wet and the game started in heavy rain. Sunderland set their stall out from the kick-off, tackling fiercely and with an uncompromising resolution. In the first minute England Under-18 defender Ritchie Pitt left Allan Clarke, the Leeds striker, limping heavily after a clumsy challenge. 'Arthur Cox had told me before kick-off', says Pitt, 'that we needed to show them we were no pushovers and while Mick Jones was a tough lad who'd bounce back, we might be able to intimidate Clarke and keep him out of our penalty box.' Sunderland's quick interceptions in midfield disturbed Leeds' customary composure and their usually accurate passes were off target. As the first half settled into a rhythm, however, Leeds, prompted by Johnny Giles' insistent probing, began to threaten but Sunderland's defence, led by the commanding figure of Dave Watson, snuffed out the fearsome striking power of Jones, Lorimer and 'Sniffer' Clarke, the archetypal opportunist. At the other end, Hughes and Halom worked tirelessly and behind them, in midfield, Horswill drove himself forward, shooting at every opportunity. They found the obdurate Leeds defence in top form, with Madeley and Hunter displaying their characteristic blend of ruggedness and positive thinking.

Then came the first of two incidents which settled the fate of the Cup. In the 31st minute Leeds keeper David Harvey tipped a long shot from Sunderland skipper Bobby Kerr over the bar. Dave Watson just failed to get his head to Billy Hughes' corner but Vic Halom, between two defenders, chested it down and the ball flew out to Ian Porterfield. With the utmost calm, the former Raith Rover killed the ball on his left thigh and, pirouetting like a ballerina, cracked the ball into the roof of the net with his right foot from 12 yards.

Stung by their opponents' temerity in breaching their citadel, the holders fought back and launched a powerful assault just before half-time. Time and again, however, they were repelled by a Sunderland defence in which Dave Watson stood like a granite cliff, keeping the Yorkshire invaders at bay. Behind him, as Leeds strove with a growing sense of desperation throughout the second half, Sunderland's goalkeeper, Jim Montgomery, defied them with a string of fine saves until the decisive moment of the game.

Twenty minutes from the end Leeds, still a goal down, were dominating play and pounding the Sunderland goal: an equaliser seemed inevitable. When Mick Jones laid the ball back for full-back Paul Reaney to centre from the right, Trevor Cherry, who had ghosted in from the blind side, met the ball with a firm diving header across goal which produced an instinctive reflex save at full-stretch from Montgomery. The Sunderland goalkeeper palmed it away with his left hand – but only as far as Peter Lorimer's formidable right foot, seven yards out with the goal at his mercy. Instead of bursting the net with his customary howitzer, Lorimer chose to side-foot the ball. 'I was shielding Jones,' recalls Richie Pitt, 'but when I turned and saw Lorimer I thought, "Oh, no, they've scored".' On ITV Jimmy Hill announced the equaliser but, back-pedalling, Montgomery pivoted up from his left elbow and diverted the ball on to the underside of the crossbar for Dick Malone to scramble clear. 'Cherry, still prone, wagged a disconsolate heel, but the ball was gone, and with it Leeds' belief.'[5]

Even after a replay, Hill could not fathom what had taken place and only on a third viewing did he finally accept that it was 'an incredible save' one that has often been compared with that made by England's Gordon Banks in the 1970 World Cup match with Brazil. Many observers believe it to be the greatest save at Wembley, and some even rate it the greatest save of all time. Montgomery himself remembers:

The ball coming in from the right, Trevor Cherry headed it and I dived to knock it out. Then I saw a Leeds shirt thundering in – I didn't realise it was Peter Lorimer at the time – and I knew I had to get up quickly so I just threw myself across the goal and tried to cover as much space as possible and the ball hit my hand, went up on to

[5] Jonathan Wilson, *FourFourTwo*.

the bar and Dick Malone cleared. I didn't think it was anything special and we just got on with the game – but I knew the Cup was ours when I saved that one from Lorimer.

As for the holders, in that moment they realised they were not destined to retain their trophy. They sensed their chance had gone, and the remaining 20 minutes were a frenzy of incoherent raids and panicky clearances as Montgomery made further saves from Bremner, Yorath and Cherry. Amid almost intolerable tension, Leeds skipper Billy Bremner beat Watson and went down spectacularly in the penalty area only to be ignored by referee Ken Bums. This reprieve gave the Black Cats fresh heart: through Horswill and Porterfield they began to regain midfield control and, though their efforts in the first hour began to sap their stamina, Sunderland held out. Their attacking spirit burned bright and the Black Cats very nearly scored again in the final minutes, Harvey deflecting a shot from Vic Halom round the post.

When Ken Burns signalled the end of a remarkable game he was drowned in the whistles of thousands of incredulous Wearsiders. Their tumult of bewildered celebration was climaxed by Bob Stokoe's one-man pitch invasion. Clad in his scruffy beige raincoat, red acrylic tracksuit and trademark pork-pie hat perched on his balding head, he leapt from the bench and accelerated across the Wembley turf in an attempt to cuddle Montgomery. 'It's all a bit hazy and I've no idea what Bob said to me at the end. When he hugged me, I don't think it was just for those saves in the second half. It was also for some important saves I'd made in earlier rounds – against Manchester City and Arsenal in particular. As we went up the steps to collect the trophy I can just remember the deafening noise from the Sunderland fans.'

Nearby, in unforgettably stark contrast, stood Revie, grey with shock and stress, unable to comprehend such a devastating reverse. Sunderland had not only provided Wembley with possibly the greatest-ever Cup Final upset, their victory underlined the value of flair, imagination and spirit over detached efficiency. It was also a notable triumph for captain Bobby Kerr, who at 5 feet 4½ was the smallest man on the field, the team's 'little general'. Towards the end Kerr's nerves were jangling: 'The ball was pinging around our area and I was convinced we had another four or five minutes to hold on. As Ken Burns ran by, I asked him how long there was to go. He just gave me a big grin and said. "It's all right, Bobby, you've won it." Twenty seconds later he blew the whistle and we had.'

Twenty years later, in the early 1990s, the Taylor Report required all top-flight clubs to upgrade their grounds to all-seater stadiums. This would have restricted the dilapidated Roker Park to a much smaller capacity than the sort of attendances that Sunderland could expect. The site was too confined for expansion, and in 1997 Roker Park was demolished after being the home of Sunderland for 99 years and the Black Cats moved to the Stadium of Light on the site of the closed Monkwearmouth Colliery. As Humphrey Lyttelton kindly observed, 'That name was borrowed from Benfica's stadium in Lisbon, because of the obvious similarity between the two cities: Lisbon is a coastal city of constant sunshine, boasting Baroque and Romanesque architecture, whose cultural heritage makes it a Mecca for writers and artists, and Sunderland is also on the coast.'[6]

Within days of the Cup win, Sunderland finished the season a respectable sixth place in Division Two: Stokoe's magic touch had taken from relegation candidates to Cup-winners. It is for May 5th at Wembley, however, that his name is carved into Sunderland folklore and his memory honoured by the erection of an 8½-foot-high bronze statue, complete with pork pie hat, which was unveiled at the Stadium of Light in July 2006. The statue was unveiled by Bob's daughter Karen Craven, and a number of fans and ex-players, including Jimmy Montgomery, Bobby Kerr, Dick Malone and Richie Pitt from the 1973 team, were present. Stokoe's unique achievement was to transcend the traditional rivalry between Tyne and Wear. These are passionate football areas whose League clubs are still based in their local community: in 2002, still 80 per cent of the Mackems' season ticket holders were born locally. Their club has a long and proud history, with six League Championships and two Cup wins – but none is remembered with more pride than the day they humbled the mighty Leeds and Porterfield and Montgomery became instant legends.

SUNDERLAND: Montgomery, Malone, Guthrie, Horswill, Watson, Pitt, Kerr, Hughes, Halom, Porterfield, Tueart
LEEDS UNITED: Harvey, Reaney, Cherry, Bremner, Madeley, Hunter, Lorimer, Clarke, Jones, Giles, Gray

---

[6] Pattinson, p. 197.

26

BRIGHTON AND HOVE ALBION 0, WALTON AND HERSHAM 4

FA Cup First Round replay, November 28th, 1973

On the opening day of the 1958/59 season, Brighton and Hove Albion took the field against Middlesbrough at Ayresome Park for their first-ever game in Division Two. It was an ignominious debut: they were thrashed 9–0, with one Brian Clough helping himself to five of the goals. Fourteen years later, the paths of the flamboyant striker and the Seagulls would cross again.

Clough eventually netted 204 goals in 222 games for the Teesside club before his promising career, which had already won him two England caps, was cruelly cut short by a knee injury on Boxing Day, 1962. He stayed in the North-East to become boss at Fourth Division Hartlepool United at the age of 30, appointing Peter Taylor as his assistant, a coaching partnership that would be the key to his future successes. In 1967 he became manager of Derby County, establishing a reputation as the most innovative and self-motivated manager in England. Clough's controversial methods became legendary, demonstrating either his obsessive madness or his drive, determination and high standards, depending on your point of view. He could undoubtedly get the best out of his players. He said once, talking about his team meetings, 'We talk about it for 20 minutes and then we decide I was right.' Despite – or perhaps because of – this utter self-belief, Clough and Taylor were hugely successful, leading the Rams to their first League Championship in 1972 and to the semi-finals of the European Cup in 1973.

For their part, over the intervening years, Brighton had undergone two relegations and two promotions and by October 1973, with gates dipping below 6,000, they languished in the bottom four of the Third Division. Enough was enough and when Pat Saward was sacked at the end of the month, the chairman, Mike Bamber, had his eyes set on a stunning coup.

On October 15, Clough and Taylor resigned from First Division Derby County, chiefly as a result of a long-standing disagreement with the club's directors over restrictions placed on Clough's media activities. Following protracted negotiations, involving Bamber's persuasive tongue, his sales talk about the club's potential – plus no mention of the media, the sensational news broke on November 1: Brian Clough and Peter Taylor had signed a five-year contract to manage the Seagulls.

During an overnight stay at the White Hart Hotel in Lewes, the new management team took stock of the Albion squad. Taylor, realising the cupboard was almost bare, decided 'they were dealing with "a bunch of amateurs and layabouts"'. He tried to curb the fans' renewed optimism: 'Forget promotion. Just be happy to avoid relegation.' His point was borne out by Clough's first game in charge, a goal-less home draw with York City, which nonetheless attracted a gate of 16,017, almost 10,000 up on the previous home game.

A good draw at Huddersfield and a sound away win at Walsall steadied the ship, but before the end of the month Clough and Taylor were faced with an awkward trip to the Amateur Cup holders, Walton & Hersham of the Isthmian League, in the First Round of the Cup. A year earlier, Exeter City had gone down 2–1 amid tumultuous scenes at Walton's delightfully named Stompond Lane and the non-Leaguers expected a crowd of around 6,500 to see if the shock win over Exeter was merely a one-hit wonder or whether the Swans could shoot down the Seagulls, who included Barry Bridges, the former Chelsea striker.

The game against Brighton was yet another milestone in the history of Walton and Hersham FC. A football club had been formed in Walton in 1895 and given the town's long association with the Thames and the graceful birds who had lived around Walton Bridge for two hundred years, it was nicknamed 'The Swans'. On the resumption of football in 1945, the club became Walton and Hersham FC, joined the Athenian League in 1950 and finished runners-up in their first season. The semi-final of the Amateur Cup was reached in successive seasons, 1951/52 and 1952/53 and after 15 mundane mid-table years, the appointment of Allen Batsford as manager in 1967 marked a new watershed in the club's history.

At the end of his first season, a splendid victory over the strong Wimbledon side won the Premier Midweek Floodlit League and the Athenian League championship followed in 1969. The Swans reached the FA Cup First Round in the next two years and, on being elected to the Isthmian League in 1971, they finished third in their first season. Then followed the First Round Cup win over Exeter City in November 1972 and the triumph in the FA Amateur Cup Final in April 1973. The trophy had been won without a goal being conceded, a unique record, and Dave Bassett, Willie Smith and Roger Connell, who scored the last-minute goal which beat Slough Town, had all played for the England non-League side.

By the end of the afternoon at Stompond Lane, Clough confessed he was 'very pleased to be still in the Cup. Walton had enough football to keep us occupied. Brian Powney earned his cash today.' The Albion keeper was indeed the man who kept Brighton in the Cup – but after only seven seconds Walton nearly had a fairy-tale start as 'Powney lay flat on his face watching in dismay as the ball snuggled in the back of the net'.[1] Straight from the kick-off, Bassett struck a long ball which beat the defence. Powney, on the edge of his six-yard box, misread the bounce and Perkins dashed in to flick the ball into the net. But to the dismay and anger of the Swans' fans, the whistle blew for a foul: as referee Mr Kew explained afterwards: 'I did not allow a goal because the centre-forward jumped at the goal-keeper.'

After that, the game 'was rent with most ungenteel tones from a district where there are more stockbrokers to the acre than you can shake a stick at'.[2] In a finely balanced first half, Walton's amateurs more than matched Brighton for determination and skill. Batsford had three players marking Peter O'Sullivan, the most skilful player on view, and the visitors created few chances. Once Bloom saved well as Robertson closed in and then clung on to a header from Bridges. For their part Walton forced a fine save from Powney at the foot the post and, just before the interval, Morris, clear on goal, had his shot blocked by the Albion keeper.

Four minutes into the restart Sargent hit a long centre from the right and Perkins' half-volley flew narrowly wide with Powney beaten. Then Brighton's busy keeper had to leap to clutch a powerful drive from Woffinden, the former Albion reserve.

---

[1] *Evening Argus*, November 24, 1973.
[2] *Evening Argus*, November 26, 1973.

Bassett, who was having a blinder as Walton's skipper, hit a left-footer wide from 40 yards, but the visitors seldom matched this kind of adventure. They were misfiring and had neither the ability nor the punch to penetrate the Swans' defence but in the last ten minutes Albion called on their reserves of stamina. Clough's last Cup tie had been the European Cup semi-final with Juventus and, as the November afternoon closed in over this tiny ground in suburban Surrey, he must have felt a frisson of Cup fever again. Pat Hilton half-hit a shot past the post, George Ley rifled a low drive only a foot wide from 25 yards and the same player forced a fine save in the dying minutes.

In the end it was stalemate and as the Swans players struggled to the dressing room through hundreds of milling fans, their faces lined with disappointment, the 'lugubrious countenance of Eric Sykes reflected Walton's feeling'.[3] The celebrated comic reckoned Walton should have won. Clough concurred, 'They did a very good job' – then he asked for a Scotch and water and retired to the dressing room. He knew that his side were lucky but the Brighton paper considered 'Albion should decide the issue in Wednesday's Goldstone replay'.

The atmosphere at the Goldstone that Wednesday afternoon had a surreal edge. The kick-off time of 1.45 was unusual and the crowd of 9,657 oddly subdued. The North Stand, denuded on a school day of its raucous youthful choir, was about as noisy as a seaside bingo hall out of season.

From the first whistle, the Seagulls swooped all over the Swans, whose defence endured incessant pressure. Schoolmaster Russell Perkins, man of the match on Saturday, was left to plough a lone furrow up front. As the visitors weathered this early storm, a mounting sense of apprehension gripped the home fans and in the 20th minute Powney flapped at a corner by Smith, nodded on by Lambert across the Brighton goalmouth. Perkins had got himself goal-side of Norman Gall and, dropping on to his knees as if in a grateful prayer of thanks, headed the simplest of goals.

Walton's moment of joy was short-lived, as for the rest of the half they were subjected to an incessant artillery barrage from the home side, during which Bassett and Edwards threw themselves into the defensive trench warfare with a will.

The pivotal moment of the game came early into the second half when

---

[3] Ibid.

Barry Bridges, veteran of many a Cup battle with Chelsea, stumbled over two feet from the line, just failing to prod the ball past Bloom. It was Albion's best chance and, despite forcing 18 corners, it was as close as they would get all afternoon. Walton had an equally golden opportunity to take the lead just before the hour when Clive Foskett took the ball round Powney but he scuffed his shot, giving Templeman time to clear.

The redemption of Foskett, a 26-year-old joiner who worked at the British Natural History Museum, came straight from 'Roy of the Rovers'. For Seagulls fans it was more like a penny dreadful as the Swans striker hit a hat-trick in the last eight minutes to put the seal on a woeful afternoon. On 82 minutes, Brighton, who had spent much of the second half hammering long balls into the visitors' packed goalmouth, were all caught upfield when Lambert hit a long ball out of defence. Foskett had hared off through the middle before the home defenders had time to turn and, running on to Perkins' precise pass from inside his own half, coolly slid the ball past an onrushing Powney.

Two minutes later, another booming clearance, this time from Woffinden, beat the defence and Powney, charging out once again, found Foskett skipping round him for an easy goal. A minute from time, just because he could, Foskett broke free again. Morris sent him through the middle and he made short work of beating Powney for his hat-trick.

Brighton had capitulated and Brian Clough could only admit: 'Walton were better than us at every aspect of the game – better technique, certainly, and better organization.' The roots of Walton's crushing victory were the clinical ability to take their chances when under pressure themselves and their dogged refusal to concede that full-time footballers might be better, fitter and more skilful than a bunch of engineers, schoolmasters and taxi drivers.

Brighton had more of the game than the visitors but lacked the decisive final pass. They were superior in fitness but Batsford's men soaked up Albion's pressure and had 'men of heart and character, and not a few players who showed a greater desire for the ball when it was obvious somebody was going to be hurt. . .'[4] Men like Foskett, only a substitute at Wembley after a season which brought him 23 goals before Christmas – only to see his goal touch desert him completely. He said afterwards: 'This is the highlight

---

[4] *Evening Argus*, November 29, 1973.

of my career, although nothing can really make up for not playing in the final at Wembley. I was left so much space at the back and I had time to think about all three goals.' For Brighton, further humiliation was heaped on their heads only three days later when the Third Division leaders, Bristol Rovers, won 8–2 at the Goldstone in front of ITV's *The Big Match* cameras.

And Walton? Drawn against Hereford, heroes against Newcastle two years before, they went to Edgar Street and were put in their place, 3–0. The Swans had become ugly ducklings once more.

The following summer Clough moved on to his 44 days at Leeds and then to European Cup glory with Nottingham Forest. At his memorial service in October 2004, he was remembered with poems and music from his favourite singer, Frank Sinatra, of whom he said, 'Frank Sinatra? He met me once.'

Ah, Cloughie, you always did it your way.

BRIGHTON and HOVE ALBION: Powney, Templeman, Ley, Spearritt, Gall, Piper, Bridges, Howell, Hilton, Robertson, O'Sullivan
WALTON and HERSHAM: Bloom, Sargent, Lambert, Donaldson, Edwards, Bassett, Woffinden, Smith, Perkins, Foskett, Morris

27

BRIGHTON AND HOVE ALBION 0, LEATHERHEAD 1

FA Cup, Round Three, January 4, 1975

'The heavy firing that had broken out while we were driving down Maybury Hill ceased as abruptly as it began, leaving the evening very peaceful and still. We got to Leatherhead without misadventure about nine o'clock. . .'[1] The attractive old Surrey market town of Leatherhead, with its narrow streets, gabled houses, twelfth-century church and its set of stocks, seems an incongruous location for H.G. Wells' powerful and apocalyptic vision of a world invaded by Martians. Yet the narrator and his wife, whose house would soon be in the range of the aliens' heat-ray, had fled to his cousin's cottage, when 'the scent of hay was in the air through the lush meadows beyond Pyrford, and the hedges on either side were sweet and gay with multitudes of dog-roses.'

Wells' novel, published in 1898, is of course one of the most influential works of science fiction: what happened to Leatherhead Football Club some 77 years later, while not belonging in the realms of interplanetary fantasy, had enough elements of the unreal and faintly bizarre to capture the imagination of both the English press and the footballing public.

The first of many clubs to spring up in the town was founded in 1886 and 21 years later Leatherhead Rose, the acknowledged ancestor of the present club, was formed as a team drawn from Leatherhead Common. The Rose were the first League Champions of the newly formed Dorking and District League in 1909: after the Great War, the club joined the Kingston and District League and won the League title three times, the last in 1938/39.

---

[1] H.G. Wells, *The War of the Worlds*, Chapter 10, 'In the Storm'.

Leatherhead United were formed in 1924 and in 1925/26 won Division One of the Sutton and District League, playing at Fetcham Grove, a ground on the Guildford Road which was regularly flooded from the nearby River Mole. In the early 1930s United joined the Surrey Junior League, becoming Champions in 1933/34. During the war, despite travel restrictions, petrol rationing and players being on active service, some kind of amateur football was possible, and in 1940/41 United beat Rose 3–2, the last ever meeting between the two sides.

The modern Leatherhead Football Club was formed by the merger of Leatherhead Rose and Leatherhead United in 1946, playing at United's Fetcham Grove ground. The Tanners entered the Surrey Senior League and won four successive Championships and then, for a season, joined the Metropolitan League, which included some professional sides such as Chelsea's A team. They later became the last champions of the Corinthian League in 1963, celebrating their new floodlights in the same year with a game against Fulham – Johnny Haynes, Bobby Robson, George Cohen and all. The following year Leatherhead topped Division One of the new Athenian League, earning promotion to the Premier Division and won the Surrey Senior Cup in 1969. If the Tanners had made solid progress through the 1960s, the 1970s were nothing short of astonishing. In 1971 they reached the FA Amateur Cup semi-final, losing 2–0 to the eventual winners, Skelmersdale United, at Bolton's old Burnden Park ground. Two seasons later Leatherhead were elected to the Isthmian League and in 1974 Ilford scotched Leatherhead's hopes of appearing in the last ever FA Amateur final with a 1–0 victory over the Tanners at Millwall's old Den.

Five months later Leatherhead found themselves in the First Round Proper of the FA Cup for the first time. They scraped a goal-less draw at their fellow Isthmian League club, Bishop's Stortford, winning the replay 2–0 at Fetcham Grove. Then, ten days before Christmas, Third Division Colchester United succumbed to a goal from John Doyle at Fetcham Grove, the Tanners' first victory over Football League opposition.

The vagaries of the Third Round draw took the Tanners to the south coast, to Brighton in winter, to a ground where Brian Clough's men had crumbled to Walton and Hersham, thrashed 7–1 by Leatherhead in the Fourth Qualifying Round, barely 14 months before. Surely it was too much to hope that lightning would strike twice – yet, in the Tanners' side who travelled to the seaside on that first Saturday in January, there was a spectre at the feast in the shape of Colin Woffinden, the former Brighton reserve, who had played for Walton and Hersham in the debacle on that embarrassing November afternoon. Much had happened to the Seagulls since. Clough had quit, lured by the glamour of the First Division and the promises of trophies at Elland Road. 'Heads had rolled and you could hear the tumbrils creaking all the way down Old Shoreham Road,'[2] wrote John Vinicombe, veteran chronicler of happenings at the Goldstone. Peter Taylor had made a clean sweep of the playing staff, beginning the new season with an almost totally new squad. By Christmas, the new broom had lost its bristles, and Albion were struggling. They had won only seven out of 21 games and were one off the bottom of the League. Nevertheless, the Walton defeat, stunning as it had been at the time, could be written off as 'one of those days'. It could never happen again. . .could it?

Well, it did. In fact, on January 4th, 1975 all five non-League clubs survived the Third Round. Wimbledon won 1–0 at Burnley[3] and Wycombe, Stafford Rangers and Altrincham drew, two of them against First Division opposition. Wycombe held Middlesbrough to a goal-less draw at Loakes Park, and, at Goodison, Altrincham took the lead before Everton equalised through a Dave Clements penalty.

And at the Goldstone Ground, Leatherhead halted Brighton's hopes of a morale-boosting Cup run and made them – and the crowd of 20,491 – 'all too painfully aware of the narrowing gap in standards between those inside and outside the Football League.'[4]

Leatherhead dominated the match, their enthusiasm and midfield control giving Brighton few chances. In the opening minutes the home defence faced a fierce bombardment for the Tanners but gradually the Albion exerted pressure of their own, pressing Leatherhead deep into their own half. Fred Binney went close, flicking a centre from Walker over the bar, and, when Wilson centred after a neat combination with Mellor, Towner stole in on the blind side and was unlucky not to put the Seagulls ahead, his shot grazing the far post.

Leatherhead had soaked up this early onslaught and were soon causing trouble of their own. Chris Kelly's determined run, in which he cruised past three defenders, was stopped only by Winstanley's last-gasp tackle on

---

[2] Vinicombe, p. 86.
[3] See Burnley v Wimbledon, pp. 199–205.
[4] *Evening Argus*, January 6, 1975.

the edge of the box. Then the same defender had to dive head first to give away a corner as the determined Leatherhead midfield started to gain control.

After half-time Brighton began to warm to their task. However, their revival was cut short in the 65th minute by Chris Kelly, an upholsterer from Croydon, who had not played a full game since a cartilage operation in November. Two excellent efforts in the opening minutes had given evidence that he had shrugged off his recent injury and, when he picked up a loose ball just inside the Brighton half, he shimmied easily past two defenders: with the defence converging on him, Kelly ran through and calmly placed the ball beyond Peter Grummitt's reach.

Kelly's goal sparked the Seagulls into a brief but tardy response. There was more punch about their attacks, especially as Marlowe had been brought on to add pace, presence and power to the forwards. Yet there was also an air of desperation about their football and their increasingly haphazard and ham-fisted assaults never seemed capable of troubling opponents, whose defence grew in confidence with every attack they repelled.

At the final whistle, with his team an embarrassing second best, a gloomy Peter Taylor said: 'I don't mind getting beaten but we were outfought, outplayed and have no excuses. I was disgusted with Brighton. We didn't play five minutes' football. Leatherhead played it honestly and showed plenty of heart and fight, exactly as we anticipated. But Cup football is a different game. Highlighting the lack of character in his side, he went on:

Leatherhead's advantage was that they appreciated what hard work means. All their players have a job in the week. It would be good for my players to clock on at eight and leave at five in the evening ... which some of them might be doing shortly. Having a job makes players realise what it is to work for a living. I've told the players there will be an inquest at the ground tomorrow to thrash the whole thing out. I thought we had seen the last of the Walton days at Brighton. Evidently we have not, but it is not the end of the world.

His bitter terseness was in stark contrast to Kelly's garrulous swagger. Later that evening he was celebrating in his local when the BBC whisked him off to appear on *Match of the Day*. 'I'm feeling a bit woozy from the drink,' said Kelly, 'and I'm in this studio with this po-faced lot including Jimmy Hill and I think: "I'll liven this up a bit." We'd got First Division

Leicester next and I said, "Oo, we'll 'ammer them, they're rubbish." Half the country must have thought "Who's this little runt?" but the rest obviously found it quite amusing.'

In 1975 the professional game – and the British public in general – viewed non-League football with a patronising amusement, occasionally indulging one of the so-called 'minnows' during a brave but ultimately futile Cup run. The 'small' clubs were supposed to know their place in football's pyramid and were expected to be seen but not heard. Kelly was different. Talented enough to score 150 goals in nearly 500 games, he freely admits that his brashness created a rod for his own back. 'I was this cocky, unbearable loudmouth who'd give people gyp, eccentric to the point of being one cog away from insanity. Can't believe now the stuff I came out with. Outrageous.'

Thus was born the legend of the 'Leatherhead Lip', a gift to the tabloids and the non-League counterpart to mavericks like Stan Bowles, Rodney Marsh and Frank Worthington. The latter, who had in his day more clubs than Tiger Woods, would actually face Kelly three weeks later, for the suits at Lancaster Gate rewarded Leatherhead for their cheek, handing them a Fourth Round plum against Leicester City. The Tanners manager, Billy Miller, was philosophical: 'Not a bad draw. If they hang from the trees we might get a crowd of 5,000 at Fetcham Grove. We might as well play at Filbert Street; I know we can't beat a First Division side.' So, to maximise their gate income, Leatherhead agreed to switch the tie to Filbert Street.

The *Match of the Day* cameras – and a 32,000 crowd – saw a dramatic match. For the best part of 50 minutes, the Tanners stood on the threshold of the Fourth Round. After only 12 minutes, Peter McGillicuddy headed home a low cross to put the Tanners ahead and on the half-hour Chris Kelly (who else?) doubled the lead with a curling back-header from a free kick. As the tie approached, Kelly had been irrepressible. He confided in one of the tabloids how upset he was that Jeff Blockley, who had just joined Leicester from Arsenal, was Cup-tied: 'I wish he was playing cos he's absolutely useless, about as mobile as a statue. I'd run rings round him.' As he came off at half-time, still in a daze at his goal, Kelly turned towards the wrong dressing room and found himself face to face with Blockley, a large man with the turning circle of a small oil tanker. 'Raging, he was,' recalls Kelly. 'Good job he wasn't too mobile, then.'

Five minutes after the restart, Kelly had the chance to put the tie beyond the Foxes' reach. Nicking the ball off Cross, he tore into the box and as City's keeper, Mark Wallington, bore down on him, he dillied and dallied, shimmied and shallied, and finally saw his shot hacked off the line by Steve Earle. With the Tanners three up, City would have been beyond recall – but Kelly's miss was to prove decisive. Class and superior fitness told in the end and goals from Earle, Sammels and Weller clinched the tie for City. Leicester may have scraped home by the odd goal but, like the names of Ronnie Radford or Dickie Guy, Kelly, 'the Leatherhead Lip', was immediately etched in the annals of the FA Cup. He was now hot property and, four days later, he signed for Millwall.

Over the next two years, victories against a Cambridge United side managed by Ron Atkinson and over Pat Crerand's Northampton Town confirmed the Tanners as one of the most celebrated post-war giant-killers. They did reach Wembley in 1978 for the FA[5] Trophy Final, where they came unstuck against Altrincham, giant-killers themselves in 1986 and one of the leading non-League outfits in the country. That season Leatherhead reached the First Round of the Cup for a fourth time, but were beaten by Swansea City and the following year Colchester United avenged their defeat in 1974/75, seeing off the Tanners 4–0 in a Second Round replay at Layer Road.

In the decades since the heady days of those Cup runs, Leatherhead FC has not escaped the inevitable financial vicissitudes which perennially beset clubs on the lower rungs of the footballing pyramid. Since the summer of 2000 the club has been run by Tanners fans, who rode to the rescue when Leatherhead FC was faced with extinction. Gradually the playing side has been consolidated and a long-term lease secured on Fetcham Grove, whose fabric, some of which stretched back to the 1940s, has been refurbished. The Tanners' ethos, 'A club run by its supporters for the benefit of its community', runs deep and today Fetcham Grove commendably hosts 'The Pitstop', a daytime drop-in centre for the homeless, unemployed and socially isolated in and around Leatherhead.

In his most famous book, set in suburban Surrey, around Horsell Common, Shepperton, Woking and Leatherhead, Wells wrote of a catastrophic interplanetary confrontation. That was science fiction: but early in 1975, the Tanners' clashes with Brighton and Leicester were flesh and

---

[5] See Birmingham City v Altrincham, pp. 35.

blood, real-life collisions between two different footballing worlds – though, sometimes, the stories of the struggles between David and Goliath are themselves the stuff of legend.

BRIGHTON AND HOVE ALBION: Grummitt, Tiler, Wilson, Mason, Piper, Winstanley, Towner, O'Sullivan, Binney, Mellor, Walker
LEATHERHEAD: Swannell, Sargeant, Webb, Cooper, Reid, McGillycuddy, Woffinden, Lavers, Kelly, Smith, Doyle

28

BURNLEY 0, WIMBLEDON 1

FA Cup, Round Three, January 4, 1975

Most footballers never slay even one Goliath in their careers. A few, who were fortunate enough to have played in a legendary giant-killing side, remain local heroes long after their boots have been hung on the dressing-room wall. Still fewer manage to do it twice but Dave Bassett, Dave Donaldson and Billy Edwards – and their manager Allen Batsford – achieved a quite extraordinary, if not unique, feat. They did it in successive seasons – with different clubs.

A defensive midfielder, Bassett had had trials with Watford and Chelsea, but without success. He moved into the semi-professional game, playing for Hayes, from whom he joined Walton and Hersham, managed by Allen Batsford, in 1970. He skippered the side which won the FA Amateur Cup in 1973 without conceding a goal: a few months later Bassett, whose uncompromising tackling and qualities of leadership had already gained him several England amateur caps, led Walton in their 4–0 demolition of Brighton. At the beginning of the 1974/75 season, when Batsford left to manage Southern League club Wimbledon, he took Dave 'Harry' Bassett, Donaldson and Edwards with him. It was the start of a crazy saga which in only 13 years took the club from suburban South London to the First Division and ultimately the FA Cup itself.

By the late eighteenth century, 'Wimbleton', as the village was called on John Cary's map of the London area in 1786, had a traditionally rural population, living cheek by jowl with members of the nobility and prosperous merchants from the City, whither stagecoaches ran from the Dog and Fox pub, running the gauntlet of highwaymen like Jerry Abershawe on the Portsmouth Road.

A century later, 1889 was a landmark year for the growing suburb (from 2,700 in 1851, the population increased 15-fold in 50 years). Rail links had grown in the half-century since 1838 when the London and South-Western Railway built a station at the bottom of Wimbledon Hill and in 1889 the Metropolitan District Railway, now the District Line, extended its service from Putney. In the same year, for sentimental reasons, the word 'croquet' was restored to the name of the All England Lawn Tennis and Croquet Club, having been dropped seven years before as tennis had become the main activity of the club. Old boys from the Central School, founded on Wimbledon Common in 1758, formed a football club known as Wimbledon Old Centrals, playing on the Common, up the hill and across the High Street from the All England Club. The players used the Fox and Grapes pub, in the same road as the school, as the team's headquarters and changing room.

The 'Old Boys' gained their first honours only seven seasons later, winning the Clapham League in 1896. By the First World War, the club had become Wimbledon FC (May 19505) and in 1912 had moved to Plough Lane, its home for the next 79 years. Down the years, of course, the name 'Wimbledon' had become exclusively synonymous with manicured lawns, wooden racquets, the Royal Box, strawberries and cream, Fred Perry, Rod Laver and Dan Maskell. The existence of the local football team, known as the 'Dons', was scarcely acknowledged. The club had led a quiet life in suburban amateur leagues, though they had won the Isthmian League seven times and the FA Amateur Cup in 1963, when Eddie Reynolds headed all four goals in the 4–2 win over Sutton United. The Dons turned professional a year later, joining the Southern League, Division One, and winning promotion immediately to the Premier Division, finishing runners-up in 1968.

The club was now clearly a power to be reckoned with in non-League football and in 1974/45, following home victories over fellow Southern Leaguers Bath and Kettering, the Dons landed a tough assignment in the Third Round against First Division Burnley. The Lancashire side, managed by its former FA Cup Final captain Jimmy Adamson, were lying seventh in the League and hadn't lost at Turf Moor since the previous September. So confident was Adamson that he jocularly quipped that his team's opponents were a tennis club. They were the division's leading scorers, their main threat coming from Welsh international winger Leighton James whose strong-running, direct style caused headaches for the best defenders in the country. Furthermore, it had been more than half a century since a non-League team had won away at a First Division club, since Darlington beat Sheffield Wednesday in 1920: thus, though Wimbledon were third in the Southern League, 55 years of football history weighed heavily against them.

Part of the history of Wimbledon was that Robert Baden-Powell wrote parts of *Scouting for Boys* while staying at the windmill on Wimbledon Common. Heeding the Scouts' motto, 'Be Prepared', the Dons' manager, Allen Batsford, had drawn up his own survival handbook – a 15-page dossier on Burnley and on the morning of the game Batsford and his coach, Brian Hall, put the team through their paces on a Burnley sports ground. As well as the three heroes from Walton and Hersham, on the left-wing Wimbledon had Mickey Mahon, a member of the Colchester United side which had humbled Leeds four years before.

In spite of this, there was barely a whiff of an upset around Turf Moor on the first Saturday in January. Neither *Match of the Day* nor *The Big Match*, the rival TV programmes, covered the game. There wasn't much drama to be gleaned from a non-League side being taken apart by a side flying high in Division One – but those who write the FA Cup script were to be confounded yet again.

In a goal-less first half, the visitors effectively shackled Leighton James, with full-back Bob Stockley and the obdurate Dave Bassett all over him like a cheap suit, so close, as the saying goes, that by half-time he and James were practically engaged. Wimbledon's stubborn defence led Burnley's prolific forwards down blind alleys and the whole team's work rate drew the home side's attacking teeth. Up front, the lone threat Wimbledon could offer the first 45 minutes was a speculative cross-cum-shot from Billy Edwards, which Alan Stevenson pushed over the bar.

Batsford's half-time talk must have been easy – 'More of the same, lads, if you will. Stop them scoring and we'll get them back to the Lane.' He hadn't bargained for what happened three minutes after the break. Burnley's left-back, Jim Thomson, hesitated, giving Ian Cooke time for shot. Alan Stevenson in the Burnley goal parried Cooke's drive into the path of Roger Connell, who took a swing at it and miscued. Loitering with intent was Mick Mahon, who rifled home a left-foot drive from close range: 'there wasn't a lot of goal to aim at but it went straight in. I will never forget the look on the faces of the Burnley team when we scored.'

While Mahon had made himself an instant hero by putting the non-

Leaguers ahead, the Dons' true superman that afternoon was their bearded keeper, Dickie Guy, a tally clerk at London docks who hadn't missed a Wimbledon first-team game for four years. As early as the third minute, he effortlessly clung on to Paul Fletcher's cross-shot; on 27 minutes he saved Ray Hankin's header from James's cross and on the half-hour Keith Newton's fierce volley produced a blinding save from the inspirational keeper. On the whole, though, Burnley just weren't at it. 'With the exception of Newton, no one looked remotely anxious enough.' As time trickled away for the First Division side, Wimbledon rode their luck. The home side were fighting for an equaliser and Guy virtually played Burnley on his own. Towards the end, with the Dons under siege, a remarkable succession of fine saves kept the Dons in front, culminating in a splendid reflex stop from Fletcher's point-blank shot. In a breathtaking final minute Guy spilled another shot from Fletcher but fortune favoured the underdogs as Doug Collins blazed the rebound over the bar.

Even as the battle raged in their own penalty box, the Dons strove to take the game to the home side, Keiron Somers sent three shots narrowly wide as he and his similarly bearded striking partner, Connell, kept beavering away, looking for the killer goal.

In the end, it was a stalemate and with the referee's final whistle Wimbledon became the first post-war non-League side to beat a First Division club away. It was a great day for the minnows. All five non-League sides – Leatherhead, Wimbledon, Altrincham, Stafford Rangers and Wycombe Wanderers – 'covered themselves in equal parts with mud and glory, and not one of them was beaten'.[1] But it was Wimbledon who were talk of the pubs that night – and not only in South London. As the *Guardian*'s Paul Wilcox put it, 'The expected Wombling taunts from the crowd faded with Burnley's reputation. And little wonder. The only rubbish that Wimbledon picked up on Saturday were the First Division team's errors.'[2]

Allen Batsford's face was a study in bemused happiness. 'We had Burnley watched,' said the ecstatic Dons boss, 'and reckoned they were rather predictable. In many ways, they only have themselves to blame . . . They were too complacent during the first 20 minutes and, once they fell behind, they panicked.' Burnley's captain, Colin Waldron, agreed. 'We played what

[1] *Observer*, January 5, 1975.
[2] *Guardian*, January 6, 1975.

I would call ignorant football,' he conceded. 'Right from the first minute, we kept hitting these long, high balls into their goalmouth in the hope that someone would make a mistake, and made their centre-halves look a cross between Jack Charlton and Jairzinho.' He went on to assess the problems he feels all First Division teams face against opponents like Wimbledon: 'These teams don't react in the same way to situations and therefore don't really make you think. For example, we have a free kick plan which every First Division team has fallen for this season. But Wimbledon – they just stood around, not knowing what was going on, and cancelled it out.'

It had been quite a weekend for the Southern League side but, having humiliated Burnley, they had to come back down to earth on the following Tuesday with a game against Atherstone at Plough Lane – and then look forward to a journey to Yorkshire in the Fourth Round. The luck of the draw had handed the Dons a tough trip to Leeds United, the League champions and 5–1 ante-post Cup favourites. The canny Leeds manager, former England captain Jimmy Armfield, viewed the tie with a pinch of northern prudence. 'We will not be in a complacent mood,' he promised, for Leeds had faltered in Cup competitions in the past – most notably at Colchester four years before.[3] At Elland Road, however, such ignominies were as rare as a Gary Lineker booking and Wimbledon's hopes for the tie might well not have been set much higher than the chance to play at a First Division ground and a handsome cheque.

True to form, however, the undaunted Dons got amongst the champions and held Leeds until eight minutes from time, when more heroics from Dickie Guy forced a replay, the keeper palming a penalty from Peter Lorimer round the post. As Plough Lane was considered unsuitable, the replay was staged at Selhurst Park in front of a 46,000 crowd when finally, after more than three hours of football against Division One opponents, Dickie Guy was beaten, the doughty Dave Bassett deflecting a shot from Johnny Giles past the local hero.

The Cup run launched an era of glory for the Dons, as they won the Southern League Premier Division three years running, took First Division Middlesbrough to a Third Round replay in 1977 and that year, under the managership of Dario Gradi, Wimbledon FC were elected to the Football League. Nine years later, with Dave Bassett as manager, a team dubbed by

---

[3] See Colchester United v Leeds United, pp. 163–168.

the press as 'the Crazy Gang', a rag, tag and bobtail crew of rejects, has-beens and never-weres found themselves in Division One. And unbelievably, 'Bassett's dogged rewriting of the rulebook via relentless hoofing of the ball downfield'[4] destroyed Liverpool's smooth passing game in the 1988 Cup Final, when Lawrie Sanchez's curling header clinched the most bizarre Wembley victory of all time.

During the 1990s, however, the club's fortunes plunged rapidly downhill. Following the post-Hillsborough Taylor Report, Plough Lane's days as a viable stadium were clearly numbered. Entrepreneur chairman Sam Hammam sold it off to Safeway and, after a decade of sharing Selhurst Park, dark rumours began to circulate about a move to Dublin, Manchester, Cardiff and, most disturbingly of all, Milton Keynes. This was a blatant attempt to cut off the club from its traditional roots in the Borough of Merton, as the money-men either knew nothing about, cared less for, or chose to ignore the organic nature of football clubs' support in this country. Increasingly intense pressure from the Wimbledon Independent Supporters' Association forced Hammam to offload the club to a bunch of Scandinavian multimillionaires. Their misguided appointment of the ineffectual former Norway boss Egil Olsen ensured relegation to Division One whereupon the new figurehead chairman Charles Koppel agitated to uproot Wimbledon FC up the M1 to Buckinghamshire. Amazingly, the FA caved in, spinelessly agreeing in effect to kill off Wimbledon and gates slumped to below a thousand. Two years later, on June 20, 2004, the Football League agreed to the club changing its name to Milton Keynes Dons FC.

There then followed an extraordinary example of 'people power' – proof, if proof were needed, of the intense, almost symbiotic, attachment of football fans to their local team. A packed meeting in the Fox and Grapes pub in Wimbledon Village – where the Old Centrals used to change – voted overwhelmingly to set up a new team, AFC Wimbledon. The highly respected football magazine *When Saturday Comes* describes the new club's swift progress:

> Their first game, against Sutton in July 2002, was watched by over 4,500 and the new team began 2002–03 in the Combined Counties League. By the summer of 2005, promotion to the Ryman Premier

---

[4] Lyons and Ronay, *When Saturday Comes*, p. 435.

League had been achieved. With crowds regularly topping 3,000 at Kingsmeadow, the stadium they now own and share with Kingstonian a couple of miles outside Merton, the club is edging nearer the ultimate aim of a return to the professional ranks.[5]

The fans' determined resolve to get their club back is now seen as a landmark and its impact has become something of a model for supporters looking for a more democratic and rational structure for the organisation of football and its clubs. As WISA's chairman, Kris Stewart, asserts, 'We're a true football club, owned by the fans, for the fans. We've built something truly precious here, something I don't believe Wimbledon's former owners, or anybody else involved with the franchise in Milton Keynes, can ever really understand.'[6] Alan Hardaker, Secretary of the Football League in the 1950s, once maintained that 'Spectators are what professional football is all about. Without them it has no point, no status and no future.'[7]

Amen to that.

BURNLEY: Stevenson, Newton, Thomson [Morris 64], Ingham, Waldron, Noble, Flynn, Hankin, Fletcher, Collins, James
WIMBLEDON: Guy, Stockley, Bryant, Donaldson, Edwards, Bassett, Cooke, Rice, Connell, Somers, Mahon

---

[5] *When Saturday Comes*, p. 436.
[6] Conn, p. 255.
[7] Irwin, p. 9.

29

NORWICH CITY 1,
BRADFORD CITY 2

Round 5, February 23, 1976

The factors which made Bradford the centre of Britain's woollen industry in the late eighteenth century read like a passage from a dog-eared geography textbook stuffed in my satchel in the 1950s. Sheep had grazed the Yorkshire moors for centuries and there had been a textile industry in the area for five hundred years. It was not, however until the mills began to exploit nearby coal to power steam-driven machinery, utilising the soft lime-free water from the Pennine streams to wash, card and comb the wool, that Bradford, specialising in dress cloths, took the worsted trade away from Norwich and the city's nineteenth-century prosperity was born. The Victorian Gothic architecture and the vast looming mills in Bradford's city centre may not possess great aesthetic appeal, but their solidity and grandeur exude an air of self-importance which cannot be ignored. From the splendour of the Wool Exchange to the labyrinth of narrow streets winding between terraced houses, it is undoubtedly a city born of the Industrial Revolution.

Manningham FC, as it was originally known, was a founding member of the Northern Rugby Football Union and the dominant sporting force in the wool city. The club had a stranglehold on football under the rugby code but, as the impact of soccer's professional game took a stronger hold on the imagination of the workers of industrial cities like Bradford, it became increasingly apparent that the amateur handling game could not remain solvent. Despite a summer archery contest that realised a sum sufficient to have ensured their survival, Manningham's members were persuaded to switch their allegiance to the game of soccer.

The formation of Bradford City FC represents one of the first attempts at missionary work by the still-fledgling Football League, spreading the gospel of the association code in what was a rugby-dominated region. At the end of the 1902/03 season Manningham changed its name to Bradford City AFC and the club was invited to join the Football League's Second Division. Along with Chelsea, who emulated City's feat in 1905, Bradford City remain the only club to join the Football League before it had assembled a team, played a single senior match, or even had the certainty of a ground on which to play. Yet in May 1903, when the club topped the poll at the FA's AGM with 30 votes out of 35, Bradford City became the pioneers of professional Association football in the West Riding of Yorkshire.

Against a backcloth of local fervour which began with a gentle ripple of enthusiasm and developed with the force of a tidal wave, Bradford City, the upstarts of this newfangled round-ball game, won the Second Division Championship in 1908. There followed ten successive seasons straddling the Great War with a best-ever position of fifth, achieved during their FA Cup Final winning season of 1911. This was the year they set the club's record attendance of 39,146 for the visit of Burnley in the quarter final – still the country's longest-standing ground record. All of this was achieved in the face of competition for their supporters' affections – another professional club in Bradford down the road in Park Avenue. That great man of letters, J.B. Priestley, native of the city, had a cosmic view of the game in his first popular success, *The Good Companions*: 'To say that these men paid their shillings to watch twenty-two hirelings kick a ball is merely to say that a violin is wood and catgut, that *Hamlet* is so much paper and ink. For a shilling the Bruddersford United AFC offered you Conflict and Art.'

City's history has oscillated down the years between success, financial crisis and even tragedy, yet the club has emerged from these vicissitudes only to frustrate its supporters time and again. The club remains nonetheless one of the pillars of the Football League: indeed, the club holds a unique distinction, unfortunately unrelated to its prowess on the field – Bradford City is the only professional football club in England to wear claret and amber, colours inherited upon the conversion of Manningham FC from rugby union to soccer in 1903. However, whereas Manningham traditionally wore hooped shirts, City have always worn stripes, which gave the club its nickname of 'The Bantams', from the imagined resemblance of the claret-and-amber colours to the plumage of those fighting cocks. Indeed,

208

contemporary reports from before the Great War refer to live bantams being taken to games by supporters as mascots for the team.

By the mid-1970s the claret-and-amber stripes were going through yet another of the lean times. In the 1974/75 season the club had considered going part-time, owing to the perennial financial pressure. Average attendance had slumped to a meagre 2,916, as City only just avoided the ignominy of seeking re-election at the foot of Division Four. On the plus side, manager Bobby Kennedy, a member of the great Manchester City side of the 1960s and a former Scotland international, had arrived in the summer and had put together a promising side, on a budget that would barely cover the weekly wage of one of today's players.

One of the surest remedies for pressure on the purse strings is a successful Cup run, yet few of the 4,352 who saw Don Hutchins' late header overcome Chesterfield in the First Round at the end of November could have foreseen the drama to come. Ten days before Christmas, City travelled down the M1 to the Don valley to face Third Division Rotherham in Round Two. The Bantams raised a few eyebrows in the nation's newsrooms as two goals from Gerry Ingram and a third from Joe Cooke overcame the Millers on their home turf. Years later, in a *City Gent* interview, Don Hutchins said of that game, 'Of all the matches in the Cup run, that was the best we played. We were like Real Madrid. We murdered them.'

Round Three is of course the 'money round', the chance to earn serious cash from a plum draw, preferably away, to the likes of Manchester United, Chelsea or, in the mid-1970s, Liverpool or Leeds United. Just Bradford's luck, therefore, to be paired with another Third Division side, this time Shrewsbury Town, at their quaintly named home, Gay Meadow, where Cooke and Don Hutchins were once again the heroes as City won 2–1. The Bantams' financial fortunes failed to turn again in Round Four as the black balls from the black bag determined that City would play at Valley Parade against Southern League Tooting and Mitcham, who had themselves beaten League opposition in Swindon in a Third Round replay. By now the Cup run was beginning to excite the Bradford faithful and 21,152 packed Valley Parade to see City win 3–1, Hutchins scoring twice more and John Middleton notching the third. Hutchins thought the game 'was tougher than Rotherham and Shrewsbury. Tooting put up a good fight. Time after time, people in Bradford had looked for good things happening, but were usually let down at the last minute, so it was nice to go through.'

It was the best of times, it was the worst of times in Round Five. It was a tale of two cities whose fortunes were made from the wool trade as Bradford were drawn to play First Division Norwich City at Carrow Road. The Canaries had been promoted the year before and had already reached the League Cup Final. The Yorkshire side had seven of their first-team squad bedridden with flu and the FA postponed the tie twice. John Bond, yes – the ex-Bournemouth man and now the Canaries' manager – garrulously tactless as ever, maintained that City were 'muddlers' who ought not to be in the League if they couldn't put a team out. Nine days later, he was made to eat his words. His side began in a hurry but Bradford defended magnificently, visiting keeper Peter Downsborough making several fine saves. Then, six minutes from half-time, Canaries full-back David Jones generously gave the ball to Bradford's diminutive winger Don Hutchins, who hurdled Jones's desperate attempt to atone for this error and let fly a dipping cross-shot which baffled Kevin Keelan in the home goal. He flapped at the swerving ball but could only palm it into his net. It was only the third time he had touched it since the kick-off. This was soon cancelled out when World Cup hero Martin Peters back-headed home a corner from Colin Suggett.

In the second half Bradford found themselves under tremendous pressure. In one harrowing minute, full-back Cec Podd cleared off the line, and Dave Stringer and Duncan Forbes hit the woodwork. To add insult to injury, the Canaries had a goal disallowed. However, in pushing forward, they left themselves vulnerable. Three minutes from time Bradford were almost out on their feet but, in their only attack of the second half, Billy McGinley, a free transfer signing from Huddersfield, intercepted a loose pass from the usually reliable Dave Stringer and should have squared the ball to Gerry Ingram, who had the goal at his mercy. But McGinley's shot was blocked by defender Sullivan and rolled back to his feet. Wasting no time, he slid the ball into the net through Keelan's legs. Incredibly, City had become only the third Fourth Division side to reach the FA Cup quarter-finals, an astonishing achievement for a club stony broke and entrenched in the bargain basement of the English game. It was the first smell of success for the post-war generations of supporters and the first time City had reached that stage of the competition since 1920.

The quarter-final, or the Sixth Round as the suits at Lancaster Gate always called it, saw the Bantams at home to Southampton and was indisputably City's post-war highlight. Once again Valley Parade was packed to the rafters. In a tight game, City, in their first quarter-final since 1920 and only the third Fourth Division side to reach that stage, lost 1–0 to a controversial free kick. Late the first half, Peter Osgood flicked the ball up for Jim McCalliog to fire home on the volley, a move that had been outlawed since Willie Carr and Ernie Hunt had used to it to great effect for Coventry a few seasons earlier. The referee allowed the goal to stand and the Saints went on to win the FA Cup.

There was a coda to this tale of derring-do. Two decades later and some 14 years after the tragedy of the fire in May 1985 at Valley Parade, City made it to the Premiership and, in their first season in the top flight for 70 years, they reached the Fifth Round following a famous 3–2 win over Everton at Goodison Park. The good times were back at Valley Parade, but not for long. The Bantams now languish near the bottom of Division Two, with only faded memories of their past glories and old programmes to remind them of their own very special 'tale of two cities'.

NORWICH CITY: Keelan, Jones, Sullivan, McGuire, Forbes, Stringer, Machin, MacDougall, Boyer, Suggett, Peters
BRADFORD CITY: Downsborough, Podd, Cooper, Johnson, Middleton, Fretwell, McGinley, Ingram, Cooke, Hall, Hutchins

30

SOUTHAMPTON 1, MANCHESTER UNITED 0

FA Cup Final May 1, 1976

In early May 1976 temperatures in Greater London and Kent soared to 29°C. Office workers sunbathed in Hyde Park, others frolicked in the Serpentine, the Government appointed a Minister for Drought and the tabloids screeched 'Phew! Wottascorcher – and there's more to come!'

It was scarcely the weather for football, yet on May Day thousands flocked down Wembley Way to see Manchester United reach the climax of an inspired and exhilarating season. They were amongst the hottest of Cup Final favourites, having finished only four points behind champions Liverpool in the First Division. Though their opponents, Southampton, were the third Second Division side to reach Wembley in four seasons, it was their first final in 74 years. As Geoffrey Green put it in *The Times*, 'Any riverboat gambler in search of the quick buck must surely back them with his last piece of silver.'[1]

Few football writers gave the Hampshire side a chance, dismissing the homely club from the city on the Solent as a hotch-potch of has-beens and journeymen. Bryan Butler wrote, 'What a fine final it might have been if Manchester United and Derby County, who finished third and fourth in the First Division, had met at Wembley in 1976!'[2] When they were drawn against each other at Hillsborough, leaving Southampton of the Second Division and Crystal Palace of the Third to meet in the other semi-final at Stamford Bridge, United's manager, Tommy Docherty, said, 'This is the first time a Cup Final will be played at Hillsborough. The other semi-final is a bit of a joke, really.'

---

[1] *The Times*, May 1, 1976.
[2] *Illustrated History of the F.A. Cup*, p. 248.

United won the toss for colours and, in their traditional red, with Southampton wearing the daffodil yellow of spring, they emerged from the gloomy tunnel into the blazing sunlight of early summer. The David and Goliath aspect lent the occasion an extra spice. Was there perhaps an omen of things to come when a single yellow balloon floated gently down between the players during the presentations to the Duke of Edinburgh? Life, after all – and football life especially – is 'a banana skin on which opinion is often liable to slip unceremoniously' and the unpredictability of so many Cup finals of yesteryear bear testimony to that immortal truth.

The underdogs hailed from England's youngest city, Southampton having achieved that prestigious status just ten years before. A Roman harbour, Southampton was an important medieval port and had seen the departure of the *Mayflower* in 1620. In Victorian times the advent of the railways made it Britain's leading base for passenger liners. A century earlier Southampton was a fashionable spa, attracting distinguished visitors like Jane Austen, who, while staying with her brother Frank, often picnicked on the banks of the Itchen. Frank's sons would row from the ferry upriver to Northam and it was near there that members of St Mary's Church Young Men's Association formed Southampton St Mary's Football Club in 1885, playing their football a stone's throw from the river before moving to a new stadium, The Dell, in 1898.

'The Saints', as they were nicknamed, joined the Southern League in 1894 and at the turn of the century, were among the top Cup teams in the country. They reached the first of their five FA Cup finals in 1899 as a non-League team, going down 4–0 to Bury, losing again in both 1900 and 1902. The club joined Division Three (South) in 1920, achieved promotion in 1922 and stayed there for 31 years. In 1960 Saints legend Derek Reeves' 39 goals helped the club regain Second Division status and two years later a young university student from Hastings watched the first of many games on the cramped, friendly, boisterous and always witty terraces in the West Stand. On one occasion, in the middle of a poor run of results, Vic, a docker, hadn't turned up for a few games. We'd heard he hadn't been too well and, on his return, we asked him about it. 'Waaall,' he replied, in a rich Hampshire brogue pitched somewhere between Worzel Gummidge and Benny Hill, 'they never cum and saw me when I wuz bad.' And when George Kirby, an old-fashioned centre-forward, strong in the air, missed a couple of sitters from David

Burnside's customarily immaculate corners, Vic roared, 'Cum aan, George, you coulden' head a queue!'

The Dell, compact and hemmed in by houses, was a ground no club enjoyed visiting. Its terraces, like those at the old Upton Park, were so close to the action, you could almost touch Terry Paine's shirt as he took a throw-in. An away player must have felt like a Christian thrown to the lions, albeit that the home fans were on the side of the Saints. By the early 1960s, it was 'a wooden, battered old ground'[4] but it had a magical atmosphere.

Run down or not, in 1950 The Dell became the first ground in England to have permanent floodlighting installed and five years later Ted Bates, a Saints player for 16 years either side of the war, began his 18-year reign as manager. In 1963, in a marathon Cup quarter-final tussle with Nottingham Forest, Terry Paine earned a 1–1 draw at the City Ground, and after a thrilling 3–3 draw at The Dell, two goals each for Burnside and O'Brien at White Hart Lane saw Saints in their first semi-final since 1927. In a grim contest at Villa Park, a goal from Denis Law took Manchester United to Wembley.

Division One football came to The Dell for the first time in 1966 when a scrambled goal from Terry Paine against Leyton Orient at Brisbane Road clinched the runners-up spot behind Manchester City. The tall, rangy and powerful 21-year-old Martin Chivers scored 30 goals that season, which also saw the debut of 17-year-old Mike Channon. Paine would win his last England cap against Mexico in the triumphant World Cup campaign that summer; later, Chivers and Channon would both play for England. In 1969 the Saints made their first venture into Europe via the Byzantine rules of the Inter-Cities Fairs Cup. By this time Chivers had left for Spurs and in 1973 Ted Bates made way for former Coldstream Guardsman Lawrie McMenemy.

An injury while playing for his native Gateshead had put an end to McMenemy's career in 1961 and he moved into coaching, taking Bishop Auckland to the Second Round of the Cup and the Northern League championship. After two years as coach at Sheffield Wednesday, he became manager of Doncaster Rovers before joining Grimsby in 1971. Although he suffered relegation at the end of his first season, the Saints becoming the first victims of the new three-down relegation system, by the mid-70s this imposing figure, who commanded instant respect, had built a side that

---

[3] Geoffrey Green, *The Times*, May 1, 1976.
[4] From Southampton PodJockey Matt Brennan, April 4, 2008.

was a judicious blend of youth and experience. Channon, Peter Osgood, Peter Rodrigues and Jim McCalliog provided most of the experience, three of them having played in the Cup Final before – Osgood had scored for Chelsea in 1970, Rodrigues was in the Leicester side beaten by Manchester City in 1969 and McCalliog had got one of Sheffield Wednesday's goals in their 1966 defeat by Everton.

In 1976 Southampton's march to their first Wembley final was more of a shifty sidle down the back alleys. After McCalliog's brace had put out Aston Villa in a Third Round replay, they rose without trace, beating Blackpool 3–1 in Round Four with goals from Channon and Bobby Stokes. In the Fifth Round, a stomach bug had run through the team and the Saints were forced to field a much weakened side against West Bromwich Albion. Stokes' late equaliser gave Southampton another bite at the cherry and a hat-trick from Channon took the Saints through to a quarter-final against Fourth Division Bradford City, who had carved their own niche in Cup history by dumping Norwich out at Carrow Road.[5] As the twin towers beckoned, tension in the city rose and the teams comfortable 2–0 win over Malcolm Allison's Crystal Palace in the semi-final fostered a genuine belief that it could be their year.

Manchester United awaited them after regulation wins over Oxford United, Peterborough and Leicester City, but it took extra time in a replay for them to win through at Molineux, Stuart Pearson's winner seeing off Wolves in the quarter-final. With Arsenal and England's Charlie George drafted into a championship-winning side, Derby looked a tough nut to crack in the semi-final. The game itself proved something of a damp squib, Gordon Hill's double strike taking the Reds through to Wembley.

On the eve of the game, the Manchester United boss who had only half-jokingly quipped that the semi-final with Derby was 'the real Cup Final' told journalists he'd give his house away, jump into the Thames, eat his hat and – somewhat alarmingly – 'mud-wrestle my elderly relatives' if Southampton won the FA Cup. His side was inexperienced, with an average age of only 24, but they were an excellent attacking side, with Stuart Pearson in the old-fashioned centre-forward role and Gordon Hill and Steve Coppell the traditional nippy wingers – and they were the out-and-out favourites as three o'clock struck on May Day.

---

[5] See Norwich City v Bradford City, pp. 207–211.

In the countdown to the Final, the press loved to portray the Saints as yokels up from the sticks. Bobby Stokes, for whom it would prove a very special day, was photographed 'shovelling horse muck at team-mate Mick Channon's stables, slouched in a wheelbarrow with a piece of straw in his teeth, and quaffing cider in a pub.'[6] According to Geoffrey Green in *The Times*, Channon, now a successful and respected racehorse trainer, held the key to the Saints' prospects of victory. 'If the shrewd Osgood and McCalliog can create the right situations with the quick through pass, then Channon is capable of escaping with the loot through the back door.'[7] Colin Irwin records Mick Channon as claiming that 'after becoming a pro he couldn't bear to watch an FA Cup Final on telly because he was so eaten up by envy watching others enjoying the drama.'[8] One of them was that Southampton University student, now teaching in Sussex and sitting on a mate's sofa glued to the TV more in hope than expectation.

My worst fears seemed to be confirmed in the opening minutes as United eased into their confident stride, playing fluent, creative football. Docherty's men enjoyed the best of the early exchanges as the ball was moved swiftly through Macari, McIlroy and Daly in midfield. Three promising moves were snuffed out as the Southampton defence worked their offside trap 'like a greased zip-fastener'.[9] The zip stuck however after 11 minutes when Pearson cleverly judged his pass through to Hill. The winger tried to chip over Turner's head as he dashed out, but from only two yards the Saints' keeper flung up his right arm to make a brilliant save. Then Coppell dribbled skilfully at speed down the right wing for Turner to beat away his fierce cross-shot – but Pearson and Macari were slow to react on the six-yard line.

By then I was hiding behind the sofa. The Saints' defence, honest and forthright but caught for pace at times, were increasingly stretched. When Buchan sent Macari 'scampering like an urchin on an errand'[10] past Blyth, a United breakthrough seemed inevitable. The little Scot reached the byline and pulled the ball back to Daly, unmarked eight yards out, but he swung hurriedly at the ball, driving it hard against Turner's legs.

---

[6] Jon Spurting, *FourFourTwo*, January 2007.
[7] *The Times*, May 1, 1976.
[8] Irwin, p. 97.
[9] Peter Corrigan, *Observer*, May 2, 1976.
[10] Ibid.

The escape inspired Southampton and as Manchester began to play with more caution, they began to delay their approach passes in midfield, enabling the Saints' back four to catch United's forwards offside. The side who had played with joyous abandon all season had failed to sweep Southampton aside and the underdogs began to play with more conviction. Though the Saints could not match their opponents for technical ability, relying on long balls and clearances, Jim McCalliog, their most skilful player, began to impose himself, probing the United defence with several 30-yard through passes to Channon and Osgood. So much so, that ten minutes before half-time Channon galloped clear, latching on to McCalliog's accurately flighted pass. As Stepney rushed out to narrow the angle, the England striker fatally hesitated, so that his shot struck Stepney's left boot and soared away for Buchan to clear.

Though Manchester had had the better of the first half territorially, they had spurned any number of chances and the second half began as the first had ended, with Channon leading a threatening attack only for Buchan to save the situation. Nonetheless, it was an ominous sign that Saints were warming to their task. United set about disconcerting them and Coppell and Peach had some fierce tussles. Once, the speedy winger scuttled past two defenders and crossed to the unmarked Pearson. However, the ball came at him thigh-high and, though he swivelled acrobatically to strike the volley, Pearson's shot flew wide.

Southampton launched a counter-attack from the resulting clearance, Channon shooting powerfully a yard high and wide of United's goal. This prompted a Saints' revival, Holmes and Rodrigues both fluffing chances when well placed. First, Holmes scuffed his shot when put through by Osgood, who then found Rodrigues with a low pass, but the Southampton skipper, with time to control the ball, screwed his shot past Stepney's post.

The Saints' recovery was short-lived. On the hour Gordon Hill's in-swinging corner was flicked on at the near post by Pearson, whose back header met Sammy McIlroy's forehead full-square. A hundred thousand Wembley fans and millions of TV viewers shared in the Irishman's cry of anguish as his header hit the post and rebounded to safety. It was the turning point of the afternoon. If United had achieved a breakthrough then they would probably have won, as Docherty confirmed. 'The sides looked so evenly matched,' he said, 'I thought the first goal would settle it, and after Sammy McIlroy had hit the post it didn't look as if we were going to score it.' But as the game wore on without a goal from Docherty's men, the more concerted and purposeful became Southampton's ripostes.

Indicative of this was Docherty's substitution of Gordon Hill for David McCreery after 66 minutes, Peter Rodrigues having had the England winger in his pocket for most of the afternoon. It was, as Geoffrey Green put it, 'the first positive sign of United's growing anxiety before the mountain was finally reduced to a molehill.' Then McCalliog gradually wrested control of the midfield from the tiring Macari and Daly, urging on 'the eager Stokes, the surprisingly industrious Osgood and the fleet-footed Channon'[11] with more purpose. With mounting confidence and a smooth rhythm Southampton moved into the last half-hour, their expansive game exploiting Wembley's open spaces, and their goal, when it came seven minutes from time, was a stunning testament to their creative control.

Channon seized on a goal kick from Turner and instantly switched the ball to McCalliog, who flighted a perfectly weighted 20-yard pass between two United defenders into the path of Stokes, streaking through the inside-left channel. The Saints' midfielder had just gone close with a lob which dropped over the bar. Now, he summed up the situation in an instant before calmly shooting low and accurately beyond Stepney's despairing dive just inside the far post. United fans claim to this day that Stokes 'shinned it in', and that he was yards offside. Stokes himself thought he was but replays showed that it was his anticipation and speed that took him past Buchan and left him with only Stepney to beat.

On the parched Wembley turf, Stokes typified the Saints' terrier-like spirit, nipping at Lou Macari and Sammy McIlroy's heels like a Jack Russell whenever they had the ball.

From a young age, Stokes' talent had made him the target for a number of clubs and when Portsmouth's youth system let him slip he joined the Saints in September 1966. He made his first-team debut at the end of the 1968/69 season, scoring against Burnley. Now, after a decade of service at The Dell, he had written his name forever in Southampton folklore.

United tried to regroup, to summon up one final effort 'but their last attack was so unlike those which have thrilled us this season as to be a true parody'.[12] The Saints coasted the remaining seven minutes and, for the

---

[11] *Daily Telegraph Chronicle*, p. 155.
[12] Peter Corrigan, *Observer*, May 2, 1976.

teacher in Hastings, sweltering in a lather of mounting euphoria, they were the longest seven minutes of his life.

Overwhelmed, perhaps, by the yoke of odds-on favouritism, United's smooth engine misfired when it mattered most, as if their spark plugs, worn down by a season in almost continuous overdrive, finally gave up the ghost. After the opening salvo, Southampton had to withstand only sporadic pressure from an anxious young team, who ultimately capitulated to the composed experience of McCalliog, whose generalship made him man of the match, Osgood, Channon and Rodrigues, who effectively shackled Hill, Manchester's much-vaunted winger. Afterwards, Docherty said that Rodrigues was the reason why he substituted Hill in the second half; in fact, he praised the entire Southampton defence.

Lawrie McMenemy, the Saints' proud manager, said calmly when it was all over: 'This sort of thing is not supposed to happen to a club like ours. But now it has.' His strategy won the match. He aimed to cut off supply to United's dangerous wingers, Coppell and Hill, and, by tight marking, to make it difficult for Macari and Daly to get behind the defence on blind side runs. So United's attack, cramped for space, held the ball too long and ran round in elaborate but ever-decreasing circles in front of a solid back four. Fundamentally, the shock victory was a team effort, in which every man worked willingly for each other, Steele, Blyth, Holmes, Stokes and the rest never allowing themselves to be intimidated by the illustrious reputation of their opponents.

The next day, nearly 250,000 people lined the streets of Southampton to greet the conquering heroes. 'They came out of hospitals and fire stations, they sat up trees, and made us all feel 20 feet tall,' Bobby Stokes said later. 'Let's be honest: we weren't the best side in the world, but this was our five minutes of fame. I thank the people of Southampton from the bottom of my heart for the best two days of my life.'

It was a life, which, sadly for Stokesy, as he was always known, would be a short one. While he naturally became an icon among Saints fans, he was barely tolerated in Portsmouth, his native city, where he worked in a take-away cafe on the harbour. Many Pompey fans could never forgive him for his goal which won the only trophy the bitter 'enemy' has ever won. Stokes died in 1995 at the age of 44, after contracting pneumonia while playing golf. In his all-too-short life, he had done what nearly every schoolboy dreams of – scoring the winning goal in a Cup Final at

Wembley – and slaying the giants from Old Trafford to boot.

Though defeat smarted for Docherty, at least for him United had already won the 'real' Final. For the Saints, whose last final in 1902 had ended in defeat by Sheffield United, it had been worth the wait. In the next two seasons McMenemy took his side to the quarter-finals of the European Cup Winners' Cup and then back to Division One under the captaincy of World Cup winner Alan Ball. Over the next decade, great names like Kevin Keegan and Peter Shilton arrived at The Dell, which, with mandatory all-seating after the Taylor Report, was becoming more and more antiquated.

In 2001 the Saints moved, in a sort of spiritual homecoming, to the new Friends' Provident Stadium in St Mary's. Many Southampton fans have applauded the stadium's architectural elegance and its atmosphere while cherishing their deep and abiding memories of The Dell, of Derek Reeves, George O'Brien, Stuart Williams, Martin Chivers, Terry Paine, Mike Channon and perhaps the most gifted of them all, Matt Le Tissier.

And none of them will ever forget little Bobby Stokes, who, on a sunlit May Day in the mid-1970s, put the Saints on top of the football world.

SOUTHAMPTON: Turner, Rodrigues, Peach, Holmes, Blyth, Steele, Gilchrist, Channon, Osgood, McCalliog, Stokes (Fisher)
MANCHESTER UNITED: Stepney, Forsyth, Houston, Daly, Greenhoff, Buchan, Coppell, McIlroy, Pearson, Macari, Hill (McCreery)

31

STOKE CITY 2,
BLYTH SPARTANS 3

FA Cup, Round Four, February 6, 1978

Northumberland – rugged uplands, waterfalls, a National Park, craggy castles on windswept coasts, coal, ships, steam – and townscapes scarred by the Industrial Revolution. All of that, yes – but in the last two decades, signs of vigorous regeneration. Blyth, an ancient settlement 13 miles north of Newcastle, exemplifies the rich industrial history of North-East England, its growth and prosperity, its decline and renewal. The port of Blyth dates from the 1100s, but the modern town developed only after 1854 when the Blyth Harbour & Docks Board was formed and a quay built for the shipment of coal. Over the next century, until it reached its peak in the early 1960s, Blyth became the major outlet for the export of Northumberland coal. For generations, the area was dominated by heavy industries such as foundry work, shipbuilding and mining – but the last of its deep mines closed in the early 1980s and the shipbuilding yard, which built the first *Ark Royal* in 1914, was the largest on the North-East coast until it closed in 1967.

With the closure of the shipyard and the pits, Blyth has had to diversify into light industries. However, it is still a busy seaport importing paper and pulp from Scandinavia for the newspaper industries of England and Scotland, aluminium ore, plywood and timber from Scandinavia, the Baltic, South America and the Far East and, ironically, coal. In addition, it began to expand its retail base and to develop a tourist trade aimed at exploiting the Blyth Valley's rich industrial heritage and the proximity of the Northumberland National Park. Offshore, nine striking windmills – the Blyth Wind Farm – generate electricity for the National Grid. The harbour is the home of the Royal Northumberland Yacht Club and, while the town would not claim to be the 'Newquay of the North', its South Beach has a long stretch of golden sands and is popular with windsurfers. With a population of thirty-five thousand it is the largest town in Northumberland and still has a market three times a week.

Only five miles up the A189 north of Blyth lies Ashington, once known as 'the world's largest mining village' and home to footballing legends Jackie Milburn and his nephews, Jack and Sir Bobby Charlton. The Northumberland area was one of many conurbations which grew and mushroomed into the metropolises of the Industrial Revolution, becoming the hotbeds of football, especially the new professional game which, along with pigeon fancying was the main cultural and recreational pastime for the working man of the late nineteenth century. Blyth, with its mining and shipbuilding base, was part of that sporting milieu. Every young lad wanted to play football in his spare time. Wilf Mannion, a wonderfully gifted inside-forward for Middlesbrough either side of the war, recalls: 'We were playing across the street with anything we could get hold of. You were mostly groomed for the shipyards, steelworks and blast-furnaces so if you did make the grade *[at football]* it would be a good way out of that . . . It was nothing else but ball, ball, ball. It was all football.' So, in September 1899, a club was formed in the town. Mr Fred Stoker, who was the first club secretary, suggested the name 'Spartans'. He thought it appropriate to name the team after the Spartan Greek army in the hope that the players gave their all as they went into 'battle' on the field of play. He died in 1943 but his legacy lives on with the name 'Spartans' unique in the annals of English non-League football.

At first the club played only friendly matches before joining the Northumberland League in 1901. For the next 70 years the club plied its trade in the Northern Alliance, the Northern Combination, Northern Counties and the Northern League, a nomenclature for fundamentally the same animal – amateur or semi-professional football north of a line from Birmingham to The Wash.

'When you support a non-League team,' writes Ken Sproat, 'it can feel enough, and be a matter of quiet pride, that the club is known and respected in its own town.'[1] That respect had been the case in the Northumberland

---

[1] *When Saturday Comes*, no. 218, (April 2005).

port for generations, but in 1978 the town's team moved on to an almost astral plane and for a brief but glorious month Blyth Spartans became one of the most famous teams in the entire football-speaking world.

Blyth's squad had been put together during the previous decade and the club's relatively large support meant that Brian Slane was the manager of a side that had the pick of the North-East's non-League talent – Dave Clarke, for instance, was considered the best semi-pro goalkeeper in the country, Eddie Alder was the midfield dynamo and full-back Ron Guthrie had played for Sunderland in one of the other great Cup upsets when they beat Leeds in the 1973 final. A crucial acquisition that season, returning homesick to his native North-East, was former Brentford and Southend striker Terry Johnson, one of soccer's nomads who usually comes with the label 'journeyman'.

The qualifying-round schedule for the FA Cup in 1977/78 gave no hint of the drama to come. Regulation wins over four local sides were followed by a victory by the only goal over another team of part-timers, Burscough, in the First Round proper. Third Division Chesterfield were the next visitors to Croft Park. Blyth beat them 1–0, a notable result but not yet out of the ordinary, as both Crewe Alexandra and Stockport County had been beaten by the same score, in 1971/72.

The Third Round draw was disappointing. A home tie, yes, but to another non-League club, Enfield. No glamour, but it gave Blyth the opportunity to progress to the potentially lucrative Third Round. The reward for Alan Shoulder's header was a trip to Second Division Stoke City, a huge anti-climax. On paper they were several classes higher than Blyth and the expected inevitable defeat would allow Slane and his men time to reflect that they had done what few other non-League clubs had achieved – reached the Fourth Round without having played a team from the top flight.

This was a bad winter for weather and a waterlogged pitch meant the Stoke tie was called off twice. Fans who couldn't get down to the Midlands for a third time were to curse the postponements – they lost out on seeing one of the biggest Cup shocks in English football history. Stoke were a recent top-flight team, had won the League Cup six years earlier and had Howard Kendall, Terry Conroy, Alec Lindsay, former Newcastle striker Viv Busby (he was playing when Hereford's Ronnie Radford scored that goal) and a young Garth Crooks. By now the draw for the Fifth Round had been made. If, by a miracle, Stoke could be defeated, then the reward would be a trip of a lifetime to Newcastle (once they had disposed of Wrexham).

The tie turned out to be a classic as 'Blyth of the Northern League earned a place in the Fifth Round with a shock victory over Second Division Stoke at the Victoria Ground'.[2] An upset looked likely as early as the tenth minute, when Stoke keeper Roger Jones fumbled a corner and Terry Johnson easily scored from close range. But Stoke came back with a vengeance, Terry Conroy going tantalisingly close. Howard Kendall saw a shot parried away by Clarke only to see Ron Guthrie head the follow-up off the line. Early in the second half the Potters seemed to have sealed the tie with two goals in two minutes. First, after 57 minutes, Busby tucked a rebound into the corner of the net from 15 yards, from Busby and then, six minutes later, Garth Crooks – yes, the same one – nodded in at the far post. This double whammy should have saved the Second Division side's blushes and polished off the non-Leaguers. But Blyth came storming back: with ten minutes left Ron Guthrie's free kick spun off the wall at a daft angle and bobbled against the left post. Alan Shoulder headed on to the other post and Steve Carney was standing in the right place to lash in the equaliser. Both sides would probably have settled for the replay at that point but, with two minutes left, a free kick from John Waterson seemed to be overhit. However, Houghton managed to head it back into the area, where Robert Carney stuck out a hopeful boot, whence the ball rebounded to Terry Johnson, and from 15 yards the centre-forward coolly slotted the ball home. So Blyth became the first non-League club to reach the Fifth Round since Colchester and Yeovil in the late 1940s.

As Newcastle had been on the wrong end of a not-quite-so-surprising 4–1 hiding at Wrexham, Blyth fans were denied a memorable day out at St James' Park. Still, the Spartans became the nation's favourite underdog. As Ken Sproat put it, 'Blyth had it all – a great and unusual name, an odd strip, a solid history to show they were no mere fly-by-nights, eccentrics in the dressing room (cue excruciating footage of the players singing Zip-a-de-doo-dah), the de facto support of Newcastle and Sunderland fans, and for the papers an easy headline – 'Blyth Spirit.'[3]

Blyth faced Third Division Wrexham in the game that by rights should have seen Spartans into the last eight. In front of the *Match of the Day* cameras, after Terry Johnson scored what had become a customary goal

[2] *Daily Telegraph Football Chronicle*, p. 164.
[3] *When Saturday Comes*, no. 218 (April 2005).

after seizing on an appalling back pass the Welshmen escaped with a 1–1 draw, courtesy of a controversial last-minute equaliser. Roared on by enormous travelling support, they held on until the 89th minute when a thrice-taken corner owing to the flag's inability to stand up in the frozen ground gave Dixie McNeil the chance to force the ball over the line at the back post. Sproat again: 'Blyth had been denied in the harshest of ways. The sense of injustice was tangible. It still is. But Blyth were in the Sixth Round draw – Arsenal at home – and there was an indignant belief that we would surely win the replay, and perhaps even the Cup.'

Police fears for crowd safety at Spartans' compact Croft Park, with its 6,000 capacity, meant that the replay was switched to St James' Park, Newcastle. The Blyth supporters had their big night out at the 'Toon' after all: 42,000 swarmed in half an hour before kick-off, leaving fifteen thousand locked out. However, the occasion overwhelmed the apparently nerveless non-Leaguers and Wrexham were two goals up in 20 minutes. Battle though they did, Spartans ran out of steam and, in spite of Terry Johnson's inevitable goal, eight minutes from time, the Cup dream had ended.

Whatever happened to the heroes? The £7-a-week part-time players each received £350 worth of bedroom furniture from a local business. Alan Shoulder, who had combined part-time soccer for Blyth with life as miner for seven years, had been under close watch by Newcastle United during the Cup run and, at the age of 26, moved to St James' Park at the start of the 1979/80 season. He soon muscled his way in to the first team and he went on to average a goal every other game during an explosive 18-month introduction to full-time football, before moving on to Carlisle United. Steve Carney, the 20-year-old central defender, was also signed by the Magpies and went on to make 125 appearances for them over six seasons before he, too, ended up at Blundell Park. Terry Johnson can still be found every Saturday afternoon in Blyth – Blyth market that is. His fruit and veg has a particular taste for Spartan fans of a certain generation.

Spartans, having embarked on the adventure in the First Qualifying Round, played eleven games in that memorable run, scoring 20 goals and conceding just 6 (5 of which were in the three games against Stoke and Wrexham). No other non-League team had been as far in the FA Cup since before the Great War. An FA Cup Fifth-Round replay is not only as good as it got for Blyth Spartans, but for every non-League team, it is the stuff that dreams are made of. . .

STOKE CITY: Jones, Marsh, Lindsay, Kendall, Dodd, Bloor, Waddington, Scott, Busby, Conroy, Crooks
BLYTH SPARTANS: Clarke, Waterson, Guthrie, Alder, Scott, Dixon, Shoulder, Houghton, Johnson, S. Carney, R. Carney.

32

HALIFAX TOWN 1, MANCHESTER CITY 0

FA Cup, Round Three, January 5, 1980

Four and six, in old money – that's all it cost me in 1962. It seemed a lot then, to a university student in Southampton – every fortnight, on the terraces of The Dell, watching Terry Paine, David Burnside, Stuart Williams, George O'Brien and, in the couple of years before the full flowering of Martin Chivers and Mike Channon, the feisty Scouser centre-forward, George Kirby. A decade and a half later, via New York Generals, Watford and Iceland, where he managed one of the country's leading clubs, IA Akranres, Kirby pulled one of the great publicity stunts in Cup football, a brilliant sleight of hand against Manchester City's charismatic leader, Malcolm Allison, one of the great showmen of the modern game.

Kirby was by then in his second spell in charge at the Shay, the League's most ramshackle ground and home to Halifax Town. In one of the most bizarre episodes in the story of a competition liberally sprinkled with tales of the unexpected, the glorious and the almost incredible, Kirby had enlisted the services of Romark,[1] the well-known TV hypnotist. He it was who four years before had put a curse on Malcolm Allison, then the boss at Crystal Palace. Allison, an innovative coach with a touch of the used-car salesman, had asked Romark to hypnotise the team for the earlier rounds but changed his mind for the semi-final, whereupon a scorned Romark put a curse on Palace, who then lost to Southampton. Romark offered his services to Halifax for free and hypno-

---

[1] Ronald Markham in real life.

tised every member of the side, making them believe they were invincible.[2] Martin Tyler, now the distinguished football commentator for Sky TV, wrote in the august columns of the *Daily Telegraph* of 'the familiar cup themes of superstition and ritual' and that Romark's presence in the Halifax dressing room was 'totally in keeping with the magical image of the competition'.[3]

But we are getting ahead of ourselves – and Halifax, the down-to-earth wool town in the heart of West Yorkshire, seems an unlikely place for such irrational flights of fantasy. Two centuries ago, steam-driven machinery powered by water from the fast-flowing Pennine streams replaced the wool-spinning and weaving of the traditional cottage industry, which had since the Middle Ages used the soft water for washing, carding and combing the wool. As a consequence, wool production moved closer to the coalfields, crowding the valleys of the rivers Colne, Calder and Aire, and, gradually, each wool town in West Yorkshire developed its own speciality. After the invention in 1813 of the rag-grinding machine, by which discarded cloth known as 'shoddy and mungo' could be ground down into a fibrous state and reprocessed for a fraction of the price of new wool, towns like Dewsbury, Ossett and Halifax, in Calderdale, became major manufacturers of quality blankets, coats and military uniforms.

Halifax's cloth trade dates back to the fifteenth century, when lads were apprenticed to wool-masters to learn the trade. In 1450 the town forbade them to play football on pain of a fine of a shilling. Other provincial towns like Leicester, Liverpool and Manchester also banned the game, the good burgesses concerned about damage, personal injury and the fact that football dragged men of military age away from essential archery practice. Moreover, the game appealed mainly to 'young, healthy men whose vigour and collective boisterousness could not easily be contained by a society which lacked effective police forces or similar agents of social control. . .'[4] Football, then a mass participation sport with no rules, also afforded an ideal excuse for crowds to gather, often

---

[2] He was less successful in hypnotising himself. In October 1977 he announced that he was going to drive a car, blindfold, through Ilford. He set off in his yellow Renault and after 20 yards drove into the back of a parked police van. Nothing daunted, Romark declared, 'That van was parked in a place that logic told me it wouldn't be.'

[3] *Daily Telegraph*, January 7, 1980.

[4] Walvin, p. 19.

a young, excitable, moody crowd at that. Apprentices, moreover, were no ordinary crowd. Overworked, exploited and generally harbouring a range of grievances, they formed a frequently disaffected body of young men, living close to each other in the same areas of the city and thus easily in touch with each other. They posed a regular threat of unruliness and often erupted into outbursts of radical agitation.

The fragility of social control was always a source of unease to the governing class,[5] an attitude eerily reminiscent of the Thatcher government in the 1980s, for whom football, 'with its robust teams and its mayhem. . . could easily become the spark for a wider disturbance'.[6]

The striking eighteenth-century Piece Hall in Thomas Street is an architectural reminder of Halifax's heyday as a wool centre and the town is unmistakably a product of the Industrial Revolution, its solid Victorian heritage most notably represented by the town hall, the work of Sir Charles Barry, who designed the Houses of Parliament. Its football club, however, emerged in the Edwardian era. Halifax Town was founded on May 24, 1911 after a meeting held at the Saddle Hotel; for a season the club played in the Yorkshire Combination and then for nine years in the Midland League. Initially, Town's home ground was at Sandhall Lane, then at Exley, three miles from the centre of Halifax. This distance became increasingly irksome and, after the Great War, the club sought a new home. On the south side of Halifax, about a quarter of a mile from the town centre on the Skircoat Road, lay the Shay Estate, a council refuse tip where once there were green fields, a Georgian mansion and the elegantly peaceful Caygill's Walk (so named after one of the estate's early owners). In August 1920 the council agreed to 'let for a period of seven years a portion of the Shay Estate to the Halifax Town A.F.C., Ltd.', at an initial annual rent of £10. Much of the work in preparing the ground was done by fans, directors and players and the *Halifax Courier* appealed for funds. Eventually, in 1923 a stand was purchased for £1,000 from Manchester City's old Hyde Road ground. It still exists and is now the only part of the ground which dates back to the early years.

---

[5] Ibid.
[6] Walvin, p. 20.

The new ground was instrumental in gaining Halifax Town League status and in 1921 the Shaymen were elected to the Football League and became founder members of the newly formed Third Division (North). The first fixture at the stadium took place on September 3, 1921, when ten thousand spectators saw Darlington beaten 5–0. It was an inauspicious first season, however, and Town finished second from bottom.

Nearly six decades later, as the 1970s drew to their close, Halifax were flat-broke and the Shay was a dilapidated monument to years of struggle in the battle for re-election. However, on Christmas Eve, 1979, in a second replay, the Town scraped past Walsall 2–1 after extra time to reach Round Three and a home tie at the Shay against Manchester City, at the time seventh from bottom in the First Division and the 'cheque-book Charlies' of the day.

Since the glory days of the late 1960s, when they were League champions and Cup-winners, as well as winning the European Cup winners Cup twice, City had been perennial underachievers and the previous season had been knocked out in the Fourth Round of the Cup by Third Division Shrewsbury. Malcolm Allison, Joe Mercer's former assistant, had been plucked from comparative obscurity at Plymouth and immediately hit the headlines in September 1979 by signing the Wolves midfielder Steve Daley for £1,437,500. Daley had been capped for England at both Youth and B level and was vastly experienced. There was no doubting either his stamina or skill but he would look overvalued at that price even today.

The average home gate at The Shay was only two thousand and a full house promised a much-needed pay day: but on the day of the game, that prospect hung in the balance. After a week of frost, followed by a thaw and an overnight downpour, the pitch was a pond. It was still being forked half an hour before kick-off after a day in which a zealous 'Heath Robinson' mopping-up operation, involving the liberal use of towels, persuaded the referee against his better judgement that the ground was fit for play. Nonetheless, it still looked like a ploughed field and in the words of the *Guardian*, 'the setting was perfectly imperfect. A ramshackle stadium with a narrow playing area that thawed in time to turn the pitch into a morass.'[7]

Kit Walton, now chairman of Town's Supporters' Club, recalls waking up in the morning to a real Yorkshire downpour and rubbing his hands

---

[7] *Guardian*, January 7, 1980.

with glee. 'We thought a mud bath would be a great leveller'. Peter Ball, in the *Observer*, wrote 'City's notorious defensive frailties away from home were always likely to be tested by a determined club playing on their own patch. . .'[8] So it proved. The First Division side picked their way gingerly through the swamp for most of the game, longing for the replay, and the lush surface that awaited them at Maine Road.

Kirby had urged his men to get into the visitors' faces from the whistle and, in the first minute, centre-half Dave Harris nodded on Mick Kennedy's long throw unchallenged and Paul Hendrie, a £5,000 signing from Bristol Rovers, screwed a volley wide from only six yards out. That set the tempo and minutes later Andy Stafford, released by City as a schoolboy, swung in a deep cross from the left which was only just hoofed away from Franny Firth by Powers's frantic boot. The young City defence, three of whom were teenagers, including Ray Ranson, who would feature in Birmingham's defeat against Altrincham six years later, failed to pick up Stafford's in-swinging corner which struck Corrigan's far post beyond the goalkeeper's groping arm.

Gradually City played more cohesively and the home side's 19-year-old keeper, John Kilner, was forced into acrobatic saves from Bobby Shinton and Michael Robinson, who three years later would go on to Cup glory with Brighton. However, Halifax held firm until the interval, organised by their young captain, Dave Evans, who, when at Villa Park, was once chosen by Ron Saunders to mark Johann Cruyff in a European tie.

The second half was less open as the heavy pitch began to sap increasingly tired legs and the game became a war of attrition in the midfield morass. Hendrie, the smallest man on the pitch, 'ploughed through midfield like a little tank'[8] but hesitated too long at City's far post 11 minutes into the half. Halifax were indebted to the sterling defence of Harris and Geoff Hutt, but as time went on City's class looked as if it would prevail. Using the wings, where there was still some grass, Bennett picked his way past tackle after tackle to set up chances and one corner from Steve Daley skidded right across the goalmouth needing only a touch. The home defence, now severely stretched, had a let-off just after the hour when the ball fell to Bobby Shinton with the Shaymen's rearguard all at sea – but from only three yards he stabbed a shot straight at Kilner's midriff.

---

[8] *Observer*, January 6, 1980.

With 15 fifteen minutes left, Kirby and his staff, along with nearly 13,000 locals, were dreaming of a midweek replay across the Pennines and another fat cheque when Halifax won a throw-in near the halfway line. It was hurled down the line towards Andy Stafford, who eluded a half-hearted challenge before swinging over a low cross which reached John Smith on the edge of the area. He played it quickly forward where Paul Hendrie, sprinting through the mud, scooped the ball on his instep and coolly clipped it past the onrushing Joe Corrigan. That winning goal encapsulated the piquancy of the game. Stafford, rejected by City, had picked up the throw; Smith, whose career at Preston had been to all intents and purposes[10] ended by the development of Robinson, 'produced a remarkably deft touch in the conditions' and Hendrie, who cost less than one three-hundredth of Daley's transfer fee, had given the Fourth Division side an historic victory.

Inevitably, the last quarter of an hour had some palpitating moments for the home crowd as City roused themselves from their lethargy, but young John Kilner stood firm. It was enough to see Halifax home.

There had been little wrong with Allison's tactics – a conventional 4–4–2 formation, with Caton and Reid coping reasonably well at the centre of defence and Daley indefatigable in trying to work the ball effectively out of the midfield, but though they had more possession, City lacked incisiveness. To give him his due, Allison faced up to the inadequacy of his team's performance. 'How many chances did we miss from eight or nine yards with only the keeper to beat? We didn't finish. Pitches are going to be like this if we play the FA Cup at this time of year.'

The Town's triumph was captured by *Match of the Day* cameras and, because the floodlights at The Shay were not up to standard, the match had started early. Thus the Shaymen had emerged as the first of the day's giant-killers before most of the other clubs had got in for their half-time cup of tea. One of the many legends which abound in Calderdale is the tale of the Cragg Vale Coiners, a notorious band of counterfeiters whose leader, 'King' David Hartley, was subsequently hanged for murder in 1770, but there was nothing phoney about Halifax's victory and Hendrie's goal 'ensured a classic ending to a confrontation that included every element of cup-tie football; the fourth division against the first; the poor of the league

---

[9] Ibid.
[10] *Daily Telegraph*, January 7, 1980.

against its biggest spenders; a quagmire of a pitch in one of the game's least fashionable settings.'[11]

The Shaymen and their supporters had been expecting a replay but three weeks later they had their day out in Lancashire after all, climbing aboard their coaches for the trip to meet First Division Bolton Wanderers at Burnden Park. On this occasion, Romark sent an invoice and Town, with the cheque for their famous victory still in the post, couldn't or wouldn't pay it. Superstition or skill, whatever had worked for them at The Shay, lightning failed to strike twice as goals from Whatmore and Greaves consigned the Town to a 2–0 defeat.

As for City, for the second successive season they had egg on their faces and the wider implications of the defeat at The Shay unfolded as January rolled on into spring. After the first week of the new decade, City could offer nothing to their supporters but a long and disheartening climb from the cellar of the First Division. Prior to the Halifax game, Allison had said, 'It won't be the end of the world if we lose, but it will be close to that' – and the moneybags of the First Division were sent back along the M62 to play out a dismal season. Come May, City found themselves struggling against relegation and finished only 17th, six points clear of danger. To cap it all, Allison moved back to Selhurst Park, succeeded by the equally colourful and loquacious John Bond. It has never been dull being a City fan, for,

> according to the business seminar thinking that dominates so much of modern football, Manchester City are the sort of club that should no longer exist... Yet, by drawing strength from their marginalized position, and recruiting amongst Mancunians with an antipathy towards United's corporate power, Manchester City have defied market logic and claimed an important place in the landscape of British football.[12]

At the other end of the scale, their conquerors on that muddy January afternoon were only six years later facing extinction. In November 1986 Halifax Town were £425,396 in debt, with just six days to come up with proposals for paying the £76,000 tax debt to the Inland Revenue. The situ-

---

[11] Ibid.
[12] Lyons and Ronay, *When Saturday Comes*, p. 241.

ation was so serious that Halifax Town manager Mick Jones resigned for a more secure position at Peterborough United and the club began looking for a new home. They looked into sharing Thrum Hall – the home of Halifax RLFC, but an old covenant banned 'soccer for profit' there. Halifax Town even looked at playing at Odsal in Bradford, though this idea met with intense local hostility.

On December 23, John Madeley announced he had signed an agreement with a local firm, Marshall Construction of Elland. They wanted to build a superstore for Gateway Foodmarkets on The Shay, though it would have involved buying the lease of the ground for £2,430,000. The scheme seemed exciting but, like the plans of Marshall's and others, it was rejected by the council. Marshall's offered to build Halifax Town a 4,500-capacity stadium next to the nearby leisure centre, though they still wanted to build a superstore on The Shay, but when that plan was rejected, Marshall Construction, who had ploughed in more than £30,000 to meet the club's running costs, cut off all links with Halifax Town and the club was no closer to salvation than they had been five months previously.

Then, out of the blue, in April 1987, Calderdale Borough Council announced its rescue plan – they would hand over £210,000 to the club and buy back the lease on The Shay, worth about £150,000. This amounted to municipal control of the club and the Board of Directors was sacked. It meant, however, that football was kept at The Shay and the club was in one fell swoop on its soundest financial footing since its formation in 1911.

Halifax Town had risen from the ashes, since when it has acquired one unenviable record – it is the only club to be relegated to the Conference twice – in 1993 and 2002. However, on that day in January 1980, it had featured in one of those bizarre episodes which adorn the history of the world's greatest tournament. Romark's curse, which had done for Malcolm Allison in 1976, had worked again.

HALIFAX TOWN: Kilner, Dunleavy, Hutt, Evans, Harris, Hendrie, Firth, Kennedy, Mountford, Smith, Stafford.
MANCHESTER CITY: Corrigan, Ranson, Power, Reid, Caton, Bennett, Henry, Daley, Robinson, Viljoen, Shinton.

33

HARLOW TOWN 1, LEICESTER CITY 0

FA Cup, Round Three, January 8, 1980

Ebenezer Howard – not a household name now perhaps, but it would be fair to say that without him, modern Harlow might never have existed. Howard's 1902 book; *Garden Cities of Tomorrow*, set out a vision of towns cleared of the slums created by the Industrial Revolution, blessed with the benefits of urban living (opportunity, entertainment and high wages) and the pleasures of the countryside (such as beauty, fresh air and low rents). The book argued for the creation of new, planned suburban towns of medium size, offering modern housing, local employment, wide streets and open space, surrounded by a permanent belt of agricultural land. His ideas were instrumental in the creation of the world's first 'Garden Cities', at Letchworth in 1903 and Welwyn Garden City in 1920, and this planning ethos later informed the New Towns Act of 1946.

Over half a million Londoners had lost their homes in the Blitz and under the 1946 Act, towns like Basildon, Stevenage, Hemel Hempstead, Crawley and Harlow were designated 'New Towns'. 'Planning' was the post-war buzzword and under the Act enormous sums of Government money were ploughed into rehousing the homeless Londoners in these 'New Towns'. In the late 1940s and early 1950s, these communities in the Home Counties, largely pre-war villages or small market towns, would see a vast expansion in employment and a growing influx of newcomers, many of whom were tough, resilient, aspirational East Enders, as homes, factories and leisure amenities were built to absorb London's 'overspill'.

In Harlow, on the border of north-west Essex and Hertfordshire just west of the M11, the master plan for the new town was drawn up in 1947 by Sir Frederick Gibberd, whose plan divided the New Town into neighbourhoods, each self-supporting with its own shopping precincts and community facilities. It incorporated the market town of Harlow and the villages of Great Parndon, Latton, Tye Green, Potter Street, Churchgate Street, Little Parndon and Netteswell. Harlow's town centre, built around 'Old Harlow', boasts Britain's first pedestrian precinct and Britain's first tower block, The Lawn, constructed in 1951, which is now a Grade II – listed building.

Originally nicknamed 'The Owls', Harlow Town FC was formed in 1879 and entered East Herts League Division One in the 1896/97 season. Down the years the club has played in five different amateur leagues based in the Home Counties: in fact, in 1909/10, as members of the Stansted & District League, the same team played in two competitive divisions at once, a practice then fairly common at the lower end of amateur football.

In 1932 Harlow joined the Spartan League, one of the strongest amateur competitions in the South of England and, though they never finished above halfway in the League, Harlow did win the first-ever Spartan League Cup in 1953. However, a year later the League changed its format and the Owls moved to the much more competitive London League. The club did not finish in the top half of the league until 1960/61, though that season proved to be a major landmark in the history of Harlow Town. Not only did they win the London League Cup, but they moved from Green Man Field, their home since 1922, to the newly built Harlow Sportcentre on Hammarskjold Road, the first sports centre in the country.

For the 1961/62 season, Harlow had once again moved, this time to the Delphian League and by the late 1970s on to the Isthmian League, having won the Athenian League's Premier Division in 1973. Under an experienced manager, Ian Wolstenholme, the club had built up a strong side and in 1978/79 the Owls romped away with the title, scoring 93 goals, conceding only 32. Thus, for the first time in their history, Harlow appeared in the Isthmian League Premier Division in their centenary season of 1979/1980, one which would turn out to be the most memorable in the club's history.

Harlow's season began promisingly but when the club beat Lowestoft Town in the Preliminary Round of the FA Cup few Owls fans could have entertained notions of the saga to come. However, wins over Hornchurch, Bury Town and Harwich & Parkeston brought Conference side Margate to the Sportcentre in the Fourth Qualifying round. A 1–0 victory meant that Harlow Town were in the First Round proper for the first time in their history, with a chance of a money-spinning draw against a leading League side.

What came out of the hat was a disappointing bread-and-butter home tie against Leytonstone & Ilford from their own league but a 2–1 win gave the Owls a promising away tie with Southend United, then near the bottom of the Third Division. Ten days before Christmas, Harlow fought out a fine 1–1 draw at Roots Hall and brought the Shrimpers back to the Sportcentre on the following Tuesday night for the replay, where a crowd of 5,000 saw Harlow win 1–0 with a goal from Micky Mann.

Harlow's reward was a visit to Second Division League leaders Leicester City at Filbert Street. By now, the Owls had become a focus for media attention. Leicester fans permitted themselves some nervous titters but after the near-debacle against non-League Leatherhead five years before,[1] they persuaded themselves that, while a game against an Isthmian League side who had squeezed past Southend United represented a potential banana skin, it was of a non-slip variety.

The optimism of the Foxes' fans seemed justified when Martin Henderson put City a goal up after half an hour following a mistake from Harlow's keeper, Kitson. The home side squandered innumerable chances to clinch the tie but Harlow, playing with a devil-may-care resoluteness, refused to lie down but did not pose a serious threat to Leicester's goal in the second half. However, in a rumbustious finish to a mundane encounter the home crowd were silenced when two minutes into stoppage time, the Owls' left-winger Griffith found Neil Prosser 'with an incisive pass. Prosser, with his socks around his ankles, spun like a top to evade May's challenge and calmly slid the ball into the net as Wallington came out'.[2]

The Sportcentre was packed on the following Tuesday night when a record crowd of 9,723 turned up to see a scrappy game – a far-from-tasty treat to set before BBC's *Match of the Day* cameras. Not that the Owls' faithful minded that as their heroes could have been a goal up after only three minutes when Leicester defender Larry May just got a foot in front of Peter Twigg, who had latched on to Micky Mann's free kick. Then Twigg went close with a fine drive from 35 yards and Mann swung over another dangerous free kick which flew across the six-yard box, evading everybody.

---

[1] See Brighton v Leatherhead, pp. 191–197.
[2] Vince Wright, *Daily Telegraph*, January 7, 1980.

At the other end, Harlow keeper Paul Kitson was in imposing form, saving well from John O'Neill. His only nervous moments came in the 24th minute when he tipped Alan Young's header over the bar at full stretch and, later, when he was forced to punch clear from another O'Neill effort. Throughout most of the first half, the visitors showed little enterprise up front, relying on high balls launched at the heart of Harlow's defence where Vic Clarke and Tony Gough whose height and strength snuffed out any danger before it occurred.

On a night when tension precluded any quality football, the only goal, when it came, was appropriately shambolic. Four minutes before half-time, Micky Mann floated yet another free kick into Leicester's goalmouth, where 25-year-old company accountant John Mackenzie tried to head the ball on. His flick towards goal bounced off Larry May and Mackenzie reacted first to prod a left-foot shot past the startled Mark Wellington. The ball crept no more than 18 inches over the line before Tommy Williams hoofed it clear. Harlow needed no video replays, no Hawkeye, no Russian linesman – the referee was on hand and instantly gave the Isthmian Leaguers the lead. Later, MacKenzie admitted his moment of glory wasn't a classic: 'It came from a free kick move we play. Micky Mann swung the ball over well, I played the ball on to a defender, it came back and I hit it – with my wrong foot! I was so pleased to see the ball go over the line!' As the crowd 'erupted in to a sea of waving red-and-white. It might have been the Stretford end in full flight, and the expressions on the Leicester faces told their own story.'[3]

After the interval, however, Leicester raised their game, spurning several excellent chances to equalise. Larry May struck a looping long-range shot just over the bar, Smith volleyed over when Young headed Henderson's cross down to him, then Young wasted Leicester's best chance of the match when his weak left-foot shot skidded past the post. Eventually however the Foxes resorted to hoisting over-hopeful high centres, which were swallowed up by Gough and Clarke in a resolute home defence.

Harlow themselves did not sit on their lead. They were always the more inventive side on the night, Prosser and Twigg continually testing the visitors' harassed defence. Before the end Leicester's right-back Williams vented his frustration on the effervescent Neil Prosser, Twigg and Wickenden shook

---

[3] Martin Penny, *Harlow Gazette*, January 11, 1980.

Wellington with dipping 35-yard efforts and MacKenzie nearly added a second when Dennis Rofe scrambled back to head his effort off the line with Wallington beaten. Seconds later referee Mr Robinson blew for time and all Harlow went wild.

It had by no means been a lucky victory for the Owls, who matched the Second Division leaders for both skill and commitment. As the jubilant fans went singing home, the party got underway at the Willow Beauty, the closest pub to the ground. In the home dressing room, goalscoring hero John MacKenzie, surrounded by photographers, was being drenched in milk by Peter Adnams and Fred Flack: presumably the Owls didn't run to champagne. While manager Ian Wolstenholme didn't see it as the highlight of his career – 'I once saved a penalty at Wembley and there aren't many people who can claim that' – he did, however, concede that it was 'a great result and a deserved one'. He went on to explain: 'We played far better than at Filbert Street. Some of Leicester's younger players appeared to show their nerves and we took full advantage. Tactically it went just as wanted. We cut off the supply from Eddie Kelly in midfield and in the end thoroughly deserved to go through.'

As for City's boss, Jock Wallace, he admitted to being 'bitterly disappointed. You make your own luck in the game and all credit to Harlow, they had the bit of luck that was going and took it. They were well organised and played hard, but so were we. The only thing they did better was to take their chance.'

The Owls were probably still suffering from the post-Leicester celebrations when, on the following Saturday, they stumbled to a 3–0 League defeat at home to Hayes. However they had recaptured their Cup-gifting spirit just over a fortnight later when they travelled to Vicarage Road to face Graham Taylor's Watford in the Fourth Round. On January 26 the *Match of the Day* cameras were at the Second Division club's compact ground as Harlow Town's dreams of Wembley were dashed in an epic performance.

From the first whistle Watford's direct approach, based on speedy delivery to the bustling Luther Blissett and the lanky Ross Jenkins, posed enormous problems for the Owls' sturdy but somewhat static defence. Nonetheless, the non-Leaguers survived this initial onslaught and, midway through the first half, centre-forward Neil Prosser sent all 10,000 of the Harlow fans at the Rookery End mad with delight. He 'harried Ian Bolton into conceding a corner, and as Mann stepped up to take the kick one could sense an air of expectancy. The corner was delicately flighted to the near post where Prosser's flick completely confused Steele and crossed the line before the keeper snatched it back. Referee and linesman had no doubt and the goal stood.'[4]

While Harlow thoroughly deserved to go into half-time a goal to the good, they knew the home side would come at them with a vengeance after the break – and Watford did not disappoint. Whatever Graham Taylor said to his team – and later he claimed he hadn't said very much – they stormed out and seized the game by the throat. Ross Jenkins fired a warning shot across Kitson's bows, his fierce drive screaming over the Owls' bar. Then, 17 crazy minutes saw Watford, seemingly, put the game beyond all reach.

On 48 minutes Wilf Rostron nodded the ball into the path of Malcolm Poskett, who calmly drove home from 15 yards. Four minutes later Jenkins flicked on a corner for Martin Patching to plant a diving header past Kitson. With the Harlow defence creaking at the seams, in the 55th minute Patching waltzed through the defence to make it 3–1: then in the 63rd minute Ian Bolton smashed a free kick from the edge of the box while Harlow were still building their wall.

The tie was settled, but the League side had two late frights as Harlow's spirit never waned. Their unwavering character was rewarded after 65 minutes when Clarke flicked a ball on for Mackenzie, who had had two stitches in a cut to his head before half-time, to nod past Steele. Six minutes from time Mackenzie doubled his tally with the goal of the match. Peter Twigg got his head to a cross to put the ball into the inside-left's stride and his stunning 30-yarder flew past Steele. In the last seconds Twigg almost grabbed an improbable equaliser, rising to attempt an almost impossible header, only to see the ball soar narrowly over the bar with all of Watford breathing a collective sigh of relief.

After these heroics, however, the rest of the 80s were a decade of struggle and, when the club's plans to leave the Sportcentre for a new stadium on Roydon Road collapsed, the Isthmian League closed down the Sportcentre after it no longer met League requirements and in 1992 Harlow Town FC went into administration. A year later Italian restaurant owner Georgio Di Benedetto and builder John Taylor invested hard cash in the club, now

---

[4] Martin Penny, *Harlow Gazette*, February 1, 1980.

dubbed 'The Hawks', and in October 2006 Harlow FC moved to a new stadium at Barrows Farm, which can hold up to 3,500 spectators.

The Hawks are clearly aiming to create new memories and new heroes but, whatever summits are scaled and whatever dramas played out at Barrows Farm, Hawks fans will never forget the night at the old Sportcentre when Leicester City, Gary Lineker and all, were done for by an accountant called John Mackenzie.

HARLOW TOWN: Kitson, Wickendon, Flack, Gough, Clarke, Adnams, Mann, Austin, Prosser, Twigg, Mackenzie
LEICESTER CITY: Wallington, Williams, Rofe, Goodwin, May, O'Neill, Lineker, Henderson, Young, Kelly, Smith

34

AFC BOURNEMOUTH 2, MANCHESTER UNITED 0

FA Cup, Round Three, January 7, 1984

When retired army officer Lewis Tregonwell visited the coast near the Hampshire/Dorset border in 1810, he found only a wasteland of fallow common between the burgeoning boroughs of Christchurch and Poole. Where a bridge crossed a small stream, or 'bourne', which led out into Poole Bay the gallant captain and his wife bought several acres and built a home, today part of the Royal Exeter Hotel. Tregonwell also planted pines near the mouth of the stream and a village clustered around these scattered trees. From a settlement which barely existed at the start of the nineteenth century, Bournemouth quickly became a destination for affluent holidaymakers and invalids in search of the sea air. In Thomas Hardy's *Tess of the d'Urbervilles* (1891) Bournemouth features as 'Sandbourne', a 'fashionable watering-place, with its eastern and western stations, its piers, its groves of pine, its promenades, and its covered gardens'. Although the number of convalescents fell towards the end of the Victorian era, the town's popularity as a holiday destination continued to grow and more hotels, theatres, concert halls and cafés appeared in the town centre.

This seaside pleasure dome seems an unlikely place to find the origins of a professional football team. 'A statistic says if every bar in Bournemouth is full, 40,000 people are drinking – a huge number for a town with a population of 163,000. However, if AFC Bournemouth's stadium is full, there are just 9,000 fans watching; Bournemouth is a resort not a football town.'[1] Nonetheless, the present football club can trace its roots as far back as 1890

---

[1] Lyons and Ronay, *When Saturday Comes*, p. 48.

when Boscombe St John's Institute Football Club were playing in local football. They disbanded in 1899 and, from the remains of that club, Boscombe FC were formed at a meeting under the streetlights in Gladstone Road, Boscombe. After enjoying many local successes, they joined the Hampshire League and were attracting large crowds. In 1910 Mr J.E. Cooper-Dean granted the club on a long lease some wasteland next to Kings Park. With their own ground, named Dean Court after the benefactor, the club gained the nickname, 'The Cherries', after the cherry-red striped shirts the side wore – or, as some would claim, because Dean Court was built next to the Cooper-Dean estate which included many cherry orchards.

Elected to the League in 1923, Bournemouth held the record for the most years in Division Three, but made a name as Cup fighters in January 1957, reaching the Fifth Round by beating Wolverhampton Wanderers, led by England captain Billy Wright and flying high in the First Division, in front of forty-two thousand at Molyneux. Left-winger Reg Cutler, who scored the winning goal, did the damage in more ways than one: he collided with a goal post, which had to be repaired. Bournemouth then accounted for Tottenham Hotspur by 3–1 at Dean Court before going down to a controversial quarter-final defeat, 2–1 at home, by Manchester United's 'Busby Babes'. One of United's goals appeared offside and the other was a dubious penalty.

In 1970, with a change of name to 'AFC Bournemouth', the club raised its sights and the flamboyant, outspoken John Bond aimed to become a First Division manager at Dean Court. Ted MacDougall was the star striker, with Phil Boyer and Mel Machin supplying him with the ammunition. MacDougall scored 49 goals in the 1970/71 season and, in the following campaign, he hit nine in the 11–0 FA Cup win over Margate. Unfortunately, MacDougall left for Manchester United after the side had finished third in Division Three at a time when only two clubs were promoted. In 1973 Bond left for Norwich, taking Boyer and Machin with him, and the 20,000 crowds dwindled to little over 3,000. The arrival of Alec Stock as manager restored some pride to the club and ex-Saints and Chelsea stalwart David Webb assembled a good side, which won promotion in 1982, whereupon he was dismissed and the club seemed to be heading back to Division Four. However, the appointment of ex-Hammer Harry Redknapp was to transform the club.

Harry's finest hour came when Manchester United arrived at Dean Court in the Third Round of the FA Cup on January 7, 1984 – a chance for the Cherries to exact FA Cup revenge, 27 years on. United were the Cup-holders, having seen off another South Coast side, Brighton, in a replayed final the previous May, and had suffered just one defeat on the road all season. They had not won a League title since the 60s and, though they were in a relative slump at the time – just before Christmas, United had been knocked out of the League Cup by Third Division leaders Oxford United – a repeat against Bournemouth looked unlikely. With Bryan Robson, Arnold Muhren, Frank Stapleton, Norman Whiteside, Lou Macari and Gary Bailey they had the nucleus of a good side. Gordon McQueen and Kevin Moran were injured, yet the team still boasted ten full internationals and an upset seemed as remote as a settlement in the miners' strike, then gripping the nation. Jim Straight, a long-time Cherries fan, recalls United manager Ron Atkinson appearing on TV the night before the game. His response to the comment, 'May the best team win', was 'Oh, we will'.

He had every right to be confident. The Cherries were fourth from bottom of Division Three, with only five home wins all season. Despite a comfortable 4–0 win over Walsall in the First Round, the Cherries had needed two attempts to overcome non-League Windsor and Eton (0–0 away before 2–0 in home replay) in Round Two, and, having lost to bottom-of-the-League Port Vale on the preceding Monday, David Swindells, a supporter for over half a century, felt 'there could not have been too much optimism in the Bournemouth camp'.

Yet Atkinson's air of confidence bordered on the complacent and Redknapp showed that beguiling mix of self-assured brashness and tactical nous that has become his stock-in-trade. He told Stuart Jones of *The Times*, 'We watched a video of United against Oxford and we noticed there was a chink in their armour. Some of them do not perform when they are closed down.' Formerly a winger with West Ham United, Redknapp 'remembered how much unnecessary respect First Division sides pay each other, and how their rhythm, and subsequently their confidence, can be broken if their freedom is suddenly limited.' According to Cherries fan Lindsey Wainwright, 'The papers had also referred to Harry's novel form of training – a stroll along the prom and a cuppa tea in a caff.'

You could buy a voucher for a Cup ticket if you went to the home game the week before and sure enough the gate swelled from 3,000 to 14,000.

When the tickets went on sale on the Sunday, Cherries fan Kevin Foote recalls 'the indignity of queuing up all around Dean Court and the surrounding leafy suburbs'. Lindsey Wainwright joined the queue before eight in the morning 'and had my four tickets by ten – £3.50 each, including the 50p programme.'

Saturday, January 7, 1984. Jim Straight recalls standing in the 'packed South End on a cold crisp afternoon, with the away fans occupying the entire Brighton Beach End.' Barrie Price took his nine-year-old son and watched the game from the New Stand, the one with the low roof. There he might have rubbed shoulders with Robert Day, who always enjoyed the walk to Dean Court 'over a golf course, through an underpass, then onto an avenue, turn left up to the ground'.

They saw an unremarkable first half, in which honours were even. From the kick-off, Bournemouth took no prisoners and their uncompromising tackles had the Reds 'visibly frightened', according to Cherries centre-half Roger Brown, who commanded his defence with a calm assurance. The rearranged United defence began apprehensively and both Graham Hogg, making his debut in the centre of the defence, and Arthur Albiston were embarrassed early in the game. With ten minutes gone, Albiston conceded a corner from 20 yards out without a Bournemouth man in spitting distance. It seemed Redknapp was right: they didn't like it up 'em.

The Cherries went close with Phil Brignull, Savage and a header from Milton Graham, who had Bournemouths best chance when his left-foot drive from only eight yards was deflected for a corner. There were some enterprising canters from Morgan up front, Ian Thompson was looking sharp, but it was La Ronde who stole the show, coolly snuffing out Stapleton's intelligent runs and reducing Whiteside to scowling impotence. United's chances were sporadic. After only eight minutes, Savage fouled Stapleton just outside the penalty area and Arnold Muhren chipped a promising-looking free kick well over the bar. Then skipper Bryan Robson shot just over the bar and, on the half-hour, Muhren floated a fine cross from the left but Brown skidded up and whacked the ball to safety before Stapleton could capitalise on it.

Robert Day recalls the half-time buzz around Dean Court: 'We came back for the second half still full of self-belief.' With Albiston unable to continue, midfielder Lou Macari reverted to full-back in an already makeshift defence, but with 55 minutes gone 'they had a marvellous chance to score themselves. In one of their few fluent moves, Whiteside back-heeled to Wilkins, who found Arthur Graham free out wide on the left.'[2] However, Cherries keeper Ian Leigh 'twisted brilliantly to paw out Arthur Graham's shot'.[3] This may have changed the course of the game for 'they were soon to be humiliated cruelly for their earlier torpor'.[4]

Five minutes later, a dull game burst into life as, said Jim Straight, 'within a mad few minutes when I thought I was dreaming', Bournemouth scored twice. On the hour, Chris Sulley took a corner at the Brighton Beach End, Gary Bailey, touted as a future England keeper, fumbled the cross and Trevor Morgan nodded the ball back for Milton Graham to hook it home. Tottenham-born Graham had spent the previous summer honing his playing skills in New Zealand: now 45 and working as a boat-builder, he suffered a serious ankle injury in 1989 and retired from professional football six years later. 'I had this superstition of putting my shorts on last. I don't know why.' On that day it worked: Dean Court exploded with rapture.

Two minutes later, while United were still coming to terms with being a goal down in such lowly company, England skipper Bryan Robson dithered with uncharacteristic hesitancy over clearing a free kick from the exotically named Everald La Ronde and Ian Thompson, a £16,000 buy from Salisbury City, stole the ball back and whacked in an unstoppable half-volley for a second goal. Robert Day, only 14 – 'but I felt younger that day' – was whirling his scarf round his head: 'I dropped my programme on the ground over the barrier, because of my excitement; and a passing policeman picked it up for me.'

With the South End in uproar, the holders had 28 minutes to stay in the Cup, but the customary assertion of First Division class after the huffing and puffing from the lower orders just did not happen. Indeed, Bournemouth could have increased their lead. The defence stood firm, with Roger Brown outstanding, and Leigh saved well from Stapleton. Even when Macari did beat him, the effort was disallowed and, as Julie Welch commented in the *Observer*, 'for all Wilkins's ultimate hard work and Whiteside's macho forays, this was one afternoon when nothing they did turned out even halfway right'. However, it was all in vain: 'the cause had been lost long before for United, who had started off timorously, played without style or daring or

[2] Nick Pitt, *Sunday Times*, January 8, 1984.
[3] Julie Welch, *Observer*, January 8, 1984.
[4] Ibid.

adventure, and finished up on the wrong end of one of the most staggering wins in Bournemouth's history.'[5]

While Bournemouth thoroughly deserved their triumph, United had barely turned up. Donald Saunders in the *Telegraph* blamed a certain inflexibility in the Cup-holders' attitude. 'Despite the presence of gifted individuals such as Robson, Muhren, Wilkins and Stapleton – all capable of turning or controlling a game – United seem incapable of adapting quickly and smoothly to changing circumstances.' While Cherries fan Barrie Price felt that Ray Wilkins 'was the only United player who actually cared about losing', Stuart Jones felt he 'faded all too soon' in a midfield where 'Robson looked unfit, Muhren unwilling and. . . Whiteside, once laughably compared to Best, continued to resemble a broken windmill, all flailing arms and legs. . .' Furthermore, as United manager Ron Atkinson said afterwards, 'You cannot assume a divine right to play well. You have to fight for it – matching fire with fire, until you get the chance to play.'

A minute from the end United fans infiltrated the South End terraces reserved for Bournemouth supporters and, as Jim Straight put it, 'a few fists were exchanged, representing the futility of a lost cause'. United 'fans' were attempting to get the game abandoned. Indeed, the tie was held up for five minutes as hundreds of Bournemouth fans spilled on to the pitch, bringing the game to an ugly and almost premature close. It was an irrelevance: United were done for and as Harry Redknapp declared: 'We don't get many days like this in Bournemouth.'

For the first time, Robert Day, Lindsey Wainwright and hundreds of others climbed over the barrier on to the pitch, where a tracksuited Harry Redknapp was talking to Southern TV. In contrast, Ron Atkinson kept his team in the cramped away dressing room, emerging after 45 minutes, boiling with anger and as the cliché has it, 'tight-lipped'. His superstars had played without style or adventure and George Best, working on radio, declared that he would have been 'embarrassed to pick up my week's wages' if he had played like some of the Reds that day. For Atkinson, it had been 'a horrible experience. We beat Barcelona not long after in the Cup Winners' Cup and I told Maradona he could think himself lucky he hadn't been playing Bournemouth.'

Still in a daze, Jim Straight headed for a few pints in the Supporters

---

[5] Ibid.

Club, where on TV, 'There were joyous scenes on *Final Score* – Robbie Savage inadvertently revealed almost all in the players' bath – and ITV's Fred Dinenage was dragged in for a full soaking.'

The little club from the Dorset coast received all the usual national media hype and the victorious Cherries team celebrated their famous victory with a holiday in Spain. For a while, supporters like Jim, Lindsey, Robert and Barrie Price could dream of Wembley, but the grim reality was an away trip to Middlesbrough in the Fourth Round. The game was postponed until January 31, a Tuesday. Jim Straight went up by train to see two goals from Sugrue put the Cherries out of the Cup. 'We faced a never-ending journey home – back to Scunthorpe away and Newport County at home.'

That season Harry's side won the first ever LDV Vans Trophy (then known as the Associate Members' Cup) and captured the Third Division championship. But the likeable Londoner could not keep them there, however. On the final day of the 1989/90 season, Bournemouth were beaten by Leeds, which gave the Yorkshire side the title and sent the Cherries back down to Division Three. Over the next 15 years they were up and down the leagues like an Otis lift, until, at the end of the 2007/08 season, Bournemouth suffered yet another relegation, down to League Division Two.

But then football is very much a game of glorious highs and unbearable lows. For Milton Graham, his goal against Manchester United at Dean Court 'has to top everything', but he was left out at Middlesbrough in the next round, 'which was a bit of a choker'. Though he has managed to adopt a philosophical stance – 'I have to remind myself that football is no longer the be-all and end-all' – his is only a superficial sanity. 'I still get carried away with football,' he says, and as Chris Oakley reminds us, 'football offers us the possibility of manageable doses of self-elected madness. A madness that is essential for a sane life.'[6]

BOURNEMOUTH: Leigh, La Ronde, Sulley, Savage, Brown, Brignull, Train, Nightingale, Morgan, Graham, Thompson
MANCHESTER UNITED: Bailey, Duxbury, Albiston, Wilkins, Hogg, Robson, Moses, Muhren, Stapleton, Whiteside, Graham

---

[6] Oakley, p. 5.

35

BIRMINGHAM CITY 1, ALTRINCHAM 2

FA Cup, Round Three, January 14, 1986

Think executive-style Tudor developments, with gated driveways and swimming pools. Think four-by-fours, Mercedes and Ferraris. Think – Altrincham, the home of modern-day 'celebrities' such as Premiership footballers and Andrew Flintoff. We are in leafy Cheshire here, but, lying about eight miles south-west of Manchester, the town owes its desirability to the Industrial Revolution. Nothing more than a small market town with a cotton and worsted trade until the mid-eighteenth century, Altrincham's fortunes improved with the arrival of the famous Bridgewater Canal, constructed in the 1760s, but it was the development of the railways, in particular the opening of the Manchester South Junction and Altrincham Railway in 1849, which sparked the town's growth. Despite the fact that mid-Victorian Altrincham endured epidemics of typhoid and cholera, the town and the older village of Bowdon near by became sought-after places for the nouveaux riches to establish grand residences, whence they could commute to the city by train. However, even with the creation of the railways, horses were still a common transport between Altrincham and Manchester as was a passenger boat down the canal and new potatoes were still carried from Bowdon Downs to Manchester on workers' heads.

Altrincham lies on the A56 south of the M63 and the suburb of Sale. The oldest surviving part of the town is around the Old Market Place and Church Street, where there are a number of Georgian buildings, and it was here, in the Red Lion, that Bonnie Prince Charlie's troops were billeted in 1745. Altrincham became a part of Trafford Metropolitan Borough in 1974, having, till then, been part of the County of Cheshire.

Indeed, though it is no longer necessary, many people still know the town's address as 'Altrincham, Cheshire'. From the 1970s Altrincham's industrial base declined and the area is now predominantly residential and commercial in nature, with large-scale retail parks growing up in Broadheath, a former industrial area west of the A56 on the Bridgewater Canal.

Broadheath had become heavily industrialised after the arrival of the railway and it was here that the origins of Altrincham FC can be found. In 1891 the club was known as the Rigby Memorial Club, formed from a local Sunday school. They went on to merge with another local club known as 'The Grapplers' to form Broadheath FC and become founder members of the Manchester League in 1893. Ten years later the club took its present name and is today the only founder member of the Manchester League still in existence.

Altrincham's FA Cup exploits started in 1934 when they reached the First Round proper for the first time, losing 1–0 at Gainsborough Trinity, though they had already notched their first league scalp in a Fourth Round qualifying tie against Tranmere Rovers in 1921/22, winning the replay 4–2 after a 4–4 draw.

By the early 1960s, however, the club was in financial trouble, the ground was in bad shape and the team was struggling. Enter two knights on white chargers, better known as White and Swales Ltd, who had built up their chain of radio, record and TV shops in Altrincham at a time when technological advance and rising affluence coincided. Noel White and Peter Swales, both ex-accountants and former players,[1] applied the same tough financial methods to running Altrincham FC that had built up their successful chain of 15 shops.

White and Swales loaned £6,000 to the club to clear its immediate debts and guaranteed the wages of the club's complete professional staff. They replaced all the exisiting directors (except Len Pollitt, a haulage contractor) with themselves and three specialist members of their own staff. They were commercially hard-headed – 'Everything has to show a profit – or we want to know why, but the only real guarantee of success is a winning team.' To this end, they brought in ex-Newcastle, Manchester United and Blackpool inside-forward Ernie Taylor, Paddy Fagan from Manchester City and Tommy

---

[1] Swales played inside forward for Ashton United and White had three years as centre-half with Chester City.

Banks from Bolton. After Charlie Mitten had come and gone after his spell with Newcastle

they had a re-think. Maybe the best man for a non-League club was a manager who knew the non-League set-up, inside out. They picked Freddie Pye – a successful scrap-metal dealer, who had played with Accrington Stanley, but who made his biggest mark in winning two Cheshire League championship medals as a wing-half with Hyde United. With two businessmen at the helm, and an equally good businessman running the team, things began to happen.[2]

They were ambitious for League football at Moss Lane and in 1966 Altrincham reached the Third Round of the Cup, knocking out Fourth Division Rochdale on the way, before crashing out 5–0 to Wolves at Molineux.

In 1968 the club became founder members of the newly formed Northern Premier League and won the FA Trophy at Wembley ten years later. In 1979 Altrincham FC became founder members of the Alliance Premier League, the forerunner of today's Blue Square Conference Premier, winning the title in its first two seasons, as well as the Bob Lord Trophy in 1980/81 and the FA Trophy once more in 1986.

By the mid-1980s, with White having moved into the hotel business and from there to the Liverpool Board and chairmanship, and Swales making a hobby of sacking managers at Maine Road,[3] having become Chairman at Manchester City in 1972, Altrincham had been for two decades one of the top non-League teams in the game and had narrowly missed election to the Football League on more than one occasion. Having put out 11 League sides in the previous two decades, the club's Cup credentials were well established. A 1–1 draw against Everton at Goodison Park in 1975 and a respectable 2–0 defeat at Old Trafford in the replay were followed later in the 1970s by games against Tottenham Hotspur and Liverpool, and excellent victories over Crewe, Rotherham, Sheffield United, Scunthorpe and York City, which only served to enhance the club's growing reputation.

At the turn of the year, in December 1985, Altrincham were fourth in the Alliance Premier League, now the Conference, and pushing hard for

---

[2] *The Best of Charles Buchan's Football Monthly*, p. 131.
[3] He appointed and dismissed 11 managers. He died in Manchester in May 1996.

promotion to the Fourth Division. Chorley, of the Northern Premier League, had been despatched in a comfortable 2–0 win in Round One and Blackpool, Cup winners themselves in the epic 'Matthews Final' of 1953, provided Alty's next opposition away at Bloomfield Road. Their Division Three status made no difference to the confident Alliance outfit, whose 2–1 victory secured their place in the hat for Round Three. The draw, which took place ten days before Christmas, gave the club the present of a potentially lucrative away tie at St Andrew's against First Division Birmingham City, who were having a ghastly season. The charismatic Ron Saunders had secured the club promotion the year before, but they were heavily in debt and propped up the old First Division, having lost fourteen and drawn one of their previous fifteen First Division matches.

In the New Year, heavy snow and a frozen pitch forced a postponement from the original Saturday, and ten days later, on Tuesday, January 14, conditions had barely improved. Only 6,636 bothered to turn up at St Andrew's, where in a gale-force wind and an atmosphere more akin to a memorial service, the Blues' crude, long-ball game was ineffective in the howling wind.

After an uneventful first 45 minutes, the visitors turned round to face the teeth of the gale, kept the ball on the grass and controlled what was in truth a dreadful game. Then unbelievably, and against the run of play, with the Birmingham faithful fearing the worst, nippy winger Robert Hopkins gave the Blues the lead in the 63rd minute, hooking the ball home from a corner kick by Ray Ranson, an advantage which proved to be short-lived. A free kick from Davidson fell invitingly in Birmingham's goal area and, with the Blues' defence standing like dummies at Madame Tussaud's, Ronnie Ellis equalised from close range. However, with a quarter of an hour left, after an inept performance from the top-flight team, came a suitably calamitous winner. Hopkins, who barely ten minutes before had been City's potential hero, decided the tie when he coolly planted an injudicious backpass past England's Under-21 goalkeeper, David Seaman. By contrast, Altrincham's keeper, Jeff Wealands, released three seasons earlier by Blues manager Ron Saunders and with a point to prove, was enjoying 'a very sweet win. The problems I had with the manager here are well known. I fancied our chances right from when the draw was made. They didn't really put us under any pressure whatsoever.' Two days later, Ron Saunders resigned as Birmingham's manager and, despite a brief improvement under his successor, John Bond, the Blues won only three more games and Hopkins, Seaman and co left for pastures new. City were relegated and it would be 16 years before they returned to the First Division.

Altrincham's achievement was unfortunately set against the unpopularity of the game in the mid-1980s. English clubs were banned from European competitions and supporters of the national team were constantly in the spotlight. The spectre of hooliganism on the terraces was at its zenith: there were no Saturday highlights programmes and very few games were shown live. Sadly for Altrincham only a local TV news crew was present to film the game and the quality of the footage matched the mediocrity of the game itself. Remarkably, however, given the notorious insularity of American sports coverage, the victory of the non-Leaguers from a Manchester suburb made headlines across the Atlantic, as UPI reported in the *New York Times* a 'Stunning Upset in British Soccer'.

Altrincham had become only the sixth team from outside the English League to beat a First Division club and it remains the last occasion on which a non-League side won away to opposition from the top division. Their reward was a home tie in Round Four against Third Division York, which they lost 2–0. Altrincham did go on to win the FA Trophy that season, although promotion to the League has proved to be the end of the rainbow which has never quite been reached.

BIRMINGHAM CITY: Seaman, Ranson, Dicks, Hagan, Armstrong, Kuhl, Roberts, Wright, Kennedy, Platnauer, Hopkins
ALTRINCHAM: Wealands, Gardner, Densmore, Johnson, Cuddy, Conning, Ellis, Davison, Reid, Chesters, Anderson

36

ALDERSHOT 3, OXFORD UNITED 0

FA Cup, Round Three, January 10, 1987

On the Hampshire/Surrey border, where the heavy clays of the London Basin give way to widespread sand and gravels, the heathland around Aldershot was the perfect landscape for the establishment of an army base. Although the name may have derived from 'Alder', indicating that it was a wet, boggy place, the heaths on which the settlement grew up were well drained and in 1854, at the time of the Crimean War, the newly expanded British Army was searching for a headquarters. The arrival of the military led to a rapid expansion of Aldershot's population, which rose from 875 in 1851 to over 16,000 a decade later (including about 9,000 from the garrison), and the impact on the local area was dramatic. Aldershot rapidly grew into a Wild West shanty town, with spivs and prostitutes moving in to help relieve the troops of their money (some would say not a lot has changed). The town even made its name in the annals of one of the great detective legends of our time – Sherlock Holmes was called in by the Aldershot police to investigate the murder of Colonel James Barclay in nearby North Camp. The town continued to grow, reaching a peak in the 1950s, its respectable suburban credentials enshrined in Betjeman's gently romantic 'A Subaltern's Love Song':

> Miss J. Hunter Dunn, Miss J. Hunter Dunn,
> Furnish'd and burnish'd by Aldershot sun,
> What strenuous singles we played after tea.
> We in the tournament – you against me!

Since then many locals would assert that it has fallen into a steady decline, claiming that the British Army has been the making and, in recent years, the breaking of Aldershot.

Aldershot Football Club does not stretch as far back as the Crimean War, however – and its formation owes almost everything to one individual, a Mr Jack White. In the early 1920s White, a sports journalist working on national newspapers, moved to the town and soon opened discussions with local businessmen regarding the forming of a local football club and in December 1926, with municipal blessing, Aldershot Town Football Club was formed and an application to join the Southern League (Eastern) was accepted. The club was nicknamed 'The Shots' for both the last syllable of the town name and its military links. The club's home ground was to be the council-owned Recreation Ground in the High Street, where Aldershot Town FC (1992) still play today. The club was admitted to League football when Thames AFC declined to apply for re-election in 1932 and the 'Town' part of the name was dropped in 1937.

Town then spent many seasons in the lower divisions of the Football League and were among the founder members of Division Four in 1958/59, but despite its humble status Aldershot has had some notable players in its colours: in 1975/76 the current manager of Crystal Palace, Neil Warnock, played 37 games for the Shots before moving on to Barnsley and Teddy Sheringham played for the club six times while on loan to the team in 1985. Brian Talbot, the former England international, Ipswich Town and Arsenal stalwart, and later West Bromwich Albion's manager, was also briefly a 'Shot'.

The club twice reached the Fifth Round of the FA Cup, once in its inaugural Football League season and once in 1978/79, but 1986/87 must rate as the most successful season in the club's history, when Aldershot were promoted to Division Three for only the second time, becoming in the process the first winners of a play-off final, beating Wolverhampton Wanderers FC over two legs. There were dramatic Cup runs as well: the Town reached the Southern Final of the Freight Rover Trophy, but it was the FA Cup which gained the Shots their short-lived moment of national glory. A routine home win by the only goal over Torquay United in Round One was followed by a close game at the Rec in the Second Round. The Shots edged past Colchester United, also in football's bargain basement, by the odd goal in five, Martin Foyle, another of Aldershot's noteworthy old boys, scoring twice. Foyle moved on in 1991 to Port Vale to become the Valiants' record post-war goalscorer and, until September 2007, the manager.

On the day before the game the *Aldershot News* ran a flag-waving editorial urging local fans to turn up and cheer the Shots on – 'Aldershot will hit the headlines on Saturday when Oxford United visit the Recreation Ground. This will be the first time a First Division team has played an FA Cup tie there for 23 years.' It's hard to believe that Oxford United, now in the Blue Square Premier (the Conference), were a top-flight outfit two decades ago. The paper goes on to say that the club had already reaped much publicity locally by charging £9 for the ticket-only game but it hoped that the Shots would 'produce a display to match the ticket prices'.

Tickets caused problems on the day of the game itself. Under a headline all too familiar in the 70s and 80s – 'Soccer fans on rampage' – the paper reported the arrest of 24 fans as trouble broke out among both sets of supporters when they were unable to get into the Recreation Ground to see the match. At 12.30 several hundred local fans were turned away by police and violence flared when some 150 Oxford fans arrived at the railway station, having caused trouble at Ascot station, where knives were stolen. Once in the town centre, they gathered in an off-licence, leaving just enough time for a spot of shoplifting in Next. Unsurprisingly, many of the fans, according to Inspector Jim Pretty, were the worse for drink.

In the event, a crowd of fewer than two thousand saw the Shots' biggest game for years. The council-owned stadium was sorely in need of refurbishment and stringent ground safety regulations which followed the 1985 Bradford fire led the police to set an all-ticket limit of 3,400. However, had the club charged a more reasonable £5 to stand and £7 to sit they would have filled the capacity of 3,400 and taken as much in gate receipts without infuriating so many of their loyal supporters. Chairman Colin Hancock denied accusations of profiteering. 'If we had played this game at a loss we would have been faced with winding-up orders.' With the club nearly £300,000 in debt, they had tried unsuccessfully for a £30,000 grant from the local council for ground improvements and needed cash to plan for the future. Nonetheless, a letter in the *Midweek News* in the week following the game complained that regular fans were being expected to 'pay through the nose' for the Cup game and that only the committed diehards would forsake TV and videos to 'stand around a cold and draughty soccer ground for 90 minutes of entertainment'.

Entertainment there was aplenty, however, at the Rec that Saturday as Aldershot, a team assembled for a mere £23,000, beat their First Division opponents 3–0. It was an embarrassing irony for Aldershot that their most memorable success since the win over Aston Villa in 1964 should be watched by the lowest-ever recorded Third Round attendance.[1] As the *Daily Telegraph* put it in a headline on the Monday, 'Missing fans sour Aldershot triumph'. Manager Len Walker and Colin Hancock admitted that the meagre size of the crowd had overshadowed the team's triumph. Hancock assured Shots fans that prices would come down for the next round and the team would not want to switch the tie if they got a good draw. 'I would rather play at home in front of 1,000 than play away,' said Len Walker, 'because we can beat anybody here.'

While Walker had always been confident of victory, he must have been surprised at how poorly Oxford played. The frosty pitch – midfielder Glenn Burvill didn't think the game would be on – and the warm reception from a home side with nothing to lose 'effectively ironed out any difference in class'.[2] In short, as Burvill put it, 'they didn't fancy it'. In one of those ties which make the first weekend in January one of the most eagerly awaited in the footballing year, all the most fluent and incisive football came from Aldershot and after six minutes they were ahead.

Their captain, Ian McDonald, floated a deep cross to the far post where centre-half Colin 'Smudger' Smith struck a precise header past Hardwick for his first goal of the season. Smith, who was only 28, had recently re-covered from Hodgkin's disease and 'played very well', according to Aldershot's coach, Ian Gillard. 'He lacks a bit of pace, but that was no problem to him because he is an intelligent lad, and reads the game well.' Throughout the first half, Oxford struggled to find any composure, until Blankley nearly equalised for his opponents when his hasty back-pass forced Lange to his one significant save. They exerted serious pressure at the start of the second half, when Aldershot 'packed their area, tackled hard, and sensibly cleared first time without much worry about where the ball went'.[3]

Langley, Ring and Barnes always threatened in attack, Ian McDonald impressed in midfield and Friar was outstanding at left-back, setting up the killer goal in the 58th minute. Glen Burvill latched on to his through pass and his drive flew past Hardwick, who was slow to take off on the slippery surface.

---

[1] Aldershot were not alone – Charlton Athletic, who were beaten 2–1 by Third Division Walsall, had their lowest FA Cup home gate since November 1927.
[2] Tony Pawson, *Observer*, January 11, 1987.
[3] Ibid.

'We were kicking towards the home fans. I was about 25 yards out and I thought, "I'll just hit it and see". It flew in under the bar.' Burvill was in his second spell at the Rec: 'I'd come to the Shots from West Ham, then spent a year at Reading and went on loan to Fulham under Ray Harford, which was great. We had some good footballers in the side at the time – Martin Foyle was the main man, the goalscorer – he'd come from the Saints. Ian McDonald was a good player, too, and Bobby Barnes, who was with me at West Ham.'

Barnes, indeed, it was who hammered the final nail into the visitors' coffin. Sprinting clear, his first shot brought a sprawling save from Hardwick and he fired the rebound into the roof of the net. Oxford's aura of impending doom was signalled by the substitution of John Aldridge, in his last game for the club before moving to Liverpool a fortnight later for £750,000. At the end, the faithful few danced the conga 'on the empty spaces of the terraces in a warming victory celebration'.[4]

Burvill was to score an arguably even more significant goal in the summer of 1987. That season the Football League turned back the clock and reintroduced end-of-season play-off matches similar to the old test matches which were features of the League in the 1890s. Bolton Wanderers had had a dreadful season: however, they were thrown a lifeline when they finished in a play-off position. Aldershot proved to be too strong, winning 3–2 on aggregate, though it was only in extra time, and after injury to goalkeeper Dave Felgate, that Burvill's goal condemned the Wanderers to relegation to Division Four for the first time in their history.

In the match to decide the final promotion spot, Aldershot overcame Wolverhampton Wanderers 3–0 on aggregate, but the club was relegated back to the Fourth Division two years later and in August 1990 they were wound up in High Court, 'hopelessly insolvent' with debts of £490,000. A white knight appeared in the unlikely shape of 19-year-old property developer Spencer Trethewy, who staved off the threat of closure for another couple of seasons. In the end, Trethewy's sticking plaster ran out and, in spite of heroic efforts from the supporters and playing staff, on March 25, 1992 Aldershot FC finally went out of business. They were obliged to resign from the Football League and the Shots' League record for the 1991/92 season was expunged.

On Wednesday, April 22, 1992 at the Royal Aldershot Officers' Club, at a public meeting attended by over 600 faithful Shots supporters still

---

[4] Ibid.

stunned by the loss of League status, Aldershot Town Football Club was formed. Its fanzine carries the appropriately evocative title of *The Rising Phoenix*. Until early 1992, when the first Supporters' Trust was formed in Northampton, 'the only serious mobilisation of fans', writes Paul French, 'had revolved around supporters' clubs and associations – sad collections of men who paid a small yearly subscription fee to become the proud owner of a wallet-sized membership card, a newsletter they'd never read and the right to brag they were the club's most dedicated supporters.'[5] The fans in Aldershot had gone one better – barely had their club been buried, while its embers were yet warm, they formed a new one from the ashes of the old.

The meeting was organised by Terry Owens, a former chairman of the Save Our Shots campaign, in conjunction with Graham Brookland, who was chairman of the Supporters Club, Peter Bridgeman, honorary secretary, and David Brookland, honorary accountant. A limited company had been formed as Aldershot Town Football Club (1992) Ltd and, at a second public meeting on June 16, 1992, another packed audience were given the news they all wanted to hear. Despite the fact that Chris Tomlinson, son of head groundsman Dave, was the only player on the books, Aldershot Town had been accepted into the Diadora Isthmian League Division Three.

On Sunday, August 16, soccer fans settled into their armchairs 'to watch the beginning of a new era in English football'. On the following Saturday, against the backdrop of 'the all-singing, all-dancing always-the-best-game-ever world of The Premiership',[6] when within a few years the £100,000 which led to the liquidation of the old Aldershot would be a superstar's weekly wage, the fledgling club played its first-ever match – and 15 years later, at the time of writing, the Shots are seven points clear at the top of the Blue Square Premier, with every prospect of League football returning next season to the Recreation Ground.

ALDERSHOT: Lange, BlankIey, Friar, Burvill, Smith, Wignall, Barnes, Mazzon, Ring, McDonald, Langley
OXFORD UNITED: Hardwick, Langan, B. McDonald, Reck, Hebberd, Dreyer, Houghton, Aldridge, Whitehurst, Trewick, Brock

---

[5] French, p. 212.
[6] French, p. 74.

37

MIDDLESBROUGH 1, GRIMSBY TOWN 2

FA Cup, Round Three, January 7, 1989

Listen! No, please, this is a good one – 'Which Football League club has never lost at home?' Give up? Thought so. The answer's Grimsby Town, because Blundell Park, their home ground, is in Cleethorpes. Like another, would you? Oh, all right. . . 'Sunderland did it in 1979, Villa did it in 1981. Who did it in 1980?' No? Well, it's Trevor Brooking – scored the winning goal in the Cup Final! Just two of the millions of snippets of useless information which delight football anoraks in clubs and pubs all over the world.

Here's one more fact. . . 'Grimsby is the largest fishing port in the world'. One of those bits of data which, for a grammar schoolboy raised in the mid-1950s on Pickles' regional geography of the British Isles,[1] seemed an immutable law of nature – like Mount Everest being the highest mountain and the Pacific the largest ocean. We assumed it had always been thus and so, we thought, for the infinite future it would remain. However, like many 'facts' in history and geography, they represent mere snapshots in time, which, as in Grimsby's case, ignore the context of an interesting past and an uncertain future.

Although there is some evidence of a small Roman town of artisans, Grimsby was founded by the Danes in the ninth century AD. The old Danish word for village was *by* and this one was probably Grim's *by* or Grimmr's *by*, or village. Located on the Haven, which flowed into the Humber, the village was listed in the Domesday Book, with two hundred people, a priest, a mill and a ferry (probably to take people across the

---

[1] Thomas Pickles, *Britain and Abroad: An Introductory Geography* (Blackie, 1928).

Humber to Hull) and became a fishing and trading port, an ideal place for ships to shelter from approaching storms. Sadly, by the fifteenth century, the Haven began to silt up, preventing ships in the Humber from docking, and Grimsby fell into a slow but inexorable decline.

By the late eighteenth century, however, Britain's Industrial Revolution offered new opportunities for enterprise and growth and in 1796 the Great Grimsby Haven Company was formed by Act of Parliament for the purpose of 'widening, deepening, enlarging, altering and improving the Haven of the Town and Port of Great Grimsby'.

As a consequence, in the early 1800s, Grimsby imported iron, timber, wheat, hemp and flax and, when the railway linking the port with London and the Midlands was completed in 1848, the town began to export coal from the South Yorkshire coalfields. Furthermore, Grimsby's proximity to the rich fishing grounds in the North Sea added to its wealth and No. 1 Fish Dock was built in 1856. The town boomed and Grimsby's population, like the fishing fleet, greatly expanded, growing from 8,800 in 1851 to 75,000 by the end of the century.

The expansion of the railway network impacted coastal communities in other ways. When the railway linked growing industrial cities like Leeds, Bradford and Sheffield to small fishing villages on the east coast such as Scarborough, Bridlington and Skegness, they were transformed into thriving resorts. Cleethorpes, physically linked to Grimsby, as Brighton is to Hove, was another such village, and in the 1850s, with the arrival of the railway, this genteel society retreat grew into a major resort, its population growing tenfold in 40 years.[2]

The railway station disgorges day-trippers directly on to the North Promenade but Cleethorpes isn't really a 'seaside' resort at all. The town actually sits on the Humber estuary and at low tide bathers are separated from the 'sea' by a vast expanse of mud. They can console themselves, however, with panoramic views of busy shipping plying the ports of Grimsby, Immingham, Hull and Goole.

As they watch the container traffic cruising up and down the Humber, they are probably unaware that Blundell Park is in Cleethorpes and is part of a delicious bit of football trivia. Grimsby Town's home ground, whose Main Stand is the oldest in English professional football, was opened in

---

[2] In 1831 the population of Cleethorpes, according to the census, was 497: in 1871 it was was 4,019.

1899 and the club itself is one of the oldest in the country. It came into being at a meeting held in September 1878 at the Wellington Arms in Freeman Street, when members of the local Worsley Cricket Club wanted to form a football club to keep them fit in the winter. With a home ground off Ainslie Street, the club was originally known as Grimsby Pelham FC, after the Pelham family who were prominent landowners in the area, but only a year later the club was renamed Grimsby Town. The club – nick-named 'The Mariners' – turned professional in 1890 and were founder members of Division Two in 1892. By 1901 Grimsby had made it to the First Division, surviving for a couple of years before plummeting down to the Midland League for a season a decade later. Former Lincoln manager George Fraser took Grimsby to third position in Division Three North in his first season (1921) but he left when he felt the board were interfering too much in team selection and the recruitment of players. He was succeeded by Lancastrian Wilf Gillow, who had played briefly for both Blackpool and Preston before the First World War, before taking over as player–manager at Blundell Park, guiding the club to Division One in 1929 for the first time in 27 years.

The next two decades were the Mariners' 'sepia glory days, a cloth-capped utopia to which it has never really returned. Legends such as the prolific Joe Robson, Pat Glover and the England international midfielder Jackie Bestall took Grimsby to fifth in Division I in 1934–5, their best-ever finish.'[3] The club also appeared in two FA Cup semi-finals, in 1936 against Arsenal and three years later against Wolves at Old Trafford: the atten-dance (76,962) is still a record for that stadium.

Those glory days seem now to be part of an alternative space – time continuum, one in which the game, played in a monochrome Pathé News world, was watched by flat-capped middle-aged men with fags in their mouths and waving rattles. The legendary Bill Shankly was briefly at the helm after the club's relegation to Division Two in 1948 but the 1950s saw a steady decline to its 1969 nadir – finishing next to bottom of Division Four. A couple of positive achievements – an excellent Fourth Division championship in 1972 under the charismatic Lawrie McMenemy (later an FA Cup winner with Southampton) and fifth position in the old Division Two in 1984 – could not obscure chronic problems of under-investment

---

[3] Lyons and Ronay, p. 176.

in playing strength and by 1988 the club had suffered two successive relegations. The heady days of Cup semi-finals were half a century away, the
team were struggling in Division Four and the club faced severe financial
difficulties.

The Cup campaign was a welcome diversion from the depressing League
form and began promisingly when Wolves and Rotherham, respective leaders
of the Third and Fourth divisions, were despatched in the First and Second
rounds. To many Mariners' fans, however, with Grimsby 750–1 shots to
lift the Cup on the morning of the game, the trip to Ayresome Park to face
a Middlesbrough side going well in the First Division was a journey more
in hope than expectation. However, Middlesbrough had an even worse
Cup record than Grimsby, never even having reached the semi-finals, and
they had been put out of the League Cup (that season known as the
Littlewoods Cup) by another Fourth Division team, Tranmere Rovers.

Around two thousand Grimsby supporters made the trek up the A1 and
Chris Dillon recalls hearing Bruce Rioch, the Middlesbrough manager,
announcing on local radio that 'If we lose today I will put all 11 on the
transfer list.' Neil Parsons, another Mariners fan, remembers being one of
the two thousand 'crammed into an open standing corner of Ayresome
Park, a typical old-fashioned ground,[4] accompanied by inflatable bananas,
an inflatable champagne bottle and an inflatable black & white penguin.'

The most that the visiting fans might hope for was a decent game. On
the one hand, Middlesbrough had some highly rated players – including
one of the most solid and reliable pairs of centre-backs in Tony Mowbray,
now manager of West Bromwich Albion, and the newly capped Gary
Pallister, subsequently a star with Manchester United – and on the other,
Alan Buckley, in his first spell as Grimsby manager, favoured a neat passing
game. Grimsby kept the Boro at bay for the first 40 minutes, being threatened only when a drive from Peter Davenport was parried away by keeper
Paul Reece.

After 25 minutes, during a spell of sustained pressure, the visitors almost
took a shock lead when Shaun Cunningham latched on to a through pass
by John McDermott, but his run, nearly half the length of the pitch, was
thwarted by Steve Pears in the home goal. Visiting fan Neil Parsons felt
that 'the Mariners' best chance had gone when we failed to score during

---

[4] It had been opened in 1903.

this period'. And then, when Grimsby seemed likely to go into the break on level terms, against the run of play Bernie Slaven, who had been consistently on target since joining Boro from Albion Rovers in 1985,[5] nodded home a Stuart Ripley cross to give the home side a fortuitous half-time lead.

After the interval, Grimsby began to get on top and to create chances, forcing Pears to save twice in quick succession from Richard O'Kelly and Keith Alexander. But they could not break down a stubborn home defence and it seemed as if the Mariners would be going out of the cup, despite outplaying the favourites in the second half.

Then, 20 minutes from the end, manager Alan Buckley gambled, hoping to exploit this attacking initiative. He decided on a change of tactics, making a substitution which must rank as the most inspired of his long managerial career. While Grimsby were taking a throw-in, Buckley replaced skipper O'Kelly with Marc North, who had begun life as a goalkeeper with Luton Town. From the throw-in, Keith Alexander evaded Pallister's tackle and slid the ball to North inside the penalty area. With his first touch, the sub twisted smartly and beat Pears with only his second touch of the ball. 'The manager told me to run around and score goals,' said North and he obeyed his boss's instructions to the letter. Three minutes from time, Kevin Jobling (who had taken the throw-in which led to the first goal) sent over a long cross, Alexander knocked the ball on and Marc North swooped to put a diving header into the back of the net.

Cue delirium in the ranks. 'Oh for the days of jumping up and down on the terraces with your mates,' sighs Mariners fan Martin Robinson, but there was no time for prolonged euphoria. Neil Parsons recalls growing 'desperate for full time as Boro' began to take control again, forcing a goal-line clearance by Paul Agnew with the goalie Paul Reece beaten, and winning several corners, Gary Pallister heading against the Town crossbar.'

'When the final whistle went,' says Parsons, 'there were unforgettable scenes as the Town players and management all rushed over to the corner where we were housed, and we sang, jumped and danced as if there was no tomorrow. I remember all hell breaking loose at that point, with Town fans jumping and dancing around the terrace in all directions.' He remembers

---

[5] Slaven, who now co-presents the *Three Legends* football phone-in on Century FM in the North-East, scored 146 goals in 381 games for Middlesbrough.

'looking up to the stand on the left, where a number of Boro' "undesirables" were throwing coins at those of us celebrating below.' In fairness, Martin Robinson's memory is that 'the home fans clapped us off that day – though it was a bit hairy getting back as some Boro' fans tried to stone the coaches, but we made it OK.'

Neil Parsons' one abiding memory was at Ferrybridge services on the way home, when about a thousand Grimsby fans spotted Marc North walking through the service station. 'The whole place erupted into "Marcy North, Marcy North, Marcy, Marcy North, he gets that ball he's sure to score, Marcy, Marcy North" as he was raised shoulder high.' It was a Roy of the Rovers moment to cap a *Boy's Own* afternoon for the late substitute, who said after the game, 'The gaffer told me at half-time that I'd go on if we were still losing. I'd not been playing well in recent matches and the fans were impatient with me. So this was a great day for me.' It was also a great day for Gillian Green and her family. 'My husband, two daughters and I drove up to Middlesbrough. Alan Buckley allowed Marc North to travel home with us, and when we stopped at the Ferrybridge services for a drink, Marc was totally mobbed. A joy to see.'

It is a football memory tinged with sadness, which puts the game into true perspective, for seven years ago Marc North died of cancer. 'He was our son-in-law but he left us with some wonderful memories, plus a grandson, Daniel, who also has his father's love of football, so it lives on.' Sadly, too, neither Marc nor Grimsby really received the credit they deserved for their victory. That very same afternoon Sutton United beat the Cup-holders, Coventry City, and took all the plaudits in the media, which still rankles with Martin Robinson. 'For us, beating a team about 70 places above you in the League in their backyard was the upset of the day.'

For Buckley's young side, including players from non-League football like Keith Alexander, John Cockerill and the young goalkeeper Paul Reece, the game against top-flight opponents was a valuable experience, as *Gazette* reporter Dave Boylen pointed out, 'the young lads in the side such as Mark Lever and John McDermott will have learnt a lot from the Middlesbrough game which will only enhance their character. . .'[6]

The proof of Buckley's pudding was seen in Round Four, when another goal from Marc North gave the Mariners a draw against Reading at Blundell

---

[6] *Grimsby Gazette*, January 13, 1989.

Park. 'We then won the replay 2–1 at Elm Park in another game which no Town fan there will ever forget,' says Neil Parson, 'but our Cup run culminated at Plough Lane, Wimbledon, where seven thousand Grimsby fans, accompanied by a thousand inflatable Harry Haddocks which inspired innumerable crazy imitations, saw Town lose 3–1, after leading at half-time through a goal by Keith Alexander.'

Neil Parsons was just 21 at the time and assumed with the naive optimism of youth that another such Cup run would be just around the corner. Spare a thought for Neil. At 39 he is still waiting. The double-winning visit to Wembley in 1998 for the Auto Windscreens Shield and Division Two play-offs, an unlikely win at Anfield in 2001 in the Worthington Cup, followed by a 1–0 defeat of Tottenham in the League Cup in 2005, were all straws to be clutched at 'in the current patchy landscape of financial difficulties, with the taxman a regular visitor and administration looming darkly'.[7]

Despite its proud past and its sporadic Cup successes since the war, Grimsby Town remains one of the country's harder, no-nonsense clubs, and Blundell Park, with its rusting turnstiles and ancient stand a stark reminder of cloth-capped black-and-white football, is a tough ground for any team to visit – a place where the locals glorify powerful, committed competitors and are sceptical of any elegant ball-players.

The town itself 'is forever redolent of fish, despite the fact that very few trawlers ever come within miles of its docks these days'.[8] As a result of the Cod Wars with Iceland, overfishing and EC quotas, the industry has declined sharply since its heyday in the early twentieth century. While the town still has the largest fish market in Britain, most of what is sold is now brought in from other UK ports. In recent years the frozen food industry has become a large part of Grimsby's economy and new industries such as light engineering, chemicals and plastics have grown. It is a measure of the decline that the fishing industry now has its own museum – the National Fishing Heritage Centre – opened in 1991.

Two decades ago, however, the Mariners enjoyed a rare triumph, a day of promise which remains unfulfilled – much like the pledge of Bruce Rioch, who never did put his team on the transfer list. And for the Green family,

---

[7] Lyons and Ronay, p. 176.
[8] Ibid.

a proud memory of Marc North, a man taken far too young, who on January 7, 1989, had his day in the sun.

MIDDLESBROUGH: Pears, Burke, Cooper, Mowbray, Hamilton, Pallister, Slaven (Mohan), Brennan, Glover, Davenport, Ripley
GRIMSBY TOWN: Reece, McDermott, Agnew, Tillson, Lever, Cunnington, Jobling, Saunders, O'Kelly (North), Cockerill, Alexander

38

SUTTON UNITED 2, COVENTRY CITY 1

FA Cup, Round Three, January 7, 1989

On Gander Green Lane, Sutton, you're in classic semi-detached suburbia – leafy tree-lined avenues, manicured front lawns, pebble-dashed fascias and quiet, secluded back gardens. Ten years ago Katie Melua, the golden-voiced beauty from Georgia, lived in the lane where, since 1912, the Borough Sports Ground has been home to Sutton United Football Club. Ms Melua's first, huge, hit was 'The Closest Thing to Crazy' and, for United fans, the events of January 7, 1989 would be the closest thing to crazy they had ever known.

Amateur football clubs in suburban South London don't really do crazy, but Sutton United has had its moments. In 1929 the club was expelled from the FA Amateur Cup because two players were found 'guilty' of also playing Sunday football. One of the game's most flamboyant characters, Malcolm Allison, was appointed manager in 1958, his first post after leaving West Ham before starting his chequered career, first as assistant at Spurs, then in 1963 at Bath City. United have made three losing Wembley appearances – in the FA Amateur Cup finals of 1963 and 1969 and in 1981, when they lost the FA Trophy Final against Bishops Stortford. However, United hold an almost unique record – they are almost the only English non-League club to lift a European trophy, winning the Anglo-Italian Cup in 1979 with a 2–1 victory in Chieti.

In the FA Cup, the club made national headlines in 1970 with a Fourth Round tie against English champions and European Cup semi-finalists, Don Revies Leeds United. Temporary benches, borrowed from The Oval cricket ground, enabled a club record crowd of fourteen thousand to see

Sutton lose 6–0. In 1987/88 Sutton drew at home against Second Division Middlesbrough in the Third Round before going down 1–0 only after extra time, at Ayresome Park.

The club was formed 90 years before, when in March 1898 Sutton Guild Rovers FC and Sutton Association FC (formerly Sutton St Barnabas FC) agreed to merge during a meeting at the Robin Hood Hotel and in the 1912/13 season the club moved to the Adult School Sports Ground in Gander Green Lane, purchased and renamed the Borough Sports Ground by the local council in 1934.

In 1921 Sutton United joined the Athenian League, winning the first of its three league titles seven years later. The club were champions again 30 years later, celebrating with a tour of Germany and Luxembourg. When they returned, their manager joined Crystal Palace and Malcolm Allison, his career at West Ham terminated by TB, replaced him. Five years later, Sid Cann, an FA Cup winner with Manchester City, took United to its first Amateur Cup Final, where Eddie Reynolds, the Wimbledon forward, scored all four of the Dons' goals with his head.

The Anglo-Italian Cup was an improbable tournament dreamed up in 1969 largely to reward League Cup winners Swindon Town with European football.[1] It evolved into a competition for 'semi-professional' sides, in which English non-League clubs played opponents from Italy's Serie C (many of whom were in fact full-time). In 1979 the former United player Keith Blunt masterminded United's 2–1 win over ASD Chieti in Abruzzo, England's only success in the trophy. Blunt then departed for FC Malmö, to be succeeded at Gander Green Lane by the idiosyncratic Barrie Williams, a qualified FA coach and an English teacher for 17 years in a former life.

The pipe-smoking Williams, whose team talks largely eschewed Anglo-Saxon expletives for quotes from Kipling and Shakespeare, took the club to the championship of the Isthmian League for the second successive season in 1986. This success secured for United promotion to the GM Vauxhall Conference: they stood on the fringe of the Football League.

Two seasons later, Sutton United's Cup run gave notice that, though Gander Green Lane had never been the venue of legends, and suburban Surrey could never claim to be a hotbed of soccer, no League club would relish a visit to play Williams' well-organised, competitive team on their

---

[1] UEFA rules excluded them from the Inter-Cities Fairs Cup owing to their lower division status.

compact little ground. That season, they made the Third Round of the competition, beating Third Division Aldershot 3–0 at home and Peterborough United of the Fourth Division comfortably 3–1 at London Road. The Third Round brought Second Division high-flyers Middlesbrough to Gander Green Lane, where Nigel Golley's late header gave United a replay at Ayresome Park. Golley headed against the bar in the last minute but Paul Kerr's goal in extra time ended the dream.

There was always next year – except that the 1988/89 FA Cup campaign was almost over before it started. What became the stuff of legend required a replay at Stompond Lane in the Fourth Qualifying Round after scrambling a home draw against Walton & Hersham. However, United were lucky in their First and Second rounds, beating Isthmian League Dagenham and fellow Conference side Aylesbury United to earn the dubious honour of facing First Division Coventry City at Gander Green Lane. City were fifth in the League and fielded seven of the side who had won the Cup two years earlier in a gripping match against Spurs, with Keith Houchen, who had scored that stunning diving header at Wembley, on the bench. Barrie Williams' team had lost heir last three games, were lying fourteenth in the Conference and included two assistant bank managers, two insurance executives, a commodity broker and a bricklayer.

The shrewd Sutton boss had perceived a weakness in the Sky Blues' defence at set pieces. With the exception of the redoubtable Brian Kilcline, they lacked height and Williams devised a cunning plan. On the morning of the big game he had his men out at 10.30 on a park pitch behind Gander Green Lane practising corners. 'Nothing went right. Corners were too short or too long, leaving Williams cursing in language which owed more to the factory floor than the Bard.'[2] Nonetheless, the compact ground at Gander Green Lane must have seemed a claustrophobic place for the First Division stars on a raw, windy afternoon. The pitch was hemmed in by the huge crowd of around eight thousand, augmented by the residents of the bungalows around the Sports Ground, who had an excellent view from their kitchens.

From the first whistle, Coventry took the game to United, Steve Sedgley and David Speedie drawing sharp saves from Roffey in the first two minutes. Their passing was the crisper of the two teams but it was soon clear that

---

[2] Tibballs, p. 181.

Sutton weren't going to be overawed. United's midfield fought for every ball, snuffed out every pass, not allowing the First Division side time to settle to their normal game. In fact, Sutton had a great chance from their first corner, which the Coventry defence failed to clear and Matthew Hanlan's instinctive low shot was well saved by Steve Ogrizovic.

For their part, City continued to create chances, with the turning point of the first half – if not the whole match – coming in the 24th minute, when Brian Kilcline headed straight at the Sutton keeper. The failure of City's skipper to bury a free header reminded Williams' men 'that First Division footballers were fallible, too, and left Coventry with a sense of foreboding'.[3] Gradually, United's Paul Rogers and Phil Dawson secured dominance of the midfield and four minutes before half-time, just after Cyrille Regis had headed wide from Borrows' cross, their persistence was rewarded. Kilcline gave a corner away on the left, Mickey Stephens floated a perfect ball to the near post corner and Nigel Golley nodded it on. Ogrizovic, committed to going for the cross, left United captain, Tony Rains, an insurance executive, playing his 613th game for the club, free at the far post to stoop and head in from five yards. The plan plotted in the park that morning had worked – it was, wrote Michel Calvin in the *Telegraph*, 'a model of professional efficiency'.

Sutton's lead lasted scarcely seven minutes after the restart. They seemed to have mislaid their first-half script, allowing City more freedom in midfield and, when winger Dave Bennett drove forward, he slipped the ball to Steve Sedgley, whose precise pass left two defenders floundering and David Phillips beat Roffey easily with a crisp drive from 15 yards. Coventry were level and the roar from City's travelling faithful was born more of relief than celebration. Sutton might have been expected to fold but their collective resilience withstood the setback.

They were still very much in the game and in the 58th minute City's vulnerability at set pieces was ultimately to prove their Achilles heel. Once again, it was a short corner from Stephens that did the damage. Phil Dawson's penetrating cross into the six-yard box confused the visitors' rearguard, McKinnon headed on for the grammar schoolboy-turned-bricklayer, 22-year-old Matthew Hanlan, to emerge from a clutch of City defenders to beat Ogrizovic with a close-range volley. 'I found myself staring at an open

[3] Joe Lovejoy, *Independent*, January 9, 1989.
[4] John Moynihan, *Sunday Telegraph*, January 8, 1989.

goal with the ball at waist height' he recalls. 'I remember thinking "Don't miss", and luckily enough, I didn't.'

Their noses in front, Sutton then played their best football of the afternoon. A few moments later Hanlan had a chance to put the game out of Coventry's reach, half-volleying over the bar from another long through-ball. Then McKinnon, twice, and Dennis both had good chances and after a fluent crossfield move involving four players, Stephens shot narrowly wide.

Inevitably, Sutton had to ride their luck in the last 20 minutes as they began to run out of steam. All hands were summoned to the pumps in the hectic denouement as Coventry sent waves of players upfield in a despairing quest for a face-saving equaliser. Cyrille Regis' cross-shot was superbly saved by Roffey. Keith Houchen came on, and at once he hit the bar with a swirling cross-cum-shot and Steve Sedgley's pile-driver from the rebound cannoned off the post. Coventry's final flourish became a frenzy, their long balls into the Sutton area growing more speculative and increasingly frantic. From one such barrage Brian Kilcline's header was cleared off the line by Jones.

All the pressure was to no avail and at the final whistle United supporters poured on to the pitch, 'the lasting image of an occasion that captured all the romance of the Cup'.[4] The 2,500 Coventry supporters generously stayed and applauded the Sutton team, 'a tremendous gesture in an era of cynicism and terrace abuse'[5] and John Sillett, the Coventry manager, was dignified in defeat. 'We weren't as good as we should have been, and so we lost. Sutton's hospitality has been superb and we weren't kicked off the park.' In the scrum beneath the stand, Sillett embraced Barrie Williams, the mastermind behind Sutton's remarkable win. 'Enjoy it,' muttered Sillett. 'Thank you very much,' replied Mr. Williams. 'You know what this means to us, don't you?' The answer glowed in the radiant faces of the small boys held aloft by their ecstatic fathers and it 'shone in the eyes of the Sutton manager's part-time players, who had showered him with champagne and were singing Jingle Bells as they danced, fully clothed, in their small, square, bath.'[6]

Despite the five divisions between the two clubs, there was nothing crude or freakish about Sutton's win. 'I am delighted that we won by

---

[5] Ibid.
[6] Michael Calvin, *Daily Telegraph*, January 9, 1989.

playing good football,' said Barrie Williams. 'You can have all the luck in the world, but still have to score goals. It was particularly pleasing to get them from moves we had been working on. We have intelligent players and they always learn set-plays well.' Though the win was testament to Williams' tactical astuteness, it was not confined to set pieces. Coventry's forwards could find no rhythm, and Stephens and Hanlan, United's two wide players, exposed the lack of pace of City's flat back four by constantly interchanging positions.

'While Coventry's players were away from their families most of the week, we've been doing our jobs and leading normal lives. We didn't feel any nerves – all we wanted to do was avoid total humiliation,' reflected Tony Rains.

We had nothing to lose. Coventry weren't very different from the teams we play every week in the Conference. We had more time on the ball than we usually get and it wasn't as hard physically as in our league. We've proved that professional sides aren't superstars. Perhaps if they had a bit more passion, a bit more commitment to what they are doing – but they're humans and can be beaten. Sometimes you're at work, and your mind drifts away. You think to yourself 'I might score, we might even nick a win.' Then you tell yourself not to be silly and drift back, content to play as well as you can. You think of the security you've got, the freedom the pros don't have. I've worked hard, waited years for this day.

The two goalscorers were in the spotlight on the *Terry Wogan Show* the following Tuesday. The team's reward was a trip to East Anglia in the Fourth Round a fortnight later. Against another First Division side, Norwich City, the wheels came off the wagon in spectacular fashion, when four goals from Malcolm Allen and a hat-trick from Robert Fleck did for United in an 8–0 hiding.

Two years later United were relegated back into the Isthmian League Premier Division and, following another championship in 1999, they found themselves again a Conference club. It was a flash in the pan, however: their sojourn lasted only a single season and they joined the Blue Square Conference South in 2004. United now play in the Ryman Premier League in front of respectable crowds at Gander Green Lane, which has seen new floodlights installed in 2000 and the welcome arrival of Rose's Tea Hut, proudly decked out in the distinctive yellow and chocolate of Sutton United.

Since the FA Cup was reorganized into its present format in 1925, non-League teams have beaten First Division opponents on only six occasions and no non-League side has knocked out one from the top flight since that memorable afternoon in Surrey. So, Sutton's victory over Coventry will be remembered as one of the greatest Cup giant-killing feats in football history. For Sutton's part-timers, any thought of financial reward was irrelevant. The club had never been able to pay players much: 'There's a great danger in regarding football as anything more than a wonderful hobby,' said Mr Williams, who had included in his programme notes an extremely apt quotation from Kipling:

> It ain't the individual
> Not the army as a whole
> It's the everlasting teamwork
> Of every bloomin' soul.

SUTTON UNITED: Roffey, Jones, Rains, Golley, Pratt, Rogers, Stephens, Dawson, Dennis, McKinnon, Hanlan
COVENTRY CITY: Ogrizovic, Borrows, Phillips, Sedgeley, Kilcline, Peake, Bennett, Speedie, Regis, McGrath, Smith

39

WEST BROMWICH ALBION 2, WOKING 4

FA Cup, Round Three, January 5, 1991

Next time the conversation flags in the Dog and Duck, toss this conundrum around the bar and see if anyone catches it. 'What has Gibraltar cricket got to do with the FA Cup?' No? Give up? Well, the answer is Tim Buzaglo. He played 32 matches in the ICC Trophy for the team of his birthplace, scoring 681 runs, before retiring in 2001: five years later, he was named among the FA's 'Team of Heroes' to commemorate 125 years of the FA Cup. It was all to do with events in the Black Country one January afternoon in 1991, when almost single-handedly Buzaglo, a 29-year-old computer operator, put Woking from the Isthmian League Premier into the Fourth Round of the Cup.

Buzaglo was a natural goalscorer – an instinctive finisher whose 34 league goals took Woking to the Division Two South title in 1986/87. But the story really starts almost a century before, when Woking Football Club, known as 'The Cards', was formed. The nickname derives possibly from the red half of the club's home strip,[1] chosen because of the town's link to Cardinal Wolsey, who once stayed with Henry VIII at Woking Palace, whose remains can be seen near the River Wey at Old Woking. Another less intriguing theory is that it simply derived from the colour – cardinal red.

The story of football in the town began, as it did in many other places, in the twilight of the Victorian age. Formed in 1889, the club won the West Surrey League in 1895/96 at its first attempt but, barely a decade later, financial problems threatened the Cards with collapse. Then a battling

---

[1] Now red-and-white halves.

run to the First Round of the Cup in January 1908, where Woking travelled to play Bolton Wanderers, brought the club to national prominence. Though they trounced the Cards 5–0, Wanderers, impressed by Woking's spirit, played a friendly match in Surrey the following season, which kept the club afloat.

Over the next 80 years Woking FC, playing at their trim Kingfield ground on the south-east side of town, rode the roller-coaster of the Isthmian League, with the vicissitudes which beset any amateur club. They had their halcyon days, spoken of wistfully in the clubhouse by rheumy-eyed ancients: for Woking the golden age was the mid-1950s. In 1957 their gifted centre-half, John Mortimore, left for Chelsea and over the next nine seasons he would make 279 appearances for the Blues: in spite of that, the Cards won the Amateur Cup in 1958, beating Ilford 3–0 before a crowd of 71,000 at Wembley.

It was the club's zenith as an amateur outfit: by 1984/85 Woking FC had plummeted to Division Two (South) of the Isthmian League. Two decades of strife and periodic flirtation with extinction had taken their toll. Then, club stalwart Phil Ledger signed the former player Geoff Chapple as manager for £12.50 a week. The recovery was underway. The club narrowly missed out on promotion at the first attempt and, in the summer of 1986, Tim Buzaglo rang Woking's assistant coach, Mick Gowan. He'd been playing for Weysiders, a small club from Guildford – but they hadn't won promotion and didn't have a pitch to play on. 'I told Mick I'll come and play for Woking reserves but instead I went straight into a first team friendly at Dulwich Hamlet.' Buzaglo didn't get much coaching from Chapple: 'All Geoff ever said to me was "go and run around".'

The arrival of the cricketer from Gibraltar sparked a dramatic improvement in the Cards' fortunes. In all, Buzaglo scored 45 goals in 50 games in his first season at the club, his fast, elusive grace and his powerful left foot endearing him to Cards supporters. His goal at Whyteleafe clinched the Division Two (South) title and he became a Kingfield legend. Two years later, in 1989/90, when Woking were promoted back to the Premier Division, Buzaglo's 49 League and Cup goals included four hat-tricks – but, according to Geoff Chapple, Kingfield's new hero 'was never renowned for being a grafter. That's just the way he was. He never wanted to work hard in life or in football. Basically he was bone-idle.' Buzaglo acknowledged that himself: 'All I wanted to do was play football and I didn't think I needed to train.'

The next season, the one in which Woking made their indelible entry in the history of the Cup, began encouragingly with wins over three Conference sides. Bath City were beaten 2–1 at Kingfield, followed by three epic games against Kidderminster Harriers in the First Round proper which attracted a total of 9,091 fans. In an emotional climax at Aggborough, a late Andy Russell header gave Chapple's side a 2–1 victory. On that dramatic night, Harriers manager Graham Allner believes, 'Woking really came to prominence. Geoff had built a brilliant side at that time. He used to have the same philosophy as me. If I didn't enjoy watching my team play then why should I expect anyone else to? He was a lovely man but single-minded and when you were up against one of his teams you knew you were in for a real game.' Conference side Merthyr Tydfil were up from the valleys in the Second Round and had two of their men dismissed as a hat-trick from Mark Biggins led the Cards in a 5–1 thrashing of the Welshmen.

Woking had hoped to draw Liverpool, Arsenal, Manchester United or even Derby, bottom of the First Division, in the Third Round, but the draw pitted them against Second Division West Bromwich Albion at The Hawthorns. Albion were on the slide, second from bottom in the League: over the Christmas period, however, they had been unbeaten in four home games. Managed by two-time Cup winner Brian Talbot and led by former Tottenham hardman Graham Roberts, they still represented daunting opposition for an Isthmian League club.

In the build-up to the tie, Talbot paid Woking the respect of watching them play at Marlow before Christmas. That night, Woking were terrible and he told Chapple, 'If my lads don't beat your lads, they want their arses kicking. After all they are full-time professionals.' Chapple was nonchalant. 'With the team we had I knew we'd have a go. There was a buzz happening at that time,' says Chapple.

> I didn't know what but I had the feeling something was happening. Gates were improving and things were moving. But hand on heart I didn't think we'd beat them. They were in the old Second Division and we were in the Isthmian League. There was a huge gap of four divisions. But I remember driving along the Hogs Back on my way home to Farnham and wondering what I was worried about.[2]

---

[2] Youlton and Chapple, p. 58.

Chapple had taken a close look at Albion and felt that a quick-moving, direct approach could overcome their solid but slow defence. But his match-winner was out of touch. Apart from a recent hat-trick against Wokingham Town and a winner at Barking, his winter had been mundane.

When Chapple strolled round the empty Hawthorns stadium on the afternoon before the game, the intimidatory air of a First Division ground sent a chill up his spine. Undaunted, as he wandered up the tunnel an hour before kick-off, Chapple noticed a few West Brom players sitting around reading newspapers instead of the match-day programme. 'I felt they thought we were just a minnow side from down south who had arrived for a pasting. Their players were totally relaxed, probably too relaxed. What with their mentality and our travelling fans, it lifted us. To have five thousand supporters there backing us was something else, albeit they were tucked in the corner.' The Woking boss was aware that for most of the Cards' supporters, the visit to The Hawthorns was merely a day out. 'All I wanted', he said, 'was to give a good account of ourselves and hear nice things said about Woking.'[3]

From the kick-off, the Cards burst from the traps and chased and harried, attempting to unsettle Albion. They steadily grew in confidence but it was against the run of play that Colin West put the Baggies in front after 34 minutes: as the half-time whistle blew, the home fans breathed a collective sigh of relief. Woking had given a respectable account of themselves and, though they trailed, Chapple was 'bloody pleased. I can't remember what I said at half-time but it would have been along the lines of "Well done, we're still in it."'

Albion picked up where they left off in the second half as Woking stuck to their game plan. Their quick passing and shrewd running, aimed at exploiting the lack of pace at the heart of the Baggies' defence, posed a growing threat. And so it proved; suddenly, the wheels fell off the West Brom wagon. The Cards' passing game had unsettled the home defence and in the 59th minute, Tim Buzaglo hit a great goal to round off a well-worked move. Woking were level and the Albion were rudderless. Graham Roberts and Gary Strodder, their centre-halves, could not track Buzaglo's runs and five minutes later he broke through to head a second. Woking were in front.

[3] Youlton and Chapple, p. 59.

For the Second Division side, it was a bad day at the office: they needed to salvage some pride and force a replay. Perhaps they could raise their game if they got the Isthmian Leaguers back to Kingfield. No chance. Sixteen minutes from time, even the most fervent home fans headed for the turnstiles as Buzaglo nonchalantly brushed off Roberts' tackle to complete his hat-trick. In 14 minutes of fantasy football, the tie was dead and buried. 'When Tim scored his third I kept thinking we could hang on for a draw here,' says Chapple. 'It was crazy thinking like that at 3–1 up but it was because of the stage we were on. Then I was thinking what will happen if we win? What will happen to me? What will happen to the club?'

The Cards' crazy day out got even crazier a minute from the end as substitute Terry Worsfold ambled on to the park to add a fourth. For the Albion, their confidence already torn to shreds, it was the last straw and their fans turned on their own players and began applauding the visitors. 'Before I went on Chaps just told me to get on there and get a goal,' says Worsfold. 'So I did, although it wasn't enough for me to play in the next round.'

There was time for a last-minute consolation as Darren Bradley scored for the Baggies, a strike greeted by scornful derision from the home supporters. At the final whistle, the loyal Baggies fans, appalled by their team's display and recognising a new hero, hoisted Buzaglo high and bore him round the ground for a lap of honour. 'All I could hear was them singing "sign him on, sign him on, sign him on,"' recalls Chapple. 'That was special, they were so kind.'

Buzaglo, only a few seasons away from county League football, where the team takes down the goal nets after the game and changes in a shed, was a reluctant man of the match. 'We played some fantastic stuff that day but the attention I got for the two weeks leading up to the next round were the worst two weeks of my life. I hated every minute of it.' The hat-trick hero, swept off to the *Match of the Day* studio, never made it to the dressing-room celebrations. Geoff Chapple did: 'I'd only got two steps in when the players picked me up and threw me in the bath.' The media were pressing for interviews, so, drenched to the skin, the Woking boss was rescued by West Brom's laundry lady. As he squelched towards the Baggies' laundry room, Chapple says, 'I was so elated I just stood there in the nude as she found me some kit to put on.'

No such euphoric exposure for West Brom's Brian Talbot, who left the

Hawthorns with all the signs of a lamb being prepared for the slaughter. Sure enough, he was sacked a couple of days later. Speaking after what proved to be his last match as Albion boss, he conceded that Tim Buzaglo had 'finished brilliantly', adding, 'We knew he was a good player and he showed it today.' Albion midfielder Craig Shakespeare, who in 1984 had been in the Walsall side who held Liverpool to a draw in a League Cup semi-final at Anfield, confessed that Albion were 'surprised' by Woking's performance, 'but perhaps we shouldn't have been. They are a good side who are prepared to play football. We seemed to go to pieces after their equaliser whereas they got better with every kick.'

Less than 24 hours later everyone connected with the club was crammed in the clubhouse to hear the Fourth Round draw. Of the 16 balls in the velvet bag, the Cards were drawn out first. The announcement took the roof off, for the reward for what the *Surrey Advertiser*'s Chris Dyke called 'Chapple's mish-mash of interior designers, van drivers, decorators, door fitters and bank clerks' was in the realms of fantasy – a home game against First Division Everton a fortnight later. Nine-times Division One champions and five-times Cup winners, Everton were one of game's aristocrats. Never relegated from the top flight, their team was packed with internationals. On police advice the game was switched to Goodison Park and on Sunday, January 17, 1991, 125 coaches took ten thousand Woking supporters up the M6 to face the likes of Sharp, Sheedy, Southall and Ratcliffe.

Chapple and his men were determined to enjoy the day. 'West Brom was always going to be special because it was the first, but this was massive,' he said. 'The players were all trying to grab programmes as souvenirs and I kept nipping down the tunnel to see how full the ground was. The players were saying "Can we go out yet?"'

Amazingly, at half-time Woking were doing the Isthmian League proud. Mighty Everton were being held, 0–0: it was a score line to raise the eyebrows of the football world. The non-Leaguers held the Merseysiders for another 12 minutes, until a characteristic left-foot strike from Kevin Sheedy gave Everton the lead. That was it. They could not breach the Woking defence again and it was the First Division side who were grateful for the final whistle.

The 34,000 crowd gave the Woking team a deserved standing ovation and Everton manager Howard Kendall and his players joined in the applause.

But, Geoff Chapple remembers, 'Howard said later if we'd have beaten them they certainly wouldn't have clapped us off the pitch.' Chapple, who before the tie feared a thrashing, would have liked another crack at the glamour boys. 'Tim [Buzaglo] and Shane [Wye] came close to scoring and the best result we could have had was 1–1,' he says. 'We had fighters in the team and although it might have been more a second time, I would have liked a second chance – but the game kicked us off as a club financially. West Brom got us going but when we got that £90,000 from Everton, that's when the ground started to improve.'

What didn't improve was West Brom's season. Bobby Gould's appointment at The Hawthorns failed to turn Albion's fortunes around and in spite of being unbeaten in their last nine games they were relegated to Division Three for the first time in their history. As for the Cards, after the euphoria of the Cup run, their League performances inevitably suffered and their challenge for the League title fell away. Today Woking is a friendly, well-run club plying their trade in the Blue Square Conference (South).

Tim Buzaglo became a marked man and soon after his FA Cup heroics he fell foul of a diabolical tackle by St Albans' Bob Dowie, brother of former Northern Ireland international and Charlton and QPR manager Iain. A cruciate ligament operation put him out for the rest of the season and the whole of the 1991/92 campaign. He did play again, in the club's first Conference year in 1992/93, but was never the same force and he drifted into junior football. He recalls the hat-trick against West Brom with natural pride: 'It was the best moment of my life' – but he does regret saying Graham Roberts was slow. 'I didn't think I'd be playing against him again. But I did, for Marlow against Enfield, about three years later and he gave me a right kicking.'

Some defenders are built like elephants – and they, too, never forget.

WEST BROMWICH ALBION: Rees, Shakespeare, Harbey, Roberts, Bradley, Strodder, Ford, West, Bannister, McNally, Robson
WOKING: Read, Mitchell, Cowler, Pratt, Baron, S. Wye, Brown, Biggins, Franks (sub: Worsfold), Buzaglo, L. Wye

40

WREXHAM 2, ARSENAL 1

FA Cup, Round Three, January 4, 1992

'Anyone got change for a tenner?' An innocent enough request, you might think, but on the Wrexham training ground, in 1992, any wide-eyed YTS trainee would have been well advised to steer clear of the old pro flashing the cash. For 37-year-old Mickey Thomas, a self-confessed free spirit whose philosophy was 'to forget about tomorrow and concentrate on enjoying today', was a loveable rogue, who, in the days before the millionaire foot-baller, thought the odd counterfeit currency scam on the side would help sustain the lifestyle of what Judge Gareth Edwards termed 'a flash and daring adventurer'. In doing so, the learned judge sternly declared to Thomas, 'you betrayed the trust of your employers and you failed in your duty as a distinguished sportsman'.[1]

Though Thomas has quipped, 'Wayne Rooney's on a hundred grand a week. Mind you, so was I until the police found my printing machine', he has always maintained he was guilty only by association. Rather unsport-ingly, the good judge failed to see the funny side of an experienced pro-fessional flogging bent tenners to teenage trainees and sent Thomas to prison for 18 months. Though he served only half his sentence, it was a salutary experience. Locked up in a tiny cell with a double murderer who had decap-itated his victims, Thomas 'slept with one eye open but I got on with everyone inside because you had to. Playing football with a team of "lifers" was an experience – every time the ball went over the fence they all wanted to go and get it back.'

In January 1992 Thomas was in his second spell at Wrexham, the terminus of an extraordinary 20-year round trip that began as an apprentice with

---

[1] From 'The Game', *The Times*, January 7, 2008.

the North Wales club and took in en route Manchester United, Everton, Brighton, Stoke (twice), Chelsea, West Bromwich, Derby, Wichita Wings, Shrewsbury and Leeds. That January, courtesy of the FA Cup Third Round draw, he had been handed one last chance to make a name for himself on the big stage when Wrexham faced Arsenal at the Racecourse Ground.

At the time, Arsenal were the League champions and lay fourth in the First Division and, though Wrexham were undefeated in their last three home games, they were fourteenth in Division Four and nobody gave them a chance. However, the aristocrats from North London had had a desolate Christmas which had produced only one point from nine. Benfica had put paid to their European Cup hopes and Coventry had dumped them out of the League Cup. In a season rapidly disappearing down the plughole, the FA Cup represented the Gunners' last hope of salvaging some silverware.

Following two financially unprofitable home victories over non-League Winsford United and Telford United in the first two rounds, Wrexham saw the fixture as a much-needed source of income, since a dour and difficult struggle in the depths of Division Four was not attracting vast crowds to the Racecourse Ground. By and large, the 1980s had been a dismal decade in the bottom division, enlivened only by two remarkable games: in 1985 they knocked Porto out of the European Cup Winners' Cup. In the next round, Sven-Goran Eriksson's Roma scraped through thanks to a couple of goals which TV replays showed should have been disallowed.

With former centre-forward Dixie McNeil as manager, fortunes looked up briefly in 1989 when Wrexham reached the Fourth Division play-offs, losing 2–1 to Leyton Orient, but by the turn of the decade the club had just three wins from 13 League games and was in desperate financial straits. After the players had been compelled by the club's penury to travel to Maidstone by train, McNeil resigned, perhaps before his inevitable sacking: 'When I left as the manager, it was for the right moral reasons – players have to be treated properly – but I regret resigning, especially after getting beat in the last play-off game at Leyton Orient.' He was replaced by Welsh international Brian Flynn and the team finished in twenty-first place, thereby avoiding relegation. In 1990/91 Wrexham finished bottom but, as Aldershot had already resigned from the League, the Welsh club were thrown a lifeline.

That lifeline was an unbroken thread stretching back over a century, when in a story which mirrors that of Cardiff City, members of the cricket club in Wrexham sought a sporting activity for the winter months. So, on September 28, 1872 Wrexham Football Club had been formed at a meeting held at the Turf Hotel on the Racecourse Ground, where the club have played ever since.

Traditionally, soccer was much more popular than rugby in North Wales, whereas in the valleys of the South Wales coalfields in the late nineteenth century rugby football rivalled Methodism as the dominant religion. However, there was no rigid regional demarcation: records show that rugby was played in schools in Beaumaris, Ruthin and Ruabon from as early as the 1870s. Conversely, North Walians, along with Englishmen, migrated to the South Wales coalfield and popularised the round-ball game in the valleys.

Historically, both codes emerged from the same tradition. In the early Victorian period, English public schools like Cheltenham and Rugby preferred the more rugged game in which the ball could be touched with the hands or even carried. Soon it was recognised in educational circles that football in whatever form was not merely an excuse to let off steam but constituted a useful distraction from less desirable occupations, such as heavy drinking and gambling.

This was hilarious, as gambling had been a national addiction for two hundred years and lay behind the stakes put up by the titled patrons of the turf and the wealthy landed gentry who sponsored many 100-guinea-a-side cricket matches in the eighteenth century. A lot of the betting on horses and no doubt football was done illegally in pubs, where bookies' runners ferried bets between punters and bookmakers. As for the heavy drinking, it had long been associated with sport. Richard Nyren ran the gentlemen's club at the Bat and Ball in Hambledon, where on Broadhalfpenny Down many fine early cricketers learned the game. One entry in the Minutes of the club reads: 'A wet day: only three members present: nine bottles of wine'.[2] For the working man of the late nineteenth century, with a bit of disposable income for the first time, the pub – and football, whether rugby or soccer – afforded ideal opportunities for him to enjoy his new-found leisure time. It wasn't much, but for 90 minutes or so on a Saturday, he could escape the mine, the mill or the foundry.

---

[2] Birley, p. 34.

Wrexham had all of those. The industrial centre of North Wales, it had collieries, steelworks and brick and tile factories. Furthermore, there were several large breweries in the town, with evocative names like the Albion, Cambrian, Eagle, Island Green, Soames and Willow. Perhaps the best known was the Wrexham Lager brewery, built in 1882. By then, four years before, Wrexham had won the first of their 22 Welsh cups: in 1890 they joined the Combination League and after the Great War, in 1921, Wrexham were elected to the newly formed Third Division (North) of the Football League and spent the next half-century see-sawing between the bottom two divisions.

They did attain the Fourth Round of the FA Cup in 1956/57 where they were walloped 5–0 by Manchester United's 'Busby Babes' in front of 34,445 people – still the Racecourse Ground's record crowd – and in 1974 Wrexham reached the quarter-finals before losing 1–0 to First Division Burnley. John Neal's arrival as manager in 1968 following a successful playing career with Aston Villa heralded a marked upturn in the club's fortunes. The following season he led them to promotion and two years later they took their first tentative steps into Europe via victory in the Welsh Cup. In 1976 they reached the quarter-finals of the European Cup Winners' Cup before losing to the eventual winners, Anderlecht. A year later, when Neal left for Middlesbrough (and eventually Chelsea), the club appointed popular former player Arfon Griffiths as manager and immediately enjoyed the greatest season in its history. Playing enterprising football, a team containing six players capped by Wales swept to the Third Division championship, won the Welsh Cup and got to the quarter-finals of both the League Cup and the FA Cup, where they were narrowly beaten 3–2 by. . . Arsenal.

So for Wrexham, when the Gunners took the field at the Racecourse on January 4, 1992, it would be a chance to avenge that defeat 14 years before – and for Mickey Thomas, who had been in the Manchester United side beaten 3–2 by Arsenal in a thrilling Cup Final in 1979, it would be especially gratifying to put one over them before he hung up his boots.

Any prospect of revenge seemed half a world away in the first half as Arsenal seized control of the game and had at least three golden opportunities to put the tie beyond the Welsh side. In the second minute Phillips cleared off the line from Alan Smith and three minutes later Jimmy Carter shot wide from 12 yards with the goal at his mercy. Then Kevin Campbell was denied by Vince O'Keefe, whose saves kept the home side in the game, but he was powerless when a moment of international class from Paul Merson created a chance for Alan Smith. In the 44th minute, just when Wrexham thought they had reached half-time unscathed, Merson 'cut in from the left and beat two Wrexham defenders before pulling the ball back for Smith to score his 16th goal of the season.'[3]

The second half saw Wrexham huff and puff but 'We then absolutely battered Wrexham', recalls Arsenal skipper Tony Adams, 'and should have been well clear.'[4] Indeed, the visitors should have settled the issue when Nigel Winterburn's fierce drive struck the underside of the bar in the 62nd minute. 'But instead of powering ahead to win the game,' wrote Clive White of *The Times*, 'as in the first half they had threatened to do, and would have done but for the defiance of O'Keefe in goal, they idled.'[5] Arsenal relied on their defensive wall, the country's meanest back four, to keep Wrexham's honest endeavours at bay, counting on Smith's strike just before half-time to take them into the Fourth Round. And then, within 120 calamitous seconds, their season collapsed around them.

With only eight minutes remaining, David O'Leary tangled on the right edge of the penalty area with 36-year-old Gordon Davies, the former Fulham, Chelsea and Manchester City striker and the other half of Wrexham's 'Dad's Army'. Referee Breen agreed with his linesman's frantic flag and awarded Wrexham a free kick, a decision described by Arsenal boss George Graham as 'mysterious'. Mickey Thomas, who 'more than anyone else in a chaotic midfield, found time and space to produce the telling pass or the neat escape route,'[6] and who 'had frolicked through the game like some up-and-coming youngster,'[7] meticulously placed the ball, took four steps back and from 20 yards unleashed a drive that flew as straight as an arrow past an astonished Seaman into the top corner. Sweet revenge indeed as, ironically enough, O'Leary, who had conceded the free kick which has now passed into Wrexham legend, was the sole Arsenal survivor from Mickey Thomas's 1979 Final.

Wrexham were level and within two minutes the fans' scarcely contained joy turned to unbridled euphoria. From Andy Thackeray's throw-in down

---

[3] Colin Gibson, *Daily Telegragh*, January 6, 1992.
[4] Adams, p. 114.
[5] *The Times*, January 6, 1992.
[6] *Daily Telegraph*, January 6, 1992.
[7] *The Times*, January 6, 1992.

the Wrexham right, Gareth Owen slipped the ball on to Davies. His turn wrong-footed Tony Adams, who muffed his clearance and 20-year-old Steve Watkin stretched out a leg round the Arsenal captain to poke Davies's cross past Seaman. 'I've found it hard to top that goal,' said Watkin in 2002. 'It wasn't a particularly good one. The cross came over from the right, I got a foot to it and it trickled in.' Ten years later, the memory had faded a little: 'I'll get the video out soon and have another look. I've not seen it for ages.'

Tony Adams won't mind if he never sees it again, for while Arsenal's Jimmy Carter did have the ball in the net in the last minute, the linesman's flag had waved for offside ages before O'Keefe was beaten and Arsenal's stumbling season had fallen apart.

Steve Watkin's scuffy toe-poke had done for the Gunners. A YTS trainee, he was a Wrexham lad who had only recently broken into the first team: for him, 'the last 10 minutes, after my goal, were the longest of my life so it was a special, special moment when the final whistle went.'

'The lowest point of my career' was George Graham's description of the defeat but, despite the fact that his team had failed to show 'the character, commitment and invention of their illustrious predecessors,'[8] he thought they played 'very well. We just didn't finish them off. It's a very thin dividing line between success and failure.' As for the Arsenal skipper

It was a major shock to us. Pride was stung. You just don't do that kind of thing with the Arsenal. An hour later we were sitting on the coach watching all those Wrexham fans banging on the windows and gloating after what had been their Cup Final. Sitting at the back, I told the boys that I would rather go out here and now than in the semi-final against Tottenham as we had done last year. I told them to remember this feeling because we didn't want it back.[9]

Gordon Davies, fresh from the fray, saw it somewhat differently. He had detected unrest in Arsenal's ranks. 'They're big stars and you can see on the television that when things don't go their way they tend to get a bit rattled,' he said. 'I thought they were going to be a lot more professional when they were leading and tighten it up. They treated it as a training match. We've

---

[8] *The Times*, op. cit.
[9] Adams, p. 115.

got a team of youngsters and two old men and perhaps our desire to win was greater than theirs.'

The desire may have been there but the bubbly wasn't. As Alan Hamilton put it, 'Sunday in Bible-black chapel-going Wales is not a day for rejoicing, celebration, partying or drunkenness. Not even when you have slain a giant in red that came roaring across Offa's Dyke to eat some natives for tea. Well, you might reasonably expect a bit of a knees-up on the Saturday night; just one teeny bottle of champagne to mark Goliath's fall.'[10] However, the result was so unexpected that Wrexham hadn't bothered to order any champagne – even if they could have afforded it. Instead, celebrations were confined to a few beers in the players' lounge.

A month later Wrexham went out of the Cup in a Fourth Round replay, beaten by a goal from West Ham's Colin Foster. At Upton Park ten days before, goals from Stewart Phillips and Lee Jones secured the Welshmen a creditable 2–2 draw. Mickey Thomas played in that match and was grinning from ear to ear as he trudged off the pitch. The West Ham supporters were waving £20 notes at him. 'We all make mistakes,' Thomas said. 'Mine was making my £20 notes an inch too big.'

WREXHAM: O'Keefe, Thackeray, Hardy, Carey, Thomas, Sertori, Davies, Owen, Connolly, Watkin, Phillips
ARSENAL: Seaman, Dixon, Winterburn, Hillier, O'Leary, Adams, Rocastle, Campbell (sub. P Groves), Smith, Merson, Carter

---

[10] From timesonline.co.uk, January 6, 1992.

41

BIRMINGHAM CITY 1, KIDDERMINSTER HARRIERS 2

FA Cup, Round Three, January 8, 1994

Saturday December 31, 1955. One of those cold, crisp afternoons and in the pale winter sun my dad took me and my brother to see Hastings United play a side called Kidderminster Harriers. Their name was unique and I just loved it – and they had the most colourful kit in the Southern League. Usually they wore red-and-white halves and black shorts. That New Year's Eve they were in green and got thumped 5–2.

I had no idea where Kidderminster was. I didn't know that Kidderminster is in Worcestershire, about 20 miles south-west of Birmingham. Neither was I aware that the town had a prosperous cloth trade between the fourteenth and the eighteenth century, that the River Stour and the Staffordshire and Worcestershire Canal both flow through the town, and that Kidderminster was the heart of the British carpet industry throughout the Industrial Revolution. Carpets had been manufactured there since 1735 and in the mid-eighteenth century the town began to specialise in new forms of carpet weaving.[1] The revocation of the Edict of Nantes by Louis XIV in 1685 had scattered skilled Protestant carpet makers over Europe and exiled Huguenots established centres of weaving in England, first at Kidderminster, then at Wilton and Axminster. The industry's raw materials, notably wool, came originally from the immediate area, but by the end of the eighteen century demand was such that the transport of resources from farther afield was facilitated by Kidderminster's position on the River Stour and by the arrival of the canals in the late 1770s.

---

[1] The demand grew for cheaper floor coverings and ingrain, or reversible, carpets began to be manufactured in Kidderminster, where weavers copied the Flanders loom, which produced a pile by looping the worsted warp threads.

In 1783 William Brinton, who ran a business dyeing and finishing cloth in Mill Street, took over the mill at Hill Pool near Belbroughton and a quarter of a century later, there were were a thousand carpet looms in the town. By the late Victorian era Brintons' was the largest company in Kidderminster and the town had become established as the centre of carpet manufacture in the country.

When in in April 1888 the Football League was formed, the Midlands, along with Lancashire, was one of the powerful heartlands of the professional game. Initially, 12 clubs were formally invited to be members – six from Lancashire: Accrington, Blackburn, Bolton, Burnley, Everton and Preston North End; and six more, broadly, from the Midlands: Aston Villa, Derby County, Notts County, Stoke, West Bromwich Albion and Wolverhampton Wanderers.

It was clear where the balance of power lay: 'No southern club received an invitation because there was no professional football south of Birmingham.'[2] This was not strictly true, however, for Kidderminster Harriers had been formed in 1886 after nine years as an amateur athletics and rugby union club. In the 1880s 'Professionalism rolled up on football like a huge black cloud in an otherwise blue sky. Everyone could see it coming, but few were sure whether it would plunge the game into darkness or simply cast a passing shadow. Its arrival, however, was inevitable'[3] and on July 20, 1885 at Anderton's Hotel in Fleet Street the FA formally legalised professionalism. There was a desperate need for a more formal structure as a 'season which consisted of friendly matches and a few Cup games was clearly not going to sustain the professional clubs of the North and Midlands.'[4] As an industrial centre in its own right, only 20 miles from the 'City of a Thousand Trades', Kidderminster could not escape that sea-change.

The Harriers were one of two professional clubs in the town. The other, Kidderminster Olympic, was an offshoot of the Harriers and local derbies attracted gates of around seven thousand. Three years later the two clubs amalgamated, playing in the newly formed Birmingham and District League (West Midland League), winning consecutive championships in 1938 and in 1939 and stepping up to play a couple of games in the Southern League before football was suspended for the duration of the Second World War.

---

[2] Butler, *The Official History of the Football Association*, p. 32.
[3] Butler, p. 27.
[4] Butler, p. 30.

Immediately after the war the Harriers played in the Birmingham League and Birmingham Combination before rejoining the Southern League in 1948/49, the season which saw the Harriers' record attendance for a game at Aggborough, when 9,155 spectators saw them lose 0–3 in an FA Cup tie against local rivals, Hereford United. Aggborough was the setting for another record six years later, when on September 14, 1955 the Harriers beat Brierley Hill Alliance 4–2 in the first FA Cup match under floodlights.

A second-place finish in the Southern League in 1983 led to promotion to the Alliance Premier League (now the Conference) and the most important appointment in the club's history, with Graham Allner taking over as manager. Allner was to be at the helm for 15 years and had an immediate impact, taking the side to two Welsh Cup finals, the first in the centenary season of 1985/86, in which striker Kim Casey set a club record in scoring an astonishing 73 goals in all competitions. Harriers reached the Welsh Cup final in 1986 and 1989, losing to Wrexham and Swansea City respectively and won the FA Trophy in 1987, with a replay victory over Burton Albion. Four years later, however, they were beaten by Wycombe Wanderers in front of a Trophy record crowd of nearly 35,000.

Only two seasons later Harriers were struggling against relegation, but chairman David Reynolds resisted calls for the sacking of Graham Allner and by Christmas 1993 Kidderminster had lost only once in 16 games and were three points clear at the top of the Conference. In the FA Cup, after comfortable home wins over Kettering Town and Woking, they found themselves drawn at home against Birmingham City in the Third Round. In one of those quirky twists of fate which happen in football, Graham Allner had lived five minutes' walk from City's home, St Andrews, and was a lifelong Blues fan.

While the omens were not propitious – Kidderminster had never beaten a League club in their history – Birmingham manager Barry Fry prophesied with his customary engaging candour: 'If I was Kidderminster boss, I would really fancy my chances.' His misgivings were well founded. He had taken over at St Andrew's from Terry Cooper only six weeks before and, despite having beaten West Bromwich Albion 2–0 in the post-Christmas local derby, his team still lacked confidence.

The League side had the better of the early exchanges as Kidderminster took time to settle, but gradually their central defenders, Brindley and Weir, came to grips with a string of crosses from Blues danger-man, ex-Rangers and Derby winger Ted McMinn.

No doubt some Blues fans still suffered sleepless nights after the ghastly defeat at the hands of Altrincham eight years before. However, their fears of another humiliation were partly allayed after only nine minutes, when Louis Donowa found Scott Hiley on the right and Paul Harding drove his low cross past Kevin Rose, courtesy of a vicious ricochet off Harriers skipper Simon Hodson.

Rose, a veteran of four League clubs, notably Hereford where he made 350 appearances, was unperturbed by this early setback and, as Birmingham pushed for a decisive second, he was in superb form. He clung on to a crisp drive from Kenny Lowe and in the 21st minute, he turned a looping header from Blues, leading scorer Andy Saville over the bar. Eight minutes later Harriers were level. Paul Bancroft overlapped like a gazelle down the left, crossed to the far post where Neil Cartwright, once a West Bromwich Albion reserve, scored with a downward header.

Harriers looked like facing a difficult second half only four minutes after the interval when referee Trevor West judged Simon Hodson's push on Kenny Lowe a deliberate foul and instantly pointed to the spot. Local fans were aghast, feeling the referee's decision unduly harsh, but at this point, Andy Saville, whose penalty kick for Hartlepool beat Crystal Palace in a Third Round shock a year before, learned how capricious Cup football can be. His shot struck the top of Rose's right-hand post, which summed up Birmingham's afternoon – misguided power, wasted opportunities and woeful luck.

After the penalty miss, the game drifted away from the League side and was settled just after the hour with the afternoon's one moment of class. Jon Purdie, 26, was a former England schoolboy international who had joined Arsenal in the same intake as Paul Merson, Tony Adams and David Rocastle. He then moved on to Wolves (where in November 1986 he was a member of the team which lost to Chorley), Oxford United, for whom five years before he had appeared in the fifth round at Old Trafford, where he admits he froze in a 4–0 defeat. He had spells at Shrewsbury and Cambridge United before joining Kidderminster. Undoubtedly an unfulfilled talent, Purdie saw his career spiralling downwards until Allner instilled him with self-belief. 'It's a pleasure', he said, 'to be able to work with someone of so much talent at this level, even if he is an idle so-and-so.'

In the 64th minute the 'idle so-and-so' bestirred himself. From an innocuous position outside the area, Purdie worked his way infield. Chris Whyte, Birmingham's experienced central defender, aware that Purdie favoured his left foot, allowed him space for a right-foot shot from 25 yards. This was a fatal error: Purdie dipped a shoulder and hit such a fierce drive into the roof of the net that Ian Bennett could only brush it with his finger-tips. Local reporter Ian White, of the delightfully named *Kidderminster Shuttle*,[5] indulged himself with this understandable hyperbole: 'A magnificent right-footer from 25 yards will surely be a contender for television's goal of the month – if not goal of the season!'

Later, Purdie admitted: 'You get in situations like that in every game, but rarely do they fly in like that. Usually they trickle wide or finish up in the stand.' Centre-half Chris Brindley agreed: 'We've been waiting for that all season,' he said. 'All the ones he's tried so far have gone out of the ground.'

With 26 anxious minutes to go Harriers diehards chewed their fingernails and the Blues threw everything at Kevin Rose's goal. Hodson nodded Whyte's header off the line, then the local hero dived full length to turn Gary Cooper's 20-yard free kick round the post and Kenny Lowe's volley struck the same post to deny the League side an equaliser.

Six minutes from time, referee Trevor West unwittingly gave Birmingham their best opportunity to force a replay when John Deakin's pass bounced off his back into the path of George Parris. He put Andy Saville through on goal and his rising drive beat Rose – only for Saville to be flagged offside.

Then, to cap it all, Graham Allner and his colleagues on the bench had to endure four minutes of injury time before they could race on to hug players and embark on the customary lap of honour. Barry Fry had been right. He had been suggesting all week that Birmingham City could be on the end of a giant-killing and the Harriers took him at his word.

Allner could not conceal his delight at putting one over the club with whom he was once on associate schoolboy forms. 'I won't tell you where I'll be celebrating tonight,' he said. 'It will be in Birmingham. With a body-guard!' Asked if he felt sympathy for the club he had always supported, he said no. 'He walked on a yard, paused, looked over his shoulder and grinned

---

[5] Kidderminster's local newspaper is still named the *Kidderminster Shuttle*, named, of course, after the shuttles used on the looms.

broadly. "Well, maybe . . . When it has sunk in and I have time to think about it."[6]

For his part, Birmingham's manager Barry Fry, as Blues supporters booed their team's second defeat in less than a decade to a team from outside the League, offered a shrewdly sombre summing-up of a miserable afternoon 'We've let the club down,' he said.

A lot of Birmingham fans will be degraded and humiliated. They will go into work and take a lot of stick. It will take a long time for them to get over it. Never mind that we had so many chances. We started well, got a goal and their goalkeeper made three, four, five brilliant saves. We had one off the line, missed a penalty, had a goal disallowed . . . it was a typical cup tie.

Walter Gammie wrote in more literary vein in *The Times*: 'Kidderminster won a match that Birmingham often dominated. Yet their self-belief never wavered; fortune favoured the brave.'

Chairman David Reynolds was in no doubt how to spend the proceeds from the side's historic win. Kidderminster's 108-year-old ground at Aggborough was in need of urgent upgrading. The terraces behind each goal needed covering, at a cost of of £500,000 – but when Kidderminster clinched their first Conference title in 1994, the ground was not considered to be of League standard and Harriers were denied promotion to Division Three. Ironically the club's successful FA Cup run had not allowed sufficient time and space for the required ground improvements to be in place by the deadline of December 31. A Harriers fan commented caustically: 'Northampton's three-sided ground with three derelict stands was deemed to be better than our four-sided ground with one derelict stand'.

By the time Kidderminster won their second Conference title six years later, with former Liverpool and Denmark star Jan Molby in charge, the ground had been upgraded. A new 1,100 all-seated main stand was built, along with the installation of new floodlights at a cost of £450,000 and, three years later, a new £1.1 million 2,040 all-seated East Stand. Molby had returned in 2004 after a brief spell at Hull City and, ten years after their triumph over Birmingham, Harriers again reached Round Three, in which

---

[6] *The Times*, January 10, 1994.

they were drawn against Premiership team and local rivals, Wolverhampton Wanderers. Few Harriers fans will forget John Williams giving Kidderminster the lead in a 1–1 draw at Aggborough, though they went on to lose the replay 2–0.

In 2008 carpets continue to be made in Kidderminster, though on a much reduced scale. Brintons still employs several hundred people, though they have moved from Weaver's Wharf, their town centre site, which is now a shopping mall incorporating two fine old industrial buildings, Slingfield Mill and the Piano Building.

Another survivor from the late Victorian era, Kidderminster Harriers now find themselves in the Blue Square Conference, after five years in the Football League. They are a club with a long history and a proud tradition, with perhaps no moment more memorable than Purdie's thunderbolt which did for the moneybags from the city up the A456.

BIRMINGHAM CITY: Bennett, Hiley, Whyte, Dryden, Cooper, Parris, Lowe, Harding, McMinn, Donowa, Saville
KIDDERMINSTER HARRIERS: Rose, Hodson, Brindley, Weir, Bancroft, Deakin, Grainger, Forsyth, Purdie, Cartwright, Humphreys

42

SWINDON TOWN 1,
STEVENAGE BOROUGH 2

FA Cup, Round Three, January 3, 1998

All of a sudden Stevenage is virtually the centre of Britain's sporting world. Hard on the heels of golfer Ian Poulter's most successful season, young Lewis Hamilton of Peartree Spring Junior School goes and becomes the Formula One world champion. Stevenage, in Hertfordshire, lies in a county whose chief claim to fame is that major roads passed through it on the way to somewhere else – and the town is no exception. A Roman road ran through its present site from St Albans to Baldock and much of the town's early prosperity stemmed from the Great North Road, today the A1(M), which was turnpiked in the early 1700s. By 1800 several coaching inns served the 21 stagecoaches that rattled through the High Street every day. The railway boom of the mid-nineteenth century ended the age of the stagecoach but, though the Great Northern Railway was built through the town in 1857, Stevenage grew only slowly through the Victorian era, with a population of only six thousand or so by the end of the Second World War.

A year later, in August 1946, the New Towns Commission designated it the first New Town and today Stevenage has around eighty thousand people and a distinctive urban landscape. Its maze of roundabouts and cycle tracks and the tallest street lights in Britain testify to its modernity, though the town development plan declared that the Old Town would not be touched: a pity then that the first significant building to be demolished was the Old Town Hall.

Rural Hertfordshire was not a traditional hotbed of football: it had none of the coal, iron or heavy industry of the North and Midlands, passionate crucibles of the modem game. However, as the new town grew during the

1950s, it absorbed Londoners, largely from the East End, imbued with football culture, and in 1963 a club called Stevenage Town were elected to the old Southern League. A third place in 1966/67 secured them promotion to the Premier Division: however, plagued with financial problems, Town went to the wall at the end of the 1967/68 campaign.

Crawling from the wreckage a new club, Stevenage Athletic, joined the Metropolitan League in 1968 and Southern League Division One in 1970/71. Their visit was only a passing one and five seasons later, in August 1976, Stevenage went into liquidation.

Following the demise of Athletic, a phalanx of JCBs ploughed up the pitch at Broadhall Way, determined that it would never see football again. Nonetheless, a dedicated band of football-crazy aficionados resolved to raise the phoenix from the ashes of bankruptcy and the club known today as Stevenage Borough was formed late in 1976. From humble beginnings – the club played in the Chiltern Youth League on a roped-off pitch at the King George V playing fields – Borough joined the United Counties League in 1980/81, playing at a renovated stadium at Broadhall Way. In their first season as a senior club Stevenage Borough won the double of United Counties Division One Championship and Cup and moved to the Isthmian League Division Two in 1984, winning the league in their first season and reaching the quarter-finals of the FA Vase.

The beginning of the 1990s saw a new era for the club with the appointment of Paul Fairclough as manager. Unbeaten at home for two seasons, winning the Ryman Division Two North Championship and then the Division One title, in 1993/94 Stevenage Borough achieved promotion to the Football Conference, winning the title in 1996. Stevenage then became the third club in successive seasons, along with Kidderminster and Macclesfield, to be refused admission to the Football League owing to strict ground regulations.

In the second half of the 1990s Stevenage Borough were also making waves in the FA Cup. In 1996/97 Stevenage reached the Third Round after beating Leyton Orient at Brisbane Road but for their Fourth Round tie at home against Birmingham City, the FA ruled Broadhall Way unsuitable. Accordingly, the game was played at St Andrew's, where the then Division One side won only 2–0. The following season's Cup campaign faltered rather at the start line, as Borough needed replays to see off Carshalton and Cambridge United, but when their ball came out of the draw's velvet bag, they faced an away trip to then Division One Swindon Town in Round Three.

'When the talk is of the magic of the Cup they don't mention the bleakness of Swindon's Stratton Bank, the rain driving in your face, the wind howling around your ears. For the Stevenage supporter, however, that inhospitable terrace became heaven on earth.'[1] The 19 coaches from Hertfordshire had swept their way along the storm-battered M4 and disgorged the two thousand fans on to the uncovered away end and, as Borough fan David Banks recalls, 'the wind and rain are remembered with a kind of affection, worn like a badge of honour amongst fans that were there that day,' like Henry Vs archers at Agincourt.

The game was played in torrential rain throughout and for the crowd of 9,422 Stevenage's attacking intent was plain from the start. They might have scored in the first two minutes as Swindon keeper Fraser Digby miscued in the howling gale but redeemed himself with a smothering save at Grazioli's feet. Almost at once, Swindon took the lead when Mark Walters' speed exposed a lack of cover in the Stevenage defence, the former Liverpool winger thundering home a drive from 30 yards. It was the prelude, the sages said, to several more from Swindon. 'Good teams would have capitalised on that,' said Steve McMahon, the Swindon manager. 'They would have gone from strength to strength but we're not a good team.' He was right. Walters' strike was the only silver lining in an otherwise wet, windy and dismal afternoon for the Robins.

Stevenage's response to the goal showed their greater stomach for the fight. At once they lifted their game: 'Smith shone at the back, heading or clouting every ball to safety. Perkins commanded the midfield, winning most tackles and creating with aplomb; and Wordsworth waxed lyrical upfront.'[2] Gary Crawshaw went close, Dean Wordsworth was on target with a couple of rasping drives and it was no surprise that Borough equalised in the 23rd minute. Guiliano Grazioli failed to connect with a header from Michael Love's cross and Swindon keeper Fraser Digby punched the ball out only as far as Jason Soloman, who hoisted a left-footed volley back over his head.

Soloman, regarded by David Banks as an 'enigmatic player who dazzled and frustrated in equal measure', was a former England youth international and, as he ruefully told the *Sunday Telegraph*, Liverpool's home defeat at the hands of Coventry ruled out any chance of a reunion with his old chum,

---

[1] Trevor Haylett, *Daily Telegraph*, January 5, 1998.
[2] Russell Kempson, *The Times*, January 5, 1998.

David James. 'It would have been nice to have smashed one past him,' said Soloman, who was in the same Watford FA Youth Cup-winning side as the current England keeper.

The raging storm intensified as the second half began and for Borough fans, on the open terrace behind the Swindon goal, 'it felt like we were sitting in a wind tunnel, having buckets of water thrown at us'.[3] Though lashed by the wind and rain, they were less discomfited by the elements than home keeper Fraser Digby, whose uncertain composure in the teeth of the gale was a constant source of hope and amusement. As Digby struggled to get his goal kicks out of the penalty area they 'became a farcical ordeal'[4] and, just on the hour, one of his kicks was seized upon by Simon Stapleton whose instant shot flew past Digby's right-hand post. Six minutes later, another goal kick succumbed to the power of the storm, eventually coming to earth on the edge of Swindon's penalty area where the excellent Gary Crawshaw latched on to the loose ball, slipped it square to Grazioli, whose accurate finish past the hapless Digby had the bedraggled Stevenage fans jumping for joy: a Cup legend was born.

Twenty-two-year-old Grazioli, born in England of Italian parents, had been signed from Peterborough a fortnight before for, as Fairclough put it, 'three packets of crisps and a Mars bar'. His mother, Silvana, a primary schoolteacher in North London, was almost hysterical. 'She's been on the phone already,' said Grazioli. 'She was screaming in English and Italian. I couldn't understand a word she was saying.'

The game now became solely a question of survival for the Conference side and, though Mark Robinson had a goal disallowed and Des Gallagher tipped over a 30-yard scorcher from Les Collins, their intense resolve saw them through.

Before the tie, Fairclough had pointed to Swindon's losing run of six games in the last eight. 'I told the team that we were probably meeting Swindon at the best possible time. We could come here next month and get murdered but on the day the best team won and won well.' Stevenage had shown 'the greater spirit and fortitude and used the unruly elements to their advantages'.[5] They played most of the game after the break in Swindon's half, compounding the home side's problems in clearing their lines against the howling wind. A dejected Steve McMahon was forced to

---

[3] David Banks.
[4] Nicholas Harling, *Sunday Telegraph*, January 4, 1998.
[5] Trevor Haylett, *Daily Telegraph*, January 5, 1998.

concede that his side had not come to terms with the conditions:

> Fraser Digby was having trouble kicking with the wind before half-time yet we spent the second half knocking the ball back to him from the halfway line. It's commonsense stuff but we lacked the necessary thought. The Stevenage players played on Thursday and then went to work on Friday morning. Don't tell me about preparations, about how hard it is. It wasn't about tactics, style or the conditions. It was 11 versus 11, men against men and who wanted it the most.

The visitors' fans had enjoyed a classic Cup clash – raw, raucous and romantic. Nick Roberts, on a hospitality package for a friend's birthday, remembers Swindon as

> friendly throughout and gracious in defeat. Before the game, they gave us an unplanned tour of the stadium, including the pitch, dugouts and changing rooms. After the match, Steve McMahon was so incensed with his team that he kept them locked in the changing room long after the final whistle – so long in fact that the Chairman decided to give their post-match meals to us, which really must have added insult to injury!

For Fairclough, the remarkable victory was not without its bittersweet overtones. He managed to retain his sense of perspective: 'We've been struggling and perhaps I've brought in too many players, made too many changes too soon. I've made more mistakes this season than at any time since I've been at the club.' Yet at the same time nothing, he said, could compensate for the club's failure to earn a place in the Football League after winning the Vauxhall Conference in 1996. The win, someone suggested, probably made it worse: 'it shows you can compete at League level.' Fairclough nodded, smiling in agreement. Having reached the Fourth Round of the FA Cup for the first time in the club's history, 'it was not a time for tub-thumping or retrospective bitterness.'[6]

It was a time for celebration and David Banks recalls a delicious scenario on his return to Stevenage, which he concedes

---

[6] Russell Kempson, *The Times*, January 5, 1998.

probably harks back to a bygone era. My mates and I went out to celebrate, but were refused entry to a bar because one of us had football
colours on (a Stevenage Borough shirt). However, the Boro players
were all in the bar celebrating themselves. When they saw the bouncer
refusing us entry a couple of them came over and explained who they
were and the bouncer let us in. It was a great night and the fans and
players were able to celebrate side-by-side.

Borough's reward for their triumph at the County Ground was a plum
home tie against Newcastle – but the attitude of the Geordies was super-
cilious in the extreme. They complained to the FA that, even with temporary seating, a capacity of eight thousand at Broadhall Way was insufficient
to meet their fans' ticket demands. Angry exchanges flew back and forth
between the two chairmen and on Sunday, January 25, the football arrived
as a pleasant antidote to the tetchy war of words. In front of the *Match of
the Day* live cameras, Borough excelled themselves. A third-minute strike
by Alan Shearer set the Magpies on their way but Stevenage's spirited
riposte thrilled the record crowd of 8,040 and millions of TV viewers nationwide. Four minutes before half-time, Grazioli scored the equaliser to take
the tie to a replay at St James' Park ten days later.

Once again Stevenage caused Newcastle a headache, and once again the
Magpies were forced to rely on Alan Shearer, as the England captain gave
them a 2—0 half-time lead. Borough were not dead yet, however: Gary
Crawshaw pulled a goal back a quarter of an hour from time but it wasn't
quite enough.

Over the last decade, Stevenage Borough have consolidated their position as one of the country's leading non-League clubs. The Broadhall Way
stadium has been redeveloped with help from the local council and now
the 7,100-capacity ground is recognised as one of the best outside the
Football League. In 2003/04 they knocked out Stockport County in the
First Round of the Cup and a year later came close to League status, losing
the Conference play-off by the only goal of the game to Carlisle. They did,
however, win the FA Trophy in 2006/07, beating Kidderminster Harriers
3–2 in the final.

In the late 1800s and early 1900s Stevenage was home to a pair of identical twins, Albert Ebenezer and Ebenezer Albert Fox. Their father, Henry,
was a devout chapel man and local farmer while their mother, Charlotte,

was a straw-plait worker. Despite their respectable background, the twins were notorious poachers who often evaded the clutches of the law by providing alibis for each other. The old reprobates might well have chuckled quietly to themselves if they knew that the football team from their home town had carried on their less than honourable way of life some 70 years later by carting home the spoils from a sporting foray into deepest Wiltshire.

SWINDON TOWN: Digby, McDonald, Culverhouse, Taylor, Robinson, Collins, Watson, Walters, Gooden, Hay, Ndah
STEVENAGE BOROUGH: Gallagher, Kirby, Smith, Trott, Love, Soloman, Stapleton, Perkins, Wordsworth, Grazioli, Crawshaw

43

LEICESTER CITY 1, WYCOMBE WANDERERS 2

FA Cup, Round Six, March 10, 2001

Brown with the free kick, Royce fists it away, only as far as Bulman, he'll clip it back in, he does – it's high, Bates heads it across – ESSANDOH WITH THE HEADER!!!!!!!!!!!!!!!!!!!!!!!!!

'It was unreal. Words actually couldn't describe it, which is never handy when you're a commentator.' Phil Slatter was working for hospital radio in High Wycombe on the biggest game in the history of Wycombe Wanderers. For Slatter, a diehard Wanderers fan, the strict neutrality of the media was impossible. This symbiosis between a team and its supporters has been explored by Chris Oakley, when he writes of football and psychoanalysis as 'instances of self-elected trauma. Both involve an identificatory and emotional tie, which psychoanalysts refer to as transference and one could say that all football fans have precisely that with regard to their chosen team. Fans are always distinct from spectators.'[1] Football at the highest level sometimes seems a marvellously choreographed piece of theatre rather than an elemental battle for survival – a subtle distinction 'exemplified by a fifteen-year-old boy talking to his father as they stumbled dispiritedly out of Brisbane Road after their side, Carlisle United, had been relegated from the Football League, "You know, Dad, at Arsenal we were just spectators. But here we are fans." That difference can be called transference.'[2]

Inherent within transference lies an element of wish-fulfilment, a projec-

---

[1] Oakley, pp. 176–7.
[2] Ibid.

tion on to another of one's hopes and dreams. Martin Ball, another Wycombe fan, was with his son in the Leicester end that day at Filbert Street. 'As we took our seats, I pulled out a picture of my great-grandfather, who was the first Wycombe captain to lift a trophy: I told Michael to kiss it and make a wish!'

The Wanderers' saga that season was certainly 'such stuff as dreams are made on'. By the time they ran out at Leicester they had already played nine matches stretching back to the middle of November and a comfortable 3–0 win over Isthmian League Harrow Borough. A glorious Cup run then, of course, was only a dream and any thoughts that the club would go on to emulate the achievement in 1937 of Millwall, their Second Round opponents, in reaching the Cup semi-final[3] were in the realms of fantasy.

The good burgesses of High Wycombe were in any case unaccustomed to dealing in fantasy. The down-to-earth market town stands in a largely agricultural county, where sheep have grazed on the Chilterns and dairy cattle and arable farming have occupied the lower slopes since Saxon times. Furthermore, Wycombe has always been a hub of commerce and industry. There has been a market in the High Street since the Middle Ages and in the seventeenth century paper-making became important but the town's most famous industry, furniture, grew to prominence in the nineteenth century and, by 1875, it was reckoned that 4,700 chairs were made every day in High Wycombe. Then, as Humphrey Lyttelton, in his whimsical notes for *I'm Sorry, I Haven't a Clue*, has helpfully pointed out, with the growth in demand for chests of drawers and fancy footstools it became the tallboy and pouffe capital of Europe.[4]

Wycombe Wanderers Football Club was founded at the Steam Engine pub in 1887 by young men working in the furniture trade. Ten years later the club attained senior status, moving to Loakes Park in 1895 and playing in the Southern League, with the inevitable nickname of 'The Chairboys' (which was soon replaced by the boringly mundane 'Blues'). Success was hard to come by in a league dominated by professional teams, so the club moved to the Spartan League after the Great War and after winning the league title, joined the Isthmian League in 1921. It was not, however, till 1956 that they won the first of eight league titles. The captain of the side

---

[3] See Millwall v Manchester City, pp. 41–50.
[4] Pattinson, p. 101.

at this time was Frank Adams, who, as club Secretary and holder of the deeds, presented Loakes Park to the Wanderers as a gift in 1947.

Between the wars, one of the highlights of the club's history came in 1930/31 when the Chairboys beat Hayes to lift the FA Amateur Cup at Highbury. Twenty-five years later, a second Amateur Cup Final appearance ended in defeat at the hands of the powerful Bishop Auckland side. The 1970s saw two heroic Cup runs: in 1973/74 the club beat Newport County and in the following season a 2–1 win over Bournemouth set up a Third Round clash with Jack Charlton's Middlesbrough at Loakes Park. A capacity 12,000 crowd – and the *Match of the Day* cameras – saw the visitors cling on for a goal-less draw before winning with a last-minute goal in the replay.

After an unproductive decade, apart from an Isthmian League title in 1987, two events in 1990 electrified the Wanderers and their fans. Martin O'Neill arrived as manager from Grantham and the Chairboys left Loakes Park for a new home at Adams Park, at the end of an industrial estate on the edge of town. It was named after the club's former captain and secretary and about that time the club's original nickname was resurrected by the fanzine *Chairboys Gas*, the suffix coming from the 'Gasworks End' terrace at Loakes Park.

During O'Neill's five years at Adams Park the club went to Wembley three more times. In 1992/93, the Chairboys became the third non-League side to achieve the 'double', winning the FA Trophy (when 28,000 Wycombe supporters were at Wembley for the 4–1 victory over Runcorn) and securing the Conference by a record 15 points, thereby becoming the first team from Buckinghamshire to play League football. A year later they moved up again to what was Division Two, narrowly missing a chance of a third consecutive promotion via the play-offs when the leagues were restructured in preparation for the Premiership.

Martin O'Neill left the club for Norwich in 1995, and Alan Smith, John Gregory and Neil Smillie came and went before ex-Wimbledon midfielder Lawrie Sanchez walked into Adams Park in February 1999. With 18 games left, it looked for all the world as if the club was heading back to the bottom tier but in the last game of the season Sanchez's men secured Division Two survival, winning 1–0 at Lincoln with a goal by Paul Emblen seven minutes from time.

The next year was a season of mid-table consolidation and 2000/2001 offered more of the same. Just before Christmas, goals from Rammell and

McCarthy beat Millwall in a replay at Adams Park and in the Third Round, a stirring performance to beat Division One Grimsby 3–1 at Blundell Park brought Dave Jones' strong Wolves side to Wycombe for a Fourth Round tie at the end of January. A crowd of 9,617 saw the Midlanders sent packing 2–1, with goals from Rammell and Parkin. The Chairboys were in the last 16.

Less than a year before, Wimbledon, Wycombe's Fifth Round opponents, had been a Premiership club. By mid-February 2001 they were at the top of the slippery slope down which they would slide through the Divisions, hitting the floor of the basement with a bump five years later, via a change of name, a barrage of animosity and a move, lock, stock and barrel, up the M1 to Milton Keynes.

With 18 minutes left at Adams Park, Wanderers trailed to two first-half goals from a well-organised and clearly superior Wimbledon side until Sanchez's treble substitution sparked a late rally. First, Sam Parkin's cross into the heart of the Dons' penalty area was headed away only as far as the onrushing Michael Simpson, whose deflected low-shot trundled almost shamefacedly past Kelvin Davis into the net. Then, ten minutes from time, Steve Brown bundled in a controversial equaliser, with the visitors pleading offside, to earn the Chairboys an unlikely replay in South London three days later.

If they had left it late at Adams Park, Wycombe cut it as fine as they dared in the replay. At a freezing Selhurst Park, Wayne Gray put the Dons 2–1 up deep into extra time and a brave and determined Wanderers performance looked doomed to end in defeat. Gareth Ainsworth had given the hosts the lead and, despite an equaliser from Dave Carroll, when Simpson was sent off midway through the second half, the writing seemed on the wall. However, in the 120th minute, Irishman Paul McCarthy converted Sam Parkin's cross. The two thousand Blues fans screwed up their courage as the penalty shoot-out went to sudden death. With the tally at 7–7 Wanderers goalkeeper Martin Taylor slotted home, and when Hawkins fired his penalty over the bar Wycombe were in the quarter-finals.

The Wanderers' opponents in the last eight were a Leicester City side who had been dumped out of the Worthington Cup at home earlier in the season 3–0 by Crystal Palace. They were lying sixth in the Premiership, however, and the more acerbic pundits were forecasting the tie as a bye into the semi-finals for City, but the canny Leicester manager, Peter Taylor, was not one either to countenance any complacency in the squad or to allow sentiment to colour his team selection, although his left-winger, Steve Guppy, was a former Wycombe player. Lawrie Sanchez was woefully short of strikers and had resorted to an internet appeal; Kevin McCarra in *The Times* reckoned 'Leicester should give him many other worries on their way to the last four.'

Things didn't quite work out like that at Filbert Street. Wycombe dominated a goal-less first half, their best chance arriving when midfielder Steve Brown tested Simon Royce with a fierce volley which the Foxes' keeper just managed to tip over the bar. It was quite an afternoon for the 34-year-old Brown, who had carried his 15-month-old son Maxwell on as the team's mascot. Maxwell had been born with a life-threatening condition known as tracheo-oesophageal fistula, which meant that his stomach was not connected to his throat and the milk he received from his mother, Nicky, went straight into his lungs. After 20 operations, it was miraculous that the toddler was there at all.

Any fears among the Wycombe fans that the Premiership side would overpower the Chairboys in the second half were dispelled five minutes after the resumption. Leicester's Andrew Impey fouled Michael Simpson on the Wycombe right. The entire Leicester defence were deceived by Brown's wickedly curling free kick and Paul McCarthy bundled past Ade Akinbiyi to head the ball wide of Royce for his fifth goal in the Cup campaign. Phil Slatter was beside himself: '. . . McCARTHY! 1–0 WYCOMBE! I screamed to the 900 patients listening in (I later learned this would result in one poor chap falling out of bed).'

Leicester responded with pace and aggression, stretching Wycombe with shrewd passing from Impey and Gerry Taggart. Once, Robbie Savage, put through by Taggart's deft through pass, seemed certain to score until McCarthy denied the Welshman with a well-timed sliding tackle. The swashbuckling Savage, niggling and pugnacious as ever, had been combative throughout, but when he limped off it produced the home side's only moment of real hope. In the 67th minute substitute Darren Eadie seized on a pass from Taggart and, from his cross into the box, Muzzy Izzet drove home the equaliser from close range. Class had told. The Foxes' faithful celebrated, anticipating a place in the semi-final and, amongst them, Michael and Martin Ball stayed seated, preparing for 20 minutes of last-ditch defence and a replay at Adams Park.

Time, thought Sanchez, to roll the dice: enter Stewart Castledine and Roy Essandoh. Their introduction brought no instant change of fortune. Far from it. Eleven minutes from time, Steve Brown's cross into the box was blocked by the arm of Stefan Oakes. A blatant penalty, cried the Wycombe fans. The officials thought otherwise and, when Sanchez stormed up the touchline to complain Steve Bennett, the referee, was having none of it. He waved the appeals away and Sanchez to the stand.

Still, Phil Slatter consoled himself, there was the replay on Tuesday to look forward to. Wycombe couldn't win now – not with a striker they'd signed via the internet. Sanchez had lost half a dozen strikers through injury and, as soon as Ian Wright and Gianluca Vialli had turned down his advances, the Wycombe manager in desperation had advertised on the club's website for a striker not Cup-tied. Roy Essandoh, a Belfast-born Ghanaian, had made a few appearances for East Fife and Motherwell before moving to Austria and thence to VPS Vaasa in the Finnish Premier League. He had returned to England to train and play with Rushden and Diamonds but when Sanchez's plight was blazened abroad on teletext it was spotted by Essandoh's agent. Within hours the two parties met and the 25-year-old was signed on a two-week contract.

With the game in stoppage time, Wycombe won a free kick, Steve Brown's cross was punched away by Royce only as far as Danny Bulman, who chipped the ball back in for full-back Jamie Bates to nod it across goal. Muscling his way past Taggart, Essandoh headed the Chairboys into the Cup semi-final with his first goal in English football. Martin and Michael Ball were the Wycombe fans in the Leicester end with the picture and the wish: 'This time we cannot be restrained. Michael and I go bananas. We don't care if we get thrown out now there are only minutes left.'

Essandoh himself recalls the free kick:

When the ball came to me I just wanted to make their goalkeeper work, but I managed to get in front of the centre-half to nod it in. It was fantastic to see it go in. You could have heard a pin drop. It was all pretty surreal, two or three seconds of emotion that I still can't explain. I haven't seen the goal for years but you know it was something special when people still want to talk about it to this day.

As soon as Essandoh's winner hit the back of the Leicester net, Brown whipped off his shirt to reveal the name of his son emblazoned on a T-shirt beneath. Since he had already been booked for a first-half challenge on Robbie Savage, he was dismissed. He departed, tears streaming down his cheeks. 'I was so disappointed, I was crying,' he said. 'Getting sent off was not a good example to set in front of my son. It just seems to me that some people do their job more ruthlessly than others.' Sadly, the referee felt he had no alternative. 'Under Football Association rules it is a mandatory instruction,' he said. After all, he was only obeying orders and, anyway, perhaps he had decided he had better even things up a bit for the Premiership side.

Sanchez, already in the stand for his protests over the penalty decision, which 'could have cost me my career, the club £1 million and the chance of promotion next season,' charged back to the touchline after Brown's red card and had to be restrained by the fourth official. 'I get more upset about injustices,' he said, 'than I do about things that happen in the normal course of events.'

As for the Leicester manager, Peter Taylor, the day was 'a nightmare I never thought would happen. We seemed nervous and I can't understand it.' From the kick-off, his side had struggled to capture the air of authority which had put out Bristol City in the previous round.

The Wanderers' conquest of the Premiership team on their own ground, where they had recently beaten Liverpool, Sunderland and Chelsea, by opponents from the lower half of the Second Division – this humbling of sixth by sixtieth – was both confirmation and celebration of the Cup's enduring appeal, something that could happen only in England, where 'such events are greeted as wondrous yet normal, like Christmas morning'.[5] The victory was no fluke by a side from 'leafy Bucks', as Sanchez put it. The Wycombe boss had been irritated by pundits who viewed his side as a quaint rustic embellishment to the last eight. His team possessed a stubborn, indefatigable streak more usually associated with teams from the traditional post-industrial heartland of the game. Wycombe's midfield, driven on by man-of-the-match Steve Brown, snuffed out the craft and passion of Taggart and Savage, unsettling the Leicester centre-backs with a series of flighted crosses: as a result, their defence was relieved of consistent threat from the home attack. 'All the way along,' Sanchez said, 'my team and

---

[5] Ibid.

myself have believed that we're writing our own page of FA Cup history.'

On April 8, when the Wanderers walked out side by side with five-time Cup-winners Liverpool at Villa Park, the page grew into a chapter. For much of a drab semi-final, Wycombe kept Liverpool at bay. The two Germans, Christian Ziege and Markus Babbel, had missed chances in a stern tussle until goals from substitute Emile Heskey 17 minutes from time and Robbie Fowler 5 minutes later put the game beyond reach. The Wanderers kept fighting and their fans were rewarded by a last-minute goal from Keith Ryan. Though the team had been well-beaten by a talented Liverpool side, Ryan's consolation strike rounded off a fabulous Cup campaign.

As so often happens, the buccaneering spirit of the Cup run did not spill over into the bread-and-butter matches in the Second Division. The Wanderers' League form tailed off and a mid-table finish was all they could achieve, as their conquerors went on to lift the trophy, Michael Owen's double strike sinking the Gunners at the Millennium Stadium.

Today, at the time of writing, Wycombe are riding high at the top of the Second Division, managed ironically by the same Peter Taylor whose Leicester side was done for by the peripatetic Roy Essandoh, whose goal etched another fairy-tale in the romantic history of the FA Cup.

And not just the Cup. For Phil Slatter, the man from hospital radio, Essandoh's goal was 'the greatest moment in history. Ever'. He was determined to celebrate it, 'come rain, or shine or being chucked out. Leaping to my feet and punching the air, I can only imagine the panic the nurses and doctors must have been in back in the wards.' For him, Wycombe's win was 'a story that nobody could make up. Or if they did, nobody would believe it. Sometimes I still don't. I'd better go and check the recording.'

LEICESTER CITY: Royce, Rowett, Elliott, Taggart, Impey, Savage, Jones, Izzet, Davidson, Sturridge, Akinbiyi
WYCOMBE WANDERERS: Taylor, Townsend, Bates, Cousin, McCarthy, Vinnicombe, Brown, Bulman, Simpson, Lee, Ryan

44

SHREWSBURY TOWN 2, EVERTON 1

FA Cup, Round Three, January 4, 2003

You say 'Shroosbry'. I say 'Shrow-sbry'. Let's call the whole thing off . . . for the fact is, the name of the town can be pronounced either way. The pupils of the prestigious Shrewsbury School have, however, always called the place 'Shrozebury' and the fact that many locals drop the first 'r' from the name, making the pronunciation 'Shoesbury', gives credence to the belief that which one you use depends on what side of the river you live on.

Whatever the pronunciation, Shrewsbury, like Durham, is renowned among geography students – or was when you had to study geomorphology – for being sited on a classic incised meander. However, where Durham's meander is dominated by its cathedral, the loop in the Severn at Shrewsbury is overlooked by its red sandstone castle. This Norman stronghold protected the only dry-shod approach to the medieval town, whose economic prosperity in the late Middle Ages was based on the wool trade. This major industry, with the River Severn and Watling Street as trading routes, gave the town a national importance and its historic significance is still seen in the splendid black-and-white houses in plaster and weatherboard. One such is the seventeenth-century Lion Inn among whose eminent nineteenth-century visitors were the violinist Paganini and Charles Dickens. The town has also played a unique role in the history of Western intellectual thought: it was the birthplace of the naturalist Charles Darwin, who attended Shrewsbury School.

Darwin is best known of course for *The Origin of Species*, but in 1886, four years after his death, old boys of his alma mater were responsible for the origins of Shrewsbury Town FC. The club was purely amateur then, as befitted its public school foundation, and it was another ten years before semi-professional players turned out for 'the Town'. While money had always been tight, the 1909/10 season was desperate. In February the roof blew off their ramshackle stand, bringing down the telephone wires above and cutting off communications between the town and the North of England. Furthermore, the club had been playing on an Army-owned ground at Copthorne on the outskirts of the town and now the military were pressing to reclaim their land. The Town was forced to cast about for a new ground. With time pressing, club officials signed a one-year lease with the local council for a site at Gay Meadow, squeezed in between the railway and the River Severn. The Town moved in for the start of the new season and though the short lease restricted building work to a pair of changing rooms, 97 years of history had begun.

The old 'Vetch Field' at Swansea is perhaps the only ground name which can hold a lyrical candle to the delightfully quirky 'Gay Meadow'. The origins of the name are not clear, though it is thought to relate to its former use as a site for medieval revelries, circuses and fairs. All went well in the club's first season until, in January, during a game against Birmingham City reserves, the Severn burst its banks and the ball began to float. The match was abandoned, setting a sadly familiar pattern for the next 97 years.

The floods were just one of the quirks that made the ground so loveable. 'Overlooked by the town's castle and abbey, it was a beautiful throwback.'[1] In the early years of this century, Gay Meadow still had a problem with squirrels, which used to chew the goalposts and dislodge the carrier bags stuffed with paper that passed for insulation in the press box. Balls were frequently kicked over the Riverside Terrace into the Severn, where for 45 years Fred Davies – a local coracle-maker – was employed on match days to fish balls from the river. Fred earned 50p for each ball he returned until his death in the mid–1990s ended this charmingly eccentric but eminently practical tradition.[2] 'And the best view of the action was never from within the ground itself, but from the classroom windows of the Wakeham School, towering over the Wakeham End.'[3]

From their windows the pupils, wresting their attention from the declen-

[1] *Observer*, November 18, 2007.
[2] Fred was succeeded by his nephew, who abandoned the coracle in favour of a motorboat.
[3] *Observer*, November 18, 2007.

sion of Latin nouns or the solution of quadratic equations, would have seen a new stand going up in 1922, American GIs playing baseball during the war, and Shrewsbury Town, also known as 'The Blues', 'The Shrews' or 'Salop' (the old name for the county of Shropshire), knocking about in the Shropshire & District Birmingham League or the Midland League and winning the Welsh Cup in 1938. When the Football League was expanded to 92 clubs in 1950, the Blues were admitted, becoming founder members of the new Fourth Division in 1958/59. Arthur Rowley, an archetypal no-nonsense post-war centre-forward, had arrived from Leicester City as player–manager and hit an astonishing 38 goals in 43 games[4] in his first season as the Blues gained promotion to Division Three. Though steadily gaining weight, he continued to take no prisoners among opposing defences and scored 152 goals for the Town in his seven seasons at Gay Meadow. Rowley had a powerful left foot and one anecdote, possibly apocryphal, claims that one of his mis-hit shots once sailed out of the ground and landed in a passing coal wagon and ended up in Newport, South Wales.

In 1961 Shrewsbury reached the semi-finals of the inaugural League Cup, but then began their life as a footballing yo-yo, up and down between the bottom two divisions until gaining promotion again as runners-up to Mansfield in 1975. By then the new Riverside Terrace, which became the home fans' favourite and the source of the ground's atmosphere, had been opened and in 1979, with player–manager Graham Turner in charge the Blues stormed to the Division Three title. It was a heady season, for Shrewsbury reached the FA Cup quarter-finals for the first time, a feat they repeated four years later.

After a decade in the Second Division, the Town lost their grip on football's greasy pole at the end of the 1988/89 season and steadily drifted down the divisions, losing the 1996 Associate Members' Cup Final at Wembley en route. Relegation to the Conference was narrowly escaped in 2000 with a win at Exeter City on the final day of the season.

Life at the bottom of football's food-chain continued to be a struggle over the next couple of seasons and it was with no great sense of adventure or optimism that 4,210 Town supporters, having seen a routine 4–0 win over Stafford Rangers in the First Round, turned up to watch their side despatch Barrow 3–1 in December 2002. However, that win brought

---

[4] Rowley holds the League scoring record of 434 goals from 619 games.

the prospect of a visit from Premiership giants Everton in early January.

At the time the Blues were lying 18th in Division Three but, in spite of having suffered a 6–0 defeat at Boston United and a 5–1 hammering at Rushden and Diamonds over Christmas, they had gone nine home games without defeat. Everton by contrast lay fifth in the Premiership: however, though they had gone five games without defeat they hadn't won an away fixture in four attempts. There were other reasons for nostalgic romantics to hope for an upset. The terraces at Gay Meadow, packed with 7,800 fans tight to the touchlines, were a throwback to the days when giant-killings took place in black-and-white – as was the muddy, bumpy pitch. Furthermore the match was personal – Shrews' boss Kevin Ratcliffe had captained Everton through the club's purple patch in the 1980s and the Toffees' boss David Moyes had led Shrewsbury at the same time.

The Everton side included English football's new *Wunderkind*, 17-year-old Wayne Rooney, taking part in his first Cup tie, and pundits around the country expected Everton, with Gemmill, Gravesen and Radzinski, alongside Rooney, to see their Third Division hosts off well before half-time.

Kevin Ratcliffe had, however, got his men well motivated against his old side and the Shrews took the game to Everton from the start. The Premiership team's defence, composed entirely of centre halves, immediately looked ill at ease: lacking pace, they played too deep, giving Shrewsbury the space to dominate in midfield. Whereas Moyes might have expected only the long ball from the home side, the experienced Nigel Jemson linked play intelligently and both Luke Rodgers and Ryan Lowe demonstrated a willingness to take on Everton's makeshift rearguard at every opportunity, Rodgers proving an especial handful to Stubbs and Weir from the kick-off.

Almost at once Jemson sent a volley wide and after 12 minutes Everton's England goalkeeper, Richard Wright, had to dive brilliantly to his right to save his flicked header from Ian Woan's free kick. Woan, like Jemson a player schooled in the right way by Brian Clough at Nottingham Forest, was also relishing one of his last hurrahs. The inexperienced Everton right-back, Peter Clarke, was having an utterly miserable afternoon as Woan's control and movement led him a merry and embarrassing dance.

With lacklustre performances from Thomas Gravesen and Scott Gemmill in midfield, the visitors struggled to create any concerted attacks, though sporadically the pace of Tomasz Radzinski offered Everton hope. He was twice denied by former Liverpool youngster Ian Dunbavin when clean through and Peter Wilding was forced to clear from the line when Radzinski threatened again after a one-two with Rooney. At the other end, Wright brought off another fine save in the 33rd minute as he turned a shot from the dangerous Luke Rodgers against the outside of a post.

Shrewsbury continued to match Everton in midfield, however, and with the visitors' defence still failing to convince the roars from the terraces grew in conviction and with half an hour gone the BBC commentary team were talking seriously of the possibility of a shock. Seven minutes before the break, their surmise became reality as Nigel Jemson, whose winning goal for Nottingham Forest in the 1990 Littlewoods Cup final at Wembley was arguably the highlight of a career that has taken him to 13 different clubs, put Shrewsbury ahead.

With 38 minutes gone Rodgers broke from deep again and headed straight for the heart of the defence. Thomas Gravesen in pursuit seemed to wade through treacle and his clumsy felling of the Shrewsbury forward cost him a booking and his side a free kick just outside the box.

Wright's wall needed repointing as Jemson struck the ball from 25 yards into the top corner with the keeper finishing wrapped around his post. 'I scored one against Barrow in the last round,' said the veteran striker, 'and though I missed badly at Rushden I was able to bend this one in. It was lovely to see it hit the back of the net.' Lovely? It was enough to send Gay Meadow wild.

Everton were stunned and anxious Evertonians consoled themselves with the thought that class would prevail in the end. At half-time Moyes replaced a Dane with a Swede, Niclas Alexandersson coming on for the ineffectual Gravesen. However, the change had scarcely had time to make a difference when, three minutes after the restart, Everton's fragility at the back should have cost them again. The combative Luke Rodgers cantered down the left and swerved inside away from David Weir. He stormed into the area and as he shaped to shoot he was upended by the luckless Peter Clarke. Shrewsbury were beside themselves as referee Steve Dunn dismissed all claims for a penalty.

Now, having been thrown a lifeline, Everton began to play with increased urgency, though they had little to show for it – until on the hour Scott Gemmill seized on a feeble clearance from the Shrews' keeper, Ian Dunbavin. He ran straight at the defence before slipping Alexandersson in on goal. The Swede's finish into the far corner was flawless and, as the Third Division side tired, the smart money was on the Toffees to seal an unlikely victory. It was the turn of the home fans to go quiet, bite their nails, hoping to hang on for the money-spinning replay at Goodison.

Their heroes were still very much in the game, but Everton were certainly more threatening and with a quarter of an hour left Alexandersson almost put Everton ahead, his cross-shot shaving the outside of the post. Then Rooney curled a 20-yard drive just over the bar. Shrewsbury responded with spirit, Jemson just missing with another free kick, Jamie Tolley forcing a good save from Wright, who a minute later bravely blocked another attempt at Ryan Lowe's feet.

Then, with a minute to go, Shrewsbury, still resolutely pressing forward, were awarded another free kick, David Unsworth fouling Steve Jagielka in a promising position near the right-hand corner of the box. Another former Forest star, Ian Woan, whipped the ball into the near post and Jemson, stealing a yard on his marker, headed home past the helpless Wright.

Euphoria erupted around three sides of the quaint old ground while the Toffees' fans plunged their heads glumly into their blue scarves. The end was nigh though there was time enough for Rooney to talk his way into the referee's notebook for complaining about not getting a penalty and for Li Tie, who replaced Gemmill, to snatch an undeserved replay but he scuffed his shot from only two yards out.

Shrewsbury were not to be denied their moment of glory, however, and Everton's former hero and captain had masterminded the saddest Cup defeat in their 124 years of history.

It had been no more than Kevin Ratcliffe's men had deserved and fully vindicated his faith in his players. 'Sometimes you need a bit of luck but I don't think we did today,' the former Everton captain said. 'We deserved it. The last thing I said was "Don't show them any respect. Get out there and get at them" – and it all clicked together.' On the other hand, David Moyes was man enough to concede that his side were outplayed for long periods. 'When you win, you take the applause, and when you lose, you have to take the boos,' Moyes said. 'We deserved the boos today.'

As for the local hero, Nigel Jemson, who had seen it all, praised his young teammates. 'We've got some great kids here and if they carry on listening to what they are told, we'll have a few more occasions like this.'

There was only one more that season. Though they were handed another 'dream' draw in the next round, at home to Chelsea, the Shrews couldn't raise their game again and Claudio Ranieri's side motored easily to a 4–0 win. Inevitably, perhaps, Shrewsbury's League form suffered too and the unfortunate Ratcliffe was shown the door at the end of the season when his team finished bottom of Division Three and were relegated into the Conference. Barely a year later they were back, when a hardworking side under Jimmy Quinn won back their League status after beating Aldershot Town in a thrilling penalty shoot-out in the Conference play-offs.

Sadly, though, the club had to confront the realities of life in the lower divisions. The Taylor Report following the Hillsborough disaster in 1989 signalled the final death knell to the increasingly ramshackle Gay Meadow. Plans to abandon the picturesque but antiquated ground had existed since 1986 but it was not till 2006, following protracted planning delays, work began on the New Meadow, a 10,000 all-seat stadium on a retail park near Meole Brace. It was opened in July 2007 with the visit of an All-Stars side captained by Gianfranco Zola.

Gay Meadow was no more. Ninety-seven years of history had seen some great games: a record 18,917 watched a game against Walsall in 1961 and in 1979 Manchester City had been beaten 2–0 in the FA Cup. In January 2003 two goals from Nigel Jemson gave the Shrews a famous win over Everton, who included the 17-year-old boy wonder of English football. He swapped his shirt with the Town's hero, to be auctioned for charity, and, as Jemson sat in the stand after the game, Wayne Rooney's shirt in his hand and a bottle of champagne at his feet, perhaps he reflected on the delicious irony of the Cup. Sometimes, just sometimes, a wise old pro can put a brash young pup in his place and the money-spinning gravy train that is now the English game can be spectacularly derailed.

SHREWSBURY TOWN: Dunbavin, Moss, Smith, Wilding, Artell, Lowe (Aiston 85), Atkins, Jamie Tolley, Woan, Rodgers (Jagielka 81), Jemson (Drysdale 90)
EVERTON: Wright, Clarke, Stubbs, Weir, Unsworth (McLeod 90), Carsley, Gemmill (Tie Li 76), Gravesen (Alexandersson 45), Naysmith, Radzinski, Rooney

45

SLOUGH TOWN 2, WALSALL 1

FA Cup, Round One, November 13, 2004

In 1943 Slough FC agreed to merge with Slough Centre FC to return to their home town from a ground-share with Maidenhead United. At the end of the war the new club, Slough United, were reluctant to rejoin the Spartan League after playing quality opposition like Barnet and Hitchin Town and led a breakaway movement to form the Corinthian League. Thus United acquired their nickname of 'The Rebels'.

Eric Collier, demobbed from the RAF in 1945, was a supporter of the Rebels even before they rebelled. In November 1947 the former Slough FC emerged with the new name of Slough Town FC and Eric, now 88 years old, still drives to watch the Town every week. He is one of those long-stay patients who follow their team from the years of youthful hope through decades of disillusion to the cynical despair of old age, one of the inmates in football's asylum who believe that they are 'witnessing a pledge of allegiance to something – whether it's team-mates, colours, a badge or a city – that will make the spectacle worth watching.'[1]

When Eric was a babe in arms, in 1921, Slough FC had just joined the Spartan League. The club had been formed in 1889 when the Swifts, Slough Albion and the Young Men's Friendly Society merged and began to play in the Southern Alliance. After the Great War, the club played in the Spartan League till the outbreak of the Second World War in 1939, when the blackouts forced greyhound racing to be held on Saturday after-noons and left Slough FC without a home. This was the aftermath of a catastrophic error which has haunted the club ever since. In 1936 the Slough FC committee made no effort to buy the Dolphin Stadium from

---

[1] Gabriele Marcotti, 'The Game', *The Times*, December 29, 2008.

the landlord, who subsequently sold it to a greyhound racing consortium. And so it was that the club, half a century old, was compelled to share with its near-neighbours in Maidenhead.

Within five years the new club, Slough Town FC, had won the Corinthian League championship, its first title, though the 1950s as a whole were something of a lean spell with only a losing FA Amateur Cup quarter-final appearance against Pegasus in 1952/53 to look back on. When the Corinthian League folded in 1963/64, the Rebels joined the Athenian League Division One, winning the title in 1964/65 and the Athenian League Premier in 1967/68. Two years later they reached the Second Round of the FA Cup, losing 1–0 at home to Barnet and in 1973/74 their third Athenian League title gained them promotion to the Isthmian League.

In 1975, with the Dolphin Stadium destined to become a supermarket, the Rebels moved to Wexham Park Stadium. They made three appearances in Round Two of the Cup in the 1980s and, at the end of the decade, the Rebels won the Isthmian League title, gaining promotion to the Conference for the first time in their history. However, not for the first time in its history[2] Slough Town became mired in controversy when, in 1997/98, in spite of finishing in a creditable eighth place in the Conference, the club was expelled. The ostensible reason was that the new consortium which had bought the Rebels were not prepared to install the additional 49 seats required by the Conference – but there were also rumours that the real reason was clandestine financial irregularities at Wexham Park.

Whatever the truth, clearly all was not well with Slough Town as the new millennium dawned and the 2000/2001 season saw the Rebels in Division One of the Isthmian League. The gloom surrounding the club was exacerbated when, at the end of the 2002/03 season, financial disagreements with the stadium's owners led to the club's eviction from Wexham Park. Slough Town have never had a permanent home and since September 2003 Rebels fans – like 88-year-old Eric – have had to travel across the Thames to Windsor and Eton's Stag Meadow ground, set amid the sylvan splendour of Windsor Great Park.[3] However, on the pitch, former Oxford United midfielder and Rebels' play-maker Eddie Denton took over that

---

[2] In the 1930s six players were deemed to be professional by the FA and banned from playing amateur football. Ironically, this was largely ascribed to sloppy bookkeeping by the club.

[3] In 2007 the club agreed a ground-share with Beaconsfield SYCOB and it seems no longer certain that Wexham Park has seen its last Slough Town match.

season as manager and he masterminded the Rebels' return to the Isthmian League Premier.

Slough may have been footballing cuckoos, sharing another club's nest, but they were paying lodgers. It cost them £25,000 a season to shack up at Stag Meadow – so, when *Match of the Day*'s cameras came calling in November 2004, the £13,000 fee was a welcome boost to the kitty.

The reason for the BBC's presence was the visit, for an FA Cup First Round tie, of Walsall, Cup giant-killers themselves some seventy years before.[4] The Beeb sniffed a 'win-win' scenario: either Walsall would score a hatful of goals or there'd be a famous upset. After all, 86 places and three divisions separated the two teams. Walsall, recently relegated, hadn't won away all season and had won only four out of sixteen games. They lay nine-teenth in Football League Division One but their player–manager was the bearded 36-year-old, Paul Merson, capped 21 times for England, who had won the Cup with Arsenal in 1993. Also in the Saddlers' side was the experienced defender Neil Emblen, ex-Crystal Palace, Wolves and Norwich, while in goal was the New Zealand international Mark Paston.

Slough included postman Ian Hodges, who had scored 39 goals for the Rebels the season before, but their run to the First Round – Croydon 1–0, Welling 4–1, Cheshunt 4–0, Salisbury 3–2 – while convincing, had hardly been the stuff of dreams. On an unseasonably warm and sunny after-noon a crowd of 2,023 turned up: Eric Collier was there, of course, a Rebels fan for nearly half a century, but Daniel Brench hadn't been watching them for long: 'It was the first season I saw Slough play. I had gone to the odd game over the years and had been at the win over Salisbury and I went to the Walsall game with my dad. I had never seen so many people at a Rebels game.'

Stag Meadow looked a picture, surrounded by autumnal tints of elegant trees and the sweeping greensward of the Great Park. The pitch, however, was rather less manicured. Its appearance put one in mind of Clifton Webb's sardonic remark in the classic 1946 film noir, *The Dark Corner*: 'The grass always looks as though it has been left out all night.'

The visitors kicked off into a low sun and in the opening minutes penned Slough in their own half, moving the ball well and threatening a nervous home defence in which 23-year-old goalkeeper Shaun Allaway was making

---

[4] See Walsall v Arsenal, pp. 33–39.

his debut. After seven minutes, he brought off a brilliant reflex save from Merson, then blocked Michael Standing's drive. At the other end, Matt Fryatt, the England Under-19 striker, shot just over the bar and soon after had a header plucked out of the air by Allaway.

Gradually Slough settled down: they began to utilise the pace of their wing backs down the flanks, forcing a corner on the left and in the 20th minute Hodges went close, bustling past Emblen and shooting into the side netting. Three minutes later, against the run of play with the Walsall defence asleep, the Rebels went ahead. The ball was shifted smoothly down the Slough right, Ryan Spencer beat the offside trap and crossed for Hodges to slide the ball under Paston from six yards.

Walsall responded vigorously and nine minutes later George Leitao, the Portuguese midfielder, fired in a shot from the edge of the penalty box which Allaway could only parry into the path of Walsall centre-forward Darren Wrack, who headed smartly past the keeper.

The half continued in the same vein, with the visitors pounding a Rebels defence in which Michael Murphy was outstanding. Merson, stouter in girth than in his prime, was clearly the best player on view but, despite his probing and harrying, he was unable to coax any coherent threat from his forwards. In fact, just before half-time, Glen Harris, the former Hayes player, in his second season at Ryman level, narrowly struck a 25-yard shot over Paston's bar.

Merson came out for the second half still pulling Walsall's strings, probing the home defence, now hampered by the sun sinking low over the park. Five minutes after the break, Leitao's header threatened – but, though the visitors had the lion's share of possession, they failed to create openings of any consequence. When Michael Standing broke through on the right edge of the box and angled the ball across Allaway's goal, Walsall's strikers had gone AWOL – and when Wrack headed down to Fryatt, he hooked it wide. Then another incisive run from Standing put Leitao through, but when Murphy blocked his shot, it ricocheted to Merson, whose goal-bound drive was cleared only for Standing to deposit the ball into the car park from 20 yards.

With 18 minutes left, and Walsall still pressing, Denton summoned fresh legs and threw Darrell Taylor on. Within a couple of minutes, Slough attacked down the left with Alex Haddow. He powered his way to the goal-line and Glen Harris, a PE assistant teacher at Wexham School, met his cross on the full. Julian Bennett scrambled it away only for Harris, racing in to the penalty area, to hit a left-foot volley past Paston from six yards.

Walsall poured everything forward, exerting relentless pressure on Slough and Leitao headed against the bar. With Walsall besieging the Rebels stronghold, they were vulnerable on the break: first, full-back Josias Carbon had a good run which ended with his left-foot drive just skimming the bar, then Harris counter-attacked after a Walsall corner but shot over and substitute Siddow burst through on the left to test Paston with a crisp low drive.

Walsall's woeful afternoon, already on the slide, slipped further downhill a minute before the end, when Julian Bennett was sent off for refusing to back away from a free kick. As the clock ticked down Merson's face grew as long as the shadows across Stag Meadow. His class had been evident but he had been unable to bring an end to his side's 13-match losing sequence away from home. Despite his persistent urgings, his forwards had proved damp squibs left over from Bonfire Night and the Saddlers' defence had collapsed under an onslaught by the Ryman Premier refugees.

The final whistle sparked the predictable pitch invasion and a manifestation of the now-endemic circular group-jumping phenomenon, followed by the mutual clapping routine between crowd and players.

For Eddie Denton, it had been

a real struggle. We were battered in the second half and had to dig deep but you expect that against professional teams and they controlled the game for long periods. The players worked their socks off in training all week and it paid off. We could have wrapped it up towards the end as we had two or three good chances to finish them off. This result was on the cards with the effort, attitude and work ethic being of such a high standard and it means a lot financially to the club. We hope the council take note and begin to realise that we need to be back in Slough.

Given the municipal leaders' archaic civic attitude, Tony Francis of the *Telegraph*[5] doubted they would. 'Saturday's heroic 2–1 win over the Saddlers is not what they wanted to hear in the town hall from hell. These are the elected representatives who told Slough Town FC to sling their hook. In the words of Richard Stokes, the council leader, 'We don't want your type

---

[5] *Daily Telegraph*, November 15, 2004.

around here. It's bad for our image.' Image? This is the place John Betjeman wanted to flatten: 'Come, bombs and blow to smithereens,/Those air-conditioned bright canteens.'

Thus, one of the most marvellous days in a town which had had little to commend it to the nation's consciousness down the years had to be celebrated in the town over the river, 'only a deer's leap away from Windsor Castle. If he hadn't been otherwise engaged at a Remembrance Day service in the Royal Albert Hall, Windsor and Eton FC's patron, the Duke of Edinburgh, could have trained his binoculars on their modest little ground and witnessed these strange goings-on for himself.'

Beneath pictures of the Prince Consort and Her Majesty, which graciously adorn the comfy boardroom at Stag Meadow, Merson was distraught. 'This is by far the toughest managerial defeat I've suffered. It's harder than it is as a player to accept these losses. I won't be surprised if I receive a phone call from the chairman when I get home.' His season did not get any better – the Saddlers soon slipped back to mid-table and were relegated to the bottom tier a season later, ending Merson's managerial career. Ben Lowe, of BBC Black Country, believes he should have gone earlier: 'In hindsight, Merson should have been sacked after our humiliating FA Cup exit to tiny Slough Town back in November 2004.'

Slough entertained Yeading in the Second Round but, for the Rebels, lightning couldn't be persuaded to strike twice as the eventual winners of the Ryman Premier won a dream home tie against Newcastle with a 3–1 victory.

As the Walsall team bus pulled out of Stag Meadow, bearing its dejected load up the M6, Jock and Vic quaffed their mugs of tea and munched slices of cake in the clubhouse. These two OAPs, along with other volunteers, had worked all week erecting crowd barriers, organising car parks and selling match tickets.

'Great day,' said Vic.

'Yeah,' said Jock, 'You can't beat non-League football.'

Eric Collier would have loved that.

SLOUGH: Allaway, Carbon, Daly, Saulisbury, Murphy, Haddow, Metcalfe, Harris, Wilkinson, Hodges, Spencer

WALSALL: Paston, Wright, Emblen, Bennett, Arunalde, Osborn, Standing, Wrack, Merson, Leitao, Fryatt

46

BURSCOUGH 3, GILLINGHAM 2

FA Cup, Round One, November 5, 2005

In the second half of the eighteenth century Britain's canals were the pulsating arteries through which coursed the lifeblood of the Industrial Revolution. This burgeoning transport network transformed the country's economic landscape, carrying commerce, wealth, ideas and a new belief in entrepreneurship and fostered the growth of major conurbations like Liverpool, Manchester and Leeds. When the Liverpool line of the Leeds and Liverpool Canal, the longest single canal in Britain, was completed in the late eighteenth century Burscough Bridge became the most important canal town in Lancashire, a staging post for the passenger boats between Liverpool and Wigan, and a transfer point for the stagecoaches travelling along the turnpike road to Preston and the North. Few villages can have exerted so crucial an influence on the industrial development of Lancashire as Burscough.

By the middle of the eighteenth century, Yorkshire was a well-established woollen manufacturing area, while Lancashire's industries were still in their infancy. The Yorkshire woollen merchants hoped to expand the market for their cloth by gaining access, via Liverpool, to the growing colonial markets in Africa and America and the cotton traders of Liverpool and the entrepreneurs in milling centres such as Blackburn and Burnley sought to exploit the prosperous markets of Leeds and Bradford. The Liverpool–Leeds Canal was built to provide the vital link in this commercial symbiosis and by the mid-nineteenth century had exerted a profound impact on Burscough, which had always been a farming community, by bringing new commercial and manufacturing opportunities.

The 1880s were a pivotal decade in the development of the game of Association football in England: in particular 1882, when Old Etonians defeated Blackburn Rovers in the Final, was a turning point in FA Cup history. A northern team had reached the final for the first time and a year later the tables were turned when Blackburn Olympic became the first northern team to win the FA Cup, beating Old Etonians 2–1. The professions of the men who made up the Blackburn side are noteworthy – three of them were weavers, one was a spinner, one a cotton worker, one an iron worker: there were also two who were clearly professionals. These were not men of leisure: they were working class. It was the end of an era. Association football clubs were springing up all over the North. Along with pigeon-fancying, the game was becoming the working man's winter pastime of choice.

A club was formed in Burscough in 1880, playing in the Liverpool & District League before folding in 1900. In 1905 Burscough Rangers were founded and moved to the present Mart Lane ground in 1908. They established many of the traditions carried on by the current club, playing in green and known as 'The Linnets', and in the 1920s Rangers won the Liverpool County Combination Championship three times. They were successful enough in 1926 to purchase a grandstand from Everton and erect it at Victoria Park. The club had overreached itself, however, and ran into financial difficulties, finally folding in 1935. Following the Second World War the present Burscough club was founded in 1946, starting life in the Liverpool County Combination, and by the end of the decade were starting to build a reputation in non-League soccer. In 1959 they reached the First Round proper of the FA Cup for the first time before losing 3–1 to Crewe Alexandra in front of a 4,200 gate at Victoria Park. The club also reached the First Round three seasons running between 1978 and 1981, going down to Sheffield United and two other northern clubs with a Cup pedigree – Blyth Spartans and Altrincham.

In 2002 Burscough appointed Shaun Teale as player–manager and the ex-Aston Villa defender led the club to its greatest triumph. Burscough became the smallest club to ever win the 2003 FA Trophy, beating Tamworth 2–1 at Villa Park. It was the Linnets' twelfth game in a memorable run which had featured a remarkable result in the quarter-finals when the 400–1 outsiders beat the runaway Conference winners Yeovil Town 2–0 at Huish Park.

Two years later Linnets fans were hoping for something special when League One side Gillingham made the trip to Victoria Park in a First

Round tie on the 400th anniversary of the Gunpowder Plot. Burscough had already won four FA Cup ties – not to mention a handy £21,000 – beating three clubs from higher-ranked leagues. The Lancashire minnows had never reached the Second Round but, true to tradition, the Cup refused to stick precisely to the script.

The teams were 76 rungs apart on the League ladder and understandably Burscough started nervously, the visitors hitting Boswell's bar. However, after ten minutes, following a cross from the Linnets' other centre-back, Adam Tong, skipper Karl Bell slammed the ball home from close range after a fumble from Gillingham goalkeeper Tony Bullock.

Burscough shaded the first half on points and, but for some wayward finishing and a goalkeeper on top of his game, could have gone into the break with a bigger lead. After the interval Gillingham began to apply more pressure on the home defence and the Linnets were bought back to earth when, after 59 minutes, substitute Mark Saunders sent Matthew Jarvis away. Jarvis headed for goal, cut inside Andy Barlow and finished well past Matty Boswell to level things up. The equaliser gave Gillingham renewed impetus but five minutes later they were a man short as midfielder Michael Flynn was sent off for a two-footed challenge on Karl Bell. Neale Cooper's side seemed to deal with this blow and, as is often the case with ten men, began to play their best football of the game. With Burscough appearing to tire, Saunders nodded the Gills into the lead in the 76th minute, guiding a well-placed header into the corner beyond Boswell.

For the first time in the match Gillingham exerted full control, keeping the ball, denying space and playing out time. It seemed as though Burscough were going to be denied, but, in a dramatic twist, the home side equalised with a minute to go. Gillingham made a nonsense of dealing with a home attack, which ended with the ball appearing to ricochet into the goal off Gills defender Ian Cox as Bullock tried to lash clear. Burscough appeared to have secured the draw that their persistence and heart deserved. The Division One side were hanging on for a replay at Priestfield but were shattered at the death when the Linnets' 23-year-old sub, David Rowan, struck a deflected winner with the last kick of the match – just reward for his patience and perseverance. Two bad knee injuries had kept him sidelined for virtually two seasons and he could have been forgiven for seeking a new club and a fresh start, but that Guy Fawkes Night he was glad he didn't.

The 1,927 fans at Victoria Park staged the obligatory pitch invasion –

and why not? The Linnets had reached the Second Round of the FA Cup for the first time. 'It equals all my career achievements,' echoed Burscough manager Derek Goulding.

> It is fantastic for us all. It was a classic Cup tie and typical of the FA Cup. The boys did extremely well in the first half and we deserved to be 1–0 up. Gillingham showed their quality in the second half but we kept our shape and kept our discipline and got ourselves back in the game. It was amazing to pinch it at the end, though. With Gillingham down to ten men we told the boys to keep pressing forward in the final minutes.

The win guaranteed Burscough another £16,000 to go with the £21,000 they had already won in prize money by battling through to the First Round for the first time in 25 years and, with plans currently being drawn up for a new £5 million stadium on land adjacent to Victoria Park, chairman Chris Lloyd saw the money-spinning FA Cup run as extremely timely. 'This kind of windfall is hugely important, and this income will be very useful in helping us to get our survey work done. You can't budget for a good Cup run, but everyone needs them. I love the romance of the Cup, but the money is imperative – probably right through to Championship level. It's not just the prize money, it's the gate receipts that are generated.'

Congratulations appeared on Burscough's website from all over the football world – many from Gillingham's fierce local rivals, Maidstone FC, as well as from Southport FC, Telford and Whitby Town FC. Also from Matlock Town: – 'I think I speak on behalf of all not only at Matlock but in the Unibond League in saying congratulations. You are the pride of the League tonight and we're all proud of you!!!' And from clubs who knew a thing or two about giant-killing themselves: 'Well done, Burscough, we're all proud of you down here in Yeovil. Great result, enjoy the ride.' And Shrewsbury: 'Hell of a result for your side, nice one.'

The Gillingham supporters faced a long and miserable trip down the M6 but the home fans were generous in their appreciation. 'They are a credit to their club and lent their own vocal support to the historic day. We hope they have a safe, if probably unhappy, journey home.' Gills fans reciprocated: 'Fair play to your boys. They wanted it more than our bunch of monkeys. Good luck for the next round!'

Further excitement was to follow, as Supporters' Club Secretary Eric Berry recalls:

In the draw for the second round on the Sunday we were drawn away to Burton Albion or Peterborough United – it turned out to be Burton. Owing to a waterlogged pitch at Burton's new stadium, the game was called off and the game was rearranged for the following Tuesday night, but at least we were in the draw for the Third Round for the first time ever. And what comes out of the hat next day – Burton Albion or Burscough v Manchester United. Total pandemonium – and at least for two days we could dream!

Then it all went wrong. After ten minutes of the game at Burton Burscough lost centre-half Adam Tong with a badly broken leg (he didn't play again for 12 months). To add insult to injury (literally), Burton went on to score the opening goal from that incident and, despite a great fight-back by Burscough in the second half, they finally went down 4–1 and the dream was over. Burton went on to force the draw with Manchester United and, says Eric Berry, 'ended up reportedly some £900,000 better off! If only!!'

'If only!' The mantra of all players, fans, managers and directors down the ages. 'What might have been. . .' – the triumph of hope over experience. . . But, of course, there's always next year.

BURSCOUGH: Boswell, Barlow, Crowder, Bell, Tong, Parry, Gray, Blakeman, Gedman, Eaton, Bowen
GILLINGHAM: Bullock, Williams, Smith, Cox, Crofts, Hessenthaler, Flynn, Hope, Harris, Jarvis, Wallis

47

CHESTERFIELD 0, BASINGSTOKE TOWN 1

FA Cup, Round One, November 11, 2006

Ask your average man on the Clapham omnibus – you know, the one in the pub who has an opinion on everything and could captain an England Boring XI – to name some New Towns in South-East England and the chances are he wouldn't get much beyond Crawley and Stevenage before uttering the word 'Basingstoke'. And there you'd have him. He's wrong. Tell him that Basingstoke has held a charter market for eight hundred years and is recorded as being a market site in the Domesday Book. Point out to your astonished interlocutor that Basingstoke was a leading brewery town in the eighteenth century. Explain to the fellow that Basingstoke was a market town of only sixteen thousand souls until the 1950s – and, while he's reeling from that, inform him gently that in the 1960s it was rapidly developed to accommodate London 'overspill' . . . But it isn't, and never has been, a New Town, as they say, 'within the meaning of the Act'.

Today Basingstoke is a town of over 150,000 people with an above-average standard of living and low unemployment. In the late 1960s the town centre was rebuilt and many buildings of historic interest were demolished to make way for a vast concrete shopping centre. At the same time the town grew to engulf several smaller villages, which became housing estates or local districts. These almost self-contained communities are linked by a large number of roundabouts, almost the only feature by which Basingstoke is nationally known.

The stark severity of Basingstoke's architecture, which was seen as an expression of its determinedly modernistic self-image, together with the perception of the town as a haven for accountants, financial advisers and insurance actuaries, has led to Basingstoke's becoming a humorous arche-type for the faceless uniformity of many modern British towns. Nicknames such as 'Boringstoke', 'Basingjoke' and 'Basingrad' have been applied to the town and, because of the many high-rise office blocks in the town centre, headquarters of companies such as Sun Life and the Automobile Association, the epithet 'Dallas, Hampshire' has also been applied to Basingstoke. The town also gets an honourable mention in Douglas Adams' *Hitchhiker's Guide to the Galaxy*:

'How did we get here?' he [Arthur] asked, shivering slightly.
'We hitched a lift,' said Ford.
'Excuse me?' said Arthur. 'Are you trying to tell me that we just stuck out our thumbs and some green bug-eyed monster stuck his head out and said, "Hi fellas, hop right in. I can take you as far as the Basingstoke roundabout?"'

Sebastian Faulks's anti-hero, Engleby, had a similarly unnerving experience:

I followed the signs for the town centre, but, after I'd spent fifteen minutes negotiating roundabouts and obediently going where the signs told me, they had brought me back to where I'd begun. The end of all our exploring will be to arrive where we started and know the place for the first time. I didn't know that T.S. Eliot had been on the Basingstoke Urban District Council Highways (Ring Roads and Street Furniture) Committee.[1]

The sandy heaths of northern Hampshire were perhaps better suited to cricket: indeed, the delightfully named May's Bounty has hosted first-class cricket since Edwardian times and the venue remains an appealing part of the Hampshire cricket calendar. The ground's trim intimacy, the tree-lined border, informal pavilion, and constant low murmur from the ubiquitous hospitality tents, gives it a unique atmosphere. It was where the renowned writer and commentator John Arlott watched much of his early cricket: however, Arlott's bucolic Hampshire brogue was also heard as a football commentator on the BBC.

---

[1] *Engleby*, p. 183.

Football was being played in the Basingstoke area in the early 1890s, but it wasn't until 1896 that a Basingstoke Town club was formed from Aldworth United and Basingstoke Albion. In 1901 the club entered the Hampshire League, and in 1909 the local Hants Ironworks team merged with the 'Town' club, with such success that the League was won in 1911/12 and 1919/20. After playing at a couple of grounds in the area, the club moved to its present site in 1946, the ground named after its benefactor, the late Lord Camrose.

After years spent trawling round the Hampshire, Southern and Isthmian leagues, the late 1990s saw Town go on two dazzling FA Cup runs. The 1997/98 season was the club's most outstanding yet, with success over Wycombe Wanderers of Division Two. After a 2–2 draw away at Adams Park in which the 'Stoke battled back from two goals down, a new record attendance of 5,085 at the Camrose saw Dean Beale save the decisive penalty in the shoot-out after the sides had again shared four goals. In the Second Round, Basingstoke travelled to Northampton Town, coming from behind to earn a replay at the Camrose, which was shown live on Sky Sports. Again the Blues held the League side to a draw after extra time, but lightning failed to strike twice and the 'Stoke went out on penalties. In the following season Basingstoke reached the First Round proper at the expense of Conference side Dover Athletic, and faced Bournemouth at home. Town lost 2–1 and it was another eight years before they reached the First Round proper.

In the 2006/07 season the 'Stoke emerged from an edgy qualifying campaign, defeating Conference North outfit Worcester City 7–6 on penalties in a Fourth Qualifying Round replay. Basingstoke, languishing at the bottom of the Conference South, were then drawn against League One Chesterfield in Round One. The Derbyshire side were 76 places higher up the League system than the 'Stoke and had an impeccable recent Cup pedigree, having despatched Premiership opposition in Manchester City and West Ham in that season's Carling Cup and having reached the FA Cup semi-final in 1997. Furthermore, the backgrounds of the two managers – Chesterfield's Roy McFarland and Frances Vines of Basingstoke – illustrated the clash between two worlds of football which only happens in the FA Cup. McFarland, a cultured and classy centre-back, was part of Brian Clough's successful Derby side of the 1970s and played 28 times for England. Vines spent five years knocking in goals for Southbank Polytechnic in the

Amateur Football Alliance before becoming a semi-pro with Kingstonian. He was eight months into his second managerial job, having taken Crawley Town into the Conference.

Basingstoke fan Joe McNulty, who had supported Basingstoke for many years, recalls talking to two policemen outside a pub at about 1.30 on match day in Chesterfield. The Spireites[2] had lost on penalties during the week against Charlton in the Carling Cup and the conversation led to the prospects for the clash at Saltergate that afternoon. Joe McNulty felt that 'Stoke should 'stick 11 men behind the ball, try and push for the draw and force a replay at The Camrose'. The good constables disagreed, one of them insisting that the 'Giant-killers would be giant-killed' but, as Joe pointed out, 'We were rock bottom of the Conference South, with the rest of the season looking bleak – I couldn't see that happening. We left the conversation with the policemen with a handshake and the wish of good luck for the game ahead.'

In the event, the boys in blue demonstrated their in-depth local knowledge. On the ground where Charlton needed a penalty shoot-out to survive four days earlier, Chesterfield were deservedly beaten, the 'Stoke running out 1–0 victors. After 25 minutes Matt Warner volleyed in Rob Watkins' cross to the delight of the 440 fans who had made the journey from Hampshire. Warner, a 21-year-old left-side midfielder, scored from close range, after which Vines' pre-match team talk came into play. He had begun to talk about Chesterfield only on the Thursday. 'It was a help,' said Vines, 'that they had been on TV so often, but I had three different people watching them at one game and they all said things that were vaguely similar. Also, I told the lads they had to play as if their lives depended on it – get a toe in there, a head in here, if you can't make a tackle, just get in a block.' It might have been a very different story if Colin Larkin had tumbled over in the penalty area when goalkeeper Stuart Searle seemed to to catch him. 'His honesty was not lost on Basingstoke captain Joe Dolan, who said: "He stayed on his feet. If he had gone down, the ref might have given a penalty and it could have been a different game."'[3] Later Searle made vital saves from Caleb Folan and Mark Hughes but Chesterfield created few chances and he was otherwise untroubled. James Taylor might have doubled the lead before the end but Basingstoke held on for the win. Roy McFarland's

---

[2] Chesterfield FC's nickname, after the famous twisted church spire which dominates the town centre.
[3] Nigel Gardner, *Daily Telegraph*, November 13, 2006.

view was that Chesterfield had slumped 'from the sublime to the ridiculous in terms of our Cup performances'. But, as 'South View Stokey' had it on the fans' website: 'as the game went on the team gave so much belief to the fans and themselves that you wouldn't have been able to separate the League and non-League side. We weren't lucky. We stuck to our game plan like a disciplined TEAM.'

They then faced local rivals Aldershot Town of the Nationwide Conference in Round Two. 'Stoke fought well to force a 1–1 draw and victory in the replay would take them to League One Blackpool, a side with an illustrious up history of their own. A 3–1 defeat put dreams of Cup glory on hold for another year, but for a week or two the Hampshire town became known for more than its roundabouts.

CHESTERFIELD: Roche, Lowry, Kovacs, Downes, O'Hare, Hall (Jackson 69), Niven, Hughes (Davies 83), Smith, Allison, Larkin (Folan 58)
BASINGSTOKE: Searle, Watkins, Wells, Dolan, Bruce, Ray, Surey, Taylor, Warner, Levis (Roach 66), Stroud

48

SOUTHEND UNITED 1, MANCHESTER UNITED 0

Carling Cup, Round Four, November 7, 2006

In Jane Austen's *Emma*, our heroine's father, the indulgent and affectionate Henry Woodhouse, shakes his head and says, 'Ah', which to Emma meant 'there is no end of the sad consequences of your going to Southend.' On the other hand, Mrs John Knightley stoutly declares that her family thoroughly enjoyed their holidays there and that they 'never found the least inconvenience from the mud.'

On the evening of Tuesday, November 7th, 2006, Manchester United's Sir Alex Ferguson must have heartily concurred with Mr Woodhouse. Ferguson had seen 'some rum places in his time and Roots Hall, all singing and all dancing, is as rum as it gets.'[1] Steve Tilson, the boss of unsung, unheralded Southend FC, would have been in the Knightley camp, having seen his side boot out the holders from the Carling Cup to secure the best win in their history.

Southend had become, by the late eighteenth century, a thriving small town, a 'watering place' with public houses, shops and private and lodging houses. By the time Jane Austen was writing, in 1816, it had also acquired the cache of royal exclusivity as in 1803 the Prince Regent had ensconced his unloved Princess Caroline in what is now Royal Terrace while he disported himself in Brighton.

Forty miles from London's East End and easily accessible by train, Southend, originally the south end of the medieval priory of Prittlewell, became a popular holiday resort during the Victorian era with all the

---

[1] Neil Harman, *The Times*, November 8, 2006.

traditional seafront attractions – funfairs, winkle stalls, cockles, jellied eels, pubs and mud. And the pier – famed as the longest in the world, complete with its railway. However, the town also had the Marine Park, opened in 1894, and the 'Kursaal', completed in 1901, with a great silver dome over the entrance to the park. The word 'Kursaal' is German, meaning a 'Cure Hall', or spa, and in its anglicised form it came to mean a place of healthy recreation – and indeed, Southend-on-Sea FC, later Southend Athletic, played at the Marine Park at the Kursaal in 1897.

The 1906 Annual General Meeting of Southend Athletic FC buried its head in the sand. Its only significant decision was to change from white 'knickers' to blue and the elephants in the room – the shrinking gate receipts, problems with their Marine Park ground and a dismal season in the unexceptional South Essex League – were ignored. For some time there had been a groundswell of support for the formation of a professional football club in the Town and on May 19, 1906, Oliver Trigg, the landlord of the Blue Boar in Victoria Avenue, Prittlewell, and a football nut, convened a meeting of fellow soccer enthusiasts to form a fully professional club. A month before, a seven-year lease on the adjacent Roots Hall field, just over the road from the Blue Boar, had been secured and the new team, Southend United FC, nicknamed the Blues – or 'The Shrimpers' – joined the Division Two of the Southern League. In their second season they were promoted and Harold Halse, who had scored 91 goals in the first season, moved to Manchester United for the maximum fee then allowed – £350.[2]

After the First World War, Southend United rejoined the Southern League, playing at the Kursaal Amusement Park for the 1919/20 season. The following season, they were elected to the Football League Division three (South), where they remained for the next 38 years. The Shrimpers had decamped from the Kursaal to the Grainger Road Greyhound Stadium in 1934 and in 1953 work began on a new stadium at Roots Hall. The whole project was financed by the supporters club who, together with the ground staff, carved a ground out of nothing, and in 1955 the club moved to its current home.

In 1966 Southend went down to the bottom division for the first time in their History. But in 1967 a Scottish striker, Billy Best, with a name like a *Boy's Own* hero, arrived from Northampton Town. In the next six seasons

---

[2] He made one appearance for England, scoring twice in an 8–1 win over Austria in 1909, and was the first player to appear in three FA Cup finals for three different clubs.

he scored 106 goals in 226 games, taking the Blues to promotion from Division four in 1971/72. Over the next 11 seasons, however, Shrimpers fans saw three promotions and three relegations between the Third and Fourth Divisions. In 1984, having just dropped down again from Division Three, they appointed World Cup legend Bobby Moore as manager, but, in common with several other great players, he failed to make his mark in management.

A less gifted defender but a much more successful coach was Chelsea Cup-winner David Webb, who had four spells as manager, winning two successive promotions in his second spell between 1989 and 1991. Then Essex butcher and nightclub owner Anton Johnson bought a majority share-holding and adopted a scorched-earth policy, leaving Southend teetering on the brink of extinction. The club was more than £700,000 in debt and the board had dipped into the SUFC Christmas Fund and taken over £70,000 – money they couldn't pay back. Johnson was arrested and Robert Maxwell and Ken Bates, of all people, rode to the rescue on their white chargers and lent Southend some cash.

On New Year's Day 1992 they briefly topped the Second Division, but their dismal late-season form ended hopes of a third successive promotion. The rest of the 1990s were a tale of relegations and rising debts. By 1999 the Shrimpers were in free fall and back in the basement, once again fighting for survival. In 2004 the club reached rock-bottom, finishing seven-teenth in Division Three and in May the popular ex-player Steve Tilson became the sixth manager of the club since 1998. A silver lining in an other-wise cloudy season was the LDV Vans Trophy Final in March when more than seventeen thousand Shrimpers fans watched their team go down to a 2–0 defeat against Blackpool at the Millennium Stadium. A year later, in the same final in the same stadium, they lost 2–0 after extra time to Wrexham. Tilson broke the depressing cycle of decline, however, when the Blues won promotion to League One, beating Lincoln City 2–0 after extra time in the 2005 play-off final and in 2006 they gained their second consecutive promotion by winning the League One championship in their centenary season.

By November, however, things again looked bleak. True, the side had found its way to the Fourth Round of the Carling Cup after a 3–1 win at Leeds, but for a club struggling at the foot of the Championship, even a home tie against the richest and most prestigious club in world football was an unnecessary distraction. Thirty-five-year-old Spencer Prior, once a League Cup-winner with Leicester, thought it was 'an absolute bloody nuisance' and Steve Tilson was concerned only with 'keeping the score down and making it respectable.' Chris Phillips, of the *Southend Echo*, felt the same: 'when the team sheets came in and we saw that Ronaldo and Rooney were playing, along with eight other internationals we feared the worst.'

They needn't have worried. For United, it was one of those nights and they failed 'to offer the kind of sustained threat that a side of their pedigree promised'.[3] Sir Alex Ferguson, celebrating two decades as boss at Old Trafford, had seen it all – including the 3–0 defeat by York City in 1995 – yet even he had not been embarrassed by the likes of Freddy Eastwood. A 23-year-old Romany and a lifelong Manchester United supporter living in a mobile home near Basildon, he was signed from Grays Athletic two years before and had burst on the Southend scene in spectacular style, scoring after just 7.7 seconds, an English League record for a debut. Nonetheless, he seized the opportunity to puncture the pride of the fancy-dans from up North, to strike a blow for the little men, the minnows forced to exist on the crumbs falling from football's top table. In the 26th minute the Shrimpers were awarded a free kick some 25 yards from goal. Eastwood coolly stepped up, taking the view that anything Beckham – or Ronaldo – could do, he could do better, and delivered a stunning strike which dipped wickedly under Kuszczak's crossbar.

It was the jaw-dropping, decisive moment of the tie. Ferguson's morose verdict – 'I bet he doesn't score a better goal anywhere else in his life' – was arguably accurate, though a trifle harsh on the young striker. However, it shocked the locals sufficiently for Chris Phillips to ring the *Echo*'s photographer: 'I wanted to make sure she got a picture of the scoreboard so we could prove we were actually winning!'

Freddy was quite a character. Released by West Ham in 2003, he had a spell as a used-car salesman before joining Grays and, when he signed for the Shrimpers, he could be seen on a Saturday morning exercising his horse with a cart on the A127 before turning out for Southend in the afternoon. 'We had to be flexible with him because of his lifestyle,' said Phil O'Reilly, the Grays secretary, 'but his father came with him to every game.' Accused by O'Reilly in the past for not taking his football seriously enough, Freddy

---

[3] Neil Harman *The Times*, November 8, 2006.

knew the importance of his goal that night: 'As soon as I hit the free kick I was happy with it.'

After Eastwood's bombshell, United threw everything they had at a side who had not won a League game in 12 starts. With the home side playing above themselves and his star players misfiring, Ferguson had to rely on the novices. Immediately after the goal, one of them, who had conceded the crucial free kick, slammed a shot against the post. His name was David Jones, who in that moment saw his team's hopes consigned to his namesake's locker. 'I didn't think the lead was going to last long but Darryl Flahavan was fantastic in goal for us,' says Chris Phillips. The Blues' keeper, who almost gave up the game after his brother, Aaron, a goalkeeper for Portsmouth, had died in a car crash five years before, was forced into two superb saves from Ronaldo, who alone that night showed any kind of form. With Rooney 'in a permanent state of frustrated indifference',[4] the Portuguese superstar led attack after attack with intelligence and vision but was foiled time and again.

The Shrimpers, however, for their resolve not to give an inch to the Barclays Premiership leaders, deserved whatever luck was going. The local paper had billed this as the 'Match of the Centenary' and, along with the entire Roots Hall crowd, the *Echo*'s Chris Phillips was 'in shock when the game ended and nobody could quite believe what had happened. The atmosphere was tremendous and it is a night that will never ever be forgotten.'

Ferguson, a football man to the core, has always known how to lose but his surprise at this defeat 'would have been all the greater because Southend have never been much good at the business of slaying the moderately tall, let alone giants.'[5] He was in philosophical mood afterwards:

That is Cup football for you. It can smack you right in the face but there will be no suicides, no mass sackings, no need for counselling. Defeat doesn't harm anyone. We will put our boots back on tomorrow and start to work again. You cannot look back in this game as I've learnt over the years. There is no need to go overboard, though I'm sure that some sections of the press will do just that. We don't go in for knee-jerk reactions. We knew that Southend were a good football team and we had to make sure we didn't give them time to play their football.

---

[4] Neil Harman *The Times*, November 8, 2006.
[5] Tim Rich, *Daily Telegraph*, November 8, 2006.

United had failed dismally to do that and Southend went through on merit to a quarter-final at White Hart Lane a week before Christmas.

'Southend had the guts, but Spurs got the glory' – so the *Guardian*'s Simon Burnton summed up the match. In a dour struggle, penalties were only five minutes away at the end of extra time when Jermain Defoe, marginally offside, slid in at the far post to put his side into the semi-finals. 'It's hard to swallow,' said Steve Tilson. 'He's half a yard offside, but that's life. It's no good making excuses. It was a fantastic performance – we matched them for most of the match and I'm just devastated we never got to penalties.' The Shrimpers' free kick hero, Freddy Eastwood, 'did little to catch the eye last night, at times appearing only slightly more mobile than his home'.[6]

Despite his anonymous performance against Spurs, Eastwood was quoted at £2 million in the transfer market and moved to Wolves in July 2007. After a season where he spent most of his time on the substitutes' bench, he left for Coventry City for an undisclosed fee. On his return to Molineux with City, his reception when he was booked provoked 'the sadly predictable chants of "Where's your caravan?" and the even less articulate "Gypo, gypo" ring around the Jack Harris stand.'[7]

Eastwood, proud of his Romany roots, will always be a hero in Southend, often labelled the archetypal working-class 'kiss-me-quick' seaside town. However, it welcomed royal holidaymakers, too, in the elegant Regency days and 'it is a town full of odd surprises'.[8] On that night in November, the Shrimpers' best win in their history was one of the more extraordinary ones.

In common with many of Britain's Victorian seaside resorts, Southend in winter acquires a melancholy air. The local Southend poet D.J. Tyrer has written:

> The resorts are dying,
> A perpetual twilight
> Of sticky rock candy
> And fish and chips.[9]

[6] *Guardian*, December 21, 2006.
[7] Josh Widdicombe, *When Saturday Comes*, December 2008, p. 28.
[8] Tim Rich, *Daily Telegraph*, November 8, 2006.
[9] From 'Twilight of the Resorts', in *Poetic Southend: A Last Resort*.

Sometimes, just sometimes, the ghosts of those resorts rise up and mock the great and the good, poking fun at the established order. And as the wise Mr Woodhouse observed to Mrs Knightley, 'If you must go to the sea, it had better not have been to Southend. Southend is an unhealthy place.'

He ought to have had the goodness to tell Sir Alex.

SOUTHEND UNITED: Flahavan, Hunt, Sodje, Prior, Hammell, Campbell-Ryce, Clarke, Maher, Gower, Hooper, Eastwood
MANCHESTER UNITED: Kuszczak, O'Shea, Brown, Silvestre, Heinze, Ronaldo, Jones, Fletcher, Richardson, Smith, Rooney

49

HAVANT AND WATERLOOVILLE 4, SWANSEA CITY 2

FA Cup, Round Three, January 16, 2008

In 1919 the Treaty of Versailles was written on parchment made in Havant. For three hundred years, from about 1500, the Hampshire town tanned the skins of sheep, goats and calves for leather. The skins were also soaked in pure water from natural springs on the slopes of the chalk Downs to make bright white parchment.[1] Though the parchment was of high quality, production ended in 1936: this was a pity as the glorious deeds of the town's football club 70 years later could be recorded only on newsprint rather than inscribed on the material once used to chronicle a piece of global history.

For nearly two millennia Havant was a working rural village between Portsmouth and Chichester, with a weekly market and an annual fair. It had a slice of the wool trade in the Middle Ages and, of course, it produced leather, but by the beginning of the nineteenth century it was still not much more than a four-horse town: stagecoaches travelling the turnpiked road between Portsmouth and Chichester stopped at the Dolphin in West Street.

The town's population was still less than four thousand at the end of the Victorian era: even so, by then it boasted a football club, Havant FC, formed in 1883, which played in the Portsmouth Football League at the cosily named Front Lawn ground. The club's most famous 'old boy' is probably Bobby Tambling, signed by Chelsea as a 16-year-old in 1957, eventually to become their leading goalscorer. Two decades later, the club, now called Havant and Leigh Park FC,[2] had progressed to the First Division of

---

[1] The Anglo-Saxon *funta* meant 'spring' and Havant was 'Hama's *funta*', or the property of a man called Hama.
[2] In 1969 the club merged with Leigh Park FC, a Sunday League club founded in 1958 who were the FA Sunday Cup holders.

Hampshire League. It soon became impracticable to play the likes of Eastleigh, Winchester City, Alton Town and Basingstoke on the Front Lawn, and in 1982 the club moved to Westleigh Park. The club, renamed Havant Town FC, became founder members of the Wessex League in 1986, and were runners up three times before winning the title and promotion to the Southern League in 1991.

After the second World War Portsmouth City Council had created Leigh Park, the second-biggest housing estate in Europe, to accommodate people made homeless by the bombing, and by the early 1970s it had a population of 40,000, working in new industries such as light engineering and plastics. Westleigh Park itself, according to Alan Lee of *The Times*, was 'framed by hideous 1960s office blocks and factories and by relentless streets created in haste and repenting at leisure'.[3] Glen Moore, of the *Independent*, was more charitable, describing the ground as 'a workmanlike low-rise arena set in a suburban housing estate'.[4]

Waterlooville, a village west of Havant, had absorbed Portsmouth inhabitants each night during the war, as they slept in sheds and garages and temporary shacks in the village to escape the bombing. Ironically, the village owes its existence to another, earlier, European conflict. The place didn't exist before 1815, when a pub named Waitland End was just one of five buildings by the side of the road through the Forest of Bere. A column of infantry, weary from the triumph at Waterloo, stumbled into the pub to celebrate England's away win in Europe. According to local legend, the pub was renamed 'The Heroes of Waterloo' in their honour and the area around the pub became known as Waterlooville.

Nearly a century later, in 1905, Waterlooville FC was formed, joining the Portsmouth League before the second World War the Hampshire League in 1953 and the Southern League in 1971. It has some distinguished alumni of its own – Guy Whittingham, Paul Hardyman and Paul Moody all moved to League clubs, Moody going to Southampton for £40,000.

The two clubs, Havant Town FC and Waterlooville FC, merged in 1998 as Havant and Waterlooville Football Club, nicknamed 'The Hawks', still based at Westleigh Park. It was more of a shotgun wedding than a marriage made in heaven. 'Both teams were in the same league,' says Trevor Brock, secretary of Havant Town. 'We got gates of 130, they got 110 and in many

---

[3] *The Times*, January 25, 2008.
[4] *Independent*, January 17, 2008.

ways it made sense but they were our biggest rivals and there were people who wouldn't cross the road to come to us.' Malcolm Jamieson, who supported Waterlooville, said: 'I was one of the loudest voices against it. . .We didn't get on with Havant at all.' Yet, as Alan Lee put it, 'somehow the jagged edges of this non-League jigsaw fitted together.'

The new club stormed to the Southern League Southern Division title in its first season and in subsequent years the Hawks have appeared in the FA Cup First Round four times, meeting a League club for the first time in a competitive match in 2006/07, when they lost 2–1 to Millwall in a home tie played at Fratton Park. Four years before, the Hawks had reached the FA Trophy semi-final, only to lose 2–1 on aggregate to Tamworth, having accounted for Conference side Forest green Rovers en route.

The Hawks were now a force in non-League football, and several former League players have turned out for the Hawks, such as Dean Holdsworth, Fitzroy Simpson, David Howells and the Irish international, Portsmouth-born Liam Daish. The club qualified for the Conference South play-offs in 2006/07 before going down to Braintree Town, whereupon manager Ian Baird departed for local rivals Eastleigh and his right-hand man, ex-Barnet and Exeter defender Shaun Gale, stepped into his shoes. No one, however, could have been prepared for the glorious winter that followed.

It all began at York, where the Hawks made history by reaching the Second Round for the first time. Conference side York City were despatched by a single goal to earn a tie against the League's oldest club, Notts County, at Meadow Lane. 'Now you're gonna believe us,' roared the Hawks fans who made the trip to the Midlands on December 1 to see Tony Taggart, then earning his living as a bin man, score the only goal.

Shaun Gale's men were now amongst the big boys and could dream of a money-spinning clash with one of the glamour teams. It was not to be and they had to settle for a long trip to South Wales and a tie with League One leaders, Swansea City. Some 80 places separated the two clubs in football's hierarchy and the Hawks had managed only one away victory in nine in the Blue Square South. The Cup, however, was a different matter: the side from Hampshire had invaded traditional football strongholds in the North and Midlands, vanquishing superior opponents in York City and Notts County with cool efficiency.

It was a narrow escape at the Liberty Stadium. Sixteen minutes from the end Swansea's Andy Robinson smashed a 30-yard free kick past Kevin

Scriven. Soon after that, Hawks left-back Brett Poate was dismissed for a two-footed tackle on Andrea Orlandi. City captain Alan Tate was also sent off after the ensuing melee that followed but it seemed the dream was over.

Not quite. With only four minutes left, Tony Taggart sent a speculative cross into the Swans' area. Alfie Potter flicked it on to Rocky Baptiste and the former car salesman with a comic-book hero's name hit a low drive into the far corner. The Hawks' determination had grabbed them an unlikely replay. They had their share of luck: Swansea struck the woodwork three times and Tate's dismissal disrupted the home defence. 'We got more bold,' said Charlie Oatway, Havant's player–coach. 'We reverted to three defenders in what was a last-chance saloon. And it paid off.'

Ten days later heavy rain had forced Havant to hire a huge tarpaulin to ensure the replay could go ahead and, though only 575 had watched the game against St Albans the weekend before, the magic of the Cup attracted 4,400 to see the Hawks take on the Swans.

Swansea's Alan Tate was automatically banned by the Football Association of Wales but, as Havant were subject to local association rules, Brett Poate's suspension didn't take effect for 14 days. Martinez, the Swans' manager, must therefore have been livid when after four minutes Poate's corner was half-cleared and Garry Monk, hampered by Richard Pacquette, glanced Mo Harkin's cross into his own net.

The Welsh side rallied and the Spaniard Guillem Bauza, latching on to a through-pass, slid the ball just past Kevin Scriven's far post. Havant went even closer when Mo Harkin, the former Wycombe Wanderers midfielder, saw his left-foot drive from 22 yards clip the bar with Dorus de Vries beaten. Insult was added to injury for Martinez' men when in the 25th minute, De Vries' punch from another Poate corner fell at the feet of Hawks skipper Jamie Collins, whose shot crept apologetically through a crowd of defenders and found itself in the back of the net.

As the Swans strikers grew more anxious and their defence more disconcerted, eight minutes before half-time Richard Pacquette's miscued shot proved a perfect pass for Rocky Baptiste, who tapped in from three yards. By now the home fans were chanting 'Easy! Easy!' but their euphoria seemed premature as, in the visitors' first real counter-attack, Bauza curled in a classy goal from 20 yards. In the 41st minute the same player was clumsily felled in the area by Phil Warner but goalkeeper Kevin Scriven became the Hawks' hero, acrobatically beating out Leon Britton's penalty.

After 48 minutes Swansea pulled another goal back. Bauza's strike from Andy Robinson's low cross hit the inside of a post and the Trinidad & Tobago forward Jason Scotland side-footed the Swans' second. The game hung in the balance: the Hawks, tenacious and aggressive, had grievously wounded their elegant prey, and with 25 minutes left they administered the coup de grace. Half-time substitute Tom Jordan stole in to meet Brett Poate's free kick from the right to plant an unstoppable header past De Vries. A deluge of delirium swamped Westleigh Park but the Division One leaders were not done with. Leon Britton, in a good position, struck the bar and then for the sixth time in the two games, the Welsh side hit the woodwork as Butler's shot found the angle of the goal.

The Hawks, the last non-League team in the competition, had a new date in the diary. Their Blue Square South fixture with Weston-super-Mare on January 26 would have to be postponed: they would be facing Liverpool at Anfield in the Fourth Round of the FA Cup. Quite apart from the money – and the club stood to gain about £300,000 from the tie – it was enough to make grown men weep. Malcolm Jamieson, the man who didn't want anything to do with Havant, had tears in his eyes. 'Drawing Liverpool is just surreal – especially as my wife, Alison, supports them. I can't sleep. I feel sick every time I think about the game.' Fortuitously, 35-year-old Rocky Baptiste, training to become a London cabbie, knew the way. 'Up the M1, M6, and turn left. This means so much to me, as a Liverpool fan.' The tie seemed a mismatch, yet the professionalism of his team's triumph over Swansea gave Shaun Gale hope of a creditable performance.

Six thousand Hawks fans, including 26 coaches which left at six in the morning, had a day out they will never forget. For the players, whose earnings equate to about 1 per cent of Liverpool's top salaries, the chance to use The Cliff, Manchester United's indoor training facility, and to listen to a motivational talk from Liverpool legend Kenny Dalglish, was living the dream.

Living the dream? Crikey! As Russell Kempson put it in *The Times*, 'Twice the tadpoles from the Blue Square South had led at the citadel that is Anfield, twice the neon scoreboard shone with logic-defying illumination.'[5] Playing with purpose and courage, Gale's men chased every ball and took the game to Liverpool from the start. First, after only eight minutes,

---

[5] *The Times*, January 28, 2008.

truancy officer Richard Pacquette should have arrested the entire Liverpool rearguard for going absent without leave. Amazed to find the defence nowhere, he had time and space to head in a corner from Mo Harkin.

Lucas Leiva equalised with an exquisite 20-yard lob 20 minutes later, only for Alfie Potter to regain the Hawks' lead with a wickedly deflected shot from 12 yards. 'Christ, lads,' a Scouse voice implored. 'Get an effin' grip.' They eventually did, a second-half hat-trick from Yossi Benayoun and a last-minute tap-in from Crouch finally asserting the Merseysiders' status.

At the final whistle, the entire Kop rose to acclaim the vanquished and the warm appreciation of the Scouse footballing tribe rolled across Anfield in waves for the visitors from Hampshire, for the side from the Blue Square Conference South. 'It was a spellbinding sight, a spine-tingling sound.'[6]

Shaun Gale, the Havant manager, summed up the measure of his men's achievement. 'People laughed when we said we'd have a go at them here but we have created chances and scored goals. Not many non-League clubs could have done this. We could have been battered but we weren't. We played the game our way and didn't sit back.'

The players, who swapped shirts with the Premiership stars after the match, enjoyed the experience, too. Towards the end, with the Kop roaring out yet another chorus of 'You'll Never Walk Alone', 'I was standing next to Steven Gerrard,' said Havant captain Jamie Collins, 'and singing along with them. He looked at me like I was a weirdo. I don't suppose he gets that in the Premier League.'

There was only one possible headline for the papers that weekend – it was in *The Times* and it summed up the Hawks' fantastic season –

'Havant they done well.'

HAVANT & WATERLOOVILLE: Scriven, Gregory, Poate, Oatway, Smith, Warner, Harkin, Collins, Pacquette, Baptiste, Potter (sub-Jordan)
SWANSEA CITY: De Vries, Rangel, Monk, Lawrence, Painter, Anderson, Britton, Pratley, Robinson, Scotland, Bauza

---

[6] Ibid.

And this is the one that started it all. . .

50

HASTINGS UNITED 4, SWINDON TOWN 1

FA Cup, Round Two, December 12, 1953

The long line of green-and-cream buses stretched along South Terrace by the Central Cricket Ground. The Maidstone and District Leyland Titans all had 'Football Special' on their destination boards: to me this always seemed less of a bus route than a universal declaration of self-evident truth. Joining the queue for the uphill journey to the Pilot Field was a ritual for hundreds of Hastings United supporters clad in claret-and-blue scarves and carrying brightly painted rattles.

It was no different on December 12, 1953. For me, ten years old and still in short trousers, the bus ride held an almost unbearable tingle of anticipation for the match ahead. I'd been going with my dad and my brother for a couple of years and I had grown to love the atmosphere, the banter and the jargon – 'Keep it on the island', 'He's playing a blinder', 'Man on' and 'Unload him'. But December 12, 1953 was utterly unique, for on that day my mum came too.

United were only five years old. In the sweltering summer of 1948 the birth of a semi-professional club in the town was the outcome of an agonising labour in temperatures close to 90 degrees. Hastings and St Leonards FC, the incumbents of the prestigious council-owned stadium, were locked in battle with the upstart Hastings United. Finally, by one vote, the council granted United the use of the pitch when the club's offer of a higher rent proved all-persuasive.

After three or four indifferent seasons in the Southern League, what happened in December 1951 changed the course of local football. Following a 7–0 defeat by Kettering Town, United appointed Jack Tresadern as manager.

He had been left-half in the West Ham team beaten by Bolton Wanderers in Wembley's first FA Cup Final in 1923 and that year played twice for England. He later managed Crystal Palace, Tottenham Hotspur and Plymouth Argyle. He came to United from Chelmsford City and the 'shilling-a-week' lottery was launched, quite illegally, and during 1952 full-time professionals began to arrive – including perhaps the greatest player ever to wear the claret and blue – stylish centre-half and club captain, Bill Griffiths, signed for £5,500 after 13 seasons with Bury. Other players with League experience to join the club were Dickie Girling, ex-Crystal Palace, Brentford and Bournemouth, Alby Parks, from Notts County, keeper Jack Ball, who had had 13 seasons with Brighton and Hove Albion, and Dennis Hillman, of Southend and Colchester United. The club's League position gained some respectability and at the end of the season the side won the Freeman-Thomas Shield, beating Crystal Palace 2–1. But it was the FA Cup which brought a stunning revival to the club's fortunes.

On September 12, 1953 United won 3–0 away to Shoreham and in four successive qualifying rounds Horsham, Eastbourne, Ashford and Hounslow Town were despatched. Syd Asher, a clinical finisher and penalty ace, had arrived from Portsmouth and scored in each of the qualifying rounds. There was something of the Teddy Sheringham about Syd: his intelligent linking play and coolness in the box made him a firm local favourite. In the First Round proper, Dennis Hillman's goal was enough to beat Guildford City at the Pilot Field. By now 'the U's were the talk of the town and Tresadern, now a local hero, prescribed his famous diet of sherry and oysters for the Second Round clash with Swindon, of the Third Division (South).

The Pilot Field had also been host to post-war speedway and for the Cup match the wooden seating built on the speedway track not only boosted the crowd to 9,917 – a ground record – but brought the action up close and very personal. We clanged through the turnstiles about two o'clock and grabbed places on the benches right on the halfway line. Many locals, like 11-year-old Alan Sutton, had been there hours. 'My mates and I arrived about 11.30 a.m. to commandeer "our spot" behind the goal at the Elphinstone Road end. Most of us had rattles but my own very heavy "noise machine" had been obtained from Malcolm Mitchell's, the old government surplus store in the High Street, and was a leftover from the war.' The visitors were not without support and the traditional Wiltshire 'moonrakers' were greeted raucously, but the loudest cheers welcomed United's mascot,

Gus Hunneman, whose regular pre-match ritual added to the already heightened atmosphere. Decked out in claret and blue, wearing a huge hat, ringing a ship's bell and waving his magic wand, he cast spells in each goal and climaxed his routine with a nifty Charleston in the centre circle.

Then, to the stirring strains of 'Sussex by the Sea', our heroes emerged into the winter sun amid what Alan Hutton remembers as 'a cacophony of noise and atmosphere and expectation', though the season thus far had held out little cause for hope: United languished in the bottom half of the Southern League, with just six wins from eighteen games. Nonetheless, as the whistle blew, we roared 'Up the U's, all nine thousand of us.

Two minutes later, we were off our feet. Dickie Girling, his spindly legs a blur, had burst throughout down the left and Swindon's right-back, George Hunt, in trying to clear the winger's cross, headed high into his own net.

Ten minutes later the lead was doubled as Girling hit a cross-field ball to Dennis Hillman. Closing in, he centred low and Tommy Huckstepp, deceptively swift for a man large enough to have his own postcode, muscled his way between two defenders to sweep the ball home in style. This was incredible enough – yet five minutes later Huckstepp took a pass from Girling and slid it through to Syd Asher, who beat Sam Burton from ten yards. United were three up and the tie was effectively over.

Early in the second half Swindon came into the game for the first and only time. After the bustling little inside-left Alby Parks had forced a good save from Burton and Syd Asher went close, 18-year-old Ray Sampson fastened on to a through-pass from inside-right Roy Onslow and shot past the advancing Jack Ball into an empty net. Swindon pressed for another but United's defence held firm. With 20 minutes left, however, the game was settled when Girling sent Hillman away down the wing: only three or four yards in front of me the flame-haired right-winger sprinted on to the pass and hit it with decisive aplomb past Burton. Just before the end Tommy Huckstepp's header missed by a whisker and the unbelievable had happened.

We surged on to the pitch amid squibs and firecrackers and we mobbed our heroes. We sang 'Sussex by the Sea' till we were hoarse and when I slapped ex-Marine Commando Dennis Hillman on the back I felt a sudden pain as the winger's boot studs crunched into my foot. Somehow I didn't care: that boot had struck the final blow. Then Bill Griffiths and Dickie Girling were borne aloft to the dressing room. Griffiths had been his usual commanding presence at the heart of a defence in which George Peacock was as tenacious and Ray Barr as cool as ever. In attack, Girling had been inspired that day and the visitors never came to terms with the subtle movement of Asher and Parks and the panache of big-hearted Tommy Huckstepp.

On the Monday lunchtime my soccer-mad teacher Mr Pilkington let us hear the ineffable Raymond Glendenning announce on the wireless another home tie, this time against Third Division leaders Norwich City. 'I hope we knock the feathers out of the Canaries,' quipped manager Tresadern. Despite increased admission prices for the January 9 clash – 1s 9d to the ground, 5s for the wing stand and 6s for the centre stand – a new record crowd of 12,727 crammed through the turnstiles.

We stood on the North bank for what was (together with England's World Cup semi-final in 1966) the most thrilling match I've ever seen. After only four minutes Alby Parks capped a smooth attack by hooking the ball past Ken Oxford, but before half-time swift, incisive raids by the visitors produced goals from Brennan and Hansell to give them the lead. That wasn't all. Parks was fouled in the area seconds before the interval. Two – two, we thought. Syd never missed: normally he rolled the ball precisely into the corner beyond the keeper. On this muddy January day, however, he didn't hit it hard enough and Oxford got down to parry his shot round the post.

United threw everything forward on the resumption and, in a crescendo of excitement, they forced yet another corner. It was quickly taken and Alby Parks, all five feet five of him, nodded Girling's centre home for the equaliser. Now the tidal waves of United's incessant attacks were pounding the Canaries' indomitable defence. The game acquired a kind of a savage beauty, Cup football at its elemental best – unyielding, heart-stopping, dramatic. City were reduced to the odd counter-attack and, with 12 minutes left, Irish international Johnny Gavin, who would become the Canaries' record goalscorer, put the Third Division side ahead.

Gallant United were not done, however. Five minutes from time, Parks seized on the ball from a throw-in and crossed for Dickie Girling to hurl himself forward, thundering the ball – and then himself – into the net for the equaliser. Then, seconds before the final whistle – and it's as vivid in my mind's eye as if it were yesterday – George Peacock hit a screamer from 30 yards which rattled the Norwich crossbar – a near-storybook ending which would have meant a trip to Highbury and a lucrative tie against the Arsenal. As it was, it was all off to Carrow Road two days later, where in heavy rain, a crowd of 17,027 saw United go down 3–0.

It had been a heady winter – but FA Cup thrills weren't over for United. In the next season, their 4–2 First Round win over Hounslow Town somehow appeared on television and the following January they – and a special train-load of supporters – made the long trip to Hillsborough for a Third Round tie against First Division Sheffield Wednesday. Amazingly, they took the lead after 25 minutes when Syd Asher capped a flowing move by heading Parks centre past keeper McIntosh. Shaw equalised for Wednesday with a header on the hour and it was only two minutes from the end when, after a fusillade of shots, Greensmith put Wednesday into the Fourth Round. Veteran reporter Francis Cornwall recalls Wednesday's 'last-ditch, desperate attack. They scrambled a hotly disputed goal which led to the referee producing his notebook and saying ominously to George Peacock "What's your name?" "George," he replied. "What's yours?" The ref laughed, put his notebook away and a disappointed United team trooped off.' Even in the heat of battle, football in the 1950s was still fun.

Despite the heroics at Hillsborough, it had been the win over Swindon which had brought United national fame. On Monday, December 14, *The Times* accorded Hastings 'the honour for the best win of the round', describing how they 'quite outplayed Swindon Town', and *The People* wrote, 'In the battle the invaders were not only repulsed but thoroughly trounced and humbled. All honour to Hastings for producing a soccer showpiece and a unruffled workmanlike performance.'

I knew little of all that at the time. Long-time supporter Alan Sutton writes, 'Hastings had not seen anything like this since 1066 – and I was there.' So was I – and if I wasn't already hooked, on that gloomy December afternoon over half a century ago, I became addicted for life to a drug for which there is – fortunately – no cure.

HASTINGS UNITED: Ball, Crapper, Thompson, Peacock, Griffiths, Barr, Hillman, Huckstepp, Asner, Parks, Girling
SWINDON TOWN: Burton, Hunt, Elwell, Cross, Hudson, Johnston, Lunn, Betteridge, Owen, Lambert, Bull

EPILOGUE

'"In the beginning was the word" and the "word" was football.' So wrote Jo Hughes, in her unpublished thesis for the University of Sussex. She describes football to its supporters as 'a religion . . . one whose high priests are venerated by millions of acolytes every Saturday afternoon to the accompaniment of chants and songs and ritualistic behaviour.' She goes on to point out that it was the FA Cup competition in the 1880s which stimulated the rise of professional football and cemented the dominance of northern and Midland clubs over the established centres of the game in the public schools and universities of the South.

While the FA Cup Final has always been the game's traditional showpiece, the heart of the tournament is its giant-killers. 'They are lustrous proof that the impossible is always possible. *[They]* shred the form book, bulldoze their way across rigidly defined social barriers. They are mice which roar and oblige the nation to listen. They prevail, like David, with a sling and a stone. They, above all, provide the fun.'[1] And 'Lord, how we love an upset.' The distinguished sportswriter Simon Barnes has alluded to 'a uniquely British taste for isolating big names and taking them down a peg or two' – evidence, as he sees it, of 'a taste for democracy, a proof that the reputation of the best must be put repeatedly to the test.'[2]

No other cup competition in world football provokes the same ardent enthusiasm to see the mighty humbled. Matthew Syed has commented in *The Times* on 'the strange zealousness of diehard fans that makes the game tick'.[3] In every one of the 50 games described in the preceding pages, the fanatical devotion of the supporters has driven their team on to remarkable triumphs of the will and, as Syed has remarked, 'Football without its furious,

---

[1] Butler, *The Official Illustrated History of the F.A. Cup*, p. 230.
[2] *The Times*, January 5, 2009.
[3] *The Times*, December 29, 2007.

chaotic and occasionally offensive tribalism would not be football at all.'

Towards the end of his splendid book, Chris Oakley writes of a young man, an enthusiastic Sunday League player in South London, whose bewildered sister could not fathom the answer to the question 'Why is football so popular?'

There was a pause and then he said, with all the fervour of the committed, 'It's because it's a bloody good game, that's why!'[4]

It really is as simple as that.

---

[4] Oakley, p. 189.

BIBLIOGRAPHY

AA Illustrated Guide to Britain (Drive Publications, 1976)

AA Illustrated Guide to Britain's Coast (Drive Publications, 1984)

Adams, Tony, *Addicted* (Collins Willow, 1998)

Armstrong, Gary, and Giulianotti, Richard, eds, *Fear and Loathing in World Football* (Berg, 2001)

Barrett, Norman, *The Daily Telegraph Football Chronicle* (Ted Smart, 1993)

Birley, Derek, *A Social History of English Cricket* (Aurum Press, 1999)

Bryson, Bill, *Notes from a Small Island* (Black Swan, 1996)

Butler, Bryon, *The Official History of the Football Association* (Aurora Publishing, 1991)

—— *The Official Illustrated History of the F.A. Cup* (Headline Book Publishing, 1996)

Butler, Richard, *Soccer and the Soul* (Queensgate Publications, 2000)

Carder, Tim, and Harris, Roger, *Seagulls: The Story of Brighton and Hove Albion F.C.* (Goldstone Books, 1993)

Cole, G.D.H., and Postgate, R., *The Common People, 1746–1946* (Methuen, 1938; revised, 1946)

Collett, Mike, *The Guinness Record of the FA Cup* (Guinness Publishing, 1993)

Conn, David, *The Beautiful Game?* (Yellow Jersey Press, 2005)

Davies, Hunter, *Boots, Balls and Haircuts* (Cassell, 2003)

Elmes, Simon, *Talking for Britain: a Journey through the Nation's Dialects* (Penguin, 2005)

Elms, Philip, *Claret and Blue: the story of Hastings United* (1066 Newspapers, 1988)

Faulks, Sebastian, *Engleby* (Vintage Books, 2008)

Ford, Mark, *Landlocked* (Chatto and Windus, 1992)

French, Paul, *Prawns in the Game* (Dewi Lewis Media, 2006)

Glanville, Brian, ed., *The Footballer's Companion* (Eyre and Spottiswoode, 1962)

——ed., *The Joy of Football* (Hodder and Stoughton, 1986)

Goldblatt, David, *The Ball Is Round* (Penguin Books, 2006)

Greaves, Jimmy, *Greavsie, the Autobiography* (Time-Warner Publications, 2003)

Hennessey, Peter, *Having It So Good: Britain in the Fifties* (Penguin Books, 2006)

King, John, *The Football Factory* (Jonathan Cape, 1996)

Irwin, Colin, *Sing When You're Winning* (Andre Deutsch, 2006)

Lloyd, Guy and Holt, *The F.A. Cup – the complete story* (Aurum Press, 2005)

Lyons, Andy, and Ronay, Barney, *When Saturday Comes* (Penguin Books, 2005)

Miles, Peter, and Goody, Dave, *A Century United: The Centenary History of Southend United* (Shrimper Publishing, 2007)

Oakley, Chris, *Football Delirium* (Karnac Books, 2007)

O'Neill, Gilda, *My East End* (Viking 1999; Penguin Books, 2000)

Pattinson, Iain, *Lyttelton's Britain* (Preface Publishing, 2008)

Pawson, Tony, *100 Years of the F.A. Cup* (Heinemann Limited, 1972)

Reader's Digest Book of the Road (Reader's Digest Association, 1996)

Rollin, Glenda, and Rollin, Jack, eds, *Sky Sports Football Yearbook 2006–7* (Headline Publishing Group, 2006)

Rose, Jonathan, *The Intellectual Life of the British Working Classes* (Yale University Press, 2002)

Seddon, Peter, *Football Talk* (Robson Books, 2004)

Taylor, Rogan, and Ward, Andrew, *Kicking and Screaming: An Oral History of Football in England* (Robson Books, 1995)

Tibballs, Geoff, *F.A. Cup Giantkillers* (Collins Willow, 1994)

Ticehurst, David, *Brighton and Hove Albion: A Portrait in Old Picture Postcards* (S.B. Publications, 1994)

Trueman, A.E., *Geology and Scenery in England and Wales* (Gollancz 1938; new ed, Pelican Books, 1961)

Tyrer, D.J., ed., *Poetic Southend: A Last Resort* (Atlantean Publishing, Southend-on-Sea)

Vinicombe, John, *An Illustrated History of Brighton and Hove Albion F.C.* (George Nobbs Publishing, 1978)

Walvin, James, *The People's Game* (Mainstream Publishing, 1994)

Ward, Andrew, *Football's Strangest Matches* (Robson Books)

Williams, Mike, and Tony, eds, *Non-League Club Directory 2006* (Tony Williams Publications, 2006)

Winner, David, *Those Feet* (Bloomsbury, 2005)

Youlton, Clive, and Chapple, Geoff, *Geoff Chapple: The Story Behind the Legend* (The History Press, 2006)